North Dakota State University Libraries
GIFT FROM

Stephen Fischer-Galati, editor
East European Monographs

ATLANTIC STUDIES ON SOCIETY IN CHANGE

NO. 80

Editor-in-Chief, Béla K. Király
Associate Editor-in-Chief, Peter Pastor
Associate Editor-in-Chief, Ferenc Szakály
Editor, László Veszprémy

War and Society in East Central Europe
Volume XXXII

TRIANON AND EAST CENTRAL EUROPE
Antecedents and Repercussions

Béla K. Király and László Veszprémy

Editors

Social Science Monographs, Boulder, Colorado
Atlantic Research and Publications, Inc.
Highland Lakes, New Jersey

Distributed by Columbia University Press, New York
1995

EAST EUROPEAN MONOGRAPHS, NO. CDXVIII

Copy Editor: Peter Doherty

Copyright © 1995
by Atlantic Research and Publications, Inc.

Library of Congress Catalog Card Number 95-67450
ISBN 0-88033-315-4

Printed in the United States of America

Table of Contents

Table of Contents	v
Preface to the Series	vii

INTRODUCTION

Zsuzsa L. Nagy
    Trianon: the Cause of the Hungarian People and Europe   3

Magda Ádám
    Delusions about Trianon   15

László Szarka
    Trianon and the Emergence of Hungarian Minorities   29

ANTECEDENTS

Hugh Seton-Watson
    R. W. Seton-Watson and the Trianon Settlement *   43

Mária Ormos
    The Military Convention of Belgrade   55

Mária Ormos
    The Hungarian Soviet Republic and Intervention
    by the Entente *   93

Ignác Romsics
    Italy and the Plans for a Romanian-Hungarian
    Agreement, 1918–1938   107

REPERCUSSIONS

Iván T. Berend and György Ránki
    The Economic Problems of the Danube Region After
    the Breakup of the Austro-Hungarian Monarchy *   149

Peter Pastor
   Hungarian Territorial Losses During the Liberal-Democratic
   Revolution of 1918–1919 *   165

Stephen Fischer-Galati
   Trianon and Romania *   185

Yeshayahu Jelinek
   Trianon and Czechoslovakia: Reflections *   201

Thomas Karfunkel
   The Impact of Trianon on the Jews of Hungary *   217

István I. Mócsy
   Partition of Hungary and the Origins of the
   Refugee Problem *   239

Lóránd Dombrády
   Trianon and Hungarian National Defense   257

CONCLUSIONS

Béla K. Király
   Total War and Peacemaking *   271

Maps   279

Biographical Index   285

László Veszprémy
   Selected Reading List on Trianon   297

Name Index   303

Place Index   309

List of Contributors   313

Volumes Published in "Atlantic Studies on Society in Change"   315

* Essays first published in Béla K. Király, Peter Pastor, and Ivan Sanders, eds., *Essays on World War I: Total War and Peacemaking. A Case Study on Trianon*, War and Society in East Central Europe vol. 6 (Brooklyn: Brooklyn College Press, 1982).

Preface to the Series

The present volume is a component of a series that, when completed will constitute a comprehensive survey of the many aspects of East European society.

The books in the series deal with the peoples whose homelands lie between the Germans to the west, the Russians to the east and the Mediterranean and Adriatic seas to the south. They constitute a particular civilization, one that is at once an integral part of Europe, yet substantially different from the West. The area is characterized by a rich variety in language, religion, and government. The study of this complex area demands a multidisciplinary approach and, accordingly, our contributors to the series represent several academic disciplines. They have been drawn from universities and other scholarly institutions in the United States and Western Europe, as well as East and Central Europe.

The editors, of course, take full responsibility for ensuring the comprehensiveness, cohesion, internal balance, and scholarly quality of the series. We cheerfully accept this responsibility and intend this work to be neither a justification nor condemnation of the policies, attitudes, and activities of any persons involved. At the same time, because the contributors represent so many different disciplines, interpretations, and schools of thought, our policy in this, as in the past and future volumes, is to present their contributions without major modifications.

B. K. K.

INTRODUCTION

Zsuzsa L. Nagy

Trianon: the Cause of the Hungarian People and Europe

Seventy-five years after the signing of the peace treaty, the complex problem embodied in Trianon is still with us.[1] It continues to concern Hungarian society, although in a different way from at the time of its signature; Europe too is still grappling with it.

Trianon was the consequence of the shift in the balance of power in Europe. Although Hungarians experienced it as the tragedy solely of their people, right from the outset it has never been merely a Hungarian cause.

All of the new and the reconstitued states owed their existence, or the frames of their existence as defined by the state borders, to the victorious big powers, even if the decisions of the peace conference were based on an objective historical process. Although the military defeat of the Central Powers did not initiate, it facilitated the welding of the non-Hungarian peoples into single nations and the creation of independent states for them. The half a century of dualism had largely contributed to this process through the capitalist transformation, one of the consequences of which was the strengthening of national consciousness.

The international function of the Austro-Hungarian Monarchy and within it, of historical Hungary was to be a counterbalancing and balancing force resisting the "temptation" of Germany, and to isolate Russia, and even more so Soviet Russia, preventing the influence of Bolshevism from spreading beyond the borders of the former empire. The Monarchy was unable to fulfil any of these functions and this decisively influenced the Entente, thus eventually leading to the creation of a new set-up in the region.

The victors essentially intended this new set-up based on new, independent small states, to have the same function as that the Dual Monarchy had been unable to fulfil: on the basis of a *cordon sanitaire* principle,[2] it was to isolate Germany humiliated and desiring revenge, and to seal Soviet Russia off from Germany in particular and Europe in general. It follows from this that the condition for the creation of this new order in the Danube

Basin was the dismemberment, not of Germany but of the Austro-Hungarian Monarchy and of historical Hungary. As a consequence, of all the members of the Central Powers, it was the Monarchy that suffered the greatest losses. The Entente powers were convinced that this settlement would solve the national problems of the region and simultaneously contribute to ensuring lasting peace.

The rearrangement of the Danube Basin was accompanied by contradictions which made it extremely difficult for the Hungarian people to register and come to terms with what had happened. While from Washington, Paris and Moscow, the period was imbued with proclaimed principles concerning the right of self-determination, and many peoples were given this right, the Hungarian people had no say in decisions primarily affecting them. While the successor states were organized on the basis of national and ethnic unity, the Hungarian ethnic group, the members of the Hungarian nation were broken up. Borders were shifted over the heads of the autochthonous Hungarian population and one Hungarian in three came under the jurisdiction of the new states. While the Monarchy and historical Hungary had been described as the prison of the peoples, a commentator writing in the liberal paper, *Esti Kurir* considered that "without asking us or hearing us, our borders have been transformed into the walls of a prison cell and the whole of Eastern Europe has been filled with the choking air of a prison which has – unfortunately, but inevitably – also infected and poisoned the life of the neighboring peoples too."[3]

In fact, two nation states emerged from this dramatic change, Austria and Hungary. These two struggled to cope with the problem of creating a new life on a greatly curtailed territory, under deteriorated economic conditions and with a reduced population. They had to weld a single entity out of regions at different levels of economic development, and peoples with a different social structure and historic past, language, culture and religion. Czechoslovakia, Romania and Yugoslavia were assembled from such varied and disparate elements that they actually vied with the ethnic diversity of the dismembered old empire.[4]

In their efforts to build themselves, all the states created from the ruins of the Monarchy used the same binding material, one which had traditionally proved successful, namely nationalism. Even economic policy was dominated by nationalism. With the dismemberment of the Dual Monarchy, the old structure of production, markets, transport, etc. also disintegrated and the entire region as well as the individual countries suffered the ill effects. All the more so since, instead of seeking economic cooperation in a renewed form, they opted for autarkic isolation at a time when the world was progressing ever more rapidly towards economic integration.

Austria survived the crisis of the collapse relatively more easily because there had been no strong, traditional Austrian national consciousness comparable to that of the Hungarians. The Austrian grievances mainly had their roots in the fact that the new state had to remove the word "German" from its name and the Peace of St. Germain excluded union with Germany, while placing the three million Germans of the Sudetenland under the jurisdiction of the Republic of Czechoslovakia and awarding South Tyrol to Italy.

The Hungarians of the Trianon country who, despite the warnings from István Tisza[5] or Oszkár Jászi,[6] were quite unprepared for the end of the thousand-year-old historical Hungary, who were deeply traumatized by the loss of three million fellow Hungarians and the way in which it had happened, who had to stand by helplessly and watch the afflictions of the Hungarians reduced to minority status, had such a deep sense of grievance that they rejected Trianon right from the outset and were ready and open to any policy and propaganda calling for revision of the peace treaty.

While Hungary was characterized by an embittered nationalism, shaped by a sense of defeat and loss, in Chechoslovakia, Romania and Yugoslavia a victorious, state-creating nationalism prevailed. This latter was not content to create state unity as soon as possible, it wanted to bring about national unity. The creation of the new statehood and various measures required for the independent country more or less, and for a considerable time, diverted attention away from the contradictions existing among the members of the ruling, majority nation, and regarding the sharing of power.

For a number of reasons the program of national unity and the beginning of its forced implementation was inevitably directed against the subjects forming the Hungarian minority. The Hungarians with their large numbers, strong national consciousness, with a level and stucture of social and economic development differing in many respects from their new environment, with the mere existence of their culture represented a challenge – or its existence was interpreted as a challenge. Sentiments nourished by real or imagined grievances, directed against former "Hungarian rule" were transferred to the Hungarian ethnic population, on whom there was a desire to take revenge, which, for the most part, was taken. The principle of collective responsibility was not yet known at that time, and its international sanctioning – later undertaken by the anti-fascist allies – was also lacking. However, in practice the Hungarian ethnic population of the new states already had to experience something similar in the aftermath of the First World War.[7]

Transylvania, together with the Partium[8] lumped together with it went to Great Romania; this proved to be far more difficult to integrate than did the Felvidék (Upper Hungary) or other regions. In Transylvania, not only did the structure that had developed over the centuries and in which the Hungarian ethnic group undoubtedly occupied an outstanding place have to be broken up, but the spirit which is generally referred to as Transylvanism, distilled through centuries of coexistence and mutual tolerance among Hungarians, Romanians and Saxons, had to be destroyed.

However, the extremely aggressive nationalism of the successor states was directed against the Hungarian ethnic minority not only as regards the conditions existing at the given time. The restriction or withdrawal of the opportunities for economic and political activity, the cultivation of culture and use of the language by the Hungarians was accompanied by a purposeful and many-sided policy which aimed at expropriating and thus destroying the past of the given territory and its Hungarian population. It was in this way that the history of Upper Hungary or Transylvania has undergone a transformation, together with the history of their literature and art: Hungarian personal and place-names have disappeared and the products of its material culture are also decaying. This serves not only the end of national homogenization. It indisputably arose from a unique constraint: to prove that the state concerned came into being not as a consequence of a decision made by outside great powers, but as the natural result of an objective course of development rooted in the past. It is as though the state's own past were not sufficiently convincing, but needed to be rounded out and propped up with myths.

Trianon is a station of exceptional significance in the history of the development of nations in the Danube Basin. Trianon opened the way for the culmination of this development and the appearance of a whole series of nation states. The creation of state and national entities that had taken place centuries earlier in the Western and Northern part of Europe now appeared to the peoples living in its Central and Eastern parts not only as the sole possible, but also as the sole desirable model and one to be followed. There was a phase lag between the situation of Hungarians and non-Hungarians as regards the development of the nation, and when internal and, even more international, conditions allowed, an effort was made to achieve a balance to the detriment of the Hungarian people. But this was not the only factor in the background of the new conflicts.

The creation of the new independent states was accompanied by compromises among the nations forming the majority, either reached voluntarily or accepted under constraint. Some had to renounce their own aspirations in the interest of attaining independence as soon as possible or of acquiring the most advantageous territory. While this renunciation appeared to be final, it was in reality only temporary. Despite the 1918 Pittsburgh agreement, the Slovaks accepted the centralized Czechoslovak state under Czech leadership in which they did not gain a role identical or equal to that of the Czechs, either constitutionally, in form or in practice. Nevertheless, in 1918 this proved to be more favorable than their status in historical Hungary. However, in critical situations, their demands for equality and even for independence soon surfaced. This led to the situation where, in 1939, the Slovak state headed by Jozef Tiso enjoyed broad mass support and appeared to be the realization of old ambitions, even though the basis for its existence was created by Hitler and by the termination of the Czechoslovak democracy.

The Croats and Slovenes had accepted the Karadjordjevices, that is, the single Yugoslav state led by the Serbs because that seemed to be the most certain path leading to the creation of the independent Yugoslav state and the satisfaction of its territorial claims. Satisfaction of the Croatian national ambitions proceeded along a similar line to the case of the Slovaks and were achieved in 1941, also by Hitler's participation. It was not this kind of national ambitions within the country that made Romania and Hungary allies of Nazi Germany, but the aim, which became increasingly contradictory from 1940, in one case of preventing territorial revision and in the other of achieving it, so that Hitler always regarded Marshal Antonescu as a closer and more reliable ally than Regent Horthy and Hungary.[9]

The new political and power relations following the Second World War, when the region became part of the Soviet sphere of interest, led to the maximum creation of centralized state power. This applied in the area of national and nationality policy too and was asserted on a scale far exceeding anything earlier, using previously unimaginable instruments and methods. Not only were the compromised efforts to achieve independence removed from the agenda (there could be no mention of Slovak or Croatian independence in this situation), but the state of affairs that resulted was nothing short of catastrophic for those in the minority. The monolithic state wished to create a monolithic society in nationality respects too, one which was not disturbed by Germans, Hungarians or others. The anti-democratic, inhuman program of recreating or creating national unity, in other words, of eliminating the national minorities appeared to be far more attainable after the Second World War than it did after the First, because it was linked to the process of defeating fascism or, rather, was used as a cover and could rely on the approval of the allies. The allied anti-fascist powers recognized and sanctioned the application of the principle of collective responsibility to entire ethnic groups, and under international law in the peace treaties they also renounced protection of any kind for the minorities.[10] This was undeniably a step backward compared to the policy of the Entente.

However, the new Trianon system was not capable either of eliminating or overcoming the tense contradictions that arose from the unfinished state of the development of nations in the region and the inadequacies of their democracy. Despite the extremely brutal methods used, nationally homogeneous societies were not created. At the cost of superhuman efforts, the minorities managed to preserve their communities, even though they were reduced. In reality the suppressed desires of the majority, ruling nations did not disappear either, they were merely dormant. As soon as the foundations of the regimes based on the Stalinist model, the monolithic states, were shaken, these desires sprang to new life under cover of the general demand for democracy.

At first the protest against the central power and the nation exercising it and against its policy appeared in the form of some kind of federalist demand; later the demands for an independent state also arose. For the first time since Pittsburgh, the Slovaks achieved the transformation of the Czechoslovak state into a genuine federation, and then full independence; the Croats and Slovenes also advanced towards the attainment of their old demand for equality. At the same time, the process of democratization that has begun in the Danube Basin is being accompanied everywhere not only by movements in harmony with democracy and aimed at equality, but also by the unleashing of nationalist sentiments. Nothing shows more clearly just how powerful and dangerous these sentiments are than the fact that the nations which are striving to improve their own status under the slogan of equality and democracy, wish to continue the old policy towards the minorities, above all towards the Hungarians, questioning even their right to survival. The Hungarian people still suffer from the old and new forms of nationalism which all follow the same path, and their fate is shared by other minorities too: Albanians, Gypsies, Germans, Ukrainians, Turks and others.

Trianon opened a new stage in the development of nations in the Danube Basin, but it did not bring the solution hoped for by those who created it and benefited from it.

Not only was the new set-up in the Danube Basin incapable of contributing to permanent peace: it became a new hotbed of war itself. In a confidential memorandum written in March 1919, the British Prime Minister Lloyd George, heading the British peace delegation, expressed his serious concern that the decisions of the Great Powers were laying the foundations for an aggressive new alliance. He considered that, in handling Central Europe and the Danube Basin on the basis of the priority of French interests and aspirations, the Peace Conference had diverted Germany, Hungary, Bulgaria and Turkey onto a path of cooperation against the entire peace construction.[11] However, Germany could not just turn the national grievances and aspirations to its advantage when it made Hungary, Romania, Slovakia and Croatia its allies. As the only industrialized state in the region with a large market, it was also able to exert an economic attraction that France was unable to neutralize, however much it would have liked to. The Versailles system was unable to fulfil the principal function that the French hoped and wished of it: increasing France's security.[12]

The great powers recognized the inherent weakness and sources of conflict in the post-war settlements in other respects too. This is why they inserted into the peace treaties the so-called clauses on the protection of minorities; these they were able to bring their small allies to accept only with the greatest of difficulty. Romania protested most persistently against signing, arguing that it was interference in its internal affairs and a serious violation of its sovereignty. Bucharest had already formulated the principle that the treatment of national minorities was exclusively an internal affair in the course of the dispute that broke out in May 1919 and continued until the autumn of the same year. It did not renounce this principle even when it signed the minority protection treaty in the interest of longer term goals.[13]

The Great Powers were neither naive nor blind; they were well aware of the new problems caused by the Versailles system. However, from June 1919 when the German peace treaty was signed, they wanted to be rid of the whole affair as soon as possible; the United States openly withdrew from the Peace Conference, did not even join the League of Nations initiated by President Wilson and signed the peace treaty with Hungary too, separately.[14] Through their behavior, the Great Powers attempted to declare that it did not depend on the system or on them if the settlement did not function in the form and manner they wished, but on those involved.

Britain and France, representatives of the civilized West for the peoples of the Danube Basin, regarded the nationality and political conflicts of the region as the manifestations of petty, provincial wrangling, the disputes of small peoples in a backward region at the edge of Europe. The haughty and disdainful view and behavior of the great powers of Western Europe ignored the fact that their part of the continent had not gone beyond a good number of nationality and ethnic problems either and that they still had territorial disputes. In this context there is little essential difference between the disputes over Transylvania and the Franco-German clashes on the matter of Alsace-Lorraine. The Irish question was and is of no less import for Great Britain, the idealized land of constitutionalism and democracy.

The unsuccessful and ill-conceived nature of the Versailles peace system and within it, of Trianon, was fully admitted in Munich in 1938.[15] A great many circumstances explain the capitulation of the Western powers before Nazi Germany, but it remains a fact that with the Munich Pact they themselves overturned their entire peace settlement and that the Munich Pact was a recognition of the failure of the Versailles construction. In Munich the Western powers handed over to Hitler the state whose creation was one of their most important goals at the end of the First World War, the state which could not have been created without the carving up of historical Hungary. Munich and the Western powers' sense of shame greatly influenced the later shaping of the Czechoslovak position.

By the end of the Second World War, all the allied powers had matters to forget and compensate for. The British and French had Munich and the Soviet Union had the Molotov-Ribbentrop pact[16] which did not merely signify an alliance with Hitler, an embarrassing fact in itself, but also participation in the destruction of Poland and the takeover by force of the Baltic states.

It became clear beyond a doubt in the interwar years and during the Second World War that the nations of the Danube Basin, so proud and particular of their independent statehood, were in reality nothing but puppets; if they had any independence at all or if they lost it, this was in fact not the consequence of their own will but of a change in the great power interests and in the balance of power.

The punishment of Nazi Germany and its allies, the need the great powers felt to compensate for their past lapses, and the well reported and deplorable behaviour of the Hungarian political elite all contributed to bringing about the result that the creation of the order in the Danube Basin following the Second World War restored the old construction, aggravated in some respects. By 1945 Hungary was no longer regarded simply as a reluctant satellite,[17] but as the last satellite of Nazi Germany. The Allies believed that Munich and the decisions made by the purely fascist states on the other, could only be corrected by restoring Trianon. The principle of collective ethnic-national responsibility already mentioned and its practical consequences affected only the German and Hungarian ethnic groups, as the exclusive allies of Nazi Germany. The Hungarian people became the victims of this policy; on the other hand, they themselves applied the same policy to the entire ethnic German population within the country, not only to the pro-Nazi Volksbund members and SS volunteers.[18]

After the Second World War, the Hungarian became the largest national minority in Europe, but it now had to struggle for its survival under more difficult circumstances and in greater isolation than earlier. The regimes built in the shadow of the Soviet Union attempted to mask their nationalism and their power interests by proclaiming the principle of internationalism. The Hungarian state and political leadership branded any mention of the genuine Hungarian grievances as nationalism and as manifestations directed against the regime. Moscow could not tolerate any open discussion of the ethnic tensions that enmeshed the region; in that case its own nationality policy and the internal contradictions that have since come to the surface would also have been raised.

The ethnic and minority problems of the Danube Basin are still on the agenda. The fact that on the threshold of the 21st century and in countries that regard themselves as European, not only in the geographical sense, the response to basic demands by minorities aimed at their survival can be pogroms against Hungarians, Albanians, Turks and others shows more clearly than anything else the uncivilized state of general relations in the region, the undeveloped state of civic values, the weakness and lack of democracy.

Despite everything, there appears to be a realistic hope that our region can advance from this low point. The harassment, and restriction of the rights of Hungarians and other minorities have become a question of international significance; the nature of the ethnic and minority policy pursued has become a yardstick of democracy. The countries of the Danube Basin, now rid of the Stalinist regimes, would like to join the democratic community of Europe and this aspiration must be manifested in corresponding deeds, meeting the conditions for entry into the European Union. It is not possible for a nation to enter the European house which is so often mentioned nowadays, if it has in its hand a club used to cudgel its minorities. Nor is it possible for Hungarian society to imagine that it can represent the interests of the Hungarian people on an emotional basis, using arguments and methods that have proved unsuccessful in the past.

The chief lesson to be learned from the past seventy-five years is that the national grievances and conflicts in our region cannot be solved on an ethnic basis, with border revisions, but only through broad democratization. A policy of grievance, lacking any constructive element, and nationalist sentiments only rebounds on the minority Hungarians.

In 1921 Count Coudenhove Kalergi launched his movement for the creation of a united Europe;[19] those in power regarded him as a dreamer, but the liberal-democratic intellectual elite of the continent enthusiastically agreed with him. It is practically beyond dispute that this utopia was based on realistic and rational elements. The many unsuccessful attempts, the tragic experiences of seventy-five years, and the favorable change in international relations have also increased the reality of the utopia once formulated by Oszkár Jászi, who dreamed of the Danube Basin as a system of countries with democratic institutions, in an alliance based on the equality of nations. Today too, the realization of that utopia would be desirable.

Notes

1. The representatives of Hungary signed the peace treaty on June 4, 1920, in the Trianon Palace in Versailles, outside Paris. For its most important provisions, see: Péter Hanák, ed., *The Corvina History of Hungary* (Budapest, 1991), pp. 176–177.
2. In the discussions of the Peace Conference concerning Soviet Russia, the French argued for isolation based on small states; this the other great powers challenged but finally adopted. See: *Papers Relating to the Foreign Relations of the United States. The Paris Peace Conference.* (Henceforth: *FRUS PPC*) Vol. XII. (Washington, 1947), pp. 373 ff.

3. *Esti Kurir*, September 21, 1938. Article entitled: "Meghallgatásunk nélkül" [Without hearing us].
4. On the composition of the successor states, see: Hugh Seton-Watson, *Eastern Europe between the Wars 1918–1941*. (New York, Evanston, London. Third ed., 1962). Appendix: Racial and Religious Statistics; Stephen Borsody, ed., *The Hungarians: A Divided Nation* (New Haven, 1988). Appendix: 1. Statistics. 2. Maps.
5. Count István Tisza was prime minister of Hungary in 1903-1905 and 1913-1917. See: Gábor Vermes, *István Tisza. The Liberal Vision and Conservative Statecraft of a Magyar Nationalist* (New York, 1985).
6. Oszkár Jászi was the leader and theoretician of bourgeois radicalism in Hungary; he drew up a plans for the democratic reorganization of the Danube Basin (United States of the Danube or Eastern Switzerland). See: György Litván, "Oscar Jaszi, 1875-1957," *The Hungarian Quarterly*, Vol. XXXII, No. 122. Summer (1991).
7. See: *The Hungarians: A Divided Nation*. op.cit. Part two: *The Hungarians of Hungary's Neighbors*.
8. The Partium is the historical name given to the territory lying between Transylvania, The Great Hungarian Plain and the north-eastern regions of the country. Since 1918 the designation Transylvania has been applied in common usage to include this considerable area.
9. Andreas Hillgruber, ed., *Staatsmänner und Diplomaten bei Hitler.* (Frankfurt am Main 1970), *Hitler hatvannyolc tárgyalása 1939–1944.* [Hitler's sixty-eight negotiations, 1939-1944] Introductory study, compilation of documents and annotation by György Ránki. Vols. 1-2, (Budapest, 1983).
10. The Hungarian peace treaty signed in Paris on February 10, 1947 – in contrast with that of Trianon – did not contain any clauses on protection of the minorities. The first program of the Czechoslovak government, published in Kassa (Košice) on April 5, 1945, held the Hungarian minority in Slovakia collectively responsible for the disintegration of the Czechoslovak Republic, and for this deprived the ethnic Hungarians of all civil rights. It was not until 1948 that they regained these rights.
11. The memorandum was dated March 25, 1919. See: David Hunter Miller, *My Diary at the Conference of Paris.* (New York, 1926.) Vol. XV, p. 367; See also: Lajos Arday, *Térkép csata után. Magyarország a brit külpolitikában 1918–1919* [Map after a battle. Hungary in British foreign policy, 1918-1919] (Budapest, 1990).

12. Magda Ádám, *The Little Entente and Europe 1920–1929* (Budapest, 1993); György Ránki, *A Harmadik Birodalom árnyékában* [In the shadow of the Third Reich] (Budapest, 1988).
13. *FRUS PPC* Vol. III, p. 391 ff.; Sherman David Spector, *Rumania at the Paris Peace Conference. A Study of the Diplomacy of Ioan I. C. Brătianu* (New York, 1962), p. 140 ff.
14. This took place on August 29, 1921, in Budapest.
15. On September 29, 1938 in Munich the British Prime Minister Chamberlain, the French Premier Daladier, Hitler and Mussolini signed an agreement which transferred to Germany the Sudetenland, which had belonged to Czechoslovakia since 1918, thereby opening the way for Germany's expansion to the East.
16. On August 23, 1939 Hitler's Germany and Stalin's Soviet Union signed a treaty of friendship and alliance (Molotov-Ribbentrop pact); it also divided Poland between them.
17. It was an ambassador of the United States serving in Budapest in the thirties who described Hungary in this way. John Flournoy Montgomery, *Hungary the Unwilling Satellite* (New York, 1947); György Ránki, "Unwilling Satellite or Last Satellite – Some Problems of Hungarian-German Relations," in *Hungarian History – World History*, ed. by Gy. Ránki, (Budapest, 1984).
18. Hungarians were deported from Czechoslovakia and Germans from Hungary. Sándor Balogh, "Az 1946. február 27-ei magyarcsehszlovák lakosságcsere egyezmény" [The Hungarian-Czechoslovak population exchange agreement of February 27, 1946], *Történelmi Szemle*, (1979); Béla Bellér, *A magyarországi németek rövid története* [Short history of the Germans in Hungary] (Budapest, 1981), p. 188 ff.
19. On the Count, the international ramifications of the movement and its Hungarian aspects, see Zsuzsa L. Nagy, *Szabadkőmüvesség a XX. században* [Freemasonry in the 20th century] (Budapest, 1977), p. 89 ff.

Magda Ádám

Delusions about Trianon

People still entertain several misconceptions about Trianon. This is due to false propaganda, to the deliberate fabrications of historiography, to the deep silence around the subject after the Second World War and last but not least to the inaccessability of the archival sources. This latter circumstance, especially the lack of available French documents has rendered an authentic and manysided approach to Trianon and the road leading to it impossible.

Still it is not true that Hungarian historians started to study the French archival sources only recently.[1] Ever since the French diplomatic and military archives were opened at the beginning of the 1970s, several Hungarian scholars have conducted research there and have published on the question.[2] It is, however, probable that their scholarly writings have not reached the public or many of their colleagues.

The preconditions for being able to achieve a manysided, tinged and authentic representation of the history of the Peace Treaty of Trianon have already been created for historians, journalists and teachers. The first two volumes of a French series of documents – the second one still in preparation[3] – are going to offer invaluable source material for this. The two volumes cover the period of October, 1918 to June, 1920, namely the period when the Carpathian Basin witnessed crutial historical events. This is what the documents from the military archives of the French Ministry of Foreign Affairs and the Bibliothéque de Documentation Internationale de Nanterre reveal. They illustrate the process why and how the fate of the Carpathian Basin took the turn it did. Such a great number of documents have never been published before concerning the circumstances of the conclusion of the Trianon peace treaty seventy-five years ago. Most of the 850 documents are published here for the first time and offer an insight into the processes leading to Trianon deeper than ever before. Accordingly, the commonly accepted version has to be modified at several points. There is concrete evidence in the sources for the following much debated statements: a) the policy of the victorious Great Powers as regards

Central Europe was determined not by their intention to be fair, nor by their morale and sentiments, but primarily by their interests; b) unexpected events often generated irrational and subjective factors that also interfered at times; c) the Great Powers had no definite plans for the future of Central Europe but were drifting with the current of the events, which gave opportunity for the so-called minor allies to profit from the situation, since they did have definite aims and they pursued them in a most aggressive manner.

The irresoluteness of the Entente or the Allied Powers regarding the fate of the region was reflected also in their policy during the war. In the first phase of the war the Entente – with the single exception of Russia – did not wish to break up the Habsburg Empire, though they "bought" allies by making promises to them to dismember their enemy. The clandestine treaties were not meant to serve the liberation of the nations concerned (Italy and Romania) but belonged to the military side of the business.

When the USA entered the war in 1917, the principles of freedom came temporarily to the fore but the idea of keeping the Austrian Empire intact prevailed and was even strengthened by the revolutions in Russia. At this time the Entente did not support the national movements for freedom and unification and did not recognize the national committees in exile, however strongly their leaders had pleaded for this. The most self-consistent in this respect was the American President Woodrow Wilson whose famous principles regarding self-determination did not mean dismemberment for Austria. He wished namely to transform the country into a federation. The Inquiry committee led by his advisor and friend dealt with the problem in detail. Charles Seymour, member of the Inquiry and later of the American delegation at the Peace Conference elaborated a plan for the reorganization of Austria-Hungary on a federal basis. (He signed the comments to the maps on May 25, 1918, i.e. five months before the end of the war). Six federative states were envisaged on the territory of the Austro-Hungarian Empire, including Austria proper, Hungary, Bohemia, Yugoslavia, Poland and Ruthenia, and Transylvania. The biggest one would have been Hungary with her 16 million inhabitants and the smallest one would have been Transylvania with hardly more than 2.5 million.[4]

In May, 1918 when the prospects of a separate peace with Austria-Hungary came to nought and the Entente's efforts regarding Russia also failed (with Soviet Russia signing the Peace of Brest-Litovsk), the Allies came to accept the idea of supporting the small nations and their separation from the Empire. Military considerations (the weakening of the hinterland of the Empire) also played a considerable part in this.

When the Entente decided to break up Austria, they had no specific plans in mind as regards the future of Central Europe. They did not know exactly what they wanted and what the Empire could be replaced by. Some felt sure that it could best be replaced by a unified Central Europe where the interdependent successor states co-operated with one another.[5] It was also evident that such a regional unit could be created if the losers were punished only moderately, which is a fact to be observed when determining both the reparations and the frontiers.

The idea of a unified Central Europe – primarily as regards the economy – was at first supported not only by the USA and Great Britain but also by France. Clemenceau wished to see Central Europe under French influence, so he tried to negotiate frontiers acceptable to the defeated as well. This was why he wished to moderate the territorial ambitions of Romania, as it becomes clear from the newly published sources. It is probable that this attitude of his contributed to his strictness in not forgiving Romania for the breach of treaty and not recognizing the validity of the clandestine agreement of Bucharest as regards the line of the River Tisza as the Romanian frontier. He did not even recognize Romania as an ally up to January, 1919.

It is also probable that the French attitude contributed to the military convention of Belgrade, favorable from Hungarian points of view unexpectedly.

The documents reveal that the dismemberment of Hungary was not the result of a premeditated diabolical plan on the part of the victorious Great Powers, as Hungarian public opinion has believed ever since. Not even Clemenceau, the statesman most condemned in this respect can be charged with wishing to detach two thirds of Hungary's territory. When he finally did so, it was not due to his hatred of the Hungarians but rather to his subordinating Hungarian interests to French security and placing the whole problem into an international context.

Contrary to public belief, the French Prime Minister did not hate the Hungarians at all.[6] The men he did hate were Brătianu and the members of the royal court of Romania. But the geographical position of Romania made the country important for France, just like Czechoslovakia, towards which Clemenceau felt sympathy from the very beginning.

The significance of these two countries from the point of view of French security was steadily growing from late 1918 owing to the French set-back as regards the German and the Russian questions.

It became evident that the USA and Great Britain opposed the French efforts concerning the Rhineland (namely that the Rhine should be the border between France and Germany and a buffer state should be created on the left bank of the Rhine). The situation was rendered even more serious by the fact that France lost her traditional allies against the Germans with the creation of Bolshevik Russia. Her efforts to support a pro-Entente government to come to power in Russia were doomed to failure. So she tried to create a Central Europe that could replace her traditional ally in the east, form a *cordon sanitaire* and be a counter-balance to Germany. So the Central Europe France envisaged was to represent French interests both in the Russian and in the German questions. Under these circumstances, geographical consideration made both Romania and Czechoslovakia strategically more valuable to France, with the logical consequence that she considered the economic, infrastructural and strategic strengthening of these countries more important than before. This could be done only to the detriment of the losers and with the dismissal of the national principle. This approach was very dangerous, since the French played a decisive role in the region at that time. The Allies accepted it after much debate and hesitation.

December, 1918 brought therefore a change in Clemenceau's attitude towards Central Europe. He gave up the idea of creating a unified region, by renouncing both Hungary and Austria; a step sharply criticized later by his successors Millerand and Paléologue.

This change was reflected also in his attitude towards the Belgrade Convention and Mihály Károlyi in general. He called the former an error and attributed it solely to Franchet d'Esperey, as action taken on his responsibility though – according to all indications – the French general acted with Clemenceau's connivance also in the case of the Belgrade Convention. Mihály Károlyi was written off in a few week's time, since the pro-Entente Hungarian Prime Minister became very burdensome for the West. He was written off with all his democratic ideals.

The demarcation line around Hungary became ever tighter and was modified more than once to the benefit of Czechoslovakia and Romania. Beneš managed to enforce his will in nearly everything.[7] He obtained a frontier line Czech politicians had not even dreamt of. Romania could, however, not achieve her original aim, namely the River Tisza as the border with Hungary, for Clemenceau never gave up his objections to it.

Contrary to common belief, the French never encouraged Czechoslovakia and Romania to violate the demarcation line. The documents in volume 1 bear witness to this. The high-ranking French officers in the region (Franchet d'Esperey, de Lobit, General Henrys and primarily Lieutenant-Colonel Vix) were definitely against such steps. The pro-Romanian Berthelot and the pro-Czech Pellé were the only exceptions, so their relationship with the others and with Clemenceau himself came to be burdened by disagreement. The relationship of the latter with Berthelot became especially tense and Clemenceau even thought of relieving the general.

The frontiers were finally determined in various committees and at the conference table. In January, 1919 the Peace Conference decided to set up a Czechoslovak, a Romanian, and a Yugoslav committee. These were expert committees, the Great Powers being represented in them by two delegates each. The chairmen of the two committees were French, that of the first being Jules-Martin Cambon and of the second André Tardieu. Their task was to prepare recommendations as to the Czechoslovak-Hungarian, Romanian-Hungarian, Yugoslav-Hungarian and the Czechoslovak-Romanian and Yugoslav-Romanian frontiers on the basis of the national principle.

The committees started their work in February, 1919 and their recommendations were controlled and sanctioned by two higher authorities, namely by the so-called frontier commissions made up of the foreign ministers of the Allied Powers and by the Supreme Council. In this process the most important role was played by the expert committees. It was they who practically determined the Trianon borders still valid today. They were really very professional, since at least one of the two experts of the individual nations knew the ethnic, economic and infrastructural conditions of the region very well. It is in fact amazing how familiar they were with the ethnic distribution of the individual villages and the transport networks. The documents thus flatly contradict the opinion that the Trianon borders were the result of the ignorance of the politicians who determined them.

One definite starting point for the committees was the principle of nationality. They relied primarily on the results of the last census of the Habsburg Monarchy, taken in 1910. It cannot be denied that in most parts of the disannexed territories the majority of the inhabitants were Slovak,

Romanian and the Southern Slav. One of the largest exceptions along the border was probably the Grosse Schütt with its 95,000 Hungarian inhabitants.

The committees had, however, another starting point as well, namely they wished to consider the economic and transport interests of their "friends" first, whatever the ethnic distribution of the territory in question should be. And this they did in several cases. The members of the committees were fully aware that their decisions were unjust and detrimental to Hungary; the long discussions invariably ended in acceptance. The delegates representing the political points of view, i.e. the French standpoints, always prevailed.

In the beginning there was much disagreement within the committees. Not a single undisputed decision was made except in the case of the Czechoslovak-Yugoslav corridor.[8] The American delegates urged for a better consideration of the ethnic principle in the east and in the north; in the latter case they were supported by the British. As regards the south and the east it was the Italians who represented a dissenting view. In the former, they supported the Hungarian case, in the latter they were against it. The Italian attitude was motivated in both cases by Italian interests. Firstly by their anti-Yugoslav feelings, then by their pro-Romanian attitude or their wish to observe the clandestine treaties concluded during the war, the Bucharest treaty being one of among them. (Italy had concluded a similar treaty in 1915). The status of Sub-Carpathia and the Grosse Schütt was especially strongly disputed. There were half a dozen draft solutions for the first, whether it should be given to Hungary, to Czechoslovakia, the Ukraine, Poland, etc. Or should it be divided between Romania and Poland or should it be left independent? The French, American and British delegates finally decided for Czechoslovakia.

The Grosse Schütt finally met the same fate. In this case there were not so many alternatives. With the exception of France, all wanted to leave it to Hungary. The committee and the sub-committee held many meetings and the long debate ended in a majority vote saying that the territory was vital for Czechoslovakia from the strategic and economic points of view and from the point of view of transport. The delegates were fully aware that their decision was in violent conflict with the principle of self-determination advocated during the war.

The frontier committee of the foreign ministers was probably also aware of this, for it did not accept the decision but sent it back for re-consideration. (This was the only occasion when such a thing happened). The expert committee and the sub-committee resumed discussion of the problem. They gave Beneš a hearing where he enumerated the reasons why Czechoslovakia was not in the position to give up the territory. Besides the strategic and infrastructural considerations, he also stressed that with the annexation of the Grosse Schütt there would be as many Hungarians in Czechoslovakia as Slovaks in Hungary. The experts were fully aware that the figures were false and the proper accounting would be 1,000,000 to 140,000. But they also knew that Czechoslovakia did indeed need the territory for strategic, economic and infrastructural reasons. Consequently, they stood by their earlier decision and this time it was accepted also by the Supreme Council.[10]

The new frontiers, transforming the region completely and mutilating Hungary, were accepted by the Council of Foreign Ministers in May, 1919 and by the Supreme Council in June. They did so on the basis of the recommendations of the expert committees.[11]

I have to add two more comments on the work of these expert committees. Their activity was a positive hindrance to a better rearrangement. First, since their members were well-prepared experts who knew the region well, their decisions were taken seriously on all levels.[12] Second, they worked separately, concentrating on a particular section of the frontier line. Each of them took only a small amount of territory from Hungary, which seemed reasonable to be taken from a defeated enemy for the sake of a friend. But all these small parcels of land finally amounted to two thirds of the country. The justness of the Hungarian protest was later taken seriously only by the British Prime Minister Lloyd George. In June, 1919 the Supreme Council notified the governments in question of the decisions regarding the new frontiers. It was imperative to be quick, since the parties at war had to be ordered to withdraw behind the frontiers determined to be final. Taking no notice of this, Romanian troops marched into Hungary and captured Budapest.[13]

The opinion is still held that Romania acted according to the expectations of the Allies and was actually their surrogate. The documents published for the first time in vol. 2 of the series mentioned above, namely, the protocols of the Supreme Council, and the reports and letters concerning the problem, reveal the critical days or weeks and the panic that broke out in Paris at the news of the Romanian occupation of Budapest. The Supreme Council was in continuous session.

As the Romanians simply ignored the protests from Paris, the American and British delegates voted for military measures against them, should they not want to withdraw on their own free will. There were various suggestions as to retaliatory measures, from the breaking off of diplomatic relations to the recapture of Transylvania. The French did not accept these suggestions, but they also considered the withdrawal of Romanian troops from Budapest important, for they feared that another war might result from this situation. Furthermore, they were aware that the presence of the Romanian troops in Hungary prevented stabilization in the country and hindered the formation of a government that could finally be recognized and invited to the Paris Peace Conference. With the formation of the Huszár government, in which the Allies played a considerable part, this condition was finally fulfilled.

The opinion is also still held that Trianon was a punishment for the Hungarian Soviet Republic. The documents in the above two volumes reveal the following. According to the protocols of the frontier committees, the major problems were decided on before March 21, 1919. These decisions were approved of by the higher forums in May and in June when Béla Kun was in power. It is very difficult to tell what would have happened if the form of government in Hungary at that time had not been a dictatorship of the proletariat.

Hazarding conjectures is not one of the historian's tools. It is, however, probable that these decisions would have been approved without the existence of a Soviet Republic in Hungary.

Kun's coming to power clearly aroused panic in Paris. The victorious Great Powers were primarily interested in Hungary's foreign policy and to the degree to which the Hungarian government would be willing to accept their decisions on the frontiers. Béla Kun followed the example of his predecessors in pursuing a foreign policy based on historical principles. The only difference was that while Mihály Károlyi demobilized the army and tried to reach this goal by means of peaceful diplomacy, his successor tried to enforce it by force of arms. Hungary started to reorganize her army and achieved considerable success in the northern campaign. So it is quite understandable that Béla Kun received much more attention in Paris than Mihály Károlyi, who, for all his democratic principles, was totally neglected. Paris renewed connections with Kun, for the Peace Conference was frightened by the Soviet Republic and what it managed to achieve, and wished to have its way with the Bolshevik country through talks or at least by promising to enter into talks with it. In fact, Kun managed to attain more than Károlyi had ever done.

Historians and publicists often raise the question if the Hungarian government had any chance of influencing the decisions at Trianon.

The documents show that the quickly changing governments of Hungary often behaved impoliticly. Mihály Károlyi kept referring to historical principles at a time when international politics were – at least nominally – dominated by the principle of self-determination. He called for French occupation when this was already an outworn idea. He did not notice that it had become unnecessary and hoped, almost up to the end, for justice to prevail.

His successor, the Bolshevik Béla Kun also left ignored the principle of self-determination. He wished to acquire Slovakia in order to help bring Communism to power there and help the country unite with Soviet Russia. It is evident that this was not the objective that a great number of those fighting in the Red Army – primarily the K.u.K. officers – had taken up arms for.

The Friedrich government, which took power in August, 1919 made Archduke Joseph of Habsburg the first man of the country, thus infuriating the Allied Powers. They did everything they could to bring about the fall of the government and help bring the Huszár government to power. This was not only to please Hungary's neighbours but also to support a government that could at last be called to Paris to sign the peace treaty.[14]

In his speech before the Supreme Council, Albert Apponyi, leader of the Hungarian delegation, stressed frontier revision in general and not just the modification of the ethnically unjustified decisions; in Paris his speech was considered a defense of historical Hungary. It elicited both criticism and praise, though not at the official meeting, which Clemenceau abruptly adjourned. Referring to Apponyi's speech, Lloyd George remarked that if the count had not urged revision in general but only for individual sections of the frontier, he might have achieved some results.

The speech and above all the abundance of maps illustrating it, prepared by Pál Teleki, also produced, however, positive responses. Some found that the Hungarian question should be reconsidered. Lloyd George advanced that idea at the London conference of the Supreme Council. His proposal was supported by the Italian Prime Minister Francesco Nitti, who shared Lloyd George's views on the subject. The Americans did not take part at the meeting.[15] The French were, however, definitely against the reopening of the Hungarian question. They argued that it had been settled in March. As the division was 2 to 1, the Conference of Ambassadors instructed the foreign ministers and the ambassadors to reconsider the question. At the Council of Foreign Ministers the Italian Scialoja sided with the French, so here the division was 2 to 1 to the French standpoint. The Italian Prime Minister, Nitti sent a cable from Rome to express his disapproval and ordered his foreign minister to reconsider his point of view. He also asked for the reopening of the Hungarian question.

The question was settled by the backing down of Lloyd George, who stated that although he fully agreed with Nitti, the documents had persuaded him that the Hungarian question had really been settled in Paris, so it could not be reopened.

The French and the victorious successor states heaved a sigh of relief. The latter had a great part in making Lloyd George change his mind. At the time of the London conference, members of the Czechoslovak, Romanian and Yugoslav peace delegations were in continuous session. They protested in joint petitions against the planned invasion. They let the world know that their countries were ready to defend the occupied territories, and what Lloyd George wished to avoid most was another armed conflict.

At the London conference it was finally agreed that in the note sent to Hungary, along with the terms of peace treaty, reference would be made to the possibility of peaceful revision.

This consignment note, to be known later as Millerand note,[16] did have some role: the Hungarian government finally signed the terms of peace they had refused to sign earlier; it also marked a turn in the French attitude towards Hungary.

Millerand, who followed Clemenceau into office, and especially his foreign secretary Paléologue, considered the policy of their predecessors concerning Hungary a blunder in that they had rejected Hungary, making the realization of the British and Italian efforts possible[17] and the signing of the peace treaty more difficult. They started therefore to make approaches to Hungary. Millerand thought of correcting some minor but flagrant cases of injustice, while Paléologue's large basis for negotiations would have been the Grosse Schütt and Sub-Carpathia. There were clandestine talks between the Hungarian and the French governments, several documents on which can be found in volume 2.

Hungary's neighbors disapproved of the rapprochement and the French policy aiming at winning over Hungary, especially when it turned out that the talks also dealt with political questions. So they combined to prevent Franco-Hungarian agreement.[18] These countries played a part also in bringing about the fall of Paléologue for pursuing a Hungarophil policy.

Millerand's policy met with full success. No doubt, his economic and political promises made to Hungary definitely played a part in Hungary's signing the peace treaty. But these French promises were never kept and Hungary had to sign the original peace terms on June 4, 1920. The terms were dictated to the defeated Hungary by the victorious Great Powers and their minor allies and became the source of renewed conflict between Hungary and her neighbours in the past seventy-five years.

Notes

1. Ernő Raffay, *Trianon titkai avagy hogyan bántak el országunkkal* [The secrets of Trianon or how our country has been mistreated] (Budapest, 1990). After the publication of this book, journalists and even historians stated that Raffay had been the first to read the French documents.
2. Magda Ádám, *A kisantant és Európa* [The Little Entente and Europe] (Budapest: Akadémiai Kiadó, 1989, in English: 1993); *Idem.*, "Confédération Danubienne ou la Petite Entente," *Acta Historica* XXV (1979) pp. 61-113; György Litván, "Documents des relations franco-hongroises des années 1917-1918," *Acta Historica* XXI (1975) pp. 904-949; Mária Ormos, *Padovától Trianonig* [From Padova to the Trianon] (Budapest: Kossuth Kiadó, 1983, in English: 1990); *Idem*, "Francia-magyar tárgyalások 1920-ban" [Franco-Hungarian talks in 1920], *Századok* (1975-76) pp. 904-949; Sándor Vadász, "Vix és Károlyi" [Vix and Károlyi], *Hadtörténeti Közlemények* XVI (1969) pp. 239-262.
3. Magda Ádám, *et al.*, eds., *Documents diplomatiques français sur l'histoire du Basin des Carpates 1918-1932*, vol. 1 (October, 1918 – August 1919) (Budapest: Akadémiai Kiadó, 1993).
4. See Magda Ádám, "Woodrow Wilson and the Successor States," *Danubian Historical Studies*, vol. 1. no. 4.
5. Several plans have been made as regards the reintegration of the region but the rising nationalism appearing also in the economic field made all of them improbable from the very beginning.
6. Hungarian histography and public opinion still hold that Clemenceau's anti-Hungarian attitude played a great part in the unparalleled mutilation of the country.
7. For the first time, the protocols of the Hungaro-Czechoslovak, Hungaro-Romanian, Hungaro-Yugoslav, Yugoslav-Romanian and Ro-

manian-Czechoslovak frontier committees are published in the first volume of the series, cf. n.3.
8. Czechoslovakia was not able to achieve its ideas for a western corridor. The plan had been worked out by Masaryk during the war. The leader of the Czechoslovak emigrés considered it important for the new Czechoslovak state to have an outlet to the sea. Beneš supported the idea at the Peace Conference most forcibly, but was not backed by any of the Great Powers. None of the victorious powers was interested in separating Austria from Hungary by a corridor and connecting the northern and southern Slav peoples. They did not wish to support a Pan-Slav revival.
9. Seeing that most of the delegates supported the Hungarian claims for the Grosse Schütt, the French, wanting to gain time, suggested to adjourn the debate till the conclusion of the Saint Germain Peace Treaty.
10. The determination of the frontiers of Hungary and her neighbors was relatively easy. To find a frontier line between Romania and Yugoslavia or Czechoslovakia and Romania was much more difficult, since the former Hungarian territories had to be devided between "friends." It was not by chance that these frontiers took so much time to decide.
11. Although the decision was taken by the foreign ministers as early as May, the Supreme Council passed its resolution and sent it to the governments concerned only one month later.
12. Revising the frontiers in favor of Hungary was generally rejected with the argument that they had been determined by experts knowing the region very well. Berthelot also referred to this, at the London Conference.
13. Paul Mantoux was an official interpreter for the Council of Four and later for the Supreme Council. He made detailed records of his activity in both. The protocols of the former were published in English and in French, though the Big Four decided never to publish them. Mantoux published his records under the title *Les deliberation du Conseil des Quatres (24 Mars – 28 Juin, 1919)*, so he did not include the ones made of the Supreme Council meetings. Vol. 2. of our series publishes those of his records that refer to the history of the Carpathian Basin, cf. n.3.
14. The fact that Joseph of Habsburg became the leader of the country as *homo regius* met with great resistance, especially on the part of

the neighbors of Hungary. They considered this as the first step towards the restoration of the House of Habsburg. Their protest contributed to the Allied warning the Hungarian government against the restoration of the Habsburgs.
15. The American delegates did not take part at the London Conference of the Allies. Davis, the American Ambassador in London was not empowered to take part, so he could not fulfil Lloyd George's demands.
16. The idea of the consignment note known as the Millerand Note was born at the London Conference and was suggested by the English delegates. The letter speaking of the possibility of "peaceful revision" played a part in that the Hungarian government finally signed the peace terms.
17. England, France and Italy started to compete for economic positions in Austria and Hungary right after the war. England and Italy (especially the former) were much ahead of France in this competition. Millerand and Paléologue wished to change this by making approaches to Hungary.
18. The clandestine Franco-Hungarian talks on economic and political matters took place in Paris and Budapest. The developing English-Hungarian relations were swept aside and Horthy's government changed to a French orientation, for they expected not only economic but also political support, i.e. the revision of the frontiers promised primarily by Paléologue.

When Czechoslovakia, Yugoslavia and Romania learned that the talks touched not only economic but also political questions, they combined their forces to prevent the realization of the Hungarian plans. They formed the Little Entente, which was initially directed against France as well.

László Szarka

Trianon and the Emergence of Hungarian Minorities

"Indeed, the ethnographic relations of Central Europe are such that the political frontiers cannot coincide all along with the ethnic borders," says Millerand's letter announcing on behalf of the Allies the completion of the definitive text of the Hungarian Peace Treaty of Trianon. It then continues, explaining the rejection of the Hungarian objections: "That said, certain nodes of the Hungarian population must fall under the sovereignty of other states – the Allied and Associated Powers had to bow to necessity with regret. However, no reference to this situation is justified claiming that it would have been better not to upset the old territorial status quo. The present state of affairs, even if it has a thousand-year past, is not qualified for the future, if it has been found unjust."[1] An investigation of the formation of Hungarian minorities in Yugoslavia, Czechoslovakia and Romania, numbering some 3 million all in all, must really take the mixed settlements of East Central Europe, that is, the objective ethnic relations, as one of its main starting points, as cited by Millerand as conclusive.[2]

It is also a fact, however, that in Hungarian-Slovak, Hungarian-Ruthenian, Hungarian-Romanian and Hungarian-Serbian relations there existed easily discernible ethnic frontiers. What is more, the greater part of the Hungarian-Slovak language frontier is one of the clearly defined language borders, along which transitional zones deeper than one or two ethnically mixed villages very rarely occured.

As the cited Millerand letter reveals, it was not a set aim of the Peace Conference to maximally corroborate the objective ethnic features of the Carpathian Basin in the peace treaties for a variety of considerations.[3]

Within the frames of pre-1918 multilingual Hungary, the constitutional relationship between the Hungarians and the other five nationalities making up one half of the population did not evolve during the centuries towards isolation or separation, but precipitated, especially in the 18th and the second half of the 19th centuries, a mosaic-like or harmonious ethnosocial structure. This multinational state community, with certain regional dimensions, provided the framework for an insular but vigorous industrialization, substantial urbanization and embourgeoisement, all entailing major changes in every stratum of society; this also brought along mass migration and assimilation (Magyarization) around the turn of the century. These social mobility processes affecting millions further tightened the connection between the nations of the Carpathian Basin, virtually raising it to the rank of blood-kinnship, as a Slovak national declaration said at that time.[4]

On the other side, in the symbolic area of national competition, the illusion of a unilingual "Hungarian Empire" and the visions of "Asian oppression," and "national extinction" pitted the representatives of the national societies in polar opposition to one another.[5]

It is unquestionable that, lacking the necessary concentration of political forces and will, the objective ethnic situation of pre-1918 Hungary was not adequately asserted in the constitutional structure of the Hungarian Kingdom and the Austro-Hungarian Monarchy. The short-lived and relatively feeble political endeavors of the Romanians, Slovaks and Serbs of Hungary to create territories of national autonomy and federalize Hungary met with insurmountable obstacles.[6]

The Hungarian Nationality Act of 1868 proposed a wide scope of language use and cultural rights for the non-Hungarian nationalities, but a few decades of assimilation-centric government policies, whose aim was to reinforce the unity of the political Hungarian nation on an ethnic basis, pushed to the background this equalitarian, practice of legal concessions. As a result of the negative Hungarian nationality policy, the outbreak of the First World War strengthened hopes among the radical national exponents in Hungary for the so-called disaster solution, that is, the military defeat and disintegration of the Habsburg Monarchy. Proof to that is the fact that the majority of opposition politicians of Hungary's nationalities adopted without comment or reservations the national state program of South Slav and Czecho-Slovak thinkers in exile in Western Europe during the World War, especially in its last months.[7]

The history of the Trianon Treaty signed on June 4, 1920, and the Hungarian minorities it created have thus a ramifying background. Without an analysis of this, today's public thinking is unable to work out the political changes of 1918-1920 and interpret correctly the indisputably central issue of 20th century Hungarian history, traumatized for such an unnecessarily long time and in such a futile way.[8]

The "year" 1919 was possibly the longest "year" in Hungarian history: lasting practically 20 months. Starting with the impetus of the democratic revolution of October 1918, it ended with the communist revolution which the country was hurled into by the bankruptcy imposed upon the now independent Hungarian People's Republic due to the defeat of the Monarchy. That was followed by a three month (at places even longer) Romanian occupation of Budapest and the greater part of the country, and the rise to power of the Horthy regime, shattering all domestic and foreign political illusions. The period quite rightly regarded as the year of collapse ended with the conclusion of the Trianon Peace Treaty. After the collapse of the liberal and proletarian revolutions the ruling elite of aristocratic or gentry origin tried, but failed, to continue where István Tisza had left off, acknowledging the military defeat on 19 October 1918. They managed, however, to preserve their hegemonic positions and tried to throw the responsibility for the disruption of the historical borders onto the leading actors of the two revolutions, who had come to grief, or at least had proved unsuccessful. During these twenty chaotic months, four systems of government were tried out by the country, with eight cabinets and two rival governments. The armies of neighboring countries often without consent from the victorious powers or the Peace Conference occupied two-thirds of the original territory of the state, including regions and towns with a Hungarian majority, encountering hardly any resistance. Externally, Hungary was almost completely isolated, maintaining contact with the decisive actors in world politics only through the military missions of the Entente and the Peace Conference.[9]

Thus, the effects of several factors of fundamental importance added up to nearly three million Hungarians finding themselves in minority situation. As it turned out later, the point of departure for the demarcation of the new border was the lists of demands and strategic proposals submitted to the Peace Conference by Hungarian's neighbors. From the Hungarian point of view, in the Peace Conference's work on borders, only a choice between bad and worse was available, due to the Czechoslovak, Yugoslav and Romanian territorial demands (and promises voiced or registered during the war). The French, English, Italian, American delegations vying with each other, as their respective spheres of interest or *ad hoc* interests dictated, were only prepared to turn down clearly excessive territorial demands when some points of the new Hungarian border became controversial. (The purely Hungarian Csallóköz (Grosse Schütt) region, for example, went to Czechoslovakia, because French diplomats, yielding to the American and Italian position, abandoned their wish to assign the Salgótarján-Miskolc coal-mining and industrial region to Czechoslovakia, and in return for this, by way of compensation as it were, the Americans gave up insisting on the Csallóköz region coming under Hungarian control.)[10]

The Millerand letter quoted at the outset tries to explain the biases of the overtly acknowledged territorial decisions by referring to an extremely polarized decision: it was not hard for the Allies to decide between the integrity of thousand-year-old Hungary and the claims of the new small allied states. Yet both the work of the Peace Conference and the alternative proposals for solutions, also adopted by the Hungarian governments, included plans and suggestions taking far more account of the ethnic relations of the region.[11]

There is nevertheless no use in putting the rhetoric question, since the answer was also unambiguous for contemporaries: the various Hungarian conceptions of confederation, personal union, cantonal administration, or the more moderate territorial solutions often proposed by the English, American, Italian diplomats of the Peace Conference stood no chance, because the Versailles peace system, of which the Trianon Peace Treaty was part, could only be based on the military and power relations at the termination of the world war, on the military *fait accompli* as it evolved from November 1918 to the autumn of 1919; Versailles tried to isolate and pacify the centres of war and revolution on these grounds as quickly as possible. At the same time, it tried to ensure the interests of the allied and associated powers for the future.

For the same reason, the odds were against proposals for condominium, themselves highly instable though undoubtedly justified for ethnic reasons, which would have prolonged local conflicts. These ideas were not adopted by the Hungarian governments consistently, nor did they find favor in the rigidly unsympathetic attitude of the Czechoslovaks and Romanians.[12]

When the war was over, the Hungarian political leadership was fully aware that without the effective support of a victorious great power, the integrity of the historical Hungarian state could not be preserved. Apart from the Americans, they could not count on anyone, so to achieve favourable negotiating positions, they both insisted on the principle of integrity and tried to work out temporary agreements which could be invoked, if they were forced to give up the principle of integrity. This is the only context in which the basic decision taken by the Supreme Council of the Peace Conference holds true which said that any rectification of the

Hungarian borders marked out by the Peace Conference would result in a worse solution for Hungary under the given power relations in the region.[13]

It is an entirely different question that the instrument of plebiscite, used on four occasions in the creation of the Versailles peace system, was only used once in Hungary despite all the efforts of the Hungarian peace delegation This was the case of Sopron and its neighborhood. It is no accident that the constantly coordinated positions of the Czechoslovak, Yugoslav and Romanian peace delegations were perhaps at their most forcible and consistent in fending off the plebiscite.[14] It can hardly be doubted that in Hungarian-majority areas and towns, it would have effected major changes in the border decided by the Peace Conference. The Hungarian peace delegation most probably missed a realistic chance by not concentrating on the subsequent revision of the fate of ethnically unquestionable, purely Hungarian areas in their petitions in Paris, instead raising this proposal only in subordination to the principle of integrity, and mentioning it in the secret Hungarian-French negotiations outside the Peace Conference.[15]

What, then, were in the interwar period the factors that promoted, or hindered the processes of self-organization of the three Hungarians minorities placed outside the borders of new Hungary in a new Central Europe created by the Versailles settlement? Which were the fundamental political and legal circumstances that under the Trianon peace treaty and the Versailles peace system afforded the possibility for the Hungarians in Czechoslovakia, Romania and Yugoslavia to organize themselves from artificially created ethnic groups into real communities? Into nationality societies which would be able to express their rights in the majority nations and in Trianon-created Hungary. The factors can be divided into three groups. The first includes the socio-psychological phenomena that helps realize a new situation in small communities. Especially in the early phase when signs of resistance (e.g. demonstration in Pozsony in February 1919, installation of Romanian prefects in Kolozsvár and the Székelyföld) elicited the new state apparatus's crude violence in all three successor states, the solidarity of the local Hungarian societies was perhaps the first positive experience of a minority community.[16]

At this juncture, mention must be made of the strong national attachment of all three groups of Hungarian minorities still a distinguishing feature of Hungarians in Slovakia as a sociological survey there found a few years ago. The primary explanation for this is the undoubted fact that the decisive 19th century period of Hungarian national development, including all its linguistic, cultural and political achievements, is a heritage common to the entire Hungarian language community.[17]

The attitude of quiet resistance to the "occupiers" was also a significant community-forming factor in the early phase, though passive resistance also became a major source of loss for the Hungarian minorities: civil servants who refused to pledge their loyalty to the new states were dismissed, most of them further increasing the threehundred thousand or so refugees settling in Hungary.[18]

A higher plane of communal organization in all three minorities is marked by the strengthening of regionalism and local patriotism or provincialism, which gradually acquired an ethnic surcharge, as well as by a sense of messianistic, heroic assignment generated early on by the minority status (a special minority version of Transylvanianism, the *Vox humana* in former Upper Hungary, the Danubian coherence, etc.). The recognition of the need for self-organization implied in all three ethnic groups a certain socio-psychological disposition towards elaborating, and collectively experiencing, the unprecedented, perfectly new minority position.

All these was made immensely difficult by the initial prohibition of contacts with the "parent state" and with Budapest which continued to be obstructed and remained improvised and contingent until very recently. In East Central Europe, for example, incredible barriers hinder the circulation of the Hungarian cultural press, let alone the dailies, right to this day. The relationship between Hungary and the Hungarian minorities has changed much and many times over the past 75 years. The period between the two world wars was dominated by the sentiments of estrangement and dispossession, and the chief goal was to put an end to this situation. In Hungarian revisionist propaganda, official Hungarian politics and arts alike, Trianon was the incarnation of all evil. It would, however, need a separate study to show that, among the Hungarian minorities and the general public in Hungary, there was a relatively narrow following for the Hungarian radical irredentists than was so often and widely envisaged.[19]

The second group of factors influencing the self-organization of a minority includes the political, economic and cultural rights granted by the new states, and generally, the attitude of the majority state towards its minorities.

The international convention on the protection of minorities, signed by all three successor states, had positive consequences in Czechoslovakia and, partly, in Romania. This affected first of all the right to use the native tongue, the preservation of a minimal network of Hungarian cultural and educational institutions and legal guarantees for the minority churches.[20]

But while Czechoslovakia tried to assert the basic principles of the international minority convention in its domestic legislation on the nationalities, Romania and Yugoslavia acted in the opposite direction, trying to limit their validity. This difference can best be seen on the operative freedom and effectiveness of the political parties of Hungarian minorities.

True, part of the reason for the success of Hungarian political forces in Cezchoslovakia was that, of all the Little Entente states, it was Masaryk's republic that was obliged to make the most concessions; the German minority of three and a half million manipulated by Hitler caused Prague an ever graver headache, especially in the thirties.[21]

All three Hungarian minority groups tried to assert all the rights contained in the convention on minority status promulgated by the League of Nations in Geneva. Oddly enough, the petitions of Romanian Hungarians were the most successful, often getting the Romanian government to back down on an anti-minority measure. This had special significance in connection with agrarian reform and the concomitant redistribution of land, as well as the remedying of grievances caused by the state supervision of Hungarian language schools. The basic conditions for the self-organization of Hungarian minorities in the interwar period was the commercial sphere, organized on ethnic grounds and school education in a national spirit. It is noteworthy that the processes of self-organization restarted after 1989 are largely hindered by the absence of both.

Between the two world wars, Budapest governments always professed their high-priority task to be the comprehensive settlement of the rights of the Hungarian minorities, though they never relinquished hope in a modification of the borders. Hungary tried to conclude bilateral agreements on the mutual protection of minorities with each of the three neighboring countries. But as the internal disputes involved in the Czechoslovak rejection of this at the time reveal, none of the successor states regarded their minorities left in Hungary important enough to be protected by giving Hungary any licence to contractually support and supervise guarantees on the rights of Hungarian minorities in their own countries.[22] Therefore the Hungarian government chiefly appealed to the League of Nations, to the Interparliamentary Union and other international forums to protect of Hungarian minorities. Never for a moment, however, did it question the fact that the real solution was the alteration of the borders.

Evaluating Hungarian revisionist politics is one of the constant moot points of Hungarian historiography; according to our present-day knowledge, the programme of total revision was a sort of diplomatic excess demand for most Hungarian governments, but after the failure of the bilateral talks in 1921-23, Hungarian foreign policy concentrated on ethnic revision, that is, the reannexation of areas populated chiefly by Hungarians.[23]

The self-organization of Hungarian minorities in the interwar years went only partly together with the integration of the three ethnic groups into the new state community. Several reasons can be adduced: from pre-1918 historical conflicts, through the Trianon decision judged by most of the minority Hungarians as unjust to their ignorance of the majority language, to the discriminative practice of the state apparatus, legislation and jurisdiction, as well as the strained relations between Hungary and the neighboring states throughout. From the very beginning, the "host" countries defined themselves as nation states, leaving very little scope for the minorities in their constitution, political establishment, public administration and legislation. Under such circumstances, the loyalty of the minority remained minimal, and could not be strengthened even in Czechoslovakia, which pursued the most openminded minority policy.

To conclude, it can be stated that the interwar development of Hungarian minorities created by Trianon exposed all the controversial points of the Peace Treaty. There is no denying that Trianon did not restrict itself to endorsing the self-determination of the former non-Hungarian national communities of historical Hungary. The provisions of the Peace Pact pertaining to territory, especially the Hungarian borders – which determined the magnitude of Hungarian minorities – realized the strategic and economic goals of the victorious powers and their small East Central European allies, instead of preparing an unbiassed arbiter's decision. The Hungarian minorities bear the mark of Trianon to this day: aware of the ambiguous experiences of the past 75 years, both minorities and majorities are afraid of any rearrangement, new political, constitutional, legal regulation. The attempts at a solution during the Second World War and the postwar years proved that the relations between the peoples of the Carpathian Basin cannot be solved by redrawn borders, local wars, exchange of population, forced resettlements, genocide – all implying the violation of human rights – for every violent attempt generates new grievances and conflicts, and any attempt at homogenization harms both the winner and the loser.

The great experiment of the post-1989 restart in East Central Europe will be characterized by a peculiar duality of democratic drives and nationalistic phenomena. This experiment offers the Hungarian minorities a chance for self-organization missing for fifty years in the teeth of repeatedly accelerating assimilation: the elaboration of the needs and opportunities of cultural and local self-government and the working out of a new set of relations with the majority societies and Hungary, based on utter openness and a continuous coordination of interests. The Hungarian minorities' certificate of baptism issued at Trianon will probably not lose its significance until the borders of the region's small states become as crossable and symbolic to the extent they now are in everyday life in the happier regions of Europe.

Notes

1. Millerand's letter of 6 May 1920 see *A Magyar békeszerződés. Traité de paix avec la Hongrie* (Budapest, 1920) p.3.
2. In his essay examining the sociological background to the demarcation of the borders, Pierre Bourdieu points out that even the factors conceivable as objective assume relative validity next to the preponderance of the subjective motives of power relations that always determine the fixing of borders. Pierre Bourdieu, "L'identité et la représentation. Éléments pour une réflexion critique sur l'idée region," *Actes de la recherce en sciences sociales* 35(1980), pp. 63-72.
3. Besides the priorities of the economic and strategic interests of the new Central European small states, an increasing role was played in deciding controversial territorial issues by the pacifying efforts of the great powers: failing the military presence of the Allies, the most effective intervention seemed to be the reinforcement of Czechoslovak and Romanian positions so as to achieve order.
4. The text of the 1861 Slovak national memorandum of Túrocszentmárton is published in Gábor G. Kemény, ed., *Iratok a nemzetiségi kérdés történetéhez Magyarországon a dualizmus korában 1867-1918* [Documents to a history of the Nationality Issue in Hungary From the Age of Dualism 1867-1918] (Budapest, 1952).
5. On this see Ludwig von Goglák's study in Urbanitsch-Wandruszka eds., *Die Habsburgermonarchie 1848–1918. Die Völker des Reiches* Bd. III.2.

6. See e.g. the studies of Károly Vörös, and László Katus, in Peter I. Hidas, ed., *Minorities and the Law* (Toronto, 1986).
7. On the reaction of Slovak politicians in Hungary, see, *e.g.*, Vavro Šrobár, *Osvobodené Slovensko* (Bratislava, 1932).
8. For a many-sided analysis of the Trianon syndrome, see Béla K.Király, Peter Pastor, and Ivan Sanders, eds., *Essays on World War I: Total War and Peacemaking. A Case Study on Trianon* (New York, 1982); Stephen Borsody, ed., *The Hungarians: A Divided Nation* (New Haven: Yale Center for International Area Studies, 1988).
9. Mária Ormos, *Padovától Trianonig 1918–1920* [From Padua to Trianon 1918–1920] (Budapest, 1984) pp. 155-160.
10. *Ibid*. On the Csallóköz region, see *A magyar béketárgyalások. Jelentés a magyar békeküldöttség működéséről Neully s/S.ben 1920 januárius–március havában* [Hungarian Peace Talks. Report on the Work of the Hungarian Peace Delegation in Neully s/S. in January-March 1920] (Budapest, 1920) pp. 448-449. Also: Géza Jeszenszky, "A csallóközi magyar-szlovák határ története" [The history of the Hungarian-Slovakian border in the Csallóköz region], *História* No. 6. (1988), pp. 28-29.
11. Millerand writes: "True, the Hungarian peace delegation argues that nowhere has a referendum been provided for by the peace terms. If the Allied and Associated Powers have judged it redundant to resort to an inquiry of this kind among the population, they must have done so in the conviction that had a survey been carried out under the guarantees of perfect sincerity of opinion, it would not have had significantly different findings from the ones the Powers had arrived at after a thorough analysis of the ethnographic relations in Central Europe and the national aspirations there. The will of the peoples was manifested in October and November 1918, when the Dual Monarchy collapsed and the long-supressed nationalities could unite with their Italian, Romanian, Yugoslav and Czechoslovak brethren." *Traité de paix avex la Hongrie*, p.4.
12. See the study of Peter Pastor in this volume.
13. Ormos, *op.cit.*, pp. 375-384.
14. The original French text of the joint memorandum dated 24 February 1920 can be found in Ion Ardeleanu, Vesile Arimia, Mirceau Musta eds., *Desavirsirea unitatii national-statale a poporului Roman. Recunoasterea ei internationala. 1918. vol.VI. Documente interne si externe, februarie 1920–decembrie 1920* (Bucuresti, 1986), pp. 32-

42. The Romanian peace delegation protested in a separate memorandum against a plebiscite in Transylvania insisted on by the Hungarian side, "Les roumains et le plébiscité demandé par la délegetion magyare, Paris, Mars 1920," *Ibid.*, pp.106-111. The Czechoslovak anti-plebiscite position is most eloquently expressed by President Masaryk's statements of January 1919: *Világ* January 6, 1919. Earlier, still in exile, Masaryk himself had been for the plebiscite, but as Premier of the Czechoslovak Republic, he flatly rejected the decision of controversial issues by referendum, referring to the propaganda of the defeated Austrian and Hungarian state apparatuses. Oszkár Jászi, the Minister of the Nationalities in Károlyi's government, sharply criticized Masaryk's position. *Világ* 1919, January 9. For the Czechoslovak peace delegation's similar position to the Romanian, see Fedor Houdek, *Vznik hraníc Slovenska* (Bratislava, 1931), pp. 345-350.

15. A most recent detailed elaboration of this question in Hungary is: József Galántai, *A trianoni békekötés 1920. A párizsi meghívástól a ratifikálásig* [The peace treaty of Trianon. From the Invitiation by Paris to Ratification] (Budapest, 1990).

16. On the Pozsony demonstration claiming 8 lives see Marcell Jankovics, *Húsz esztendő Pozsonyban* [Twenty years in Pozsony] (Budapest, 1939) vol. I, pp. 18-24. On the Transylvanian incidents, see Ernő Raffay, *Erdély 1918–1919. Tanulmányok* [Transylvania 1918–1919. Studies] (Budapest, 1987).

17. Zelová, Alena, "A nemzeti kisebbségek identitása Szlovákiában" [The identity of national minorities in Slovakia], *Regio* No. 1. 1991, pp. 57-65.

18. On the refugees, see Gyula Popély, *Népfogyatkozás. A szlovákiai magyarok a népszámlálások tükrében* [Popular Eclipse. The Hungarians in Slovakia as Reflected by the Censuses] (Pozsony-Budapest, 1990); Árpád Varga E., *Népszámlálások a jelenkori Erdély területén. Jegyzetek Erdély és a kapcsolt részek XX. századi nemzetiségi statisztikájának történetéhez* [Censuses in the Present-Day Area of Transylvania. Notes to the History of the 20th Century Nationality Statistics of Transylvania and the Attached Areas]. (Budapest, 1992); Károly Mirnics, *A vajdasági magyarok asszimilációjának történetéhez.* [To the History of the Assimilation of Hungarians in Voivodina] (Manuscript).

19. An expert and full description of the history of Hungarian revisionist politics is still missing, but on the basis of the political program of the minority Hungarian parties, their contacts with Hungary, etc. a more cautious, reserved attitude can be reconstructed on the part of Hungarian minority politicians concerning the issue of the revision of borders.
20. On this see *Fejezetek a csehszlovákiai magyarok történetéből* [Chapters in the History of Hungarians in Czechoslovakia] (Pozsony, 1993).
21. On the cooperatives of the Hungarian minority in Slovakia, see László Pukkai, *A Hanza szövetkezeti mozgalom története* [A history of the Hanza cooperative Movement] (Pozsony, 1994) (In press)
22. On this see in detail: László Szarka, "Kisebbségvédelem, reciprocitás, revizió. Megyegyezési kisérletek a nemzetiségi kérdés terén" [Protection of minorities, reciprocity, revision. Attempts at agreement on the nationality issue] in *Békétlen évtizedek 1918–1938. Tanulmányok és dokumentumok a magyar-cseh-szlovák kapcsolatok történetéből a két világháború között* [Restless Years. Studies and documents on the history of Hungarian-Czech-Slovak relations between the two world wars] (Budapest, 1988) pp. 47-53; "Revizió és kisebbségvédelem (A nemzetközi kisebbségvédelem és a magyar külpolitika az 1920-as években)" [Revision and the protection of minorities. (International protection of minorities and Hungarian foreign policy in the 1920s)], in Ferenc Glatz, ed., *Szomszédaink között Kelet-Európában* [Among Our Neighbors in East Europe]. Festschrift on the 70th birthday of Emil Niederhauser (Budapest, 1993) pp. 333-338.
23. To the evaluation of revision, see the foreign policy of Pál Köteles, *Teleki Pál, a politikus* [Pál Teleki, the Politician] (Budapest, 1992); Lóránt Tilkovszky, *Revizió és nemzetiségi politika Magyarországon 1939–1941* [Revision and Nationality Policy in Hungary 1939–1941] (Budapest, 1967).

ANTECEDENTS

Hugh Seton-Watson

R. W. Seton-Watson and the Trianon Settlement

The following is a provisional estimate of the attitude of R. W. Seton-Watson to the Treaty of Trianon. This is of course a part of his general relationship to Hungary, and it is necessary in this article to refer from time to time to that wider background.

Seton-Watson completed his studies of History in Oxford in 1902, and a year later, on the death of his father, inherited an income which relieved him from any immediate need to enter a regular profession, thus enabling him for some years to devote himself to the study of European history and contemporary politics. After two and a half years in Germany, France and Italy – mainly in Berlin and Paris – he came to Austria-Hungary at the end of 1905.

At that time he was very favorably disposed both to the Monarchy and to Hungary. His view of the Monarchy was based on respect for the Habsburg dynasty and its historical achievement, as well as on sympathy for a European state which had long been Britain's ally, and seemed by its very nature to be committed to the sort of European balance of power which it was then considered to be Britain's interest to support. In the Hungarians he saw a nation which had made great sacrifices for the cause of liberty, and also had traditional links with Britain. Hungarian liberalism, whose parliamentary style seemed to resemble the British, and Hungarian Calvinism, which had much in common with the Presbyterian culture of his native Scotland, attracted him. He arrived in Vienna when the conflict between the Hungarians and the Habsburg dynasty was at its height, and he came to Budapest at the time of the 1906 election which gave a big majority to the nationalist Coalition. Seton-Watson's sympathies were thus divided.

After some weeks in Budapest he travelled for some weeks more in the provinces. It was in Transylvania, where he met first Saxon and then Romanian spokesmen, that he first realized the acuteness of the "nationality question." It became clear to him that there was a three-cornered struggle between Vienna, Budapest and the Nationalities. He would have liked to see all three reconciled with each other. In particular, he hoped that agreement between Hungarians and Nationalities would make possible pressure on Vienna to institute more liberal government. As it became clear to him that this was not possible – and his second journey to Hungary in 1907, to the Slovak regions, Ruthenia and Budapest, confirmed this belief – then his hopes were placed on the alternative of joint pressure by Vienna and the Nationalities on Budapest. This combination was associated with hopes of reforms by the heir to the throne, Archduke Franz Ferdinand, when he should succeed the old emperor. These hopes were most forcibly expressed to Seton-Watson by Milan Hodža, the Slovak Agrarian, and Alexandru Vaida-Voevod, the Romanian nationalist leader. However, this combination also was disappointed: the Archduke was kept waiting, and Vienna antagonized at least three of the nationalities – Croats, Serbs and Czechs – no less than Budapest antagonized the others. One may in fact argue that the persistent conflict between all three elements – Crown, Hungarian leadership and Nationalities – in the end destroyed the Monarchy.

Seton-Watson's most active period of concern with Hungarian problems was in the years 1906-1908, culminating in the publication of his book *Racial Problems in Hungary* in the latter year. In the remaining years before 1914 he became more and more absorbed by Croatian and Serbian affairs, on which he published *The South Slav Question and the Habsburg Monarchy* in 1911 (enlarged German edition 1913).

In these problems the role of Hungary was much smaller than that of Vienna, in which the leaders of the growing Yugoslav Movement saw their principal enemy. In 1910 there was an interlude, when Seton-Watson once more concentrated on Hungarian affairs. This was his study of the Hungarian parliamentary election of that year, which he personally witnessed in Szakolca (Skalica). His short book *Corruption and Reform in Hungary* appeared in 1911.

It is difficult to reconstruct precisely Seton-Watson's political hopes in relation to Hungary on the eve of the Great War. The notion of "Trialism," which would have replaced the Dualism of 1867 by adding a third unit, consisting of all the South Slav provinces,[1] attracted him; but of course it would not have solved the nationality problems of Hungary. He continued to have hopes of Franz Ferdinand. Even after his assassination, in the brief period before the outbreak of war, he believed in the maintenance of the Monarchy.[2] Probably his hope was that combined pressure from a new emperor and from the Magyar and non-Magyar peoples of

Hungary would compel the introduction of universal suffrage in Hungary; and that not only the consequent enormous increase of non-Magyar representation, but also the entry of new democratic and socialist Magyar forces into the Budapest parliament would make possible far-reaching reforms. Certainly he had hopes of Oszkár Jászi and of the Hungarian socialists, and in this was encouraged by Hodža, who considered that the land-hungry Magyar peasants were natural friends of the Slovaks.

This is the best estimate I can make. Understandably, as he was concerned with day-to-day problems, as well as with the impending appearance of a new international periodical, to be edited by him, entitled *European Review*,[3] he had neither time nor inclination to record his overall view of Hungarian political prospects in the summer of 1914. What is certain is that, at this time, he had no expectation, or indeed desire, that either Slovakia or Transylvania would be removed from Hungary. He never referred in his correspondence of this period, to a new Czech-Slovak unit to be formed within the Monarchy; and as for Transylvania, not only did he himself not advocate incorporation into Romania, but he had good reason to believe that statesmen in the Romanian Kingdom, though desiring it in general terms, were opposed in practice because the consequent weakening of Austria-Hungary would strengthen Russia, and make Romania unhealthily dependent on the Russian Empire.[4]

*　　　　*　　　　*

All this changed when war broke out in Europe, and the Monarchy became the enemy of Britain. Seton-Watson regarded Austria's declaration of war on Serbia as proof that the Monarchy had abandoned its role as a major independent factor in the European balance of power, and had become an instrument of Pan-German expansionism, in which he considered the Hungarian ruling class to be willing accomplices. He therefore assumed that Entente victory must bring large-scale losses of territory to the Monarchy; and later, convinced by T.G. Masaryk's arguments for an independent Bohemia to include the Slovak lands, he became an advocate of the complete dissolution of the Monarchy.

In a letter of 6 August 1914 from London to his wife, we find the words: "Dalmatia, Bosnia, Croatia, Istria must be united to Serbia ... Romania must have all her kinsmen."[5]

During the first half of the war, Seton-Watson had no official status, but was a sort of unofficial adviser to the British Foreign Office (with which he had had no connection at all until that time). In 1917 and 1918 he was in official employment, first in the Department of Information Intelligence Bureau (DIIB) under the War Cabinet and then in the Enemy Propaganda Department, headed by Lord Northcliffe. His correspondence and papers show that his main concern was with Yugoslav affairs, affecting policy to both the enemy state Austria and the allied state Italy, and to a lesser extent with the Czechoslovak movement headed in exile by Masaryk and Beneš. Hungarian problems played a smaller part, except in relation to Romania. The Slovak lands, which were politically quiet in these years, feature less. His weekly reports to DIIB on Austria-Hungary mention political events in Hungary, but they are less prominent than the affairs of the Cisleithanian Slav territories.

Seton-Watson visited Serbia and Romania in January and February 1915, with the encouragement of Sir Edward Grey. In Bucharest his main aim was to persuade the Romanians to come to the aid of Serbia. In an interview with the daily paper *Adeverul* he declared: "What Prussian militarism is for us, Magyar hegemony is for you: these are the principal obstacles to European progress. We together with our French and Russian allies must fight the German danger; but you with the Serbs must put an end to the brutal and artificial domination of the Magyar race over all its neighbors."

He was thus bitterly hostile to the dominant policies, and the dominant political leadership, of Hungary. At the same time, however, he was against excessive expansion by neighboring states at the expense of Hungary.

On 4 January 1915 he had a long conversation after dinner with Crown Prince Alexander in his HQ at Kragujevac. Alexander's map showed the borders which it was hoped to attain, and which included the annexation not only of all Bácska but also of the cities and districts of Nagykanizsa and Pécs. Seton-Watson argued that "if there are to be tolerable relations between the new state and the new Hungary, Serbian claims in Bačka must be very considerably reduced, if not altogether abandoned" and that "Pécs and all its district are mainly Magyar and German, and must be left to Hungary under all circumstances."[6]

As regards Romania, Seton-Watson was convinced that Transylvania and most of Banat must be ceded to Romania, but he did not accept the most extravagant claims of the Romanian government at the expense of Hungary. He was in no way involved in the diplomatic negotiations of 1916, but he learned the approximate terms of the treaty that was being prepared. On 21 July 1916 he wrote to his wife: "We seem – to my horror – to be promising them the Theiss frontier for immediate entry. That will put an end for ever to Magyar intrigues. Unhappily it will also make an independent Hungary almost impossible, and so might upset the whole balance further West."

In October 1916 Seton-Watson published the first issue of a weekly periodical, *The New Europe,* which lasted for four years, and in which he himself wrote many articles and small news items. He was allowed to continue this work after he became a government official, on condition that he ceased to be Editor and that his contributions were not signed with his name. At the end of the war, leaving government service, he resumed the formal editorship and signed his main articles again.

In the more than 200 issues of the periodical which appeared before it ceased publication in October 1920, Hungarian affairs are frequently discussed, and there is both general and detailed discussion of possible future frontiers. Seton-Watson assumed that Croatia, Banat, Transylvania, the Slovak and Ruthene provinces would be detached from Hungary, but was much less certain about Bácska. His principle was to make the frontiers coincide as far as possible with the ethnic distribution of the population, though certain cases were noted where injustice was inevitable for geographical reasons, by far the most important being the Székely territory.

*   *   *

Seton-Watson was not a member of the British delegation to the post-war Peace Conference; but he spent several months of the winter of 1918-1919 in Paris as a member of the office of *The Times* in close partnership with that paper's Foreign Editor, his old friend from Vienna and colleague in the Enemy Propaganda Department, Henry Wickham Steed. Seton-Watson and Steed were in constant contact with members of the British, American and to a lesser extent, the French delegations, as well as with Czechoslovak, Romanian and Yugoslav representatives. Seton-Watson was respected as an expert on Austria-Hungary, and probably had a certain amount of influence on the general attitudes of the professional diplomats and specialists; but in the only case in which he and Steed made a strong and sustained effort to propose a solution of a difficult problem – the drawing of the frontier between Yugoslavia and Italy in Istria – they failed.

Seton-Watson detested the political climate of the Peace Conference. He was indignant that decisons were made not on the merits of each case but in accordance with the party interests or even personal whims of the leading Allied politicians. He expressed his feelings in *The New Europe* of 1 January 1920, in a review of the recently published and later widely famed work of John Maynard Keynes, *The Economic Consequences of the Peace*. Fully agreeing with Keyne's description of the atmosphere of the Conference, he wrote: "However long I may live, I hope I shall never breathe such an atmosphere again. The true Paris had been submerged by a wave of fetid intrigue, and a babel of small men in big positions surged round a few big men whom the strain of an unexampled crisis had made small and sterile."

His attitude to Hungary in these months was strongly influenced by the changes in its rulers. The presence of Oszkár Jászi in Mihály Károlyi's government briefly awakened hopes of a better Hungary. (At this time, however, he regarded Károlyi himself with suspicion as a great landowner and a pre-1914 nationalist. It was only in the 1920's that he got to know Károlyi personally and the two men became firm friends). However the advent to power of Béla Kun aroused his worst fears. Seton-Watson shared the view, widespread at that time though subsequently shown to be unsound, that the Russian Bolsheviks were agents of Germany. He feared a resurgent unholy alliance of German and Hungarian militarism in co-ordination with Bolshevik revolution. The fact that Hungarian former officers supported Kun, in the belief that he would with Russian help maintain Hungary's territory, lent plausibility to these fears. His first visit to the new republic of Czechoslovakia, in May 1919, coincided with the successful Hungarian counter-offensive in Slovakia. After two weeks in Prague and two more in Slovakia, he returned to Paris to urge the allied authorities to give aid to the Czechoslovak forces.

Kun's replacement by the regime of Admiral Horthy gave Seton-Watson no satisfaction at all. As he saw it, the dangerous Bolshevik regime had been replaced by the old political class, and Hungary seemed likely to be a centre of reaction and chauvinism in the future too.

Undoubtedly these events tended to preserve Seton-Watson's effective political hostility. His hopes of democratic forces in Hungary appeared unreal; and though he recognized that there were avoidable injustices in the frontiers which were now proposed by the Peace Conference for Hungary, he felt no inclination to battle on behalf of Horthy's Hungary against his friends in the succession states. In a full discussion of the proposed frontiers in *The New Europe* of 15 January 1920, with population figures for each of the counties of old Hungary (excluding Croatia), he noted that the settlement was "unduly severe to the Magyars," especially in the region of Subotica (Szabadka); in the Grosse Schütt island; and in the region of the frontier with Romania, which "could undoubtedly be pushed further east in such a way as to leave considerable numbers of Magyars in Hungary, without sacrificing more than a few thousand Roumanians." However, it was at least gratifying that "the idea of ceding Miskolcz and the Salgótarján mines to Czechoslovakia, and Pécs (Fünfkirchen) with its no less important mining district to Jugoslavia, would seem to have been abandoned. Both would have been acts of crying and gratuitous injustice." The arguments used by the spokesmen of Horthy's regime, and of their sympathizers in Britain, in order to modify the frontiers, infuriated him. In *The New Europe* of 22 April 1920, he referred to the argument of Count Apponyi that the cultural superiority of the Hungarians over neighbor peoples was proved by their higher level of literacy and the scanty number of non-Magyars with a middle-school training. "Such an argument in such a mouth is nothing less than infamous, for it was Count Apponyi himself who, by his Education Acts of 1907, carried to their utmost limit those methods of Magyarisation of the schools, to which above all the bakwardness of Roumanian and Slovak education was due."

*   *   *

Between the world wars, Seton-Watson's attitude to the Trianon settlement was consistent. He continued to be aware of its injustices. Some of these he considered irremovable (above all, the Székely situation). Others could be improved by frontier revision, to which he was not dogmatically opposed. However, he did not believe that the way to improve Hungary's relations with its neighbors was to begin with frontier revision, but rather that political conciliation should be the aim, and that if once the political climate were improved, then revision could be one of the matters to be discussed.

However, he remained profoundly distrustful of the Horthy regime. He was convinced that the Hungarian leader's aim was not mere frontier revision, but a restoration of the old borders, regardless of the national aspirations of the non-Magyars. And indeed the statements of Hungarian leaders were profoundly ambivalent. The fact that revision was supported by Mussolini and by Lord Rothermere made it seem even less desirable to him.

More urgent, he believed, was the effective implementation of the rights of the Hungarian minorities, as provided by the peace treaties. In 1928, in a visit to Slovakia, his main purpose was to study the situation of the Hungarian minority. He met a number of Hungarian representatives, and received a number of written statements from Hungarians, some of which remain in the papers in our possession. After his inquiries, he wrote a long memorandum for President Masaryk, of which a copy also went to Foreign Minister Beneš. There is a copy in the papers, together with a handwritten draft of a letter to Masaryk. There is no record of a reply from either of them; but this may be explained by the likelihood that they discussed it when they met in the following year.

He was also interested in the Hungarian minority in Romania, and on at least one occasion was able to intervene successfully on behalf of a Hungarian journalist. However, his opportunities were limited by the fact that his relations with the Liberal Party governments of the 1920's, dominated by the Brătianu family, were not good. Only when the National Peasants led by Maniu came to power in 1928 was there a better opportunity, but at that time the disputes about the return of King Carol II, and still more the onset of the world economic depression, drove Hungarian minority affairs into the background.

In Yugoslavia he was unable to do anything. In the 1920's the Serb-Croat conflicts absorbed almost all his attention. The dictatorship of King Alexander, introduced on 6 January 1929, developed in such a way that, in Seton-Watson's view, almost the whole population of Yugoslavia became victims of repression. If nothing could be done for the Croats, or even for the Serbs, it was hopeless to think of the Hungarians.

In 1930 Seton-Watson had a conversation in London with Count István Bethlen, of which a few notes have survived in his papers. The most interesting point which emerged was Bethlen's insistence on a high priority for the improvement of relations with Romania. The advent to power of Maniu, for whom Bethlen expressed respect, seemed to hold out hopes. Seton-Watson was impressed by Bethlen's personality. They did not discuss revision of frontiers, on which they simply "agreed to differ."

The economic depression, the rise of Hitler to power, the ascendancy of Gömbös in Hungary, and the retreat of western statesmen before German and Italian claims, made frontier revision seem even less expedient to Seton-Watson. He argued against it in his short book *Treaty Revision and the Hungarian Frontiers*, published in 1934.

The cession of territory by Czechoslovakia to Hungary after the Munich agreement of 1938 was a source of deep disagreement between Seton-Watson and his younger colleague C. A. Macartney. These two had long known, respected and liked each other, and the differences between their views of the past and present of Central Europe were comparatively small. However, Macartney felt that, though Hitler's victory at Munich was bad, at least some good had come of it through the return to Hungary of territories with a mainly Magyar population; whereas Seton-Watson felt that Hitler was a deadly menace to all Europe, that any surrender to him was a disaster, and that any government which accepted favours from him was making itself his satellite and undermining its own national independence. Macartney put his view in an article in *The Times* shortly after Munich, and there followed a painful interchange of private letters between the two men.

During the Second World War Seton-Watson advocated the restoration of Czechoslovakia, Yugoslavia and Romania. In particular, he insisted in 1940 that Transylvania should be part of Romania. This by no means implied that the Romanian-Hungarian frontier of 1940 was sacrosanct in every detail. However, the views of Seton-Watson, Macartney and any other western scholar or politician on desirable future frontiers for Hungary were of absolutely no importance, since the post-1945 frontier settlement was imposed unilaterally, by force, by the dominant Soviet empire.

*   *   *

Looking back over Seton-Watson's relationship to Hungary, and in particular to territorial problems, there can be no question that he was a consistent political opponent. This does not however mean that he hated Hungarians. On the contrary, he had Hungarian friends whom he greatly esteemed, especially Károlyi and Jászi, and did his best, both between the wars and during the Second World War, to help Hungarians who had preferred exile to life in a Hungary increasingly dominated (though not with the consent of all Hungarian political leaders) by Hitler. The tragedy was that those Hungarians whom Seton-Watson respected – the radical liberals, socialists and believers in equal status for nationalities – were never in power in Hungary. When it briefly appeared that they might have some influence, they were summarily dismissed either by the old Right or by the extreme Left obedient to Moscow. István Tisza and István Bethlen, Béla Kun and Mátyás Rákosi, all rejected, though in different degree, the values of Seton-Watson's Hungarian friends.

This summary, which is intended neither to criticize nor to defend but to explain, and which inevitably leaves a good deal still unexplained, is the best that I can do on the basis of the evidence known to me.

Notes

For more than ten years I have been studying – together with my brother Christopher, Fellow of Oriel College, Oxford – the papers of R. W. Seton-Watson in our joint possession, as well as searching for related documents in other archives, in the United Kingdom and abroad. The main result of these labors is a political biography written by us jointly, on the period of his life in which he was most active in political affairs: *The making of a New Europe: R. W. Seton-Watson and the last years of Austria-Hungary*. It was published jointly by Methuens (London) and the University of Washington Press (Seattle) in April 1981. Apart from this, two volumes of correspondence, together with some other miscellaneous documents, relating to Yugoslav matters, were published in Zagreb (Institute of History) and London (British Academy) in 1976. Edited jointly by us and by our Yugoslav colleagues, Ljubo Boban, Mirjana Gross, Bogdan Krizman and Dragovan Šepić, the volumes are entitled *R. W. Seton-Watson and the Yugoslavs: Correspondence 1906-1941*. Both these books contain much material relating to Hungary. Three further articles by myself, containing excerpts from original documents or full texts, are: "R. W. Seton-Watson and the Romanians," *Revue roumaine d'histoire*, no. 1 (1971), pp. 25-42; "R. W. Seton-Watson's Einstellung zur Habsburger-Monarchie 1906-1914," *Österreich in Geschichte und Literatur*, no 6. (1973), pp. 361-381; and "Anton Štefánek and R. W. Seton-Watson," *Bohemia* (yearbook of the Collegium Carolinum in Munich) (1977), pp. 226-254. Further documents are contained in *Századok*, no. 4, (1977), pp. 749-774 entitled "Jászi Oszkár és R. W. Seton-Watson levelezése az első világháború előtti években," [The Correspondence of Oszkár Jászi and R. W. Seton-Watson in the Prewar Years] with an excellent introductory essay by Géza Jeszenszky. I am, at present, engaged, with Romanian colleagues, on the publication of a volume, similar to the Yugoslav volume of 1976, of documents relating to Seton-Watson's relations with Romanians. I also hope to produce a substantial study, probably a long article with documentary supplements, on his relations with Hungarians. Colleagues at the Historical Institute in Budapest have long expressed an encouraging interest in such an article, and it is my strong hope that I shall produce it soon. Unfortunately the burdens of life in our increasingly despised, obstructed, and bureaucratised universities (a phenomenon which of course also has its counterpart in the United States), together with the weaknesses to which all flesh is heir, have delayed me. Meanwhile, I am most grateful to Professor Király for giving me the opportunity to offer this provisional, and insufficiently documented, contribution.

References

1. Probably not including Vojvodina, since the incorporation of the Serbs of Bácska and Banat in the South Slav unit would have been extremely difficult. See also below.
2. See his article "The Archduke Francis Ferdinand," *Contemporary Review*, August 1914. The article was written before outbreak of war.
3. For details, see *The Making of a New Europe*, pp. 98-100. He counted very much on the co-operation of Jászi.
4. See especially the statement to him in June 1909 of Take Ionescu. *Ibid.*, p. 72.
5. *Ibid.*, p. 102.
6. *R. W. Seton-Watson and the Yugoslavs: Correspondence 1906-1941*, Vol. I, no. 117, pp. 192-193. This document is a memorandum written in Niš and dated January 12, 1915, intended for the Foreign Office.

Mária Ormos

The Military Convention of Belgrade

On 13 November 1918 in Belgrade General Henrys, Commander of the French Eastern Army and Duke Mišić, Commander-in-Chief of the Serbian army, representing the Allies and Béla Linder, representative of the Hungarian government signed a military convention "to carry out" the armistice agreement, which put an end to the war.[1] Since the convention fixed the demarcation line, behind which the Hungarian Army had to be moved back within Hungarian borders (although the Agreement of Padua, signed on 3rd November, did not include[2] such a line) public opinion and historiography has always been concerned to know why Hungary signed the Convention. What makes the question even more interesting is that the government had an armistice, which was formally valid.

After two weeks it became clear that the Convention did not satisfy French interests. Another problem arose. Why did the Allies – more precisely, France – make an agreement, which proved to be such a damaging mistake from the point of view of what happened after?

This time I do not want to discuss the viewpoints of the Hungarian government; these have already been cleared up by historians. They found several reasons to explain Károlyi's move to build up relations with the representative of the French army, to win recognition for his Goverment's foreign policies, to stabilize its internal basis, and to influence the form of the expected intervention.[3] For these reasons, the politically emotional statments of the Horthy era, that the contacts with Belgrade and especially the signing of the Convention were fatal political mistakes or even treason by Károlyi,[4] do not deserve attention.

My aim is to explain France's moves, and I would like to do this in a way which is different to usual practices in the history of diplomacy. Mainly, I do not aim to describe the French-Hungarian relations in detail (although, at some points I do), but I try to put the Hungarian question in its place within the general political situation and efforts of France. Since the length of this essay is limited, it will only outline this question without giving a full and detailed explanation.[5]

There are two basic historiographic explanations of France's role in the Military Convention of Belgrade. One of them says, that at the time when the Convention was signed, its text and the demarcation line described in it were satisfactory for France. Within this explanation there are big differences in opinions about the creation and the future of the Convention. Some historians think that the conditions of the Convention were more disadvantageous for Hungary than the provisions of Padua, because the latter were worked out by all of the Allies (perhaps by the Italian Government, the Italian Army or by General Diaz alone) while the Convention was France's work. Later the French government had the chance to enforce even more effectively its hostile plans. This theory established the charge against Károlyi, which said that Károlyi, if he was looking for relationships, should have turned to friendly Italy and not to hostile France.[6]

According to another theory of the same basic explanation, the Convention was made in the spirit of rational consideration, and what became fatal for Hungary, was not the signing of it, but its gradual annulment, dictated by the French government afterwards. This opinion makes it possible for its representatives to explain the Convention as a compromise among the Allies, and within this compromise as a concession of France, or as a deliberate deception. Both these opinions regard the annulment of the Convention as a deliberate political game. This explanation goes back to the memories of leftwing bourgeois republicans and social democrats.[7] Its motives are emotional and it is difficult to analyze these experiences on account of feelings of betrayal, self-justification and isolation.

French policy changes made on the basis of November 13 have been examined more objectively in recent years. Attention has been focused on Hungarian-Romanian relations. There are larger and smaller differences of opinion among historians, but the latest researches agree that the gradual French annulment of the Convention was caused by the gradual development of the policy of a Romanian alliance, and from this point of view the interest of France in the intervention against the Soviets was decisive.[8] The merit of this viewpoint is that it clearly emphasises one of the important determinants of the events; but in some works (not generally though) makes other, more traditional characteristics of the policy of the Romanian alliance seem less important. Directly or indirectly, the above explanation suggests the opinion that the Convention itself coincided with a political concept. Opinions vary whether this political concept is connected to one individual, to the French government or to the Allies.

So, the explanation that the annulment of the Convention is closely connected to the interest in a Romanian alliance, can be connected to the second basic explanation for establishing the Convention, which thinks that the Convention was established as a result of a – technical or deliberate – mistake. General Franchet d'Esperey was supposed to have made the mistake, according to the first version, because of his lack of information, or according to the second version, because of his own inspirations, different to his government's.[9] In both versions, we have to suppose that between the 3rd and 13th of November the Commander of the Eastern Army of the Allies did not receive any orders about the Hungarian question, that he wrote the text of the Convention, and that he did not even know the text of the armistice. If we go along with this opinion, we now also meet the belief that some aspects of the Convention reflected the personal goodwill of the general. According to this, the signs of goodwill were the abandonment of the so called "order clause" and that the public services of the territories, which the Allies planned to occupy, were to be left under Hungarian supervision. The explanation, according to which the Convention was a mistake, tacitly or deliberately concludes that the conditions of the Convention did not express France's viewpoint, were not in harmony with her political conceptions, and were contradictory.

To reconsider the above problem, first of all, we have to remember the circumstances under which the date and conditions of the Peace Treaty were decided. In the summer of 1918 French politicians were seeking unconditional surrender, which was based on the elimination of the Central European Powers and which, for this reason, could include extensive demands, such as the conditions of a political settlement in Central Europe. Several earlier plans[10] were made in this connection but at the end of the war, more precisely, in October 1918 they started to become less important.

The most important question is what were the reasons for such a substantial change in the Convention? Historiography emphasizes one of the reasons, America's political vision, expressed by President Wilson and Colonel House, which, already at this time – with British support – would have opposed extensive French demands. I also believe that, to some extent, American views also played a part in changing France's viewpoint, but not through direct opposition, but because of other differences. There are several signs which reveal that the French government was influenced by other major motives, when it made the changes mentioned.

Obviously, the American viewpoint had to be considered by Paris, because of the considerable financial support of the United States, and primarily because of the major role of the American Expeditionary Force in the victory. Although the French government was listening to Washington, it was far from accepting the president's political ideas. How did the French government show its dissatisfaction in connection with Wilson's moves in October-November? The French government first protested against Wilson's message to Karl on 21 October, 1918. According to the French minister of foreign affairs, the message was offensive to France, because the president made the decision without consulting the Allies, though the French government is of the opinion, that "... one of the most serious, perhaps the most serious problem of the war is the Austrian question."[11] The text by Pichon, the minister of foreign affairs, generally lets us think that the French government did not want to settle the problems of the Dual Monarchy through internal negotiations and agreements, as suggested by Wilson's message, but wanted to keep the question under the control of the Allies, and especially of France.

On the same day, the 21st of October, France also protested against the president's offer to mediate in the armistice to be signed with Turkey. In the two versions of the instructions made for Washington, Ambassador Jusserand, the following French standpoints are expressed: the French government does not desire mediation, because "the mediation of the United States would ensure the rights of a judge to the President, which he wants very much to acquire and soon we would see him intervening in all areas, and taking away the initiative and the right to decisions in our affairs." In the end, instead of this blunt text, the Ministry of Foreign Affairs sent instructions to the ambassador, which were more finely worded, but which contained the most important points.[12]

Consideration of these arguments in connection with the armistice with Germany started much earlier, but only the president's decisive note of 23 October caused conflicts between America and France. On 6 October the German government approached the president for the first time. On the same day Clemenceau asked Marshal Foch whether the French government could approve an armistice with Germany. Marshal Foch could not know the president's – qiute rigorous – answer, when, on 8th he answered the question with a confident yes, adding that suitable conditions had to be reached, which he also outlined.[13] In their telegraphs, neither the prime minister, nor the commander-in-chief mentioned any of the Allies' opinions or viewpoints and did not discuss any political questions.

The question was only discussed and considered within the frames of French political interest.

After the French government and High Command – in complete agreement – had accepted the earliest possible armistice under certain conditions, no conflict arose, even, if there had been conflict earlier. But after the American president's note of October 23 the same problem mentioned earlier came up: Wilson's demand to act as an arbiter, and as an additional difficulty, his wish to make the armistice conform to the Fourteen Points he had issued in January 1918.[14] The French Ministry of Foreign Affairs stated that the armistice was not to be signed on the basis of the above, and the British cabinet took a similar position.[15] The Supreme Military Council was appointed to decide the question. At its session of 29th-31st, Colonel House represented the president.

Apart from the fact that Wilson wanted to act as a judge, the question of using the Fourteen Points was the main reason why the British and the French government decided for a "purely military" armistice. Although the term had been introduced earlier, the details of the armistice became final at the conference of the Allies. On October 29, during the fierce debate between House and the European politicians, the representative of the president – as a threat – raised the possibility of the United States leaving the war; he finally became satisfied, when Great Britain and France, with some reservations, theoretically accepted the Fourteen Points as the basis for making peace.[16] House gave evidence of a rich imagination by interpreting this as an American victory.[17]

So, the American-French clash influenced the details of the armistice as outlined above, but it did not directly effect its date. The acceptance of the armistice was influenced automatically the same way by the French decision itself. The situation was the following: the political demands had to be given up, because this was the only way to side-step Wilson's political vision; indeed, they had to be put aside temporarily anyway, because, at the beginning of October the French government – whether was influenced by the other allies, or not – had decided to make peace as soon as possible. So, this brings us back to our original question: what were the reasons for the decision?

The above suggests that English and American aspirations, the state of the French army and of France all played a part in making the decision, but the most important role was the evaluation of German military forces and of the German situation. To this we have to add that in the case of the Dual Monarchy, there were special elements influencing the decision.

At this time the French Headquarters and government saw a greater danger for the future in not making the most of the victory over Germany. This was based on the assumption that a disintegrating German army – as Clemenceau put it to Foch – would draw the country into revolution, and a German revolution would establish a German-Russian alliance.[18] In other words, a German-Russian combination would be formed, against which French diplomacy had been directed for decades, and which would be dangerous with or without a revolution. In the present case, this collaboration was even more frightening, because one of the states was on her way to a proletarian dictatorship, and it was impossible to guess where the other state would stop. At the same time, French headquarters were convinced that "the continuation of the military success of the Allies in the West would speed up the social transformation in Germany, and would provide an opportunity for a union imagined by Lenin."[19]

In theory there were two ways to avert this danger. One was to limit the victory over Germany to a certain extent, that is, not to maximize the causes for a revolution in Germany. The other was to intervene in Soviet-Russia, overthrow the Bolsheviks or, at least, separate the two states from each other. The French government tried to combine the two. Everything suggests that it started preparations for the Soviet-Russian intervention at the same time as dropping the idea of a total victory over Germany.[20]

All the reasons which hastened an armistice with Germany played a part in the case of the Dual Monarchy. But there were also special aspects which contributed to the quick, in some points, too quick, signing of the armistice. One of these was that the Dual Monarchy's departure from the war could have put pressure on Germany and could have helped France to reach her aims in the region. If the German government had proved recalcitrant, military pressure could have been applied on Germany from the South-east, through the territory of the Dual Monarchy. But there was one even more important and pressing aspect.

Because of its internal situation, there was a danger that the Dual Monarchy as a sovereign state, would disappear. In the last third of October, the French Ministry of Foreign Affairs and Ministry of Defense received several indications of signs of decay. The possibility was raised that within a very short period of time there would be no authority or person in the Dual Monarchy to sign an internationally valid document. Between October 21 and 25 it became evident to Paris that the Habsburg Monarchy was just a fiction.[21] Historians have ever since emphasised how urgent it was, or would have been, from the point of view of a last attempt to save the Dual Monarchy, to sign the armistice quickly.[22] Less attention was paid to the other side of the question, that this would also have been of the highest importance and urgency for the Allies, if they did not want one of the belligerent parties to collapse in ruins before signing the document.

The French government did not want this to happen and did everything to prevent it. The French Ministry of Foreign Affairs declared that if an independent Hungarian government was established, it had to be considered as non-existent, and that they would not sign an armistice with it. With regard to the Austrian decision of 21 October, made by the provisional National Assembly, the decisions of an "illegal" body could not be regarded as legitimate.[23] At the same time certain officials of the Ministry of Foreign Affairs tried to find a way to persuade the government in Vienna to sign the armistice at once. Promises to support the House of Habsburg, help the re-establisment of economic relations with the breakaway states and the cooperation with them, and so forth, were raised.[24]

Why did the collapse of the Monarchy seem so damaging for the French government that it would have been ready to sign the armistice at a time which was disadvantageous from a military point of view? The ending of the Dual Monarchy had legal and, more importantly, political consequences. Later the conference twisted its principles so that it found a way to sign a peace treaty with two states in the name of one, but this was inconceivable in connection with the armistice. One of the reasons for this was that an armistice signed in the name of the Dual Monarchy gave a basis for the above. In October 1918, a disappearence of the Monarchy would have created a situation, where instead of the "old offender" there would be two "innocent" non-belligerent states. In this case who could be dictated to, who could be penalized, and how would it be possible to prevent the validation of "autonomy" for Austria? Pichon's indignation against President Wilson's message of 18 October to Austria proves what serious trouble the latter problem caused in Paris. The outline made for the ambassador included the following: "We cannot let Germany strengthen itself with the German elements of Austria, in a new form, which she might take up as a necessary result of the war, after the break up of Prussian hegemony."[25]

Finally, there was only one possible conclusion: no matter what it might cost, an armistice agreement had to be made with Vienna, while the Imperial Government was able to sign it. For the armistice there was no other solution than to adapt to the front as it stood. As a consequence, in the case of the Dual Monarchy, most of the conditions developed by the Headquarters on 15 October had to be dropped. First, let us look at this plan, which is also highly interesting from the point of view of the principles of a political rearrangement. One of its main points was the ensuring of free passage; according to several French documents, this served two main purposes: to clear the way for the Eastern powers of the Allies, if they had to engage Germany, and to ensure the route to the Ukraine.[26] The plan fixed the main points of the demarcation line to be followed on each front line. The Dual Monarchy was involved in three: the Italian front, the Balkan front and, connected to it, the Eastern Romanian front. In the Italian Sector the demarcation line was fixed as the line accepted in the secret Treaty of London in 1915, and in the South – avoiding the question of Croatia – the evacuation of Syrmia was demanded.[27]

We have to discuss the problem of the supposed Romanian front in more detail. In 1916, during long negotiations conducted to involve Romania in the war, the Allies greatly committed themselves to this state. Under the secret pact signed in Bucharest on 17 of August 1916 Romania were to get Bukovina, Banat and the Eastern part of Hungary, which not only included Transylvania, but also the Partium, and significantly large parts of the Great Hungarian Plain. They fixed the border line – as an average – 50 kilometers to the West of the borders set finally in Trianon. The secret pact made the specification that Romania would not make a separate peace with the Central Powers.[28] But as a result of the military situation, the Romanian government was forced to ask for an armistice in 1917, and in May 1918 it signed a Peace Treaty with Germany and Austria-Hungary.[29] As a consequence, the provisions of the secret pact ceased to have effect.

But it was a premature conclusion to claim Romania was judged according to its shaken legal situation. Neither the French government, nor the other Allies came to this conclusion. After Romania had signed the armistice agreement, the French Minister of Foreign Affairs assured the Romanian minister that nothing had changed in the relationship between the two countries, and after Romania had signed the peace treaty, the French government started to concentrate on assisting the Romanian politicians diplomatically and later militarily, to bring Romania back into the war.[30] What had changed in French-Romanian relations? The Romanian peace treaty made it possible for the Allies, and especially France, to change the promises made under the secret pact, if they thought it essential and to lay down certain conditions to Romanian political circles.

The French government tried to make use of both opportunities. Firstly, it laid down the condition that the Romanian government that had signed the peace treaty, had to resign, and Romania had to set up a new government, friendly to the Allies and return to the war. The French government could not lay it down as a condition, but made it clear that it would have prefered to see Take Ionescu in an important position, and avoid Brătianu.[31] At the end of September, it made a step to involve Romania in the Bulgarian armistice, but the changes demanded of Romania did not happen at this time.[32] After this, the French decided to take military action in order to encourage Romanian political circles into the required decision. This was to be carried out by the newly structured Army of the Danube, under the command of General Berthelot. Another task of this army group was to take part in the intervention. For this, the Supreme Command used about half of the French Army of the Orient.[33] But, by the time they concentrated, organised and despatched the new army, it was already too late, even from the point of view of the armistice signed with the Dual Monarchy. The fact that the French government, which in order to involve Romania in the armistice, had sent its own soldiers at the double through Bulgaria towards the Romanian border, was finally ready to sign the armistice agreement without waiting for its plans concerning Romania to be fulfilled, reinforces what we have so far said about the urgency of the signing of the armistice. We have to add that the French government was consistent on this question. Although, in its declaration of 5 November, the American government recognized Romania's status as an ally and the jusice of her demands and promised to support these,[34] Paris saw the situation as before; in other words, since the demanded change of governments and declaration of war had not taken place in Romania, there was no front there and thus it was not possible to make an armistice agreement for a front that did not exist.

So, previous conceptions about the Romanian front had to be discarded. Another reason for these was that on 31 October, when the Allies accepted the conditions of the armistice agreement, the French forces under the command of Berthelot, were not in positions which would allow them to be used as the occupation army of the Eastern demarcation line. Nevertheless, it is very instructive to see the armistice line in the plan of October 15 in the Eastern parts of Hungary. It ran through Temesvár (Timişoara), Nagyvárad (Oradea) and Nagybánya (Baia Mare). These towns and the area between them had to be evacuated for the Romanian Army.[35] This suggests that the French Headquarters altered the demarcation line of 1916. They did not want to give the whole of the Banat to Romania, but to divide it between Romania and Serbia, so that the line went west of Temesvár from the Danube to the Maros. From here running east to the Nagyvárad heights, it was basically the same as the border fixed by the conference, but north of Nagyvárad, it deviated in Hungary's favor.

What were the considerations for this alteration of the border of 1916? I believe that the legal point of view dominated. But it is also possible that some French individuals – like several other Allied politicians – regarded the promises of the secret pact as excessive,[36] and now that the legal position had changed, wanted to take advantage of the opportunity to alter it. A more important argument, also emphasized by the Ministry of Foreign Affairs, might have been that meanwhile Romania had occupied Besarabia, which, naturally, was not and could not have been mentioned in the Secret Treaty of Bucharest, so Romania's demands on the West had to be moderated.[37]

After it had become clear, that the Romanian front could not be reopened before concluding the armistice, General Guillaumat, predecessor of Franchet d'Esperey on the Balkan front, worked out a new plan for the armistice. The document of October 28 pointed out two main goals: to develop a military situation, in which it would be possible to re-start operations, if necessary, and to extend the operational areas to Romania, and later to Russia. To achieve these goals Guillaumat wanted to establish five bridgeheads on the left side of the Danube in order to be able to control Hungary (Palánka, Újvidék, Pancsova, Kubin, Báziás), and wanted the German troops to retire within 15 days. He also wanted the Balkan states under attack, Serbia, Albania and Montenegro, to be evacuated.[38] This plan reflected the current military situation; it did not mention the areas of the Dual Monarchy which the Allies had not invaded yet, and it also did not mention the Eastern front, which had not been formed yet.

At the last moment another modifying circumstance came up. On 29 October according to the Allies, on the Italian front, General Diaz had responsibility, on the Balkan front, General d'Esperey; the representatives of the Monarchy had to submit to them their request for armistice, and they had the authority to sign it.[39] But on the 31st, when the conditions were accepted, not only the demands of October 15, but also General Guillaumat's plans were dropped and a demarcation line was fixed only on the Italian border, and the text to be signed was only sent to General Diaz. There was no word about the Commander-in-Chief of the Allied Armies of the Orient on the Balkan front making another armistice.[40] What caused these newest modifications? The clear answer is the events in Hungary. The Hungarian liberal democratic revolution had started, so the previous decision came into effect: no separate armistice agreement to be concluded with an independent Hungarian government. But, since it was not possible to make arrangements on this front without involving the Hungarian government, the Eastern front, as well as the Balkan front was left out of the text of the armistice agreement. The text included in theory the whole of the Danube Monarchy, but, in practice, only the sector of the front where Vienna's authority was primary, and where the military situation was clear.

We are of the opinion that Serb interests were not left out from the text of Padua, because of Italian wishes, but because of the aspiration to sign the armistice agreement as soon as possible and without involving the Hungarian government.

The text of Padua was basically determined by three factors: the principle of a purely military armistice, the extreme urgency to have an armistice agreement with the Dual Monarchy and the outbreak of the Hungarian revolution. As a consequence of these three, the demarcation line on the East and in the Balkans was left out from the text and the plan for a dual armistice was dropped. It is automatically clear that the problem of Slovakia was not neglected because of forgetfulness or haste, but because since there was no front, they could not make any arrangements. As soon as the conception of an armistice agreement which contained general and political conditions was dropped, it became clear that the problem of Czechoslovakia could not be solved within the framework of the armistice agreement and that a different solution had to be found. It seems that after they had signed the armistice, but before they made the convention, the Allies unsuccessfully tried to open up a "Czechoslovakian front."[41]

Although the Armistice of Padua did not have any real effects on Hungary, the Allies refered its general provisions to her,too. This reference was automatic and it did not need the agreement of the Hungarian government, which was not even recognized by the Allies. The Allies could not and did not ask for Hungary's agreement, but the fact that Hungary gave her agreement, helped them a lot. The Italian officers, conducting the negotiations reported that only one armistice agreement would be signed, and the Austrian General Weber announced this to the Hungarian organizations on November 2nd.[42] On the basis of earlier information, the commission of the Dual Monarchy responsible for the Balkan front and which had been set up only a few days in advance, sent a delegation to this front, too, and the two delegates received General d'Esperey's conditions in Belgrade. Following his earlier instructions, d'Esperey announced that on the Balkan front he was authorized to negotiate and sign the armistice agreement.[43] But before negotiations could be continued or could have any consequence, in the early morning of November 4 the Hungarian central military organizations informed General Weber via telegraph, who was on his way to Padua, that they, as the Hungarian party, authorized him to sign the armistice agreement.[44] General Weber had already signed the armistice agreement on the previous day, but the document's provisions had not yet come into effect. Although, the Hungarian declaration was problematical from a legal point of view and the Allies did not remark upon it from this point, they were relieved that the Hungarian government did not wish to continue hostilities.

What did the Hungarian government think about this declaration? It had informations from two sources: one of them came from Padua and said that only the armistice agreement signed in Padua would be valid, the other came from Franchet d'Esperey and announced that concerning the Balkan front sector, the Hungarian government had to sign an armistice agreement with him. This question could not have been decided in Budapest.

Hungarian historians analyze the difficulties which Károlyi's government would have had to contend with, if the Allies considered Hungary as belligerent.[45] These can be summarized. In this case it was obvious that the offensive of the Balkan would have continued, and not only French, but also Serb troops would have entered the country with unknown strategic – and possibly political – aims. To avoid this, the Hungarian government immediately accepted the Croatian secession declaration of 29 October. At this time Croatia, which seceded from the empire, but did not join Serbia, which belonged to the Yugoslav state, was a buffer state. It was in the interest of the Hungarian government to maintain this situation. The question of Transylvania needed urgent solution, too. The Monarchy's collapse was likely to be followed by action from Romania. If the armistice agreement was not signed, she could re-enter the war and move against Hungary. It seemed most important for the Hungarian government to clear this situation, before the Romanian political circles could make a move. Károlyi had a third problem which had to be solved, regardless. The German forces under the command of Marshal Mackensen were – from the Ukraine to Banat – collecting themselves, and on their way to the

West. They could not possibly avoid Hungary, and Germany had not signed any armistice agreements at this time. If Hungary, as a state friendly to the Allies, opposed these well armed and almost intact force of around 170,000 soldiers, she would break existing trade relations with Germany and as a result of the blockade, the country would be without coal and other raw materials within days. But if she did not take action against them, she would become the supporter of a belligerent Germany. The latter did not suit Károlyi's view of foreign affairs.

The question of Mackensen's army had to be sorted out, even if the Armistice of Padua had applied to Hungary. In this case, the strategic points mentioned in the armistice agreement, the size of the armies and the details of occupation had to be fixed, too. Taking everything into consideration, it was in Hungary's – legal, military and political – interest to clarify her situation and establish it in a way which still benefited her to some degree.

How the other side came to its viewpoint is our next question. We do not know exactly when the formula for the application of the armistice was established or which French organization's idea it was. But already on November 6 Clemenceau, repeatedly emphasizing that they had made the armistice agreement with the whole of the Dual Monarchy, authorized Franchet d'Esperey to make an agreement about the military application of the armistice with the Hungarian government, as the representative of the "local organization."[46] We – at least now – cannot establish, which Allied governments the French consulted on this question; but the events following suggest that the British cabinet was informed about it, but the Italians were not. It is natural that Serbia, was informed.

Secondly, we have to mention Franchet d'Esperey's role; and the idea put forward by French politicians and the Allies, and of publicists and historians, who followed them, that the General acted arbitrarily, without instructions, or ignored the instructions, without knowing his government's intentions.[47] Let us see how events can be reconstructed from the French sources. Immediately after the armistice delegation had arrived at Belgrade on November 3, Franchet d'Esperey asked his superiors in Paris whether the document signed by Diaz was valid for Hungary, or whether he had to carry on with the negotiations, if the Hungarians came back to him.[48] Clemenceau's answer has already been mentioned: the General had to carry on with the negotiations as required by the armistice agreement.[49] On the 7th Franchet d'Esperey reported that he had been informed of the arrival of the delegation led by Károlyi in Belgrade. From Niš, he would also go to Belgrade, and according to his instructions, he would discuss with Károlyi the application of the armistice agreement, especially the ownership and use of the railways and water ways, and the question of military protection for Serbia.[50] Meanwhile the Ministry of Defense sent a packet to Niš, which, according to the shipping document, was supposed to be handed over to the General. The consignment contained two documents, the text of the armistice agreement signed in Villa Giusti, and another document, which was explained by the shipping document as "a text for General Franchet d'Esperey".[51] It is difficult to imagine that, at the given time and in the given situation and context, this document was not the text of the military convention to be signed. The documents of the General prove that he went to Niš and then had negotiations with Károlyi and the Hungarian delegation.[52] The General's telegramme of 8 of November supports this idea. In it he asked whether it would be reasonable to add the condition, which was left out of the text, that if German forces did not leave Hungarian territory within the time period given to them, the Hungarian government would be obliged to disarm and intern them.[53] This brings us to two conclusions. In his telegraph, the General could not have refered to the Armistice of Padua, because it contained the above condition. On the other hand, he must have realized that the text of Padua contained this condition, but the other text did not. The other conclusion is that if he had not received a prepared text, but had written the Belgrade text, he would not have asked such a question. Finally, there is the General's instruction to General Henrys on November 12. He ordered Henrys to go to Belgrade and sign the military convention with the representative of the Hungarian government. And he added – without further comment – that there were some changes in the text. The title was changed (originally it had been an armistice agreement, but it was changed to a military convention), point 11 gave 15 instead of 10 days for the German forces to leave, and point 18, which stated that "the hostilities between Hungary and the Allies ceased" was left out from the text.[54] This telegram suggests that the changes were made in Paris. The title was in the category "application," the deadline for the Germans to leave was the same as in the Padua document, and finally, since the armistice had already ended hostilities, its repetition was avoided. The change suggested by Franchet d'Esperey was not made, probably, because the Ministry of Defense did not think that its application was important. So, it seems that Franchet D'Esperey did not take the freedom to put in even half a sentence arbitrarily. There was another small motive, proving that the General was indifferent to the whole question, that he was not arbitrary and he did not initiate. When he made his report on the negotiations with Károlyi and at the request of Károlyi he sent it off to the Hungarian declaration via telegraph, he did not comment on it. All he wrote was that if Paris gave a positive answer, the convention could be signed; anyway, he would continue the occupation.[55]

We believe, that the documents described above give us reasonable enough evidence to drop the theory which suggests that Franchet d'Esperey made a mistake or that he had intentions different to the Governments. Some points are worth examining separately, to clear up the misunderstandings in connection with this theory. As a test, we can compare the texts of Padua and of Belgrade. The biggest formal/technical error of the Convention is in its first paragraph, which states, that the civil services of the territories, occupied by the Allies, remain under the responsibility of local organisations. This paragraph was regarded as showing the goodwill (serious mistake, etc.) of Franchet d'Esperey. In reality it was not a "concession." Paragraph 6 stated: "In the evacuated Austrian-Hungarian territories, temporarily, local organisations would take over the administration under the control of the occupying armies of the Allies." The text of Belgrade also contained the above sentence, except for the word "temporarily." But the military convention connected to the armistice cannot be considered final.

Károlyi, and after him, many historians, believed that it was a concession to the Hungarian government that the arrangement clause was left out of the text of Belgrade. Afterwards it is difficult to reconstruct whether the text originally contained a separate paragraph on this question or if paragraph 3 was shortened. We do not want to speculate. What is important is the precedents and a thorough comparison of the two texts (the text of Padua and the text of Belgrade).

Concerning the precedents, the British and French governments, knowing that the armistice agreement would not solve the problems of any rearrangement of the Dual Monarchy's realized that they could make up for this deficiency by occupying strategic points. This requirement was, actually, the result of the free passage, but Paris realized that, by occupying these points, they would be able to solve the problem of rearrangement in Central Europe. Several documents, dated the last days of October and the first days of November illustrate this realization. The most significant of these is an account of foreign affairs, signed by chief of section de Caix. This document declares that the Allied occupation of the territory of Austria-Hungary is essential in order to satisfy the claims of national minorities.[56] A long study by an unknown writer explained the political importance of the French occupation of this sector. It took into consideration French troops stationed in Romania, Czechoslovakia, Hungary and also possibly in Austria, and saw this as the guarantee of French influence in Central Europe. It stated that the military occupation of Hungary had to be completed by civilians sent to Hungary and regarded the occupation as taking advantage of the pro-French political direction of the new Hungarian Republic. At the same time it was of the opinion that one of the tasks of the military presence in Romania was to take part in the occupation of parts of Transylvania, because the handing over would cause difficulties and grievance for the minorities which might be lessened by the presence of the French. The whole concept of the document is no less than the interpretation of the occupation of the strategic points as made by the French Ministry of Foreign Affairs.[57] The French (and also English) interpretation is reflected in the dispute of 31 October over the conditions of Padua between the Allies. Serb representative Vesnić took part in this sitting and asked for the armistice agreement to respect Serb interests. Clemenceau and the British Minister of Foreign Affairs Balfour had two arguments for not accepting this demand. They both pointed out that an armistice agreement was not the equivalent of a peace treaty and that with the occupation of the strategic points all requirements could be satisfied.

To satisfy Vesnić and the Serb politicians in general, Balfour raised the so-called organization-requirement. As a result of the meeting of 31 October, there was only one change in the text written by the French Ministry of Foreign Affairs. They completed paragraph 4 on the occupation of the strategic points, which had already contained military reasons, with the term "pour maintenir l'ordre," *ie.* they justified the occupation of strategic points by two factors: military interests and the maintenance of order.[58]

Whether there had been a whole paragraph about it originally, or whether it had been part of paragraph 3, where it logically belongs, this reasoning was left out of the text of the Convention of Belgrade. All other reasoning was left out as well. In other words, the text of the Convention dealt with the occupation not through logic, but purely on the basis of the orders of the Commander-in-Chief. At the same time there were other ramifications. While the armistice agreement mentioned only strategic points, the Convention contained the following: "Droit d'occupation par les Alliés de *toutes localités* (emphasised by the author) ou tous points stratégiques." Thus the Convention ensured the right of the Commander-in-Chief to occupy any Hungarian farm or village without these being strategic points. In the above context we cannot speak of a concession to the Hungarian government.

After making it clear that when Franchet d'Esperey acted in connection with the Convention, he did not follow his own thoughts but probably received a prepared text, and pointing out that in the text Hungary did not get a concession, we get back to our original question: what was the aim of the French government in signing this document? The first aim, which was afterwards pointed out by Clemenceau, was a military one.[59] What could have been the particular military concept?

Earlier Hungarian historical literature considers that the French Government offered the Military Convention of Belgrade, so that free passage through the territory of Hungary would make it possible to cut off Mackensen's army and the Allies could also advance against Germany. They supported this with the documents of the meeting of the Allies on the 4th of November, where the question of opening a new front against Germany from this side, was raised. Those arguing for this interpretation thought that with the German Government signing of the armistice agreement on 11 November, Hungary's political aims had lost their way.[60] It is a fact, which is also proved by other documents that, in theory, the French government did not give up the idea of opening up a "second" front, until they had made a decision about the question of Germany. But it is very doubtful that they could have counted on the participation of the French forces in the Balkans. It seems that, in theory, French Headquarters wanted to maintain the possibility of a South-Eastern front against Germany, but since only the Italian army could have provided the forces for it, they wanted to take this action only in the last resort. The relevant documents of the Allies' discussions suggest that this topic was not discussed as a theoretical operation against Germany, but to try to declare Czechoslovakia a belligerent state. Attacking Germany from Prague and the participation of the units formed from Italy's Czech prisoners of war in a military operation against Germany arose as possible strategies. The Czech Minister of Foreign Affairs, who was deliberately invited to the conference, was shocked to hear these suggestions. He did not help the Allies to solve their problems with Czechoslovakia. At the same time the suggestion that Allied troops enter certain sectors of Czechoslovakia and Poland in order to prevent oil being transported from Silesia and Galicia to Germany was accepted. Prime Minister David Lloyd George was very active in these discussions.[61] Leaving this question open for further research, our conclusion is that, on the basis of the negotiations of November 4, the necessity of passing through Hungary pointed in two directions, towards Germany and also towards Czechoslovakia, and the latter was more clearly delineated.

Since the roads and railways of Hungary could not be by-passed either in the West-East direction, or in the South-North direction, it cannot be said that after the need to mount an attack against Germany was discontinued, interest in the passage through Hungary also ceased. The Czechoslovakian route, the Eastern route and the position of Hungary were all of geographical importance. French military thinking about Hungary was linked to their intentions towards Hungary's neighbours. As is shown by the above, they could have been important from the point of view of the approach of Galicia, and, as stated in Guillaumat's armistice plan made on 28 October, from the point of view of expanding the operational area to the East, towards Romania and Soviet Russia. At the same time the occupation of the strategic points – according to the above mentioned documents – was of political importance, too. The political rearrangement of Central Europe was to be carried out with the help of this occupation in order to support the establishment of French political hegemony. So, the French government had many good reasons to clarify the Hungarian question and in particular to procede with the invasion quickly and without further difficulties.

With the Convention, the French government succeeded in establishing the most advantageous military conditions for an invasion, but on the other hand, it also established a situation which removed the need for violence. The Convention fully dealt with the Serb army and in Transylvania it also abandoned the one defendable line, the Carpathian Mountains. The signing of the Convention also ensured that Hungary would not try to prevent the occupation of the strategic points, or the use of the country's traffic lines or vehicles. And if French troops occupied Hungarian strategic points, such as Budapest, they would be able to control the solving of the Transylvanian question, they would have a starting basis for Czechoslovakian deployment and they would be able to remain within a very short distance from Vienna. To sum it up, they would be able to reach the heart of Central Europe under the most advantageous conditions.

We cannot say why they fixed the demarcation line where they did on the East. The problem is, why they did not present the line, which was defined by the presentation of the Headquarters on 15 October, and why the French military leadership was satisfied with a temporary solution which was much more beneficial for Hungary. A further note from Headquarters concerning the regulations of the armistice, dated the 3rd of November, makes it more difficult to answer the questions. This document signed by General Georges stated that the armistice, unlike the Headquarters' note did not represent Serb or Romanian interests, and adds that although Romania was not belligerent, but aimed to be, it would be reasonable to confirm her efforts. According to General Georges the best way for this, was to include Újvidék (Novi Sad), Temesvár (Timişoara) and Nagyszeben (Sibiu) among the strategic points to be occupied.[62]

It is clear from this document that, in drawing up the military convention, the French Headquarters wanted to enforce Serb and Romanian interests. They succeeded in enforcing Serb interests. What happened with Romanian interests, we do not know. It is questionable why Nagyszeben (Sibiu) was mentioned in the document of the 3rd of November instead of Nagyvárad (Oradea) and Nagybánya (Baia Mare) of October 15th. We can only suppose that this moderation was caused by the fact that the French were interested in encouraging Romania's political leaders, but they did not want to satisfy most of Romania's demands, without Romania fulfilling French conditions. It is also possible that military considerations played a part in this moderation. We do not know what information France had on Hungary's military situation. So, the possibility that they did not satisfy these demands because of military motives cannot be excluded.

In any case, the Convention relied on the strategic points, and most of all, the occupation of the Hungarian capital, as the basis for a further political solution. This plan, up to now a summary of general principles, set an operational task with the signing of the Convention. Unfortunately, we do not have any direct documentation on the most important negotiation on this question between Károlyi and Franchet d'Esperey. There are several records of this meeting, but none speaks of this part of their discussion. There are only documents dated a few days after the meeting, which took the occupation of Budapest for granted. It is clear from these documents that General Henrys and the Minister without Portfolio Béla Linder agreed in several details of the occupation. Henrys officially informed the government of the dispatch of one division to Budapest and asked Linder to give him more details on transport between Újvidék (Novi Sad) and Budapest. The answer was taken by a Hungarian officer to Captain Ameil, sent to Szabadka (Subotica) by Henrys.[63] These discussions and their immediate effectiveness is completely unthinkable without preliminary agreement between Károlyi and d'Esperey, at least in principle.

The immediate occupation of Budapest, ordered by Henrys, was delayed, because Franchet d'Esperey was forced to call some forces to Fiume, because of Italian-Yugoslavian disagreements. However, he ordered Henrys to continue the concentration of troops, and until the occupation became practical, to send a mission to Budapest, which was also ordered to prepare all the details for occupation.[64] On 18 November, Clemenceau expanded the Commander-in-Chief's plan to some extent. He gave an order to allocate one division to the occupation of Budapest and another to the invasion of Vienna.[65]

Though Henrys thought that all delays were unnecessary and harmful, he followed orders and he sent Vix military mission to Budapest, also to prepare for the occupation.[66] Lieutenant-Colonel Vix, in cooperation with the Hungarian government completed his task within days. The French soldiers were received with empty barracks, fully equipped canteens and money exchange stands at Budapest's Keleti railway station.[67]

But by this time it was already too late, the French had changed their plans completely. The moment had passed which could have been regarded by the Hungarian government as an advantage from the point of view of foreign affairs. The government would have been able to determine the strategic points to be occupied (it had determined them very carefully, most of them at the most endangered places) and it had even won guarantees that these would be occupied by French troops.

What seemed to be an advantage in the Convention, became a disadvantage within a few days. All France's allies except for Serbia, who benefited the most from it, attacked the Convention. The Czechs protested, because, according to the Convention, the civil administration stayed with Hungary, so no practical union with Slovakia was possible.[68] On November 8 to 10, the Romanian Headquarters and government made the changes required by France and, since they did not have anybody to declare war on, sent an ultimatum to Mackensen.[69] If Károlyi had been urged to anticipate the Romanian move, his negotiations in Belgrade with the French Commander-in-Chief was probably one of the reasons, why Romania quickly moved to have herself regarded as an enemy of Hungary at the signing of the Convention. Romania protested against the Convention, because it did not give her all the territory demanded, according to the pact of 1916.[70] But, since this was not in the interests of the French, nor of the British government, Romania's leading politicians sought to enforce it, from this time. The first difficulty to overcome was the Military Convention of Belgrade. The Italian government also attacked the Convention on several points. It pointed out that the document had been signed without its knowledge, and it also protested that, by signing the document, France had de facto recognized a government, which, according to the Allies, did not exist. In reality, the major Italian complaint was that only French forces were supposed to occupy Hungary, though the Italian government was of the opinion that Italy had serious interests in the country.[71] At this point Italy began an independent policy towards Hungary. In her special way, Britain was also against French occupation. She officially protested against the news that Franchet d'Esperey wanted to involve British forces in the occupation of Budapest.[72] The source of this information is quite mysterious, because, according to all signs, the French government had no intention of doing that. What is more likely is that Britain might have realized that d'Esperey ordered troops, including some British units, to move, which, by helping French troops in other sectors, enabled the move to Budapest. This would have been without any political benefit to Great-Britain, while there was urgent need for British troops in other parts of the German Empire and in future intervention in Soviet Russia. The British government "opposed" a French objection which had not even arisen,[73] probably in order to make the French government abandon its plans.

The general attack of the Allies on the Convention made the French prime minister think again, especially when he compared this attack and its possible consequence of French isolation to the French military force available. He came to the conclusion that the two divisions would not be sufficient for the tasks to be done. In this context, the most amenable side of the Convention, to take control of Budapest without difficulties, in a friendly way, became the largest obstacle to its design. The journey and the friendly reception was no problem, but on 26 November it occured to Clemenceau that the whole Hungarian question was far from being solved. In this fashion Slovakia did not become part of Czechoslovakia and Transylvania was not handed over to Romania. On the same day, the Prime Minister was forced to inform those responsible that there was insufficient French military force available for the occupation of Slovakia.[74] What might have made the French Prime Minister think about the Romanian question was Mihály Károlyi's letter of 12 November to Lansing about the question of Transylvania, as a response to the declaration of the American government, made public on the 7th. The essence of the long historical 'rationale' of this letter was that there was no Hungarian government which could accept the loss of Transylvania.[75] On the basis of this letter, Clemenceau, who had only this document by Károlyi, could easily have come to the conclusion that goodwill towards French policies might cease at this point, and that in this question the possibility of concessions might not exist for the Hungarian government. Accordingly, he asked Marshal Foch, whether it was essential, from a military point of view, to occupy Budapest. He was afraid that at the point of handing over Transylvania to Hungary, the occupation of Budapest by insufficient French forces might cause difficulties.[76]

We are not going to analyze any further moves in detail. As a result of them, Paris suspended the occupation on 26 November, and temporarily declared it a dead letter on the 30th.[77] Later, in spite of constant French attempts to win authorization from the Allies, the temporary ban became final.[78] With this, the frame of the Convention collapsed, its provisions became an unnecessary burden and the Convention itself became fiction. It is not the purpose here to detail the absurd situation of the Hungarian government, of the local French military leaders and of the whole of Central Europe.

One thing concerning should be pointed out, however. Naturally, afterwards the government did not want to make public France's intentions, which had been carefully prepared, but which had collapsed, and did not want to admit that it had collapsed in particular, that it was far from French policy to recognize the political changes made as a result of their change of interest. French policy regarded this kind of procedure as the epitome of German and Anglo-Saxon cynicism, and could not accept it for a nation brought up on Cartesianism. Since the French government was also bound to make political changes, like anybody else, in the given situation there was nothing else left to do except to cover up mistakes. They started looking for a scapegoat, and this could not have been anybody else but Franchet d'Esperey and Károlyi. The legend that the General was uninformed and arbitrary was born at this time. But the Prime Minister and the Minister of Defense did not fully give d'Esperey to the Ministry of Foreign Affairs for this purpose, probably because they knew very well that the steps taken at that time by the General were in line with military strategy and the political plans of the Ministry of Foreign Affairs, too. So, there was only Károlyi left, who from being the pro-French representative of the Hungarian Republic became the "perfidious" Károlyi. He became the individual who ostensibly twisted the original meaning of the Convention and misinterpreted it, trying to make it serve Hungarian – and according to Czechoslovakia – German imperialism.[79]

Finally, we can say that it is not only the idea that the Convention was a mistake, which is misconceived, but also the belief that the text of Belgrade was mainly political. Generally it served military aims, and it left the political preparation for peace to the occupation of strategic points. From the point of view of French interests, it was closely connected to the French occupation of a part of Hungary, above all of Budapest, but political reasons and the Allies' motives made it impossible. Paradoxically, Károlyi's pro-French policy was against it, too, because this caused moral inconsistance in the French government. As a result of all this, we cannot speak about an evaluation of French policies during the proceeding period. The most important modification was made – as we have already pointed out – in the triangle of Nagyvárad (Oradea), Szatmárnémeti (Satu Mare) and Nagybánya (Baia Mare) in January or at the very beginning of February 1919, but this question would lead us very far from the Convention itself, or from its interpretation. This is not the story of the Convention itself, but of the burial of that Convention while it was still alive.

Notes

1. See the text of the military convention in: *Documents concernant l'exécution de l'Armistice en Hongrie (novembre 1918 – mars 1919)* (Budapest, 1919); H. W. V. Temperley, *A History of the Peace Conference of Paris* (London, 1920-1924), vol. IV. pp. 351-352; Général Jean Bernachot, *Les Armées Françaises en Orient aprés l'Armistice de 1918, vol. I. L'Armée Française d'Orient, L'Armée de Hongrie (11 novembre 1918 – 10 septembre 1919)*, (Paris, 1970), pp. 235-237. One copy can be found in box no. 6 N, fonds 71 of the Military Archives Ministère des Armées, Etat-Major de l'Armée de Terre, Service historique. (In the following, each reference, which contains the letter "N," marks a document from these archives. The number, before the letter "N," refers to the fonds, *ie.*, to the box behind it. This is followed by the number of the file [doss.], if there is a file in the box. The origin and date of the document give further information).
2. The text of Padua: Mermeix, *Les négociations Secrètes et les quatre Armistices avec pièces justificatives* (Paris, 1921), pp. 345-347.

3. The latest interpretations of the Károlyi era: Zsuzsa L. Nagy, *A békekonferencia és Magyarország 1918-1919* [The Peace Conference and Hungary 1918-1919] (Budapest, 1965); Tibor Hajdú, *Az 1918-as magyarországi polgári demokratikus forradalom* [The Bourgeois Democratic Revolution in Hungary in 1918] (Budapest, 1968); András Siklós, "A polgári demokratikus forradalom" [The Bourgeois-Democratic Revolution], in *Magyarország története* [The History of Hungary], vol. VIII., President of the Committe of Editors: Zsigmond Pál Pach, Editor in Chief: György Ránki (Budapest, 1977); Peter Pastor, *Hungary between Wilson and Lenin: The Hungarian Revolution of 1918–1919 and the Big Three* (New York, 1976); János Jenmitz and György Litván, *Szerette az igazságot* [He Loved the Truth] (Budapest, 1977); Tibor Hajdú, *Károlyi Mihály* [Mihály Károlyi] (Budapest, 1978).
4. This theory is also propounded by: Ferenc Nyékhegyi, *A Diaz-féle fegyverszüneti szerződés (a paduai fegyverszünet)* [The Diaz Armistice Agreement (The Armistice of Padua)] (Budapest, 1922); Zoltán Szende, *A magyar katasztrófa 1918–1919* [The Catastrophe of Hungary 1918–1919] (Budapest, 1937). The signing of the Convention is described as a political mistake by Jenő Horváth. In his work, *A trianoni békeszerződés megalkotása és a revízió útja* [The Creation of the Peace Treaty of Trianon and the Story of the Political and Territorial Restoration] (Budapest, 1939), he states that the Convention had been originally regarded as a temporary solution by the Allies, so the Hungarian Government was not able to influence its implementation.
5. I only wanted to interpret France's opinion on this question. Aside from this, I did not wish to write a synopsis, but only a limited article describing the source. I am not going to describe the whole text, but, with regard to the central question, only the most important works, which are listed as sources, or which contain explanations, worth considering. Nor am I going to mention other countries' secondary sources or texts, ie. works which only give an interpretation.
6. On this point, see the text given under note no. 4.
7. Vilmos Böhm, *Két forradalom tüzében* [In the Crossfire of Two Revolutions] (Budapest, 1946), pp. 96-104; Ernő Garami, *Forrongó Magyarország* [Rioting Hungary] (Leipzig-Vienna, 1922), pp. 106-108; Oszkár Jászi, Magyar Kálvária, magyar feltámadás [Hungarian Calvary, Hungarian Resurrection] (München, 1969), pp. 67-69. It is

worth mentioning, that in his last work, which was published in Hungarian in 1977 with the title *Hit illúziók nélkül* [Faith without Illusions], Mihály Károlyi did not repeat the charges against France's military leaders. He made these only against Lieutenant-Colonel Vix, whom he believed to be the forerunner of Pétianism. Pp. 69-178 and 190-191.

8. Zsuzsa L. Nagy, *op.cit,*. pp. 9-12 and 74-75, Siklós, *op.cit,*. pp. 187-188, Pastor, *op.cit.*, pp. 120-122 and also his "Franco-Rumanian Intervention in Russia and the Vix Ultimatum: Background to Hungary's Loss of Transylvania", *The Canadian-American Review of Hungarian Studies*, Vol. I. Nos 1 and 2, pp. 14-27, Sándor Vadász, *Vix és Károlyi* [Vix and Károlyi], in *Hadtörténeti Közlemények*, No. 2. XVI (1969). Vadász points out that the fate of the territory had already been sealed.

9. This theory was based on the official French view which was developed during the last days of November 1918. It was supported by Claude Durand in his manuscript work *La politique française en Hongrie de l'Armistice à la chute de Béla Kun*. Pastor was of the opinion that the Convention showed Franchet d'Esperey's personal intentions and the paragraph on the occupation of strategical points was included in the text, because the General wanted to occupy Munich. *op.cit.* I. pp. 64-65. Siklós also wrote concerning the "mistake" made by Franchet d'Esperey; *op.cit.*, p. 96; General Bernachot, *op.cit.* does not take sides, he regards Romania's and Czechoslovakia's political demands as independent from French policy.

10. Concerning France's peace plans, see Paix 1914–1920, vol. 67 (the German question and the problem of the 'Anschluss') in the Archives of the French Ministry for Foreign Affairs. Hereafter AE Paix 1914–1918.

11. Archives diplomatiques, A. Paix (in the following as A. Paix), vol. 203 doss 12. ff. 24-26, instructions for Jusserand, October 22nd 1918. – also the President's message of October 18th *ibid.* (ff. 14-15).

12. *Ibid.* vol. 203. doss. 2. ff. 34 and 35, instruction plan and instruction for Jusserand, October 21st 1918.

13. 7 N 6, on the cover of file, no.135. According to Foch, October 8th, the conditions were as follows: the evacuation of the occupied territories and Alsace-Lorraine, creation of the Allied bridgeheads on the Rhine and obtaining pledges of compensation. On the same day, Allied military experts accepted a more detailed plan, which was

based on Foch's basic principles. Neither plans mentioned the Dual Monarchy.
14. Lansing sent the full text of the American-German exchange of notes to the Allied governments, pointing out that he had extensively taken into consideration the president's interests. The collection of notes is in: *A. Paix* vol. 199, doss. 2. *ff.* pp. 21-31. The American note of October 23rd pointed out, that the president could not refuse to examine the application for an armistice, after the German Government had accepted President Wilson's programme of January 8, 1918. So, he sent the text of the exchange of notes to his allies to work out the conditions of the armistice, if they thought, that it was possible: *ff.* 37-38, Jusserand on Lansing's letter of October 26, *ff.* 42-43, the French translation of Lansing's letter.
15. *Ibid.* f. 41. Handwritten notes, without a date, on the relationship of the president's armistice plan to point 14. *Ibid.*, 32-33, London Ambassador, Cambon, October 25th 1918. According to his notes, the British Cabinet's principles were completely different from those of the President, which was also shown by the fact that the European powers had not reacted to Wilson's many speeches on peace.
16. According to the dispute of October 29th-30th, three variants were prepared for the answer. All of them can be found among folios 50-56, in doss. 2, of *A. Paix*, vol. 199. Two main questions were raised in the text of October 29th: whether armistice and peace meant the same to the President, and whether the laying down of conditions on Germany by the Allies, meant – according to Wilson – that the Allies automatically accepted the Fourteen Points. The document said that General House gave a positive answer and added, that had there been a different interpretation, the USA's departure from the war would have become a possibility. Later he changed his view and thought that the president might have informed the German government, that the Allies had not accepted the armistice plan. In the following, the document lists the objections against the Fourteen Points (it was impossible to stop the blockade on the basis of the freedom of the seas, as it did not contain the principle of compensation) and finishes as: "Il est vraisemblable qu'il ne s'agit que d'un malentendu. Le Président Wilson ne peut être à la fois belligérant et se constituer lui-mème arbitre; il est impossible que cet arbitre impose simultanément aux ennemis et à ses associés des conditions de paix, sans avoir consulté ces derniers. Cela ne s'est jamais vu et c'est

une position irrégulière, contraire au droit et au bon sens." – Clemenceau made a note of his thoughts on this, and the Minister of Foreign Affairs Pichon used these in preparing the new text of October 30th. This document did not question whether armistice and peace were the same, but stated that they were not, and the two were not intended to be so interpreted. The Allies – with some reservations – accepted the Fourteen Points for peace. But the Fourteen Points had to be discussed in detail. The document also stated exactly what the president could do. There was a typical part of the text, which prohibited "d'admettre sans discussion, explication ou précision...des conditions acceptées d'emblée par l' Allemagne, l'Autriche-Hongrie en même temps que par tous les pacifistes, défaitistes et anarchistes, dont le but est de finir à tout prix la guerre sans assurer ces conséquences et ses garanties nécessaires à la victoire des Alliés." The third document, signed by Clemenceau, Lloyd George and House, is the answer finally accepted; this said that the Allies were ready to make peace with Germany on the basis of the Fourteen Points.

17. *The Intimate Papers of Colonel House, Arranged as a Narrative by Charles Seymour* (Boston and New York, 1926-1928), vol. IV. pp. 148-187.
18. On the relationship of the question of armistice and the Soviet question, see also Mária Ormos, "The French Intervention in the Ukraine and its Effects in Central Europe, October 1918–April 1919," [in Hungarian] *Történelmi Szemle*, Nos. 3-4 (1977), pp. 401-439.
19. The document quoted above is: *A. Paix*, vol. 201. doss. 8. ff. 24-28, Etat-Major de l'Armée, 3e Bureau, Group de l'Avant, A. Troisième note au sujet d'une action de l'Entente en Russie Méridionale, 30 October 1918.
20. Between 6 and 8 October it was made clear that the armistice with Germany was – from a military point of view – immediately possible under the appropriate conditions. The dividing the military forces into two groups and withdrawing four divisions from the advance on the North was dated for 7 October. From these divisions the formation of four so called Danube Divisions was ordered and sent these towards Romania, through Bulgaria. One of the duties of the army was to prepare (and later to carry out) the intervention. – 4 N 53, doss. 2 "Instruction personnelle et secrète pour M. le Général Franchet d'Espérey et M. le Général Berthelot, chargé de mission en Roumanie," 7th of October 1918. – A part of the document is con-

tained in: Général Jean Bernachot: *Ibid.* vol. II. "L'Armée du Danube, l'Armée Française d'Orient (28 octobre 1918 – 25 janvier 1920)" (Paris, 1970), p. 65; One of Berthelot's duties was the following: "entrer en liaison avec les éléments russes susceptibles de cooperer à l'action de l'Entente dans le cadre du Plan général d'opération établi par le Général Franchet d'Esperey."

21. We have selected one text, dated 23 October, from among several documents, which contained relevant news about the disintegration of the Dual Monarchy. "On peut dire, qu'à l'heure actuelle l'Autriche se présente comme un corps politique artificiel avec lequel, pratiquement, il est impossible de traiter car sa signature collective n'engage nullement ses parties séparées." 6 N 124, report of the intelligence service.

22. On this matter, see, in particular, Márton Farkas, "A Monarchia megmentésének kísérletei és a páduai fegyverszünet" [Attempts to Save the Monarchy and the Armistice of Padua], *Századok* Nos. 2-3 (1969).

23. H. vol. 44. f. 60, 22 October 1918. It contains: "L'Etat hongrois n'ayant pas d'existence reconnue, dans le droit des gens, aucun armistice particulier ne peut être conclu avec lui." See the temporary Austrian National Assembly's decision of the 21st of October in Rudolf Neck, *Österreich im Jahre 1918* (Munich, 1968) pp. 76-78. France's point of view is contained in: *Paix 1914–1920*, vol. 67, ff. 245-246, note of De Caix, without a date.

24. De Caix made notes to this effect on 25 and 30 October. In the first note he recommended to the Allies — against the danger of the "Anschluss" — that they turn to the elements still loyal to the Habsburgs. A. Paix, vol. 203, doss. 12, f. 33. – In his work, "Note sur les demandes d'Armistice," he also wrote the following: "On pourrait, pour faciliter la signature d'un tel armistice par l'Empereur Charles, lui faire dire que les Allies n'occuperont l'Autriche-allemande que pour y maintenir la maison de Hapsbourg, ce qui est notre intérêt." *Ibid.*, ff. 49-50.

25. *Ibid.* ff. 24-26, Pichon, 21 October 1918. – We should note, that at this time, in the Ministry of Foreign Affairs there was no unanimous opinion established against the "Anschluss." For example, on the 25th of October a long study, complete with facts and figures, was made on the possibility of the "Anschluss," in case France were able to move its borders to the Rhine and Germany had become a demo-

cratic federation. It was made clear that France, without the Rhineborder, would not approve of a union of Austria and Germany.
26. Both point of views are included in Poincaré's letter, 6 N 71, which was written to Clemenceau on the 29th of October 1918. The Headquarters' report, "Note au sujet de la situation créé par la capitulation de l'Autriche," made on 30 October, puts the case for a possible move against Germany. The following was included among the duties listed in it: "2e-d'imposer à l'Autriche, dans les clauses de l'armistice qu'elle sollicite, le libre passage de nos troupes sur son territoire et la mise á notre disposition des voies ferrées qui nous sont nécessaires." This document proves that the idea of the advance towards Munich had not been dropped or that it had been raised again on the basis of the opportunity provided by the Monarchy's surrender. This raised hopes that French troops might reach the Rhine easily, and that France might achieve her aim, which was also important in the event of quick armistice. The document said: "La menace en direction de Munich aurait donc vraisemblablement comme résultat immédiat un repli de l'Armée allemande sur le Rhin, seule position où elle puisse réaliser une sériuse économie de forces." 6 N 71. The document, de Caix' "Note sur les demandes d'Armistice," written on the 30th, points out the importance of ensuring the routes towards the Ukraine. – A. Paix, vol. 203, doss. 12. ff., pp. 49-50.
27. A. Paix, vol. 201, doss. 8. ff., 10-15, "Conditions à poser dans la convention réglant la suspension des hostilités entre les puissances alliées et les puissances centrales," 15 October 1918.
28. See the text in *Paix 1914–1920*, vol. 69, ff., 85-88; in print: Temperley, *op.cit.*, vol. IV. pp. 216-217; N. Dascovici, *Interesele şi Drepturile în texte de drept internaţional public* (Iaşi, 1936), pp. 9-11; On this question see also: Comte de Saint-Aulaire, *Ambassadeur de France, Confession d'un vieux diplomate* (Paris, 1953), pp. 324-343; Sherman David Spector, *Rumania at the Paris Peace Conference. A Study of the Diplomacy of Ioan I. C. Brătianu* (New York, 1962), pp. 29-37.
29. The text of the Peace Treaty in Dénes Halmos, ed., *Nemzetközi szerződések 1918–1945* [International Treaties 1918–1945] (Budapest, 1966), pp. 29-35; Also see: *La paix de Bucarest* (Paris, 1918).
30. On Pichon's declaration, which was often quoted by Romanian politicians, see: Saint-Aulaire, *op.cit.*, p. 461. According to this, with

Clemenceau's agreement, Pichon stated the following in Parliament: "Je suis intervenu à Jassy pour faire connaître au gouvernement roumain que tous les engagements pris envers la Roumanie à son entrée en guerre, seront maintenus." In June 1918 the French minister of foreign affairs instructed the Washington ambassador not to follow the American line in Romania's search for economic relations. In explanation he said the following: "La Roumanie est un des pays qui s'offriront le plus naturellement à l'influence et à l'action économique de la France après la guerre; et de fait, nous avons l'intention d'y pousser le plus possible l'une et l'autre." R. vol. 31. ff. 59-60, Pichon the 30th of July 1918. Diplomatic action was organized by the minister of foreign affairs at the end of September 1918. He sent former Paris Ambassador Victor Antonescu to Saloniki through Rome "pour se tenir prêt à se rendre en Roumanie dans le cas, où les pourparlers d'armistice proposés par les Bulgares auraient une suite." *Ibid.* 104, Pichon to Rome, the 27th of September 1918.

31. These principles had already been established by the Ministry of Foreign Affairs, before the American government asked the Romanian government's opinion on the question of armistice. L. R. vol. 31, f. 145, Pichon 1 November 1918. Although the principles were maintained after the American declaration had been handed over, it was concluded that even bigger support had to be given to Romania, and that her interests needed to be considered in the question of the German armistice. On the 7th of November Franchet d'Esperey was instructed to "de donner tout aide possible aux Roumains pour pouvoir surmonter les difficultés de la mobilisation." To hand over airplanes together with their crews, and to send advisory officers. 4 N 58, doss. 10, a copy of the letter of the minister of foreign affairs in the document of the Conseil Supérieur de Guerre. The text was sent to the general, on 7 November 1918. On 5 November a note, with reference to America's views on Romania, established the principle that the German military evacuation of this country had to be demanded in the armistice. A. *Paix*, vol. 210 doss. 8 ff., pp. 77-80.

32. See note no. 30.

33. This military action was explained in Paul Azan, *Franchet d'Esperey* (Paris, 1949) pp. 213-216; Bernachot, *op.cit.* vol. II, p. 65; Vadász, *op.cit.* Everybody wrote on the instruction of October 7, but none of them mentioned its chapter on Romania. According to this General Berthelot went to the Balkans "en vue de préparer et diriger ...

l'action militaire destinée à faire entrer de nouveau la Roumanie dans la lutte aux côtés de l'Entente." Clemenceau divided the mission into two parts. In the first phase his duty was the following: "de préparer notre intervention ultérieure en Roumanie par une action à la fois politique et militaire visant: à provoquer l'avènement d'un Gouvernement favorable à l'Entente, à organiser la résistance à l'emprise allemande et le soulèvement général du pays. – La deuxième phase sera caractèrisée par une intervention militaire directe des Alliés en Roumanie, seul moyen qui, dans la situation actuelle de ce pays, permette de la libérer de l'emprise ennemie..." – 4 N 53, doss. 2.
34. A. Paix. vol. 201, doss. 7 f. 2 and f. 8. Two reports on the American note, written by Jusserand on 6 and on 9 November. He gave the exact French translation of the text. A part of it was as follows: the American Government "exercera le moment venu son influence pour que les justes droits territoriaux et politiques du peuple roumain soient reconnus et mis à l'abri de toute agression étrangère."
35. A. Paix, vol. 201, doss. 8., ff. 10-15, Condition à poser dans la convention réglant la suspension des hostilités entre les puissances alliées et les puissances centrales, the 15th of October 1918. – The third point of the document was as follows: "C. – Front balkanique et roumain. – 1° Libération commançant immédiatement et devant être terminée dans un délai de 15 jours des territoires serbes, monténégrins, albanais et roumains. – 2° Évacuation dans un délai de 30 jours et occupation temporaire à titre de garantie par les troupes alliées: a) de la Bosnie et de la Hercégovine, b) de la Syrmie avec Peterwardien et Neusatz, c) de la Transylvanie jusqu'à la ligne incluse Temeswar, Nagy Varad, Nagy Bania, d) de la Bukovine. – 3° Livrasion immédiate aux Alliés des ports et de la flotte du Danube en aval des Portes de Fer."
36. AE Paix 1914-1918, vol. 69, 84, Saint-Aulaire the 22nd of August 1916. According to Saint-Aulaire, the Italian ambassador stated the following after the signing of the Convention: "Il n'y a vraiment aucun inconvéniant à garantir à la Roumanie des concessions tout à fait impossibles à réaliser: nous manquerons à nos engagements sans remords puisque nous n'aurons aucun moyen de les tenir. Cette clause de garantie eût été bien plus gênante si les demandes roumaines eussent été plus modérés." The Russian ambassador approved this agreement. Next to the report, there is a copy of the Secret Pact (ff. 85-88).

37. It was recorded in Lacombe's note of the 22nd of December 1918, which provided the basis for approval of Romania's ally status, R. vol. 32, ff. 32-33, and expressed in Pichon's recommendation, made on the 30th of December, that the Allies recognize Romania. The latter said: "Toutefois le traité du 17 août 1916 ayant été en droit abrogé par le traité de Bucarest, conclu avec nos ennemis, il y aura lieu pour les Alliés de formuler une déclaration nouvelle prenant pour base le traité de 1916 pour l'examen des revendications roumaines, compte étant tenu de l'annexion ultérieure de la Bessarabie et des intérêts généraux des Alliés sur lesquelsles puissances aurunt à se prononcer dans leurs pourparlers prochains." – *Ibid.*, ff., pp. 67-68. On the 25th of December the British Government asked Paris a distinct question regarding this problem (f. 44). The French Ministry of Foreign Affairs answered that, with some reservations, they recommended the recognition (ff. 69-70). The French plan was accepted by the Italian government on the 1st of January 1919 (f. 72), and by the British government on the 4th (f. 74).
38. A. Paix, vol. 197, doss. 3. ff., pp. 8-11, General Guillaumat's note, the 28th of 1918. The document was remarkably similar to another plan, which was recommended by British Prime Minister Lloyd George. For example the five bridgeheads relevant to Hungary were the same. But this plan also demanded the evacuation of Poland, the Ukraine, Russia and Romania, too. Ibid. ff. 26-28.
39. According to the text, made for Jusserand on the 29th of October, "le Président, s'il juge bon de nous transmettre la demande d'armistice de l'Autriche, pourrait lui répondre de suite que la demande d'armistice peut être adressée par les chefs des armées autrichiennes d'une part au Général Commandant les armées alliées sur le front italien, et d'autre part au Général Commandant les armées alliées d'Orient, sur le front balkanique. Ces deux généraux feront connaître respectivement les conditions d'armistice nécessitées pour la garantie de chacun des fronts; l'ensemble de ces conditions formera les conditions à accepter par le Gouvernement austro-hongrois." – *A. Paix*, vol. 199, doss. 2. ff., pp. 50-52^A.
40. Other documents, in connection with the armistice, are as follows: a version with a few changes was made by the Ministry of Foreign Affairs on 30 October; a renewed version, with further small changes was made on 31 October; the final version was made after the dispute, on the 31. – A. Paix, vol. 197, doss. 3. ff., pp. 12-22. There

is also a document on the fact that the text had been accepted by the Conseil Suprême de la Guerre on the 31st of October, and that the Italian government would send it to General Diaz, who was authorized to announce the conditions. *Ibid.* p. 23.
41. The material of the Allied negotiation on 4 November provides a basis for this. Later I will come back to this.
42. 6 N 71, Copies of General Weber's telegram, the 2 and 3 November 1918. One of them was sent to Budapest on 2 November: "En conséquence, d'après ce que me communique l'Etat-Major Général, on n'accepterait pas de commisssion d'armistice austro-hongroise sur les fronts balkanique ou roumain. Il en résulte qu'un armistice conclu ici devrait être applicable à tous les fronts de l'Autriche-Hongrie."
43. Jenő Horváth wrote with regard to this action: *op.cit.*, p. 9. He could not find an explanation for application by the two Hungarian delegates, Lieutenant-Colonels Dormándy and Kozmovszky, for an armistice, because he believed that the Hungarian governemnt had already accepted the conditions of Padua on the 3rd of November. In reality, the government had only acknowledged the conditions. Also see L. Nagy, *op.cit.*, p. 9, and Siklós, *op.cit.*, p. 90. On 4 November d'Esperey reported that the two Hungarian delegates had appeared in Belgrade at 11 o'clock a.m. on the 3rd. Besides handing over the Danube flotilla and ensuring free passage, he demanded the following, as conditions: "Retirer ses troupes au-delà d'une zone de terrain de quinze kilomètres de largeur au Nord du Danube-Save et à l'Ouest de la Drina et frontière Serbe et Montenegro jusqu'à l'Adriatique à partir de frontière Roumanie à l'Est, y déposer ses armes et matériel de guerre et permettre occupation de cette zone par armées alliées." 4 N 58, doss. 10, Franchet d'Esperey, the 4th of November 1918.
44. 6 N 71, one of Weber's telegram, sent by Hungarian radio in the early morning of the 4th of November.
45. On this question, see first of all Siklós, *op.cit.*, pp. 90-91.
46. 4 N 58, doss. 10, Clemenceau, the 6th of November 1918. It was recorded that the Armistice of Padua was valid for the Dual Monarchy and: "Il est bien entendu que pourparlers engagés avec représentants Maréchal Koevess ne doivent porter que sur applications de ces clauses, qui sont seules valables pour tous théâtres d'opérations."
47. See note no. 9.
48. 4 N 58, doss. 10, Franchet d'Esperey, the 5th of November 1918.

49. See note no. 46.
50. 4 N 58, doss. 10, Franchet d'Esperey, the 7th of November 1918. In it: "Je traiterai avec lui toutes les questions de l'application à la Hongrie des clauses de l'armistice signé par le Général Diaz en m'inspirant de vos instructions..."
51. 20 N 234, doss. 2.
52. According to most books, the date of the meeting is the 7th of October, but to others it is the 5th or 6th. According to Franchet d'Esperey's papers, Károlyi arrived at Belgrade on the 6th, the meeting had been scheduled for the 8th, but d'Esperey managed to arrive at Belgrade in the late afternoon of the 7th. But Saloniki was only able to telegraph on the negotiations on the evening of the 8th. This corresponds to Károlyi's notes, which said that Károlyi and the delegates had been able to meet the General after the day of their arrival (*op.cit.* page 171), and had gone back to Budapest on the 8th (*ibid.* page 176). I would like to note here that we did not find any trace of Clemenceau's telegramme, which had stated again that the Convention had only contained military questions, but it is certain that its date could not have been the 12th of November, as is given in most books, because Károlyi had already refered to this telegraph at the sitting of the National Council on the 10th.
53. 4 N 58, doss. 10, Franchet d'Esperey, 8 November 1918.
54. 20 N 528, doss. 3., Franchet d'Esperey, 12 November 1918.
55. A. Paix, vol. 203, doss. 12. ff., 83-84 and 4 N 58, doss. 10, Franchet d'Esperey, the 8th of November 1918. The document is published in Gy. Litván, "Documents des rélations franco-hongroises des années 1917-1919," *Acta Historica* 21 (1975) pp. 191-192.
56. A. Paix, vol. 203, doss. 12, ff. 49-50, Note sur les demandes d'Armistice, the 30th of October 1918. In this text, De Caix pointed out the necessity of the signing of the armistice and under point 4, he wrote: "4° parce qu'il est impossible de permettre à l'Autriche – à la Hongrie l'opposition de nationalités, maintenant nos alliés suffirait à l'empêcher – de prétendre régler le sort des nationalités et qu'il faut que les Alliés pénètrent dans le pays pour diriger l'émancipation de ces nationalités et leur servir d'arbitres dans la détermination de leurs frontières."
57. *Archives diplomatiques*, Europe Z. Autriche, vol. 61, ff. 107-111. On Hungary: "Notre objectif doit être ... chez les Magyars positif – faire dominer dans la nouvelle république hongroise (magyare) l'influence

française, et profiter de la préférence que les Magyars nous ont marquée en demandant à être occupés plutôt par nous." On the Romanian question among others: "En Transylvanie, le gros point est d'éviter que les populations non-roumaines, surtout le million environ de Magyars, ne soient molestées."

58. Mermeix, *op.cit.*, pp. 207-215. It reports on the dispute of the 31st of October. According to this, in connection with paragraph 4, before the reference to maintain order was accepted, Clemenceau had stated the following: "Ceci doit donner satisfaction à M. Vesnitch; vous voyez que nous réservons le droit d'occuper tous les territoires qu'il nous plaira." Serb politicians were not satisfied with this interpretation. – See, also, on this, Bogdan Krizman, "The Belgrade Armistice of 13 November 1918," *The Slavonic and East European Review*, January (1970).

59. Clemenceau gave his permission to send the notes of the Ministry of Foreign Affairs to Franchet d'Esperey that were relevant to him, but only those remarks which he knew about. He defended the Convention itself, much later, too. *E.g.*, on the 16th of January 1919 he wrote the following to General Berthelot: "Transylvanie. – La délimitation de cette région a été réglée par le Général Commandant les Armées l'Orient, conformément à des nécessités de fait et à des considérations d'ordre militaire ... " – R. vol. 32. ff. 116-117, Clemenceau, the 16th of January 1919.

60. J. Horváth, *op.cit.*, pp. 12-13. He refers to Tardieu, who as a defence against the accusations that it had been a mistake not to destroy the whole of the German army, refers to the negotiations of the 4th of November, and to Clemenceau's order of the 5th of November, based on the negotiations. But, since Marshal Foch signed the armistice with Germany, the operational plan of 5 November became pointless: André Tardieu, *La paix* (Paris, 1921), pp. 465-466. Although these aims were relevant to Germany, nothing proves that they depended on the occupation of Hungary.

61. For further information on this meeting, see Seymour, *op.cit.*, pp. 107-109. – Clemenceau's order 5 November: Tardieu, *op.cit.*, p. 466. According to this, French and British troops in the Balkans had to be concentrated in "the largest possible numbers," for an invasion towards Salzburg-Brunau, and for the same reason, the Belgrade-Budapest-Vienna line had to be occupied, too. This order was not

cancelled after the armistice with Germany had been signed, and later Clemenceau confirmed it for the French troops.
62. 6 N 71, "Etude sur les conditions d'armistice avec l'Autriche-Hongrie arretées par le Conseil Suprême de la Guerre à Versailles, le 31 octobre 1918," 3 November 1918.
63. 20 N 528, doss. 3. A note on the phone conversation of Henrys and Franchet d'Esperey. In *op.cit.*, S. Vadász referred to this conversation. The source must have been a short summary, because there were no dates on the documents that we found (he mentions 17 November), and it is obvious from this that the two generals had had a dispute. Henrys said that his troops could have arrived in Budapest within 48 hours, and since Franchet d'Esperey wanted food supplies to be organized, it was Henrys who said that this would be solved in Hungary, but neither of them mentioned that Hungary had to be occupied, in order to ensure the supplies. Henrys did not want Franchet d'Esperey to move troops from occupation of Hungary to Fiume and Raguza, but he was unable to convince Franchet d'Esperey. During this conversation Franchet d'Esperey gave instructions for a mission to be sent to Budapest. The document proves that he did not appoint his own staff officer to lead this mission, but only a member. Henrys reported that he had come to an agreement on the occupation with Linder. *Ibid.*, doss. 2. Henrys to Linder, 14 November 1918. He asked him to send a Hungarian officer to Szabadka on the 17th, with the neccesary information on transport, food supplies, accomodation of troops and accomodation of German troops. Henrys to Károlyi, 20 November. He informs him about the Vix mission. This letter, among others, also said: "Il est chargé outre, de régler d'accord avec votre Gouvernement toutes les questions relatives au transport et à l'installation en Hongrie des troupes françaises."
64. 20 N 528, doss. 3, phone conversation between Henrys and Franchet d'Esperey.
65. 4 N 58, doss. 10 Clemenceau, 18 November 1918.
66. The first three points of the instruction was quoted by Bernachot, *op.cit.*, I. Point no. 4, which has not been published yet, are as follows: "IV - Il devra prévoir l'occupation du territoire hongrois, et le fonctionnement et la sécurité des lignes de ravitaillement dans les conditions fixées à l'annexe 3." – Supplement no. 3 details these duties until the questions of health and hygiene. 20 N 497, doss. 2. Instruction signed by Henrys, 19 November 1918.

67. Many of Vix's reports include this question. The copies of the reports sent are in box no. 20 N 528, the Budapest copies are in box no. 17 N 514.
68. Prime Minister Kramář's reaction to the Hungarian government regarding this, and Károlyi's answer: H. vol. 44. among the copies of Róza Schwimmer's documents; on the complaints of Beneš to Minister of Foreign Affairs, Pichon: Archives diplomatiques, Europe Z. Tchécoslovaquie, vol. 44. ff. 1-2, Pichon's letter to Clemenceau on the 22nd and 23rd of December 1918.
69. On Romania's moves: R. vol. 31. ff. 183-188, Saint-Aulaire, the 8th of November 1918; ff. 204-207, the joint telegraph of the four Allied ambassadors, 10 November; 4 N 58, doss. 10 Berthelot ref., 11 November 1918.
70. R. vol. 31, ff. 208-209, Saint-Aulaire, 11 November 1918.
71. *I Documenti diplomatici italiani, Sesta serie*, vol. I. (4 novembre 1918-17 gennaio 1919) (Roma, 1956), document no. 264, 279, 334, 359, 372, 397, 416, 423, 431.
72. Lajos Arday, *Térkép csata után. Magyarország a brit külpolitikában 1918-1919* [Map after a Battle. Hungary in British Foreign Policy 1918-1919] (Budapest, 1990).
73. *Ibid.*, in which he interpreted Clemenceau's explanation and statement that France was ready to carry out the occupation on her own.
74. 4 N 51, doss. I. Clemenceau to Pichon, the 26th of November 1918.
75. 6 N 71. Several copies of the French translation of Károlyi's letter to Lansing. In English, the document arrived on the 14th of November.
76. "Primo: J'ai conçu craintes sur difficultés qui pourraient résulter d'une occupation de Buda-Pest par troupes insuffisantes au moment où la question Transylvanie sera résolue contre Hongrie." 4 N 58, doss. 11.
77. *Ibid.*, Clemenceau to Franchet d'Esperey, 26 November 1918, *ibid.*, Foch and Clemenceau to Franchet d'Esperey, 30 November 1918.
78. He tried to create recognition for the French government's own sphere of influence and operations at the Allied conference on 2 December, and in the negotiations at the end of December, he tried to gain the authority to occupy Budapest.
79. From this point of view, one of the most typical of several documents is the Minister of Foreign Affairs, Pichon's telegraph of 29 November, which was published by Gy. Litván, *op.cit.*, pp. 192-193.

Mária Ormos

The Hungarian Soviet Republic and Intervention by the Entente

In this paper I would like to shed light on the question of the intervention against the Hungarian Soviet Republic as it appeared to the French government and the French General Staff and reflected in their own records.[1]

Until now assumptions regarding French politics were usually based on the actual events, on the debates at the Peace Conference, or on records in the archives of other countries. Of course, these sources reflect the reality of the situation, but do so with certain adjustments, not to say distortions. The materials in the French archives now make it possible to see certain aspects of the intervention in a new light. This applies particularly to the French plans themselves, and to the motives underlying the changes in these plans. Since I intend to deal with these changes, certain introductory remarks seem to be in order.

A perennial problem in historiography has been the question of alternatives, the "What would have happened if?" syndrome. How to deal with those political or military plans which were never fully carried out and which, with the benefit of hindsight, now appear to have been unrealizable, exaggerated, irrational? And how to deal with contingencies which did not arise under the circumstances but are simply reconstructions after the fact, on the basis of rationalizations which for some reason or other could not have occurred to the participants at the time. In fact, these did not even constitute true alternatives. Hence, perhaps a word of explanation is in order: Why should we bother with, or give significance to, plans which either were never carried out, or which were realized only in a modified form? I believe it is necessary to draw a sharp distinction between the two kinds of alternatives, the actual contingency plan, and the one based on ulterior construction. A plan that has been formulated is a real alternative; an elaborated military or political project becomes a conditioning factor even if it is modified, even if it proves mistaken and is discarded. The elaboration of the plan and its adoption exclude other plans, exclude alternative courses of action, hence influences the situation fundamentally.

Such was the entire plan of intervention designed by the French General Staff and the French government, including intervention plans against the Soviet Russia. This plan was never carried out in its entirety, while those aspects of the plan which applied to Hungary were carried out only after considerable modification. Nevertheless, it undeniably affected the climate in Europe, including Central Europe, in a powerful and lasting way.

One aspect of the project of intervention revealed by the French records was its constant dichotomy, as opposed to what was formerly perceived as an undulating line, a sinusoid. More specifically, the constant of economic coercion was accompanied first by military force, then by political promises, then by waiting, then again by military compulsion, and finally by political manipulation. The French documents indicate, however, that the French government and General Staff never abandoned either the military or the political options as parallel expedients. Military intervention and political negotiations do not figure as alternatives in these plans, but were present together all along, and the occasional changes were merely on the surface, in appearance.

The first French project which dealt with the Hungarian Soviet Republic, in addition to the Soviet Russia issue, was dated March 24, 1919. It focused on the danger presented by the spread of Russian Bolshevism and the complementary Hungarian one, including the threat to Poland and Romania. The General Staff noted that the means of compulsion applied or contemplated had not proven effective with regard to Hungary, and came to the conclusion that military force should be considered. It proposed three anti-Bolshevik fronts; one of these was already in existence in southern Russia, centered around Odessa, the second was to be set up with Romanian assistance along the Dniester, starting in Bessarabia, and the third would come into being on Hungarian territory. For the execution of a march on Budapest, the project counted on three Serbian infantry and one cavalry divisions, four Romanian infantry divisions, as well as the two French divisions and cavalry brigade stationed in the Balkans.[2]

The project presumed a considerable multiplication of the forces actually available. It was based, first, on the assumption that the bridgehead at Odessa could be maintained until fresh and more significant forces could be dispatched; and this implied, in turn, nothing less than the guaranteed resupply by sea of the units encircled by the Bolsheviks there. A second precondition would have been a fully equipped Romanian army which was then only in the process of formation. Yet another assumption was the consent of the Yugoslav government to significant participation in the intervention against Hungary. This last condition appeared important to the French General Staff as it did not see its way clear to including the Czech army, in its present state, in its calculations; in addition to its lack of training and equipment, there was the problem of the leadership of the Czech army – an issue, however, which the plan did not discuss.

The French project of March 24 was defeated at the meeting of the Supreme Council of the Peace Conference the following day; or, to be more exact, the plan was altered. The Council created the basis for the organization of two fronts rather than three. Indeed, it decided on the evacuation of the bridgehead at Odessa. While the Council made no mention of the other two fronts, the one along the Dniester and the one in Hungary, it did provide for their establishment. It accomplished this by rerouting an important British convoy reserved for General Denikin, which included materials and clothing for 100,000 soldiers, to the Romanian port. It thus created the basis for the active participation of the Romanian army at the Dniester and on Hungarian territory. This decision was probably a matter of priorities, and the Supreme Council opted to bolster the Romanian interests because they seemed more urgent. (I should add, parenthetically, that it soon became evident that this choice was not final, for the British had the capacity to arm the counter-revolutionary forces in Hungary as well. The objective of the maneuver, therefore, was rather to justify the withdrawal of the Entente troops, as well as to cut down on the enormous expense which the supply of Odessa would have warranted.)

Because of the weight given to Romanian interests, this choice implied that the main concern of the Entente forces was Hungary. A simple fact may explain this concern; while the Romanian government was "satisfied" with defending the boundary of Bessarabia against Soviet Russian forces, its ambitions were to acquire further territories at the expense of Hungary. To be more exact, Romania meant to secure the boundary line it was promised under the secret Bucharest Treaty of 1916: this line led from near Vásárosnamény south of the Tisza River, passed five kilometers east of Debrecen, and reached the confluence of the Tisza and Maros Rivers once again near Szeged. The French General Staff harbored no doubts about the operation: it could always count on Romanian participation in this area, whereas Romanian participation in the anti-Soviet action could not be taken for granted.

On March 27 Marshal Foch, before ordering the execution of the resolution of March 25 taken by the Supreme Council, again tried to convince the Supreme Council to grant an increase of the forces available for intervention, and to obtain in some manner the material contributions of the United States. The attempt of March 27, however, failed completely. Another difficulty had to arise before Clemenceau would order, on March 29, the complete evacuation of the Odessa zone.

The negotiations conducted by Franchet d'Esperey about the forces available for intervention ran into difficulties in Belgrade. Although the Yugoslav government gave no definite reply, its extreme reluctance to participate in the intervention was obvious enough. Prince Regent Alexander let it be known that since the Great Powers had not authorized the conversion of the Serbian army into a Yugoslav army, that is, it did not authorize an increase in its effectives through the addition of military units conscripted in the newly acquired territories of Croatia, Slovenia, and elsewhere, he was "unfortunately" not in a position to order intervention against Hungarian Bolshevism at the moment.

The French had to reckon with these factors – i.e., with the impossibility of securing American financial aid and the refusal of the Yugoslavs – as early as March 29, when the Supreme Council undertook to discuss Béla Kun's offer to take up negotiations. A closer look at the situation revealed that the Romanian army would have to bear the main burden of the attack along both fronts, an undertaking which, in the opinion of the French General Staff, would have exceeded its capacities. Clemenceau based his next moves on this opinion. On the one hand, after four days of delays and hesitation, he ordered the evacuation of the Odessa zone; but, rather than recall the troops, he redirected them towards the Dniester.[4] Thus he decided that France would take part in the defense of Romania's eastern frontier while facilitating the movements of the Romanian army in the West. At the same time, he gave up the Odessa front once and for all. On the other hand, at the Conference table Clemenceau agreed to the Budapest mission of General Smuts; he did not hesistate in reaching that decision, since the conditions necessary for a military intervention had not materialized for the time being because of the reluctance of the Yugoslavs.

Thus political manipulation rather than military offensive became the order of the day. But while Clemenceau temporarily barred an offensive in accordance with the spirit of the decision at the Conference, at the same time he instructed Franchet d'Esperey to proceed with the negotiations for the organization of the attack. While Smuts was negotiating in Budapest,

Franchet d'Esperey was trying to convince the Yugoslav officials in Belgrade of the absolute necessity of Serbian participation. But since this attempt did not work out, the plan for an open, concentric military action under French command had to be dropped for the time being.

This was when the first significant modification of the French plan took place. It was not a matter of political moves replacing military ones outright; rather, instead of a concentric attack, the modified plan contemplated a limited offensive utilizing the forces of the Romanian army.

I wish to emphasize once more that one of the conditions for such an attack was the transfer of forces from Odessa to the Dniester, initiated shortly thereafter, on April 6. The modification in the French plan was revealed, for the first time, in a telegram from Clemenceau to the commander-in-chief in the Balkans, dated April 14. In this telegram, Clemenceau, who was both Prime Minister and Minister of War, reacted to a worried report sent by Franchet d'Esperey regarding the contemplated Romanian offensive. The latter had requested Paris to dissuade the Romanian Chief of the General Staff from taking the offensive as it might have disastrous consequences. For the benefit of the general, the Prime Minister summarized the French views in the following terms: "First: If the Hungarians attack the Romanians, the latter are fully justified in retaliating. Second: Since the decision taken by the Peace Conference of February 26 was not further modified, the Romanians have likewise the right to occupy the area allocated to them, up to the eastern border of the neutral zone."[5] As we know, the eastern border of the neutral zone corresponded essentially with what was to become the national boundary line.

Such was the theoretical framework within which the Romanians launched their offensive on the night of April 15-16. Clemenceau's stand was easy enough to defend at the Conference table since it derived from decisions the Conference itself had reached earlier. But the Romanians reached the line of demarcation they could legally claim already by April 25, and then a new justification had to be found. The Romanian General Coandă, who represented his government in Paris on a number of issues, called on General Alby, the French Chief of the General Staff, on April 26. He informed Alby that the Romanian General Staff had decided to cross the demarcation line designated in the Vix memorandum. The Romanian forces intended to advance as far as the Tisza River, and were ready to build bridgeheads on the right bank of the river as well. The French Chief of the General Staff relayed this information without any comment to the pertinent section chief of the Ministry of Foreign Affairs. In other words, the French General Staff acquiesced in the plan.[6]

This definite and explicit change in view was occasioned by Romanian military success. On the day the Romanian army reached the Tisza, the French General Staff put its views on paper. The gist of the newly elaborated plan was: "The Romanian advance, brilliantly executed, without intervention on the part of French forces concentrated in the Szeged area (two infantry divisions and a cavalry brigade), entitle us to believe that there will be no need to resort to these forces even if it does become necessary to compel Hungary to carry out the peace decisions by military force. The concentric action of the powers directly interested (Romania, Czechoslovakia, and Serbia), will be amply sufficient for the purpose."[7]

According to the new French military plan, the French forces at Szeged could be pulled out and transferred to Bulgaria. By so doing, argued the General Staff, France could exert pressure on Bulgaria to sign the peace treaty and, at the same time, relieve the Romanian army of another burden by pinning down the Bulgarian forces.

The execution of this plan, however, became highly problematic as a consequence of the formation of the Soviet front at the end of April and the beginning of May. The Soviet Russian government sent an ultimatum to Romania and gathered significant forces along the Dniester. Under the circumstances, Paris did not venture to give its blessing to the most recent Romanian request, namely that the Romanian army be authorized to continue its advance and march on Budapest. On the contrary: the French authorities insisted that the army be halted along the Tisza and that part of it be transferred to Bessarabia. Even the Romanian Chief of the General Staff felt the situation was serious enough to warrant rescinding the May 4 resolution of the Romanian cabinet regarding the action against Budapest. General Prešan emphasized that Romania did not have territorial claims against Hungary beyond the Tisza, hence the military effort was unwarranted; moreover, the army would not find a better line of defense than the Tisza, hence the action would entail certain military risks as well, while the situation along the Dniester was deteriorating. On May 5 the Romanian government resolved to stabilize the front along the Tisza in Hungary, and to retrieve three divisions for transfer to the Dniester.[8]

This transfer gave rise to bitter reproaches on the part of the Czechoslovakian government. The temporary stabilization of the Romanian front made it possible for the Hungarian Red Army to concentrate its efforts on one front in Slovakia and to attain significant successes against the

Czechoslovak forces. As mentioned, as a result of these successes the president of the Conference, Clemenceau, personally decided in favor of a political solution, and he himself persuaded the Supreme Council to endorse his message to Béla Kun. Thus, it was a military dead end that led to this message, but at the moment it was sent the French Prime Minister attributed no greater importance to it than would have been warranted by a well-chosen excuse or alibi; for it was expected that Budapest would reject the proposal.

Such an interpretation is justified by the text of the message itself, which demanded Hungarian withdrawal but gave not even a hint as to how far the Hungarian troops were expected to retreat. It is also made obvious by other measures Clemenceau adopted on the same day. While he persuaded the Supreme Council to endorse the so-called Clemenceau letter, he sent the Hungarian-Romanian file to General Belin and instructed him to work out plans for military measures in case the Hungarians rejected the letter as expected. Belin did not require much time to carry out these instructions. The General Staff was practically ready with the plan, and was able to relay Clemenceau's instructions to Franchet d'Esperey that very day. The essence of the plan was to concentrate the Romanian forces in the northern sector in order to relieve the Czechoslovak forces and, once this was accomplished, to advance towards Budapest. In the meantime the Serbian units would have to advance directly towards Budapest, while the two French divisions would operate between the two armies and ensure coordination.

The function of the message of June 8 as an alibi is confirmed by the exchange of telegrams between the French ambassador in Prague and the Ministry of Foreign Affairs. Clément-Simon reminded the Ministry that it should require the Hungarians to withdraw to a specific line; Pichon replied that the ambassador should make inquiries regarding the French plans from General Pellé, stationed in Prague.[9] In plain words, this meant that a line of demarcation no longer had any relevance, since the whole country would be occupied. Furthermore, the above interpretation of French intentions is confirmed by the fact that after almost two weeks spent on preparations for the intervention, the excuse considered necessary for the launching of the action did not materialize: the Hungarian government decided to comply with the French demand, and the Conference immediately began to search for a new excuse.

It became clear at this time, as the Hungarian troops were evacuating Slovakia, that Clemenceau, unlike the Parisian representative of the British government, and unlike the British and French military strategists, ceased to insist on military intervention against Hungary. As of July there no longer was a strict parallel between the French military and political plans. While the General Staff did not discard the military plan, its practical value and significance diminished because of Clemenceau's attitude. To find the motive behind the change in the attitude of the French Prime Minister, we must look for the factors revealed by the French documents.

Clemenceau's disillusioned remarks at the Conference in the second half of July cannot be attributed to a single factor. First of all, he was prompted by the circumstance that while France was advocating a policy of intervention, her allies, although constantly harping on intervention, were unwilling to share the military and financial burdens, or even the responsibility for the act. Clemenceau was also swayed by the failures for which the French military and political leadership were ultimately responsible. He was influenced by the fact that he did not have useful, adequate, sufficient military power at his disposal. Moreover, he was reluctant to assume the responsibility for the ill-fated policy of intervention in face of French public opinion, emanating primarily from the left.

In addition to these factors, which are discussed by other historians in far greater detail than my thumbnail sketch can hope to do, there was yet another factor which played a role in Clemenceau's stance, one we had little knowledge of until now. This factor was the French appraisal of the attitudes of the small countries adjacent to Hungary. We have mentioned that the French views changed, in the course of April, expecting the neighboring small states to overthrow the Hungarian regime and make Hungary bow to the resolutions of the Peace Conference even without French contributions.

During the subsequent months, however, it became clear that these countries were far from being completely prepared to achieve these ends and, what is more, they expected a reward for their anti-Bolshevik intervention. As regards the former, the problem was still mainly Yugoslavia. The French exerted themselves considerably to interest Yugoslavia, but the Yugoslav government did not budge from its neutral position. The Entente powers finally recognized the existence of Yugoslavia at the insistence of the French, and tried to whet the appetite of the Yugoslav government with promises of greater or lesser territorial change. None of these efforts, however, was crowned with success. Belgrade never promised the French General Staff to furnish the troops it expected. We need not discuss the reasons for the Yugoslav attitude here.

The prospects of Czechoslovakian participation and the substitution of the Serbian force with a Czech force remained problematic for the French General Staff. This alternative was raised by Franchet d'Esperey as early as the end of March and the beginning of April, whereas General Pellé was constantly urging Paris to give its consent to a Czechoslovak operation that would take place simultaneously with the Romanian operation, but there is no trace of French authorization to that effect in this period.

On the contrary, during the month of April Clemenceau reiterated several times that neither the southern, i.e., the French, nor the northern front should move. The March 20 resolution of the Czechoslovak government, taken before the proclamation of the Hungarian Soviet Republic, to extend its line of occupation, had to be suspended; because of the veto from Paris, the Czech government hesitated to initiate military action until April 26. The time for the final decision and for the launching of an attack came on April 27 when, because of the Romanian offensive, the Czechoslovak government felt its own interests jeopardized in Ruthenia and certain other areas.

To be sure, in the days immediately preceding, Pellé kept insisting that Paris finally hand down a verdict, but I have found no trace of any such decision in writing. It is possible that the Czechoslovak government did receive some kind of encouragement, but the French authorities did not wish to assume responsibility for this military operation.

Thus military inadequacy remained an obstacle to intervention. There remained yet another obstacle which, in fact, became increasingly decisive, namely the territorial claims of the neighboring states vis-à-vis Hungary; more exactly, those claims which exceeded French expectations regarding the peace terms as well as the frontiers designated at the Conference.

During the period of the Hungarian Soviet Republic, the French government did take the initiative to rectify the demarcation line in one area, the southern frontier of Hungary, and part of its proposals were actually adopted. Two factors were involved: one of the reasons for the initiative must have been that the most important role in the intervention – as attested by several French documents – was assigned to the Serbian army. The other was a technical circumstance: namely, that along this front line, because of the confusion created by Austrian and Italian intrigues, no final decision had been reached as yet, while the pertinent territorial committees did sanction the new Hungarian frontiers in the north and in the east even before the proclamation of the Soviet Republic. There is no evidence that any of the Entente powers, including the French government, subsequently intended to change these lines at the expense of Hungary. Both the socalled Territorial Committee and the Supreme Council stuck to their decision regarding these frontiers during the Council's regime.

Neither the Czechoslovak nor the Romanian government was satisfied with these decisions. In fact, it would be more accurate to say that they were intensely dissatisfied. Czechoslovakia launched an active propaganda campaign against the plan at the beginning of March. Its method at this time was to raise a lot of dust about a supposed Hungarian-Austrian-German conspiracy which the three republican governments were to organize with the dismemberment of Czechoslovakia in mind. Since the Conference gave no credence to the Czechoslovak accusations, the Prague government began to claim rectification of the borders for economic and even military reasons, and reached a decision regarding military action to that effect on March 20. Beneš succeeded in obtaining the assent of Marshal Foch for the operation, but after the proclamation of the Soviet Republic, this proposal was voted down by the Czechoslovak committee at the Conference on March 24. This was done at the suggestion of Jules-Martin Cambon, the French chairman of that committee.[10] Later on, the Czechoslovak government restricted its participation in the intervention on the grounds that it would occupy only those areas to which it lay claim, regardless of the nature of the Hungarian regime. President of the Republic Masaryk and some members of his cabinet explained on several occasions that Czechoslovakia's internal difficulties prevented it from marching into the Hungarian capital or from participating in the overthrow of the regime. On the other hand, it was quite willing to occupy Miskolc, Sátoraljaújhely, the coal basin at Salgótarján, the foothills of Tokaj, as well as the entire left bank of the Danube down to the level of Vác, in addition to Ruthenia. All this convinced the French government, as the French ambassador in Prague was wont to remark, that the "imperialism" of the Czechs knew no bounds, yet they were not prepared to make sacrifices for the sake of invention, even if their claims were to be satisfied.

It was even more obvious that the measures undertaken by the Romanian government were based on the already mentioned boundary line decided by the Secret Treaty of Bucharest in 1916. The decisions of the pertinent Romanian authorities, military as well as civilian, made this clear.

Because of the victories of the Hungarian Red Army, and for the sake of the stabilization of the Czechoslovak situation, the decision of the

Conference to inform the Czech and the Romanian governments about the irrevocability of the already approved boundaries assumes its full significance. This took place in Paris on June 11. Following this, and particularly in July, the French organization of intervention encountered serious obstacles. When the British Foreign Secretary Arthur Balfour was urging intervention, Clemenceau mentioned several times, among his counterarguments, that the small states involved were demanding compensation. The problem was so obvious that even the French General Staff made allowances for it. It pointed out that should the time for a concentric attack against Hungary finally come, it will become necessary to clarify the French conditions, considering that the interested parties have come up with excessive demands for compensation.[11] If we might conclude from such a formulation of the problem that the General Staff was inclined to give in to these "excessive demands," the French documents and the minutes of the meetings of the Council tend to indicate that Clemenceau was not inclined to undertake the satisfaction of new claims beyond those the Conference had already granted.

Hungarian historiography has often and emphatically pointed out the gap between the measures undertaken at the Paris Peace Conference and the principles it represented and advocated, particularly in the application of the national ethnic principle. Let us add the following: in the name of another proclaimed principle, that of anti-Bolshevism and the defense of democracy, small-state nationalist imperialism forced the Conference to depart in even greater measure from the ethnic principle. Considering that, all in all their claims were substantial, it behoves us to point out that, in spite of its determination to defeat Hungarian Bolshevism, the Conference did not satisfy these claims. While the Hungarian Soviet Republic elicited this determination by its very existence, it played on the other hand the role of a stabilizing force thanks to its successful military ventures.

As far as Clemenceau's attitude in the matter is concerned, we must not interpret it as mercy towards the Hungarian regime. The French Prime Minister was guided by entirely different considerations. In truth, he had confidence that the relations of power in Central Europe would sooner or later, in one way or another, grind the Hungarian Soviet Republic to bits, and from this he derived the conclusion that there was no need to commit the French government, and especially no need to let himself be blackmailed by his own minor allies. He felt the Soviet Republic was near its demise, for the economic conditions surrounding it would not let it survive long. He also hoped that either the Hungarian or the Romanian government would lose its patience, that the momentary cease-fire would be replaced by renewed hostilities in which the Hungarian side, presumably, would fall as victim. If this be the case then, once again, the issue would be resolved without the French having to intervene. Finally, when news was received concerning the negotiations between Vilmos Böhm and the leaders of the British and Italian missions in Vienna, Clemenceau could also expect that the leaders of the Hungarian Soviet Republic would, without further ado, draw the logical conclusion regarding the hopelessness of their predicament, and would simply depart from the scene for some kind of coalition government.

Thus, the French prime minister adopted a wait-and-see attitude, and expressed at the same time certain basic principles of the French government. One of these was the preservation of the Conference and of the integrity of the decisions taken by the great powers vis-à-vis the small allies. (Indeed, it would be difficult to understand Clemenceau's politics unless we considered France as a great power, a power that would not allow its decisions to become the subject of open bargaining between France and the "states with particularist demands.") Another and equally important principle concerned the reorganization of Central Europe along French lines; this required that some kind of harmony prevail in this area in spite of the transitory antagonism and troubles aroused by the Hungarian proletarian state.

All things considered, while Paris retained all the means for action against Hungary in its hands to the very end, its plans alternated as the situation warranted. The plan for military intervention, overt and concentric with French participation, or covert and without the French, or even disjointed in appearance; furthermore, the economic blockade and twisting the arms of the Hungarian regime, or the excuses for further steps or delays – all these contemplated measures had two inseparable objectives: the overthrow of the Communist regime and the acceptance of the decisions and conditions of the Peace Conference by all parties concerned. The Entente achieved both these objectives.

The peace delegation finally sent by the Horthy regime did not succeed in obtaining better conditions along the two most debated boundary lines, the northern and the eastern. Nor did the conditions become worse than those which the Conference had elaborated during the Károlyi regime, and which it maintained during the Soviet Republic, thanks in part to the efforts of the latter.

Notes

1. The limits of this article do not allow for the usual scholarly apparatus. As a matter of general information I would add that this summary is based on historical studies and documentary publications, as well as on materials found in the following French archives: Archives diplomatiques: Paix 1914-1920; Conférence de la Paix (mostly the minutes of the Czechoslovakian and Yugoslav-Romanian committees); Europe Z., Autriche, Hongrie, Roumanie, Tchécoslovaquie, Yougoslavie 1918-1919; Armée de Terre, Service Historique; Conseil Supérieur de Guerre; Ministère de la Guerre; l'Etat-Major; Armée Française d'Orient; Armée du Danube.
2. "Note sur la situation en Orient," March 24, 1919, Service historique, 4, n. 53, doss. 1.
3. Concerning the Yugoslav stance: Archives diplomatiques, Europe Z,Y, vol. 45, 40-41, note for March 29, 1919; 10-11, 12-13 and 14, telegrams from Fontenay dated March 29 to April 1, 1919.
4. Clemenceau, March 29, 1919, Service historique, 4 n. 53, doss 1.
5. Franchet d'Esperey, April 12, 1919 and 86, Clemenceau, April 14, 1919, Archives diplomatiques, Europe Z, R, vol. 47, 83-84.
6. *Ibid.*, 95. Notes concerning the report of General Alby, dated April 26, 1919.
7. "Etude sur la situation militaire en Hongrie et en Bulgarie et sur l'emploi des Forces Françaises d'Orient," April 30, 1919, Service historique, S.N. 53, doss. 1.
8. Graziani, May 3, 5, and 6, 1919, *ibid.*, 5, n 202 Roumanie; memorandum of the Romanian government, May 5, 1919, Archives diplomatiques, R, vol. 47, 102-104; 122-124, military attaché Pétain, May 5, 1919.
9. Service historique, 4, n 51, doss. 1. Clemenceau to Belin, June 7, 1919; Clemenceau to Franchet d'Esperey; Archives diplomatiques, Europe Z., T., vol. 44, 62-63, Clemenceau to General Pellé, June 7, 1919; Clément-Simon, June 8, 1919, 70-71; June 9, Pichon to Clément-Simon, June 8, 1919, 70-71; June 9, Pichon to Clément-Simon, 72.
10. Memorandum of the Czechoslovak committee, session of March 24, 1919, Archives diplomatiques, Conférence de la Paix.
11. "Note sur le conflit entre Tchéco-Slovaquie et Hongrie" summary from the second half of June, Service historique, 6, n 75.

Ignác Romsics

Italy and the Plans for a Romanian–Hungarian Agreement, 1918–1938

Origin in Rome and Budapest of the idea of the Italian-Hungarian-Romanian cooperation, 1918–1919

The Mediterranean is the natural zone for the spread of Italian imperialism, which took wing from the achievement of Italian unity between 1861 and 1871, and impetus and self-confidence from the subsequent spectacular growth of industry in Northern Italy. Right from the outset Italian foreign policy interpreted this zone in the broader sense, to include the countries in the northern hinterland of the Mediterranean Basin. That Italy was a party to the Triple Alliance did not alter the fact that, besides North Africa, the coastal region and islands of Asia Minor, Italian diplomacy also cast its eyes on the southern provinces of the Dual Monarchy. It would have liked to gain hold of the northern coast of the Adriatic, or at least bring this region within its sphere of interest. Precisely this intention was expressed in the fact that, after winning recognition of its "Ethiopian interests" (1906) and acquiring Libya (1912), in the secret agreement reached in London on 26 April 1915 Italy extracted promises from its new partners specifically on the Adriatic in exchange for which it abounded its allies and entered the war on the side of the Entente. These promises concerned South Tirol, the Dodecanese and Valona (Albania), as well as Trieste, Istria and practically the entire dalmatian coastal region and islands. Although the Italian army was not notably successful in the field, Rome's appetite grew even futher during the war: Fiume was added to the menu.[1]

Many obstacles lay in the path of these Italian aspirations. One of the greatest of these was the well-intentioned efforts being made by the Allies to bring to birth a Yugoslavia in the form of the Kingdom of the Serbs, Croats and Slovenes and here Istria and the Dalmatian coast were regarded as ethnically unquestionably South Slav and politically taken for granted as Yugoslav. In the interest of asserting its claims, the Belgrade government referred to the memorandum of 18 August 1915 of the Entente powers, which promised part of the disputed Adriatic regions to Serbia. To overcome this obstacle, Rome obviously needed helpers and supporters, not only among the great powers but also among the smaller states emerging in the place and sphere of interest of the Dual Monarchy. Since it could not count on Austria for the moment because of South Tirol, it drew closer to Romania and Hungary above all the states bordering on the Kingdom of the Serbs, Croats and Slovenes. To Romania which had taken offence at Belgrade because of Yugoslav claims to the Banat, and to Hungary which had reason for anger because of the occupation in November 1918 of the territories south of the Szeged-Baja-Pécs line.[2]

The Italian-Hungarian search for a common platform in face of the South Slav drive for unity had actually begun in the first months of the war. The Hungarian Prime Minister Count István Tisza, naturally could only reply at the time to the "probe" by the Italian Foreign Minister Baron Sonnino in 1915, that Italian-Hungarian friendship could not be directed against Austria or the Monarchy because "it is only in unity with Austria that Hungary can represent an obstacle to the Slav flood threatening the eastern shores of the Adriatic."[3] However, from the autumn of 1918 there was nothing to stand in the way of making concrete of a sympathy that until then had been largely only platonic. The Károlyi government responded favorably to a renewed expression of interest by Italy and in December 1918 sent Lajos Fülep to Fiume.

According to the reports from Fülep in January 1919, the Italian leaders – including Sonnino and even Prime Minister Orlando – wished to hold high-level talks on the questions of closer political ties between the two countries and they would be willing to send smaller troop contingents to Budapest, to counterbalance the British and French military presence. But the provisional head of state, Mihály Károlyi, hesitated and did not mandate his semi-official delegate to continue the talks. Two circumstances were the cause of Károlyi's hesitation. One was that he was wary about committing himself prematurely to one of the victorious powers that were quickly beginning to show rivalry, and moreover to the weakest of them. The second was that there were the obvious attempts at rapprochement being made by the Yugoslavs who, with French support, wanted to prevent the hostile ring taking shape around them from closing.[4] At the same time, Károlyi's wait-and-see attitude certainly did not mean that the Italian contact had been entirely forced into the background. A number of advisers close to him recommended an Italian orientation and even suggested that the potential Italian-Hungarian alliance be expanded into Italian-Hungarian-Romanian cooperation. Talks in this connection began in early February and lasted until the end of March when the Soviet Republic was proclaimed.

A conclusion based on compromise and acceptable for both sides in the Romanian-Hungarian struggle for the possession of Transylvania was an obvious precondition for the establishment of a Rome-Budapest-Bucharest triangle. It has been established that in the half century after 1867 conciliation and the search for compromises characterized the Romanian side to a greater extent, while up to the Balkan Wars Budapest was hardly even willing to enter into negotiations. But the tables were turned in the autumn of 1918. As a result of the new balance of power that emerged at the end of the war, the Romanian nation found itself in a position of power overnight, while the policy pursued up to then by Hungary appeared to have lost all external and internal support. As a consequence there was a sudden increase on the Hungarian side in the previously almost imperceptible readiness for compromise and this gained concrete expression in numerous plans for "conciliation" already in late 1918 and early 1919.

The first offer of a new type was made by Oszkár Jászi in Arad on 13-14 November 1918. This in essence concerned the transformation of Transylvania along the lines of cantonal autonomy and the guarantee of equal rights for the three nations within the territory of historical Hungary. Following this, and still in November, a plan was put forward for the transformation of Székelyföld, as a compact Hungarian territory "into a sovereign republic independent of all states." Bucharest replied to these initiatives with a military occupation of Transylvania beginning on 12-13 November 1918, and the Romanian elite of Transylvania responded by convening the "national assembly" of Gyulafehérvár (Alba Iulia) on 1 December where secession from Hungary and union with Romania was declared. Despite this, the Hungarian proposals for a mutually acceptable modus vivendi continued in late 1918 and early 1919, becoming more generous as the Hungarians sensed a hardening on the Romanian side.[5]

One of the most detailed proposals, which has largely been forgotten by Hungarian historical memory, was put forward by András Békési, who was one of Jászi's circle, in a pamphlet published in early 1919 under the title "*Erdély megmentése*" [The Salvation of Transylvania]. In it, Békési proposed a confederation for Transylvania and Hungary similar to what the Monarchy had been before 1918. Defence, finances, foreign affairs, as well as postal services and transport would have enjoyed state independence. In keeping with Jászi's ideas, the "Transylvanian League of Nations" would have been built on blocks as ethnically homogeneous as possible, that is, on cantons. Where this could not be achieved, small "language autonomies" could have been formed with limited jurisdiction and powers. "Let the Romanians make concessions in their highly ambitious plans, the misleading brilliance of which tempts and misleads them into the excesses we experience daily. But let the Szeklers, the Saxons, and the Germans too, abandon the efforts at separate organization they are proclaiming with growing stridency because these are entirely superfluous and serve only to increase the harmful dissension," wrote the author in warning to both sides.[6]

The memorandum "*Az erdélyi három nemzet uniójának alapelveiről*" [On the basic principles of the union of the three nations of Transylvania], a memorandum by Elemér Gyárfás, the revolutionary Lord Lieutenant of Kis-Küküllő county, dated 24 March 1919, was also conceived in a similar spirit. Citing the traditions of Transylvanian autonomy, Gyárfás recommended the soonest possible establishment of a governing council composed of representatives of the Romanians, Hungarians and Saxons and the election of a separate Transylvanian parliament. It would have been up to this democratically elected diet to decide on the extent of autonomy (an independent Transylvania or broad autonomy within the Romanian state).[7]

The third initiative, less well elaborated in its details, but one which was the object of concrete diplomatic feelers, is associated with the name of Oszkár Charmant, the revolution's ambassador to Vienna. The former lawyer to the Károlyi family was one of the first to link the plan for a Romanian-Hungarian "compromise" to the Italian orientation. Before leaving to take up his post in early 1919, Charmant twice met and exchanged ideas on foreign policy with Károlyi. On both occasions he tried to win over the Prime Minister, who tended to favor the Yugoslav orientation, to the idea of a Romanian-Hungarian rapprochement.

Like many other prominent figures in Hungarian politics, Charmant considered that the Romanians were the most dangerous of all the ethnic irredentists. "We do not have to fear Serbia," he argued in a manner that now appears very naive, "and the Slovaks, faced with the attempts of the Czechs to assimilate them, will not want to leave the protection of our sheltering wings." But "there are no grounds for any optimism whatsoever as regards the Romanian aspirations for secession"; this issue "should have been solved in the interest of the consolidation of our own state, even if we had not had to cope with the war." He stressed that the Pan-Slav threat and common economic interests provided a good basis for the idea of a rapprochement between the two states to be favorably received in Bucharest too. They both considered that Italy could be won – in view of Rome's known expansionist aspirations and the gestures it had made up to then – as a great power support for Romanian-Hungarian rapprochement, treated as an alternative to a possible Yugoslav-Hungarian cooperation.[8]

Oszkár Charmant first succeeded in finding a connection to the chief of staff of the Italian forces occupying Tirol. In early February 1919 he informed General Rossi that, in contrast with the French, who were thinking in terms of a "union" of Yugoslavia, Hungary and Czechoslovakia, Károlyi would like to set up a "Hungarian-Romanian union" in close political alliance with Italy. At the same time he requested the Italian government to exert pressure on Bucharest to call off the further advance of the Romanian army into Transylvania.[9] Two days later, on 8 February, Charmant also presented the idea of a Romanian-Hungarian "confederation" to Marquis Tacoli, the Italian member of the Allied military mission in Budapest. He considered the following preliminary steps necessary for its realization: 1. Hungarian action in Paris to ensure that the French did not block the plan; 2. Italian pressure on Bucharest to bring the Romanian government to recognize the "voice of history" and to desire unification; 3. the preparation of public opinion in Romania and Hungary. He added that in Paris the Hungarian government would argue above all that a Romanian-Hungarian union would be a stronger bastion not only against Panslavism but also against the Pan-Germanism that was a source of greater concern to the French than a possible Hungarian-Czechoslovak-Yugoslav alliance.[10]

From mid-February the Italian observers stationed in Budapest (Tacoli and Prince Livio Borghese) were in direct contact with Károlyi too. As we know from one of his confidential letters, Károlyi continued to give priority to the Yugoslav orientation because he assumed that "the Serbian friendship can be put to good use against the Romanians".[11] He did not say this to the Italian intermediaries though, but like Charmant, he too took the identity of Italian-Hungarian interests as his point of departure and tried to bring this into harmony with his ideas for a confederation. "Count Károlyi," reported Tacoli on 17 February, "first thought of the Hungarian-Romanian solution advocated by the Italian government," but that was not possible because of the aggressive policy of the Romanian government. Instead, continued the report, Károlyi should work on the creation of an Adriatic confederation, under Italian leadership, with the participation of Yugoslavia and Hungary, and at a later stage perhaps also Austria and Poland.[12]

The discrepancies between what was said by Károlyi and his ambassador to Vienna raises the question of how far Charmant's communications can be regarded as the official government position and how far they are his own personal views. It seems to us that this is not a matter of a private initiative on the part of the ambassador in conflict with Károlyi's intentions, but rather an alternative in the official foreign policy a rising from the situation and which could not be simply brushed aside under the influence of various anti-Romanian prejudices and emotional attitudes. There is a good reason to suppose that Károlyi tried to play several cards and that he gave one of these, in his view of lesser value, to Charmant. The fact that Charmant was already conducting his negotiations in Rome from late February, as ambassador plenipotentiary and with Károlyi's letter of accreditation in his pocket, points to this probability.

Charmant put forward all that he said in Rome as being Károlyi's own opinion and plan: the Hungarian leaders accept the planned annexation of two-thirds of the country's historical territory solely under the constraint of circumstances and if this annexation is carried out it will follow from the logic of things that Hungary will inevitably throw itself into the arms of Germany. On the other hand, if it could keep Slovakia, Transylvania and the southern region (without Croatia, but including the Banat), Károlyi would federalize the historical Hungarian state and would enter into an alliance with Romania. This bloc would then enter into an alliance with Italy.[13]

The most dedicated supporter of an Italian-Hungarian-Romanian combination among the Italian military and diplomats was Marquis Tacoli who was stationed in Budapest. In the interest of promoting the plan and derailing Yugoslav-Hungarian cooperation which had become more concrete in the meantime, his reports of early March requested immediate food and financial assistance for Hungary, and that Italy take a position in support of Hungary's territorial claims at the Peace Conference, and also offer the Hungarian government free use of the port of Fiume. He argued that all this is in the Italian interest too, since Hungary would in fact be an ideal trading partner for Italy and at the same time also a barrier that would "halt the march of the Slavs towards the Adriatic." And to ensure that Hungary would not "regret" having sacrificed the Yugoslav orientation on the altar of Italian friendship, Rome should actively support the idea of closer Romanian-Hungarian ties, the concrete plans for which had either met with no response or with rejection from Bucharest. The key question, he informed his superiors, is obviously Transylvania, which should be placed under the joint control of Hungary and Romania within its old, historical borders, with its own legislation and administration, in which the Hungarians, Germans, Romanians and Szeklers would all be represented.[14]

The Italian political leadership looked favorably on the proposals of Charmant and Tacoli. On March 13th Sonnino telegraphed the following to the Hungarian capital: 1. Italy urges the lifting of the economic blockade and the sending of food aid and assistance to Budapest; 2. In face of the Serbs, Czechoslovak and Romanian demands, in the territorial committees of the Peace Conference "Italy supported the conception of creating a Hungary whose borders coincided with the ethnic borders, which retains its economic resources and is strategically defensible;" 3. In return for suitable guarantees it is prepared to ensure favourable conditions for Hungarian trade in either Fiume or Trieste; 4. Although the Italian goverment is for the time being unable to extend loans or credit, the private banks may be able to do so.[15]

Sonnino's indications of the position to be adopted on Hungary by the Italian peace delegation were fully in line with the reality. The Italian delegation not only demanded ethnically just borders for Hungary as far as possible in the case of the borders with Yugoslavia and Czechoslovakia, but also, after some hesitation, supported the more equitable American proposal in the American versus French-British dispute that arose in the course of drawing the Romanian-Hungarian border. In practice, this would have meant awarding to Hungary the strip of the Partium lying West of the line running from Szatmárnémeti (Satu Mare) to Nagyvárad (Oradea).[16] It is interesting that this change of direction, or more precisely, the clarification of the Italian position occurred only in the last days of February, that is, shortly after the first reports were received from the Italian diplomats in Budapest. Thus Charles Seymour, the expert on Central Europe in the American delegation was not far from the mark when, seeking an explanation for the Italian delegation's attitude, he noted in his diary: "the Italians may have signed a secret treaty with the Hungarians to play them off against the Yugoslavs."[17]

No proof or serious reference can be found to the Italian leaders embracing the plan for Romanian-Hungarian union at that time. However, the idea was undoubtedly widespread and popular among the Italian military and diplomats stationed in the region. In a report sent to Sonnino on March 23, Machioro, a member of the military mission in Vienna, in part attributes even the proclamation of the Soviet Republic to the fact that Italian diplomacy did not devote adequate attention and energy to the preparation of the union between Hungary and Romania, which he presumed could have directed the Hungarians away from the Soviet orientation.[18]

The plan for Romanian-Hungarian federation (personal union), 1919

The proclamation of the Soviet Republic did not put an end either to Italian-Hungarian political consultations or to Romanian-Hungarian cooperation nor within this frame, to the drafting of Hungarian plans on the future of Transylvania. This clearly shows that an identical geopolitical situation can force widely differing political regimes into the same foreign policy course: only the actors change, the roles remain the same. Accordingly, Károlyi and his diplomats were replaced in April and May by conservative politicians who in part were still men of the old order but in part were already acting as the potential leaders of the new Hungary to follow the predictable fall of Bolshevism.

One of the new plans dealing with the fate of Transylvania and the future Romanian-Hungarian relationship was drawn up by the commanders and political advisers of the Szekler Division facing the Romanians in the vicinity of Csucsa (Ciucea) and, from April 16th; actually engaged in combat with them. Similarly to one of the directions pursued in earlier plans, they too recommended the proclamation of an independent Szekler Republic. Of the 26 counties in Transylvania, the Partium and the Banat marked for annexation in part or in full, the Szekler Republic would have covered 8 entire counties and part of 5 others. Its borders would have largely followed those of the Hungarian *Eidgenossenschaft* outlined by Jászi and his colleagues in Arad on November 13-14, 1918. This meant that its core would have been the Székelyföld proper and a few districts of the surrounding counties in such a way that a corridor leading through Kolozs, Bihar and Szilágy counties would have ensured a direct link with Hungary. The "Szeklers" promised that if their plans was adopted, they would establish friendly relations with Romania, enlarged to include the other counties of Transylvania and the Partium, and also go over to the attacking Romanian army and turn against the communist government in Budapest.[19]

The next memorandum dealing with Transylvania came before the leaders in Bucharest and the Romanian leaders in Transylvania in May 1919, a few days after the Romanians occupied the region east of the Tisza (Tiszántúl). Its author was István Rugonfalvy Kiss, a university professor from Debrecen who, like Oszkár Charmant took as his point of departure not the historical traditions of Transylvanian self-government but rather the "Slav peril" threatening both the Romanian and the Hungarian nations. He pointed out that this treat had been greatly strengthened with the collapse of the Monarchy. To avert this he proposed not simply Romanian-Hungarian cooperation but a Romanian-Hungarian personal union; in this, he was – to the best of our knowledge – the first to do so. There was no direct mention in this memorandum of a Szekler Republic or of an independent or autonomous Transylvania. However, the wording makes it appear almost certain that this was also part of his idea of personal union. Rugonfalvy wrote, for example, that Hungary could only follow the Romanian orientation "if there are undoubted signs that the Romanian nation is capable of exercising restraint in its good fortune, if the Hungarians of Transylvania and the Szeklers are able to send word to their Hungarian brothers that the Romanian nation has become not just the well-wisher but also the friend of Hungarians."[20]

Rugonfalvy's memorandum, which was also supported by one or two public figures in Debrecen, met with a response mainly among Romanian leaders in Transylvania. In declarations made at the end of May, Gyula Maniu (Iuliu Maniu), chairman of the Consiliul Dirigent of Nagyszeben (Sibiu) and Tivadar Mihályi (Teodor Mihali), head of the Romanian National Council of Transylvania – for the first time since the autumn of 1918 – began to stress the mutual dependence of Romania and Hungary. In this connection they even regarded the possibility of a constitutional link as not entirely out of the question.[21]

From the summer of 1919, Ion I.C. Brătianu, head of the government in Bucharest also indicated that the Hungarian memoranda had reached him. Contrary to Take Ionescu, his former minister and increasingly his rival, who was arguing in Paris for a future Little Entente, that is, for Yugoslav-Romanian-Czechoslovak cooperation, Brătianu tended to be in favour of the plan for an anti-Slav Romanian-Hungarian-Polish alliance. Besides the general Pan-Slav "peril," Brătianu also considered that this possibility should be examined because, despite their promises made in

1916, the influential powers at the Peace Conference not only rejected Romanian claims to the territory extending as far as the Debrecen-Szeged line, but did not even give their unreserved support to Romanian claims to the whole of the Banat, South Dobrudja and Bessarabia. From a certain point of view, Romania was thus in a situation of constraint in the same way as Hungary or Yugoslavia. It had to make peace with at least one of the hostile neighboring states if it was to take a firmer stand against the rest and against the Peace Conference. It is indicative of the Romanian Prime Minister's deep dissatisfaction that he walked out of the Peace Conference in early July and for the time being was not prepared to sign any peace treaty whatsoever.[22]

The combined effect of all these factors was that Hungarian initiatives meeting with no response gave way, from June, to bilateral Romanian-Hungarian talks of an exploratory character. Contact was made in Vienna, where the leading political figures of the Hungarian anti-Bolshevist forces were staying. It was in this same city and at the same time that the "Romanian" line of Hungarian foreign policy was linked with the Italian.

The first approach was made by Constantin Isopescul-Grecul, Romanian high commissioner in Vienna, who met with a number of Hungarian politicians there in early June. "... the Romanians are beginning to make offers and the Italians are making very strong approaches towards us. Would an Italian, Romanian, Hungarian alliance be possible?" Gyula Andrássy was informed by his son-in-law György Pallavicini who requested instructions from him, in a letter from Vienna dated June 15th.[23]

With the aim of sounding out the Romanian position, István Bethlen, leader of the Hungarian politicians in Vienna, sent Count Imre Csáky, later to become foreign minister, to Bucharest. In connection with Csáky's mission, Allizé, France's political representative in Vienna, reported that the Hungarian politicians "consider closer Romanian-Hungarian ties (at first based on common economic interests, but later also supplemented with a political agreement), which in the final analysis would culminate in a personal union between the two countries, to be possible".[24] Shortly afterwards, János Erdélyi (Ioan Ardeleanu), a lawyer and uncle of Maniu, arrived in Vienna and replied to the Hungarian proposals with a concrete counterproposal.

The conditions raised by the Romanians for a Romanian-Hungarian alliance were harsh. In addition to a break with the pro-German and pro-Slav policy, which the Hungarian side could have accepted without difficulty, Erdélyi also asked for cession of smaller Hungarian territories to the West of the demarcation line indicated in the Vix memorandum (Békéscsaba and Makó, together with the land between the Maros and Tisza rivers), and recognition of the Romanian claim to the whole of the Banat. In return, Romania would undertaken Hungary's "liberation from Red rule and would be ready to assist reconstruction of the Hungarian economy with loans."[25]

Just as in the case of the Hungarian proposals, the ulterior motives behind the offer transmitted by Erdélyi were quite transparent. Above all the Romanians would have liked to attain prior recognition of the *fait accompli* in Transylvania and the guarantee of a Romanian-Hungarian border more favorable than that in the decision of the Peace Conference, in essence approaching that set out in the Bucharest Treaty of 1916. In addition – with the aim of obtaining the Western Banat that had in the mean time been awarded to Yugoslavia – they intended the entire cooperation to have a definite anti-Yugoslav character. At the same time they made no mention of Transylvania or Transylvanian Hungarians. Thus the Romanian-Hungarian negotiations of July did not produce any concrete result, but only simply revealed the general outline of the positions of the negotiating partners.

On instructions from his government, Prince Borghese also joined in the talks in Vienna. He warmly supported the proposal for Hungarian-Romanian and for Italian-Hungarian-Romanian economic and political cooperation, and promised that his government would make approaches in Bucharest in the interest of shaping a "more rational" Romanian position than that figuring in Erdélyi's proposal.[26]

The Romanian-Hungarian talks continued in Budapest from August. The negotiations were pursued along several lines. The Hungarian politicians in Vienna were joined on the Hungarian side by István Friedrich, head of the government and his ministers, and Erdélyi was joined by a few generals from the Romanian army of occupation, and by Constantin Diamandi, previously Romania's ambassador to St. Petersburg, in the capacity of chief commissioner.

In the first stage of the Budapest talks the Romanian side appeared to be setting the following alternative, one which had an air of blackmail: signature of a new armistice agreement to replace the Belgrade Convention, and as part of this, recognition of the Romanian-Hungarian border defined in the 1916 Secret Treaty of Bucharest, as a demarcation line, and the acceptance of occupation costs and reparation obligations set at an abnormally high level; or political alliance (according to some sources, personal union under the crown of the Romanian King Ferdinand and his son, Prince Ferdinand) and within this frame, territorial concessions and economic preferences for Hungary, as well as the phased withdrawal of the Romanian forces.

The Hungarian cabinet first dealt with the Romanian offers on August 16 and then on 19th discussed them in detail. Characteristically, it was the Minister of Defense, Ferenc Schnetzer who was most alarmed by the threat. Accepting in good faith that in the case of "personal union and alliance" the Romanians "would return the Hungarian counties, and even Transylvania too and that they wish only Romanian autonomy," he threw his full weight behind "agreement" with the Romanians and a "defensive and offensive alliance." Although they showed less enthusiasm, in the end István Friedrich, István Nagyatádi Szabó and Károly Huszár also adopted a position in favor of beginning formal talks. The latter was informed by Erdélyi on the afternoon of 19th that "he would give the government food, armed forces, everything, within 24 hours if it negotiated with him, but 24 hours later everything would be too late." Only one member of the government, Foreign Minister Márton Lovászy pronounced himself specifically against it. Károlyi's former second in command considered that "if we reach an agreement with the Romanians, we will be on the edge of a precipice, we will become part of the Balkans and ruin our national future". He declared that he would not give his consent under any circumstances to a separate agreement between Romania and Hungary. Instead, he proposed waiting and – like Károlyi's idea in the spring – he would secretly have liked to enter a "defensive and offensive alliance" with Belgrade.[27]

Of the three Entente powers, Italy continued to support the idea of a Romanian-Hungarian alliance; at this stage France did not block it either. Italy's chief consideration was still to keep Yugoslavia in check and; as against its allies, who tended to favor Yugoslavia in the border disputes, to stengthen its positions in the Danube basin. Ensuring support for Romania and/or Hungary became all the more important from mid-September, because d'Annunzio and his irregular troops had occupied Fiume on the 12th and were openly aiming for its annexation to Italy. In the hope of crippling Yugoslavia, the Italians therefore urged the continuation of talks in both Bucharest and Budapest. But behind the "understanding" French position was the idea, now was beginning to take shape, of a *cordon sanitaire* against Soviet Russia, in which Paris intended an important role for Romania. The extent of the French political support was that the French ambassador to Bucharest unambiguously encouraged Brătianu to prolong the occupation of Hungary and to collect as much rolling stock as he could and bring it over to Romania.[28]

Britain made a declaration firmly opposing the closer Romanian-Hungarian ties. It was motivated in this by two circumstances. Firstly it did not welcome any further expansion by its rivals in the region where it would have liked to gain influence itself. Secondly, there was the planned Romanian nationalization of the oil industry and the notice given in the course of the summer of the termination of the concessions that had been granted to Britain. In his discussion with Brătianu on August 19th, William Rattigan, the British ambassador to Bucharest called the plan for a personal union a "very tragic stupidity." He considered that if it were to be realized the result would be, in effect, the rebirth of the Austro-Hungarian Monarchy within changed borders and that this new state would almost certainly be dependent on Germany in the future. In his discussion with the ambassador, Brătianu denied that the personal union "is regarded as timely at the moment by any serious person." He acknowledged, however, that he was striving for cooperation and even friendship with Hungary and that his goal over the long term was the creation of the "closest possible" Polish-Hungarian-Romanian alliance. As he saw it, this could represent a counterbalance not only to Pan-Slavism and within this, to the emerging Yugoslav-Czechoslovak alliance, but also to Pan-Germanism, and it would naturally strive to establish friendly, not hostile relations with Great Britain. But Rattigan raised objections to this too, and strongly cautioned him against setting up an "anti-Slav bloc."[29]

In Budapest, Admiral Troubridge, a member of the British military mission to Hungary, passed on the Foreign Office's warning. He stated that the Peace Conference had already decided on the withdrawal of the Romanian forces. There was therefore no need for Hungary to make separate agreements in the hope of freeing itself from the occupying Romanian military forces.[30]

The British objection was unable to halt further planning for the Romanian-Hungarian agreement. Among the members of the government, Ferenc Heinrich, Minister for Trade, was the most active from the end of August in urging the beginning of formal negotiations. As the political representative of the middle and high bourgeoisie, it was mainly the economic advantages – sources of raw materials and a market – inherent in the cooperation that appeared attractive to Heinrich. He did not express an opinion on the territorial or minority aspects of the agreement while, as a politician of legitimist sentiment, he rejected the personal union outright. "... Italian-Hungarian-Romanian policy is needed, an economic union and military convention. There is no question of Romanian personal union, only of economic federation," he declared at the cabinet meeting on August 21. Friedrich also made a declaration in favor of continuing the talks and at a higher level. He was informed by General Holbán, Commander-in-Chief of the Romanian forces in Budapest "that they and the Italians will have the agreements reached between the Hungarian and Romanian governments recognized by the Entente." On the basis of all this, the cabinet decided on August 29th to set up committee to carry on the negotiations and requested Heinrich to head it.[31]

We do not know the exact composition of the Hungarian committee negotiating with the Romanians, in particular with Diamandi and Erdélyi. We do know however, that Bethlen was definitely a member and Pál Teleki was probably among its members. We also have detailed exposé of the Romanian and Hungarian positions dating from mid-September, and the mutual observations made on these. In view of the fact that this documentation in French is still little known, even to Hungarian researchers, it is worth presenting it in detail.

The document consists of three main parts. The first contains Romania's demands and offers, the second Hungary's wishes and the responses to the Romanian demands, while the third contains the outlines of cooperation between Italy and Hungary.

The Romanian claims were the following:

1. The formation of a government meeting the demands of the Entente, Romania and Hungarian public opinion.

2. Exclusion of the possibility of a Habsburg restoration; a return to a monarchy is, however, possible.

3. "Rejection of a pro-Slav and pro-German policy of any kind; secret military treaty against the Slavs."

4. As a compromise between the 1916 Treaty and the decision of the Peace Conference, the acceptance of a border which gives Makó and Békéscsaba to Romania, but which would leave the territories north of Nagyvárad (Oradea) and west of Szatmárnémeti (Satu Mare) (promised to Romania in 1916) to Hungary. Romania needs Békéscsaba only temporarily, until the creation of a direct railway link between Nagyvárad and Arad.

5. Hungary formally renounces all irredentist policy.

6. In the matter of sovereignty over the Banat, Hungary recognizes Romania as the legal inheritor. In return, Romania supports Hungarian efforts to obtain a Hungarian-Serbian border following the line of the Danuba and the Dráva.

In the case its demands were accepted, Romania offered the following:

1. Signing of the broadest possible economic agreement, or even the creation of a customs union.

2. An immediate loan of 50 million lei and further financial assistance later.

3. Further development of the economic cooperation into a lasting political alliance.

4. Guarantee of the rights of the Hungarian population in the territories ceded, as follows:

a) full equality of rights, regardless of nationality and religion;

b) Hungarian public education at all levels, including a Hungarian university supported, or at least subsidized, by the state;

c) guarantee of the right to use the Hungarian language in public administration and justice;

d) regional autonomy for the Hungarian counties, or application of the Renner "ethnic cadaster" principle;

e) full religious freedom.

Six of the Romanian demands, the first, third and fifth, were accepted by the Hungarian side unconditionally. On the matter of Habsburg restoration it gave an evasive answer, emphasizing that "the free decision of the Hungarian nation" will be decisive in this. It would accept the demand in the sixth point only if the Peace Conference did in fact decide to annex the Banat from Hungary. It rejected the fourth point, that is, a prior bilateral decision on the Hungarian-Romanian border. However, at a time determined by the decision of the Peace Conference – which was not yet final – it was prepared to enter into bilateral negotiations on the basis of mutual concessions.

Hungary's demands were the following:

1. Withdrawal of the armistice conditions, a halt to the requisitions and return of the items seized earlier.

2. The renunciation of war reparations and the proportionate sharing of the state debts.

3. Guarantee of the free circulation of persons, goods and postal services.

4. Immediate withdrawal of the Romanian forces to the demarcation line; simultaneous agreement on maintaining internal order in Hungary.

5. A secret military agreement as part of the political treaty, in accordance with the Romanian proposal.

6. The immediate termination of political harassment in the territories occupied and claimed by Romania, opening of the closed Hungarian schools and provision for the former recipients of Hungarian state pensions.

7. Broad autonomy for Transylvania within Romania, as follows:

a) from the constitutional point of view there will be a common ruler, army, currency, central bank, customs system and foreign affairs; establishment of a common central legislative and government to handle matters related to these;

b) in the other matters Transylvania is to enjoy full autonomy with its own legislative and government, on the basis of full equality of the three nations and the various religions; in the interest of guaranteeing autonomy of the local administration and of church and cultural affairs, the Transylvanian state will be based on cantons corresponding to the language borders.

The third part of the document outlined the Hungarian idea of the platform for the Italian-Hungarian alliance. It declared that "Hungary is ready to sign a secret military treaty with Italy and coordinate its foreign policy with Italy." In exchange, it asked that Italy support Hungary at the Peace Conference and renounce its demands for war reparations; sign a trade agreement with Hungary; extend economic and financial support, and commodity credit; supply war material after signing the peace agreement; grant a concession for use of the Fiume port; and finally, not prevent the signing of a separate agreement between Croatia and Hungary, or possibly their unification.[32]

Erdélyi submitted the ideas of the two sides to Bucharest on September 18th. He received an answer the following day and informed the Hungarian committee of it as follows:

> ... among the points of the draft, only those which concern the Banat and the headwater region of the Tisza correspond fully to the wishes of the Romanian government. As the Romanians see it, the point concerning the section of the border between the Tisza and Maros rivers is undefined, and the Hungarian wish concerning autonomy to be given to the areas breaking away

from Hungary is unacceptable: the Romanian government does not yet wish at the present time to enter into details of the self-government to be given to the non-Romanian-speaking population in this area and is only prepared to make a general declaration to the effect that full ethnic freedom would be ensured for this population in the areas of religion, public education and justice, as well as public administration.[33]

Basically it was thus the differing assessment of the future of Transylvania that lay in the path of Romanian-Hungarian agreement. The two parties were essentially in agreement on foreign policy and economic questions; it would have been easy to bridge the differences here. However, the positions on the constitutional status of Transylvania and on protection of the rights of the Hungarian minority appeared to be irreconcilable. This was so despite the fact that the Hungarian negotiating delegation had abandoned not only on an autonomous Transylvania within Hungary, but also an independent Transylvania and Szekler Republic. For the Romanians, even an autonomous Transylvania within Romania and the program outlined for Transylvanian-Romanian dualism were too much to accept. Although the proposal made by Erdélyi – which presumably reflected the opinion of the Romanian leaders in Transylvania – did not reject the possibility of "autonomy of the Hungarian counties," it would appear that the centralist Bucharest government did not support that. This meant that Brătianu conceived the Romanian-Hungarian cooperation not on the basis of an equitable agreement, but under the exclusive hegemony of Bucharest, with Transylvania fully integrated into a united Romanian state.

Despite the cool reply from Bucharest, on September 20 the Hungarian delegation adopted the position that the talks should be continued. The cabinet also decided the same on 22nd. It called on the Foreign Minister, Count József Somssich – on September 11th he had replaced Márton Lovászy who had been much criticized both for his sympathies with Yugoslavia and his revolutionary past – to continue the negotiations.[34] In view of what had happened, Somssich had little confidence that he would succeed in reaching an agreement with the Romanians on the question of Transylvania. However, he too was in favor of negotiations because of the increasingly alarming scale on which the country was being plundered and also because of the ineffectiveness of the Paris Peace Conference. "... Only agreement with the Romanians holds out any hope of preserving what still remains of the country," he declared in announcing his intention to the British and American members of the Allied Military Commission on September 24. He added that the Italians (General Mombelli and Lieutenant-colonel Romanelli) had called for the same, that is, acceptance of the Romanian conditions.[35]

There are no authentic sources available on the negotians conducted by Somssich. However, a few diplomatic reports appear to indicate that in the last days of September and first days of October the Romanians – with Italian support – would have liked to impose at all costs an agreement on Hungary that was unilaterally favourable to them. Admiral Troubridge reported this on October 1st as follows: "The Romanians are demanding immediate acceptance of the following conditions by the Hungarian government. Immediate customs union with Romania. The occupation of Hungary for a year with the aim of preparing the personal union. The cession of Békéscsaba and the strategic points close to Szeged of the area around the mouth of the Maros. No agreement of any kind with Yugoslavia and Britain. They claim that they have formed an alliance with Italy with the aim of encircling Yugoslavia which Hungary must also join." Similar information was also sent to Paris in the first days of October.[36]

The unexpected recall of János Erdélyi put an end to this third stage of the Romanian-Hungarian talks on October 8th. The precise reason for this recall is not known. Presumably, Erdélyi went beyond the point Bucharest regarded as still acceptable in concessions and also that Diamandi succeeded in removing his rival who, in the view of the chief commissioner, did not have a mandate to conduct formal diplomatic negotiations. At all events, the Romanian intention to form closer ties still existed, at least on the part of the Transylvanian leaders. The fact that they prepared a secret cross-border meeting for Maniu and a few Hungarian politicians (Andrássy, Bethlen, Teleki) for mid-October points to this. After this meeting failed to take place, Maniu and one of his associates, Tivadar Mihali, came to Budapest to negotiate at the end of October.[37] The alleged aim of the mission – according to the Austrian ambassador Cnobloch – was "to raise the idea of a Romanian-Hungarian personal union once again".[38]

Despite the repeated attempts, by the end of October 1919 the Romanian-Hungarian talks had ran out of steam and by November-December were wrecked. The most important cause was the triumph of the British position, which was also supported by the Americans, and the defeat of the Italian-French axis at the Peace Conference. After lengthy discussion and after mutually quashing each other's ideas, on October 11th the Allies finally sent a stern memorandum warning Romania: 1. it could not make further territorial demands on Hungary beyond the decision of the Peace Conference; 2. it had to sign the peace treaties and the annexed Convention on the Protection of Minorities which provided, among others, for local autonomies for "the Transylvanian Szekler and Saxon public bodies;" 3. it must halt requisitioning without delay, a separate commission would decide on the fate of the assets already removed; 4. the occupation of Hungary could not be prolonged; the Romanian forces had to withdraw after the conditions for maintaining order had been provided and the new government formed. The Peace Conference also informed Hungary of the contents of the memorandum. At the same time it indicated that it was sending a special envoy to Budapest to discuss the details and coordinate the whole process.[39]

A new situation for Romanian-Hungarian relations too was created with the Budapest mission of Sir George Clerk beginning on October 23. As a result of his negotiations and the firm stand of the Peace Conference, Romanian troops evacuated Transdanubia, Budapest, Northern Hungary and the region between the Danube and Tisza rivers by mid-November. At the end of November a new Hungarian government was formed; it was the first one since the autumn of 1918 to be recognized by the victorious powers. At roughly the same time there was a change of government in Bucharest too. Brătianu's National Liberal Party was defeated in the elections held on November 18, and at the end of the month the Transylvanian Sándor Vajda (Alexandru Voivod) formed a government. Fearing that the Hungarian border could be drawn even further to the east and that they would not be given Bessarabia either, the new Romanian government broke with the obstructionist foreign policy of Brătianu and, in compliance with the latest memoranda of the Peace Conference, in early December signed the peace treaty with Bulgaria and Austria, together with an annexed convention on the protection of minorities. In this, as already noted, it undertook an obligation to ensure " local autonomy" for Székelyföld and to guarantee numerous other (cultural, religious and language use) minority rights. In its practical policy, however, the Vajda government gave very little sign of taking these obligations seriously. Its measures in January and February signalled the end of the provisional situation in Transylvania between Hungarian and Romanian rule, and its intention to fully incorporate the territory into the Romanian state, regardless of the traditions of self-government. These measures included the suspension of

Hungarian public administration and its replacement with administration from Bucharest, the introduction of Romanian as the official language, the conscription of men subject to military service and the beginning of the forced lease of the large Hungarian estates. In late 1919 and early 1920 the idea of reconciliation and agreement appeared to have lost all its attraction, both in Bucharest and among the Romanians in Transylvania.[40]

There was as yet no change of direction in Hungarian policy comparable to that in Romania. A few of the ministers in the new government, particularly Ferenc Heinrich and the Smallholder Gyula Rubinek, continued to regard the Romanian and the Italian orientation as correct. Heinrich, obviously entirely misunderstanding the situation, assumed that in August the Romanians "would have even agreed to the River Maros as the country's border," and in his opinion "we must still orient towards Rumania and Italy." Rubinek recommended the same thing. At the same time, there was an increase in the number (and influence) of those who judged a shift towards Romania to offer no prospects. Besides the Foreign Minister Count Somssich, the opponents of the Romanian orientation included the Social Democrat leader Károly Peyer, Minister of Welfare. As he stressed at a cabinet meeting on December 19: "If the Romanians set such heavy conditions in August and September for the creation of a Romanian-Hungarian alliance, they would set even heavier conditions today." Together with the Foreign Minister, he therefore recommended pursuing a Czech-Yugoslav direction. The fact that the future head of state, Miklós Horthy also opposed resuming the negotiatons was also a large factor. "The hatred we cannot help feeling towards Romania which is actually our greatest enemy, makes it practically impossible for us to enter into an alliance with them," he declared at that time. This could possibly still have been conceivable in August-September, he added, if the matter had been presented as the Romanians liberating us from the Red rule. After the plunder and pillage of the last months however, this is now inconceivable.[41] Count Miklós Bánffy also abandoned his earlier position of support for the Romanian orientation due to the scandalous behavior of the Romanian army, and Lieutenant-colonel Romanelli likewise blamed the behaviour of the Romanian army in Hungary for the failure of the talks. He remarked to Admiral Troubridge on one occasion that the hatred which had arisen between Romania and Hungary because of this "will live on for half a century" and "it has also made agreement among the three countries hopeless."[42]

The failure to form closer Romanian-Hungarian ties, and Rome's unsuccessful attempts at mediation in this connection temporarily cooled down Italian-Hungarian "friendship" too. "The Italians, who strove so actively and not without results to win Hungary in the time of Béla Kun, have spectacularly lost their positions," is how one of the German diplomats evaluated the state of Italian influence in Budapest in mid-December.[43] But since Italian-Hungarian relations were not burdened with a contradiction comparable to that between Hungary and Romania in the matter of possession of Transylvania, this cooling down could give way at any time to a warming up. However, for a Romanian-Hungarian rapprochement to gain new impetus, some quite extraordinary discernment, or some irresistible constraint on Bucharest was required. Due to the still amorphous European situation, this external constraint was created very rapidly, by the spring of 1920.

The Soviet threat and the resumption of Romanian-Hungarian dialogue, 1920

The cause which led to a new stage in the Romanian-Hungarian dialogue, extending from spring 1920 to autumn 1920, was the fear aroused in Bucharest government circles by the Soviet military manoeuvres in Ukraine. First of all, South Ukraine neighboring on Bessarabia became a theatre of war in January-February 1920 (Wrangel's forces were driven towards the Crimea); following the Polish intervention in April, so did the regions of Western Ukraine and Belorussia extending from Northern Bukovina to Minsk. It could be assumed from the Soviet declarations that Moscow would launch a drive for Bessarabia too as part of its operations against the Polish army. It was a consequence of this that as the Italian ambassador in Bucharest reported at the end of March "in responsible Romanian circles" once again "a real desire was beginning to show for a *modus vivendi* with Hungary." King Ferdinand himself was among those who supported the resumption of the dialogue, although naturally only on the condition that "Hungary abandon all actions directed towards recovery of the lost territories."[44]

This time too, the Hungarian government responded favorably to the Romanian intention of rapprochement which was brought to Budapest's knowledge through Italian mediation. In connection with the situation in Ukraine, the Hungarian peace delegation had already informed the Peace Conference that Hungary was ready to support Romania and Poland in "the struggle against the Russian Red Army."[45] This idea was also warmly supported by Pál Teleki, the new Foreign Minister who replaced Somssich on April 19.[46] Together with Bethlen, Teleki was a dedicated proponent of the Romanian orientation. Like Oszkár Charmant, he was convinced that rapid reintegration would take place between Slovakia, Croatia and Hungary. However, he regarded the annexation of Transylvania to Romania as "final" and therefore sought agreement with Bucharest in all possible ways. Immediately after taking up office he informed the Italian ambassador on his ideas as follows:

> ... it is his intention to reach an agreement with Romania and he is counting very much on the support of Italy in this. Beacuse of its monarchic form of government and old traditions, Romania is the only one of the states surrounding Hungary with which Hungary is able to reach a rapid rapprochement – despite the regrettable behavior of the Romanian army in Hungary.[47]

(The last Romanian units occupying the region east of the Tisza, left Hungary in mid-April).

The Romanian-Hungarian dialogue began again in Graz at the end of April 1920 and then continued at Semmering from mid-May. The Hungarian delegation was headed by Károly Soós, Minister of Defense, while Romania was represented by Isopescul-Grecul, ambassador to Vienna. In this instance too, there is no primary source available on the talks, only a French intelligence report dated May 14th. Disregarding the suppositions at the level of gossip, two things can be established from this with certainty. One is that the positions continued to differ on the question of territory and the other is that the talks "did not lead to any result."

Parallel with the Romanian-Hungarian exchange of views, Italian-Hungarian talks were also conducted in Austria. According to the French report, the Italians not only promised a substantial quantity of war material to Hungary, but the first deliveries had already reached Hajmáskér in May. At this same period, that is, in the spring of 1920, Italy supported Hungary in the closed forums of the Peace Conference too. Francesco Nitti, the new Italian Prime Minister, and his Foreign Minister Vittorio Scialoja, together with Lloyd George called for the revision of the Hungarian Peace Treaty and the drawing of new, ethnically more equitable borders for Hungary. The resulting compromise of this Italian-British initiative was the so-called Millerand covering note issued on May 6, 1920, and later attached to the Peace Treaty as an annex, which ensured the theoretical possibility for a later modification of the Hungarian borders.[48]

In the closed sessions of the Peace Conference, France consistently opposed any change to the Hungarian borders drawn in the spring of 1919. At the same time it suggested to the members of the Hungarian peace delegation the possibility that if Hungary stood behind France or joined France's alliance system in Eastern Europe, it could count on a revision. A few of the high-ranking heads of the French Foreign Ministry, which came under new leadership in early 1920, thought in terms of creating an Austrian-Hungarian-Czechoslovak-Romanian-Yugoslav bloc, or as a minimum goal, a Polish-Hungarian-Romanian bloc. Within this frame, France too attempted to mediate between Romania and Hungary from the summer of 1920.[49]

The first French mediation was in July 1920, immediately after the first successful offensive of the Soviet army against Poland, launched on July 4th. Moreover, this also increased Romanian readiness to negotiate. It is characteristic that in August even Take Ionescu (then Foreign Minister) who was otherwise one of the chief Romanian proponents of the proposed Little Entente and consistently opposed Brătianu's Romanian-Hungarian-Polish idea, made a declaration on the importance of rapprochement to Hungary. As Maurice Paléologue, French chief secretary for foreign affairs, informed Count Imre Csáky who was engaged in talks with him on August 18th, partly due to the "imminent Russian threat" and partly to the lack of interest on the part of the British government at the moment, the Romanian government was unable or did not want "to occupy a place in the political interest group" whose chief aim was to force Hungary into a pincers. This meant that the chances for an agreement were now very good. This appeared to be confirmed by the fact that the Rumanian government was for the moment resisting the siren voices coming from Prague, calling on it to join the treaty of alliance signed between Czechoslovakia and the Kingdom of the Serbs, Croats and Slovens against Hungary on August 14th, 1920.[50]

At the urging of the French government, representatives of Hungary and Romania once again sat down to negotiate in early September 1920. Shortly after it was rumored in diplomatic circles in Vienna and later also reported in the press that the talks held in Gödöllő had ended in an agreement. This agreement was said to have contained the following:

1. Hungary renounces once and for all the Hungarian territories annexed to Romania;

2. Hungary will not conduct irredentist propaganda directed against Romania;

3. In the case of a Russian attack, Hungary will extend prompt military assistance to Romania;

4. Romania is to return Hungarian rolling stock taken out of the country;

5. Romania undertakes an obligation to allow Hungary to exploit certain deposits of raw materials (the Petrozsény (Petroşani) coalmines, the saltmines of Marosújvár (Ocna Mureş) and Parád, certain oil and gas fields) and to operate the Resica (Reşiţa) metallurgical plant;

6. Romania will remain neutral if Hungary becomes involved in war with a third country.[51]

A number of sources prove that talks did in fact take place between Hungary and Romania in early September. However the agreement itself is almost certainly apocryphal. At the most it can be thought that these (or similar) were the Romanian demands and offers. Only partial credence can be given – and this is a "distortion" in the opposite direction – to the French news agency report of September 9th according to which not only were talks being held "between King Ferdinand, or his representative Take Ionescu, and Horthy," but also that "if certain preliminary conditions are met, Romania is not averse to returning the Hungarian territories outside Transylvania."[52] In the light of the Romanian position in the earlier stages of the negotiations, this latter assumption must be regarded as entirely improbable. If there was one issue on which the Romanian position was intransigent, it was the border question; it had always stood and continued to stand in the future in the way of substantive rapprochement. This claim seems especially unlikely when it is known that in August the Soviet army suffered a defeat outside Warsaw and by this time was in rapid retreat.

True to its traditional flexibility, Romanian foreign policy immediately responded to the change in the course of the Polish-Soviet war. Bucharest's readiness for a dialogue once again evaporated. But in Budapest optimism continued to prevail – as though nothing had happened. The otherwise Hungarophile German ambassador to Budapest, Prince Fürstenberg, fully sensed this mood and pointed out how unjustified it was. "Romania is clearly in the focus of political interest here....On the basis of prompting from the French they still have hopes here that Romania will make no inconsiderable territorial concessions to Hungary in Transylvania. As I know from a public figure who has good relations with Bucharest and was there only recently, in influential circles there, at least for the present, any kind of territorial concession regarding Transylvania is rejected, all the more so since no danger at all threatens from the Russian front now that it has become entirely calm....There is every reason to assume that Romania will not warm towards Hungary as easily as it is hoped here. As long as the Bolshevik danger threatening Romania from Russia does not increase again Romania will be capacle of continuing the foreign policy tactic it has been following and as far as it can will pursue a policy of double-dealing," reported the ambassador on September 22.[53]

Besides the end of the Russian danger, another factor contributing to the evaporation of the Romanian readiness to negotiate and reach an agreement was that, in the Paris Treaty of October 28th, 1920, the Allied Powers finally recognized Romania's 1918 annexation of Bessarabia. In these weeks it was now only a few Romanian leaders in Transylvania (mainly Maniu) who used a conciliatory tone with the Hungarians and towards Hungary: disillusioned with Bucharest's centralization, they hoped in this way to make some progress towards ensuring autonomy for Transylvania within Romania. However, they too were entirely against "autonomy" for the Hungarians within Transylvania.[54]

Despite the refusal of the now sell-confident Romanian policy to consider the matter, the idea of a Romanian-Hungarian alliance arose once again in late 1920 and early 1921. Following the Italian and then the French meditation, Poland took upon itself the hopeless task of bringing about a reconciliation between the two countries.

The plan for a three-member bloc which had been supported by the French and earlier by Brătianu was fully in harmony with Polish security policy ideas. Warsaw considered that such an alliance could be used to keep both the Soviet Russia and Czechoslovakia in check. In December 1920, when Take Ionescu visited Warsaw, several Polish papers quite unambiguously carried articles on the lack of Romanian self-moderation and called on Romania "to reach an agreement with Hungary if it wishes an alliance with Poland," because for Poland the Hungarian alliance is just as important as the Romanian. But, in contrast with his wavering in the summer, the essence of the opposing conception of the Romanian Foreign Minister was to divert Poland from its pro-Hungarian policy and bring it closer to the Yugoslav-Czechoslovak axis, and in this way to sign a defense treaty with it. He thus envisioned a variant of the later Little Entente in which Poland would also have been a member.[55]

Since, in the absence of the means of exerting constraint, Poland was unable to induce Romania to make concessions to Hungary, and Romania was in the same situation with Poland as regards to Czechoslovakia, neither of these two concepts was fully realised. While Romania and Poland did in fact sign a defensive treaty on March 3, 1921 (providing for mutual military assistance in the case of an unprovoked attack), Poland did not join the Yugoslav-Czechoslovak axis, but Romania did. Bucharest dissociated itself in two steps. Firstly (on April 23rd, 1921) it entered into a defense alliance with Czechoslovakia and then – setting aside the debate over the status of the Banat and accepting the division – on June 7, 1921, with Yugoslavia. The treaties not only called for mutual assistance in case of a Hungarian attack, but also obliged the signatories to coordinate their general policy on Hungary. In view of the tension that had arisen in Austrian-Hungarian relations over the question of the status of Western Hungary, this meant that the circle around Hungary had closed.[56]

In practical and technical matters Romania showed no ill will towards isolated Hungary. Regular railway traffic and postal services between the two countries were resumed from January 1921; in the spring talks began on the exchange of political prisoners. But Bucharest gave no further thought to a political alliance linked with a satisfactory settlement of the situation of Transylvania and of the Transylvanian Hungarians, which had been so frequently discussed in 1919 and 1920. It became an unshakeable basic principle of Romanian policy that reconciliation between the two countries was only possible if Hungary gave up its claim to all or part of Transylvania and demonstrated its peaceful intentions with deeds. In spring 1921, shortly after his arrival in the Romanian capital, András Hóry, Hungarian chargé d'affaires in Bucharest was informed by Maniu, leader of the Romanians in Transylvania to this effect, and this can also be seen behind the "measured courtesy" of Take Ionescu, and the words of King Ferdinand: "I know how much Hungary suffered and lost in the war. But the struggle is over and now, however sad it is, the situation must be accepted....Time and good will are needed to create good neighborly relations" thus Hóry noted the king's words.[57]

The Hungarian leadership was unable to meet the expectations of Bucharest which had become quite clear by 1921, and given the ungenerous nature of Romanian policy on the minorities that would not have been possible. Consequently, by 1921 the opinion had crystallized among the realists who held no illusions – and from this point of view Miklós Horthy was one of them – that nothing could be done for the time being: they must wait and gather strength. "As long as the Romanians are stronger than we are, they will possess Transylvania. But of the Hungarians become stronger than the Romanians, they will take Transylvania away from them. Since this is a clearcut situation, all negotiation is without purpose," is how Antal Lehár records Horthy's words on March 8, 1921, in his memoirs.[58]

But among the naive who expected miracles – including many Transylvanian refugees – the belief in, or rather the hope of the possibility of compromise persisted. In late 1920 and early 1921, for example, they took, quite seriously a declaration made by a French senator, Anatole de Monzie, and were confident that Transylvania could be made an independent buffer state placed under the protection of the League of Nations.[59]

For a while Italy watched France's efforts to foster Romanian-Hungarian talks in the summer and autumn of 1920 with the jealousy and envy of a cuckolded husband. Italy cooperated with Britain and even with Germany to prevent the French mediation from succeeding. However, when it perceived the first signs of the emergence of the Little Entente and Hungary's isolation, it beat a rapid retreat and, making a sudden about-turn in its foreign policy, began to make spectacular approaches to the neighbors it had been treating as enemies. Under the terms of the Tirana agreement of August 2, 1920, it evacuated Valona as a first step, thereby ensuring for Albania the possiblity of independent statehood. It then reached an agreement with what had been its principal enemy, Yugoslavia. In the Treaty of Rapallo of September 12, 1920, in return for the greater part of Istria it renounced the whole of Dalmatia with the exception of Zadar and one or two islands, and agreed to the proclamation of Fiume as a "free state." The treaty was also recognized by Britain and France on February 14, 1921.[60]

The significance of Tirana and especially of Rapallo from the viewpoint of Hungarian foreign policy lay in the fact that with these treaties Italy recognized the new arrangement in the Balkans and the Danube Basin worked out at the Paris Peace Conference and, with this, the Hungarian policy of grievance and revisionism lost what had been its main external supporter. The attempts made by Charles IV to return in 1921, raising the possibility of the rebirth of the Monarchy and in which Budapest's role was unclarified, increased Rome's coolness towards Hungary. From then on, for close to half a decade, Italian foreign policy in the Danube Basin strove to bring the region within its zone of influence with Italy either leading the Little Entente or at least relying on it.

Attempts at rapprochement in the 1920s and 1930s

Many concrete affairs in the first half of the 1920s showed that Italy had turned away from Hungary. One example in the summer of 1921 was the rejection or postponement of Hungary's admission to the League of Nations, which depended principally on Italy. The Italian diplomats stressed that such an act would be "scandalous" because of Hungary's behavior in Burgenland and would endanger the region's stability.[61] At first Italian diplomacy did not support a compromise solution in the question of Western Hungary either but, together with Britain and in opposition to France, urged the cession of the entire territory to Austria. It was actually for reasons of prestige that it changed its position in early September. It did not want a possible compromise to come about against its will, nor did it want the mediator – if mediation was inevitable – to be Czechoslovakia rather than itself.[62]

Bethlen took advantage of the Venice negotiations, where the decision on the Sopron referendum was made, to discuss with leading Italian diplomats the possibility of strengthening relations between the two countries. He did not obtain more than general promises for the future. Contarini, the Italian first secretary for foreign affairs, also advised the Hungarian ambassador to Rome to be patient in October 1922.[63]

Italy continued to pursue its new Danube policy after Mussolini came to power in 1922. In reply to an exploratory step by Bethlen seeking a supporter for normalization of the very tense Romanian-Hungarian relations, in January 1923 Mussolini replied with instructions to the ambassador, calling on the Hungarian government for moderation and warning it "not to upset the Danube-Balkan status quo." Nor did Mussolini show any special sign of good will in the process of obtaining a loan from the League of Nations in 1923-24. And he insisted that Hungary make its war reparation payments, in which Italy had a direct interest.[64]

The Little Entente orientation of Italian foreign policy reached its peak with the treaties on friendship and cooperation signed between Italy and Yugoslavia in January 1924 and between Italy and Czechoslovakia in July 1924. Italy's policy on Hungary at that time was summed up in a note made by Mussolini: "Oppose revision of Treaty of Trianon. Do not oppose demands of neighboring states for control [over Hungary]."[65]

Despite its unilateral annexation of Fiume in 1923, Italy's policy of orientation towards the Little Entente continued until the autumn of 1926 when it again began to engineer a change of direction. The change was sparked by the Yugoslav-Greek Agreement of August 17, 1926 which Italy regarded – not without justification – as being directed against itself. In response, on November 22, 1926, it once again placed Albania under "protection." Following this, Italian-Yugoslav relations became so tense that for weeks there was danger of military conflict on the Italian-Yugoslav and the Albanian-Yugoslav border. The deterioration of Italian-Yugoslav relations also affected Italian-Czechoslovak relations and all these factors together meant the end of the Danube policy Italy had been pursuing since the Treaty of Rapallo. From that point Rome regarded only Romania as a partner of the three Little Entente countries and once again turned towards Hungary with the aim of encircling Yugoslavia.[66]

Apart from the concrete territorial dispute, there were naturally deeper underlying causes for the change of direction in Italian foreign policy. Foremost among these were the structural weaknesses of the Italian economy and its inability to cope with the British and French competition. For all these reasons Italy was not able and could not have been able to become the leader of the Little Entente. Mussolini wanted to compensate for the failure that had become obvious by the mid-twenties by adopting increasingly aggressive positions.

Within the framework of Italian-Hungarian cooperation that began to unfold from the spring of 1927, the idea of Romanian-Hungarian rapprochement, almost entirely forgotten after 1920, gained new life. It was raised at the meeting between Mussolini and Bethlen in Rome in April 1927 and was one of the central themes of their talks in Milan in 1928. As Bethlen argued: "If a right-wing regime could be brought to power in Austria and on the other hand a rapprochement achieved between Hungary and Romania, a new situation would be created in Central Europe because the Little Entente would disintegrate. Romania could be regarded as no longer a member and a new Central European bloc comprising Austria, Hungary and Romania could be formed under Italian leadership." Mussolini and those responsible for Italian foreign policy fully shared Bethlen's views. As the Italian dictator said: "this was fully in line with the construction he had elaborated and on which he was already working." They agreed that Mussolini would exert pressure on Bucharest in the interest of this rapprochment and that he would also ask the Polish Foreign Minister to act as a go-between.[67]

In keeping with the program of action adopted at the Milan meeting, in the second half of 1928 – for the first time since 1920 – Hungarian, Italian and Polish diplomacy once again attempted to make Romanian-

Hungarian relations more friendly. The conditions set by Bethlen for the agreement were: compensation for the Hungarian owners of medium and large estates expropriated under the land reform in Romania (the so-called optant issue), substantive improvement in the situation of the Hungarian minority and finally, Romania to distance itself from the Little Entente. In exchange, he offered neutrality in the case of a Soviet-Romanian war. Romanian Foreign Minister Titulescu showed readiness to sign a treaty of friendship and non-aggression if two conditions were accepted: if Hungary guaranteed the inviolability of the Romanian border and if it moderated its demands for compensation of the optants. Bethlen would have agreed to guaranteeing the Romanian-Hungarian border, since he had already done so a number of times under the constraint of circumstances and Mussolini also made the same request of him. On June 4 he informed the Italian ambassador that he would renounce the territorial demands in return for the political agreement he hoped to achieve. However, in exchange he asked for something that Romania was almost certain to refuse: autonomy for Transylvania within the Romanian state. The positions came no closer together on the optant issue either. However, it turned out that the Romanians wished to inform their allies on the establishment of this contact. In mid-June Hungarian diplomacy therefore informed both the Italian and the Polish intermediaries that "under such circumstances the Hungarian government was obliged to abandon any continuation of this action."[68]

Analyzing the nature of the Romanian-Hungarian differences and evaluating the failure of the attempt at mediation, the Italian diplomats also agreed with this Hungarian step. With resignation and not without a touch of cynicism, Dino Grandi, the secretary of state for foreign affairs, reached the same conclusion as the German Ambassador Fürstenberg at the end of 1920. He recorded that there would only be a realistic chance for Hungarian-Romanian rapprochement if "Russia once again becomes a power factor and Romania lies at our feet."[69]

Despite the failure of the 1928 attempt, Bethlen once again tried to draw closer to Romania in the spring and summer of 1928. He was motivated in this mainly by the fact that the previous Romanian government had been replaced by Iuliu Maniu's cabinet at the end of 1928. Bethlen was closely acquainted with the new prime minister, since the latter had begun his political career in the Hungarian parliament before 1918. The Hungarian prime minister presumed that he would perhaps find it easier to communicate with his former fellow MP who stressed the regional interests of Transylvania in contrast with Bucharest's aspirations for centralization. When he met with the Polish Foreign Minister August Zaleski, in May 1929, he therefore asked him to mediate once again. He declared that if Romania distances itself from the Little Entente, shows a readiness for compromise on the optant issue and gives cultural concessions to the Hungarian minority, then Hungary is ready for "serious rapprochement with Romania," leaving out of consideration the territorial issue. He sent his message to Bucharest through other channels too in the course of the summer. But he was once again deceived in his hopes. The answer of the new Romanian government was no different from that of the previous one. As the French ambassador in Bucharest reported: "Monsieur Mironescu received this proposal with the greatest mistrust and said that he is not prepared to make concessions, to cause the opening of a crack within the Little Entente."[70] As a result, by the autumn of 1929 the idea of Romanian-Hungarian rapprochement was once again shelved as an unfeasible plan.

The repeated failure of the plan for Romanian-Hungarian rapprochement showed not only how serious were the differences between Romania and Hungary, but also the feebleness of Italy and the weakness of its positions in the Balkans and the Danube Basin. The bilateral treaties between Italy and Turkey, Italy and Greece, Bulgaria and Turkey, and Turkey and Hungary signed between 1927 and 1929, all directly or indirectly aimed against Yugoslavia, were of little value and did not prove to be sufficiently effective either. Rather than encircling Yugoslavia or causing the break-up of the Little Entente, in reality they contributed to the strengthening of the alliance binding the three states. At their conference in 1929 they signed a collective security agreement and adopted a resolution that their Chiefs of Staff would meet annually for consultation and to coordinate their military doctrine.[71]

As a consequence of the unadmitted but obvious latest failure, Italian foreign policy reduced its activity in the Balkans from 1929 to 1932. In contrast, the plan for an Italian-Austrian-Hungarian bloc came to the fore and by 1934 led not only to the creation of quite close economic cooperation among the three countries, but also to regular political consultations. The leaders of the three countries wished to give their political cooperation a character that was in part anti-status quo (directed against the Little Entente) and in part defensive (against Germany).[72] But this aim too, proved to be illusory because of Italy's foreign trade commitments elsewhere and its political weakness, which was not changed but, in fact, emphasized by its colonization of Ethiopia in 1935-1936. It is characteristic that even at its peak in 1934, Italy's share of Hungary's total imports was only 11.9% (before that it had ranged between 5 and 7%). In the same period (1930-1938), Germany's share of Hungary's imports rose from 20% to 30%, and Austria's fluctuated between 10 and 20%. The distribution of Hungarian exports showed a similar pattern. While only 10-13% went to Italy, Germany's share was over 20% from 1934 and more than 50% from 1939, while Austria took 10-20%.[73] The Berchtesgaden Protocol reflected this weakness of Italy. In signing it on October 25, 1936, Mussolini not only accepted the Anschluss but also recognized that, after squeezing out the French and the British, the Danube Basin and the Balkans would also become a German sphere of interest, within which there was scope for Italian expansion only where and to the extent that it did not conflict with German interests. For this reason, the efforts made by Italian foreign policy between 1936 and 1939 to create regional alliances led by Italy within the German sphere of influence (horizontal axis and the plan for a bloc of neutral states) were no more than weak attempts and inevitably doomed to failure.[74]

The possibility of a Romanian-Hungarian rapprochement also arose from time to time in some of the twists and turns of Italian foreign policy in the thirties which aimed at changing the status quo and at the same time at moderating the emerging German hegemony. However, since Romania's readiness for compromise remained minimal and Italy still had no means at its disposal of obliging Romania to be more flexible, these possibilities very rapidly evaporated – without leaving any tangible result or even achieving any substantive rapprochement in the positions. This was the case, for example, in 1932-1933, when the new Romanian King, Carol offered "spiritualization of the border" in the hope of closer economic cooperation, but was not prepared to accept, even as a basis for negotiations, the guarantee of "full cultural and political freedom" for the Hungarian minority in Transylvania requested by the Hungarian partner in negotiations. Or in 1936 when, in the shadow of the growing German threat, Bethlen revived the plan of 1920 for a Polish-Hungarian-Romanian bloc backed by Italy. Bethlen's offer at that time was an easing of revisionist propaganda and the exclusion of revision as a concrete issue from the negotiations, in return for which he asked for an improvement of the situation of Hungarians in Transylvania in the spirit of the 1919 Convention on the Protection of Minorities. But even in the situation which was progressively changing from the viewpoint of security, Romanian policy would not budge. It wanted to receive guarantees on the inviolability of the Trianon borders without having to undertake any accountable obligations for the guarantee of minority rights. The same thing was repeated in 1937-38 in the course of the negotiations between the Little Entente and Hungary.[75]

It was Britain that imposed the negotiations of 1937-1938 between the Little Entente and Hungary, in an unprecedented way, with Italian and Soviet support. In the eyes of many this appeared at that time to be the last chance to somehow stem the "brown tide." The offer of the Little Entente was that it was prepared to recognize Hungary's equality in armament in return for a non-aggression treaty. Hungary's answer was that it would accept the offer only if the leaders of the three countries began negotiations with the leaders of the Hungarian minority, accept their rightful demands and also undertake a commitment to guarantee them in a separate bilateral agreement.[76]

Of the three countries, Romania showed the least readiness to settle the minority question. In the meeting between Kánya and Antonescu in September 1937, the Romanian Foreign Minister argued that while Czechoslovakia would probably not be able to avoid rethinking its minority policy because of its German minority and the same was the case for Yugoslavia, because of the Croatian separatists and their support from the Germans and Italians, in the case of Romania no comparable constraint existed. "It follows from this situation," argued Antonescu, "that it is impossible for the Romanian government to accept any obligation towards Hungary on treatment of the Hungarian minority." Like his predecessors, Titulescu, Mironescu, Take Ionescu, Brătianu and the other Romanian political leaders, he too regarded the minority question as an internal affair, and considered the international or bilateral reregulation of protection for the minority to be the first step in the direction of revision.[77] Titulescu had said somewhat earlier in the parliament in Bucharest that the minority was a way of forcing Romania to "have a foreign nail in the house when the great day of revision comes."[78]

By insisting on this position Romania succeeded right up until the autumn of 1938 in preventing the more understanding and conciliatory Czechoslovak-Yugoslav approach from becoming the official view of the Little Entente. It later relaxed its rigid stance but by then there was no longer a Little Entente which could have represented a uniform position in face of Hungary. From autumn 1938 events escalated: the status quo was disturbed and then disrupted; in the new situation Hungary too formulated more far-reaching goals than it had in the period of close to two decades between 1920 and 1938. From then it was not minority protection or the modalities of a Romanian-Hungarian rapprochement based on the status quo that were on the agenda, or even bringing the political and ethnic borders into line, but rather the establishment of a radically new order in the region within which each side concerned strove to acquire or keep as much territory as it could. In this way Horthy's prophecy made in 1921 was fulfilled: Transylvania will belong to the stronger side and will belong to it to the extent that it is stronger. Germany played the leading role in this tragedy, which at the time still appeared to be a new beginning and the events after 1938 increasingly reduced Italy to a bit player, a role both Romania and Hungary had always had.

This examination of the twenty-year history of attempts to reach a Romanian-Hungarian agreement, and the role Italy played in them rise to two negative conclusions. One is that without effective external pressure, threat or constraint, an agreement between the two rival countries, Romania and Hungary, based on a mutually acceptable equitable compromise was inconceivable. The other is that because of its economic and political weakness and its geographical position, Italy proved over a long period to be incapable of exerting such pressure. Temporarily, in still amorphous situations or in a vacuum, it may occasionally have appeared that Italy was the leading power in the region, but this was just an appearance that lasted until the power that was geopolitically predestined for the role and had the strength to match this, developed the political will to create a new order satisfying its own interests and considerations.

Notes

1. Maxwell H.H. Macartney, Paul Cremona, *Italy's Foreign and Colonial Policy 1914-1937*, 2nd ed. (New York, 1972), pp. 6-8, and Giovanni Zamboni, *Mussolinis Expansionspolitik auf dem Balkan* (Hamburg, 1970), pp. X-XI.
2. Ivo J. Lederer, *Yugoslavia at the Paris Peace Conference* (New Haven, London, 1963), pp. 3-53.
3. *Gróf Tisza István Összes Munkái* [Complete Works of Count István Tisza] Vol IV. (Budapest, 1926), pp. 263-264.
4. *Károlyi Mihály levelezése I. 1905-1920* [Correspondence of Mihály Károlyi Vol. I. 1905-1920] ed. György Litván (Budapest, 1978), pp. 366-367, 380, 393-395 and 402-403. *Cf.*, Zsuzsa Nagy, "Az olasz

érdek és Magyarország 1918-1919-ben" [Italian Interest and Hungary in 1918-1919], *Történelmi Szemle* (1965), pp. 259-261.
5. Ernő Raffay, *Erdély 1918-1919-ben* [Transylvania in 1918-1919] (Budapest, 1987), pp. 76-194.
6. András Békési, *Erdély megmentése* (The Salvation of Transylvania) (Budapest, 1919), p. 11.
7. Béla Pomogáts "Válasz a történelemre. Autonómiatörekvések a romániai magyarság körében" [Response to History. Aspirations for Autonomy among the Hungarians in Romania.], *Alföld* No. 6, (1986) pp. 70-71.
8. Oszkár Charmant, "Az októberi forradalom után" [After the October Revolution], *Új Magyar Szemle,* November (1920), pp. 1-4.
9. *I Documenti Diplomatici Italiani* (hereinafter: *DDI*), Sesta serie, Vol. 2. No. 246.
10. *Ibid.,* No. 273.
11. Litván, ed., *op.cit.,* p. 444.
12. *DDI Sesta serie*, Vol. 2. No. 365.
13. *Ibid.,* No. 559.
14. *Ibid.,* Nos. 655 and 670.
15. *Ibid.,* No. 793.
16. Francis Deák, *Hungary at the Paris Peace Conference* (New York, 1942), pp. 45-47, and most recently: Mária Ormos, *Pádovától Trianonig, 1918-1920* [From Padua to Trianon, 1918-1920] (Budapest, 1983), pp. 155-204.
17. Charles Seymour, *Letters from the Paris Peace Conference*, ed., H.B. Whiteman. (New Haven, 1965), p. 173.
18. *DDI Sesta Serie,* Vol. 2. No. 942.
19. *Archives de la Guerre*, Paris. *20N513*. Dossier Szeged. Nr. 188.
20. Veszprém megyei Levéltár [Veszprém County Archives]. *Papers of Károly Kratochwill. Memorandum of Dr. István Kiss Rugonfalvy, retired university professor, to the Romanian Prime Minister on the question of the Romanian-Hungarian personal union.*
21. Géza Veress, *Hatalom és politika Debrecenben az ellenforradalom első évtizedében, 1919-1929* [Power and Politics in Debrecen in the First Decade of the Counterrevolution, 1919-1929] (1982), pp. 26-27. (Manuscript, doctoral dissertation).
22. Sherman D. Spector, *Romania at the Paris Peace Conference* (New York, 1962), pp. 73, 159-173.

23. Országos Levéltár, Budapest. [National Archives, hereinafter: OL] P 4. Papers of Gyula Andrássy. Item 330. Diary of Mrs. Gyula Andrássy, 15 June 1919. Cf.: Béla Kelemen ed., Adatok a szegedi ellenforradalom és a szegedi kormány történetéhez, 1919 [Data on the History of the Counterrevolution in Szeged and the Szeged Government, 1919] (Budapest, 1923), p. 254.
24. Archives Diplomatiques, Paris (hereinafter: AD) Europe Z. Hongrie. Vol. 45. p. 145.
25. Ibid., p. 172.
26. Aladár von Boroviczény Der König und sein Reichsverweser. (München, 1924), pp. 53-54.
27. OL K 27. Cabinet minutes, 16 August and 19 August 1919.
28. Ivo J. Lederer, op. cit. pp. 246-275, and György Ránki, "A Clerkmisszió történetéhez" [On the history of the Clerk mission.], in György Ránki, Gazdaság és társadalom (Budapest, 1974), pp. 380-383.
29. Documents on British Foreign Policy (hereinafter: DBFP). First Series, Vol. 6, pp. 172-173.
30. OL K 27. Cabinet minutes. 20 August 1919.
31. Ibid., 21 August and 29 August 1919.
32. Ibid., K. 64. Foreign Ministry political documents 1918/1920.
33. Bases des pourparlers entre la Hongrie et la Roumanie. – I have published the document in the original, French text as an appendix to my essay: "Graf István Bethlens Konzeption eines unabhängigen oder autonomen Siebenbürgen." See: Ungarn-Jahrbuch 15 (1987), München, pp. 90-93.
34. OL K 27. Cabinet minutes, 22 September 1919.
35. Public Record Office, London (hereinafter: PRO), Foreign Office (hereinafter: FO). 371/3516. Report of General Gorton, 24 September 1919.
36. Ibid., Telegram of Admiral Troubridge, 1 October 1919 and AD Europe Z. Hongrie. Vol. 46, p. 2.
37. OL. P 4. Papers of Gyula Andrássy. Diary of Mrs. Gyula Andrássy. 9 October 1919.
38. Österreichisches Staatsarchiv, Wien, Neues Politisches Archiv. Liasse Rumänien. Kart. 730. VIII/1.
39. György Ránki, op. cit., pp. 392-395.
40. Viore V. Tilea, Románia diplomáciai működése 1919 novemberétől 1920 márciusáig [Romania's Diplomatic Activity from November

1919 to March 1920] (Lugos, 1926), p. 29; Etédi, *Románia története a világháború után* [History of Romania After the World War] (Budapest, 1931), p. 23.
41. OL K 27. Cabinet minutes, 19 December 1919.
42. *DBFP. First Series*, Vol. 6, p. 414, and Ráday Archives and Library, Budapest. Papers of Count Miklós Bánffy. *Huszonöt év.* [Twenty-five years]. Manuscript. p. 22.
43. OL Film Library. Reel 8765. Report of the chargé d'affaires in Vienna, 18 December 1919.
44. Mario Toscano, "Failure of the Hungarian-Rumanian Rapprochement in 1920," in Mario Toscano, *Designs in Diplomacy* (Baltimore, 1970), p. 10.
45. *Magyar béketárgyalások.* [Hungarian Peace Negotiations.] (Budapest, 1920), Vol. I, pp. 480-481.
46. Mario Toscano, *op.cit.*, p. 11, and AD Europe Z. Hongrie. Vol. 30, p. 77.
47. AD Paix. Vol. 139, pp. 113-114.
48. Francis Deák, *op.cit.*, pp. 213-214, 239-240, and more recently: József Galántai, *A trianoni békekötés* [The Trianon Peace Treaty] (Budapest, 1990), pp. 101-112. *Cf.*, Francesco Nitti, *Nincs béke Európában* [There is no Peace in Europe] (Budapest, 1923), pp. 127-132.
49. For further details, see Mária Ormos, "Francia-magyar tárgyalások 1920-ban" (French-Hungarian negotiations in 1920), in *Századok* (1975) No. 5-6, pp. 904-949, and Magda Ádám, "Dunai konföderáció vagy kisantant" [Danube Confederation or Little Entente], in *Történelmi Szemle* No. 3-4, (1977) pp. 440-448.
50. OL K 64. Foreign Ministry political documents 1920 – 11 – res. 280. *Cf., Ibid.*, K 27. Cabinet minutes, 21 July 1920, and statement by Ionescu. *Budapesti Hírlap*, 22 August 1920, "Románia közeledése Magyarországhoz" [Romania's Rapprochement with Hungary]
51. OL Film Library. reel 10 925. (Auswärtiges Amt, Politische Abteilung II. Report of the ambassador to Vienna, 7 October 1920).
52. *Budapesti Hírlap*, 10 September 1920. French report on the Romanian-Hungarian talks.
53. OL Film Library. Reel 7067. Report by Fürstenberg, 22 September 1920.
54. *Friss Hírek*, 15 December 1920. Separation aspirations of the Rumanians in Bessarabia and Transylvania. The agreement on the an-

nexation of Bessarabia is published in Dénes Halmosy, *Nemzetközi szerződések, 1918-1945* [International Treaties, 1918-1945] 2nd ed. (Budapest, 1983), pp. 151-155.
55. *Magyar Külpolitika,* 13 December 1920. Romania, Hungary, Poland. *Cf.,* Endre Kovács, *Magyar-lengyel kapcsolatok a két világháború között* [Hungarian-Polish Relations between the Two World Wars] (Budapest, 1971), pp. 42-43.
56. The treaties are published in Halmosy, *op.cit.,* pp. 157-159.
57. András Hóry, *Bukaresttől Varsóig* [From Bucharest to Warsaw] ed., Pál Pritz (Budapest, 1987), pp. 46-50 and 64-65.
58. Anton Lehár, *Erinnerungen* (München, 1973), pp. 168-169.
59. *Erdélyi Hírek,* 21 November 1920. "Reorganization of the Danube States."
60. Ivo J. Lederer, *op. cit.,* pp. 276-308.
61. PRO FO 371/6139. C 17075 and 17665/11840/21.
62. *Ibid.,* 371/5760-5763 and 5799.
63. *Iratok az ellenforradalom történetéhez* [Documents on the History of the Counterrevolution] II, ed. and intro., Dezső Nemes (Budapest, 1956), pp. 206-208, Mária Sz. Ormos, *Az 1924. évi magyar államkölcsön megszerzése* [Obtaining the 1924 Hungarian State Loan] (Budapest, 1964), pp. 21-22.
64. *DDI Settima serie.* Vol. 1, Nos. 115, 240 and 381 (quotation from here), and Mária Sz. Ormos, *op.cit.,* (1964), pp. 21-22.
65. *DDI Settima serie.* Vol. 3, No. 486.
66. Zamboni, *op.cit.* XIV-XV.
67. *Iratok az ellenforradalom történetéhez* [Documents on the History of the Counterrevolution] Vol. IV, ed., Elek Karsai (Budapest, 1967), pp. 50-54 and 173-177. (Quotations on p. 175).
68. For further details and the sources, see Ignác Romsics, *Bethlen István. Politikai életrajz* [István Bethlen. Political Biography] (Budapest, 1991), pp. 186-188.
69. *Documents on the History of the Counter-revolution.* Vol. IV. *op.cit.,* p. 203.
70. AD Europe Z. Hongrie. Vol. 57, p. 195. *Cf.,* Ignác Romsics, *op.cit.,* p. 187.
71. Magda Ádám, *A kisantant* [The Little Entente] (Budapest, 1981), pp. 141-143.
72. Pál Pritz, *Magyarország külpolitikája Gömbös Gyula miniszterelnöksége idején, 1932-1936* [Hungary's Foreign Policy during the Prime

Ministerhip of Gyula Gömbös, 1932-1936] (Budapest, 1982), pp. 150-167.
73. New Hungarian Central Archives, Budapest. Foreign Ministry. Preparation for peace. Item III-40. *Cf.*, Michael Riemenschneider, *Die deutsche Wirtschafspolitik gegenüber Ungarn 1933-1944* (Frankfurt, 1987), pp. 388-391.
74. Zamboni, *op.cit.* pp. 493-501.
75. For further details, see Ignác Romsics, *op. cit.*, pp. 238-239, 270-271; Pál Pritz, *op. cit.*, pp. 95-97.
76. Gyula Juhász, *Magyarország külpolitikája 1919-1945* [Hungary's Foreign Policy, 1919-1945] 3rd ed. (Budapest, 1986), pp. 166-171.
77. Magda Ádám, ed.,*Diplomáciai iratok Magyarország külpolitikájához* [Diplomatic Documents on the Foreign Policy of Hungary.] (Budapest, 1965), vol. 2, pp. 246-248.
78. Imre Mikó, *Huszonkét év* [Twenty-two Years] (Budapest, 1941), p. 290.

REPERCUSSIONS

Iván T. Berend and György Ránki

The Economic Problems of the Danube Region After the Breakup of the Austro-Hungarian Monarchy

In October 1918, the Austro-Hungarian Monarchy collapsed. The Monarchy had previously provided a broad framework within which a number of nations had undergone social transformation, and modern capitalist economies had come into being. The strains and tensions engendered by the internal economic contradictions characteristic of the twentieth century, and which were reflected in the level of economic development as compared with more advanced powers, were no doubt a contributory factor in the breakup of the Monarchy, but its main causes should rather be sought in the political and social contradictions of the time and their reflection in public consciousness.

After the 1914-18 war, the political map of Europe was completely transformed. The decay of the Austro-Hungarian Monarchy had significantly contributed to this. Instead of large areas, each uniform in colour, smaller units appeared, each of a different hue. These small countries with populations ranging from seven to fifteen millions, entered on the struggle for an independent existence. On the territory of the former Monarchy, three successor states emerged – the Austrian Republic, the Czechoslovak Republic, and Hungary. Other important sections of it were incorporated into neighbouring states: newly resurrected Poland, an enlarged Serbia (now Yugoslavia), and Romania. The enormous extent of this redistribution of territories and populations denoted in itself a radical transformation of economic conditions.

The changes in territory and population did not, of course, account completely for the changes in the economic situation of the countries concerned. The economic potential inherited by the successor states bore no relation to their inheritance of land and people. Czechoslovakia, for example, came into possession of a disproportionately large share of the Monarchy's industrial potential. From the statistical calculations (which differ in some respects), we can conclude that 70 percent of the entire industrial capacity of Cisleithania was concentrated in the new Czechoslovak state: 75 percent of the coal mines, 63 percent of the lignite, 60 percent of the iron industry, 75 percent of the chemical industry, 75-80 percent of the textile and shoe industries. With its 13.6 million inhabitants – hardly more than a quarter of the population of the defunct Monarchy – Czechoslovakia disposed of an economy on a western European level, and of a powerful industry producing a large surplus for export.[1]

Similarly, the economic structure of Hungary, underwent considerable change. It gained in industrial strength, for within its new boundaries, which enclosed about a third of its former territory, there remained about 55 percent of its industry, and 41 percent of its population. There was, however, a marked disproportion between its sources of raw materials and its manufacturing capacity; in other ways, too, the internal economic balance had been seriously upset: for instance, only 11 percent of the iron ore and 15 percent of the timber was left within the new boundaries, while it retained 80-90 percent of the engineering and printing plants.Thus, even from the territorial standpoint alone, the postwar economies of the states of central, eastern, and southeastern Europe were not just continuations of the prewar economic setup.[2]

The creation of independent states in the place of great empires, the dissolution of large territorial and economic units, the contraction of some countries to a third of their former area and the expansion of others to twice or even three times their former size in land and population, the economic condition of countries pieced together out of territories at different stages of economic development and taken from different states – all these circumstances created a radically new situation. Even under normal circumstances, a considerable period of time, in fact an entire historical era, would have been required to complete the adjustment to new conditions, the integration into a unified economic whole, the opening up of new development possibilities and the attainment of a steady and sustained rate of economic growth. But history did not allow the problem to be presented in this fashion. The needs of the new order became apparent at a moment when the problems of the transition from a war to a peace economy were being added to the already difficult problems faced by an economy crippled by war, and all clamoured for immediate solution. The simultaneous appearance on the scene of all these problems brought about complete economic chaos, almost inextricable confusion, and a state of utter hopelessness.

TABLE I. Area and Population before and after the War

Country	Area in sq. km. 1914	Area in sq. km. 1921	Population in 100,000 1914	Population in 100,000 1921
Austria-Hungary	676,443 *	—	51,390 *	—
Austria	—	85,533	—	6,536
Hungary**	325,000	92,607	20,900	7,800
Czechoslovakia	—	140,394	—	13,613
Bulgaria	111,800	103,146	4,753	4,910
Romania	137,903	304,244	7,516	17,594
Yugoslavia (Serbia)	87,300	248,987	4,548	12,017
Poland	—	388,279	—	27,184

* *Including Bosnia and Herzegovina*
** *Hungarian Kingdom in the Austro-Hungarian Empire*

The most difficult conditions were to be found in the countries which had suffered the worst upheavals, Austria, Hungary, and Poland. By 1917, it was already plain that the Monarchy's Austrian territories were at the end of their economic tether. In the summer of 1918, the economic experts were unanimously of the opinion that Austria could not face another winter of war. Agricultural production had sunk to about 50 percent of its prewar level, and at their best the Austrian territories were far from self-sufficient; they had always been dependent on imports, especially from Hungary. Hungary, however, could not come to the rescue, for she was not even in a position to satisfy her own requirements.

In many industries, production fell because of the shortage of raw materials, and even those branches of industry – such as coal and iron – which were essential for the prosecution of the war did not reach prewar production levels. Hence the young republic of Austria, created in the autumn of 1918, found itself in a catastrophic economic situation. To add to these difficulties, food supplies in the country were at a dangerously low level. The bread and flour rations were – to quote Schuschnigg – too big to die on, but too small to live on. At the beginning of 1919, the consumption of milk in Vienna was only 7 percent of the prewar figure. The supplementary foodstuffs sent in aid secured, at the best, a condition of bare existence; agricultural output even by 1920 did not exceed 50 percent of what it had been before the war. For lack of coal, the railways had, for the most part, been brought to a halt. Furnaces could not be fired. In the summer of 1919, 200,000 factory workers were unemployed. Inflation had started long before as a result of the enormous war expenditure. By the end of 1918, the value of the crown, eroded by numerous war loans, had fallen by two-thirds. In 1919, the situation continued to deteriorate, for the country had been bled white and was now to all intents and purposes cut off from the other parts of the former empire. In these circumstances, economic decline could not be arrested; on the contrary, it grew worse: industrial production was hardly more than one-third of the 1913 figure.[3]

Conditions in Hungary were similar. Here, agriculture was the main source of the national income, and because of labour shortages, the requisitioning of horses by the army, and the fall in the number of cattle, it had suffered a sharp decline. The production of grain fell from 142 million cwt. in 1913 to 84 million cwt. in 1918, maize from 96 million to 48 million. There was a comparable industrial decline. In 1918, many consumer goods industries, long deprived of raw materials and fuel supplies by the war industries, showed a fall in production of 60-70 percent. Even coal-mining, essential to the prosecution of the war, showed as early as 1917 a decline in production of about 17 percent, and by 1918 the output of iron and steel had fallen by half.

By 1918, the decline had reached such a nadir that the needs of the army could no longer be satisfied and the civilian population had to endure severe deprivations. Expenditure on the war swallowed up 40-50 percent of the national income and was financed largely by the issue of paper money. Inflation had become as rampant as in Austria.

The short-lived success of the revolution had, naturally, hardly any effect on the economic difficulties, and after the counterrevolution had gained the upper hand in the autumn of 1919, conditions became even more chaotic. The Romanian forces in the country which had helped to overthrow the Hungarian Soviet Republic contributed to this situation by dismantling and carrying off a not inconsiderable quantity of machinery and rolling stock. By 1919, Hungary's agricultural output had fallen to about a third, and by 1920, to about 50-60 percent of the prewar figure. In the autumn of 1919, industrial production was only 15-20 percent of the peacetime level, and by 1920, it had risen to only 35-40 percent.

Even Czechoslovakia, which started on its way in more favourable circumstances than any of the other states in the area, could not avoid a temporary recession. The utter exhaustion and the inflation which in 1917-

18 were characteristic of the monarchy in its death throes, had, of course, also involved the Czech and Slovak regions of the empire. At the end of 1918, in the months following the creation of the Czechoslovak Republic, industrial production was only half the prewar figure, and even in 1920 it rose only to about 70 percent. (Of the more important indicators, steel production was around 78 percent, iron about 72 percent, and cement about 85 percent.) Owing to its greater strength and its more favourable situation of being on the side of the victors, the Czechoslovak economy had access to quicker and better possibilities of rehabilitation. By 1921, when Austria and Hungary were just beginning to emerge from their critical economic condition, Czech industry was already reaching 75-80 percent of its prewar output, and on this foundation the republic could successfully tackle its currency depreciation.[4]

The whole production situation of the immediate postwar years, more especially the ubiquitous and steep decline in agriculture, dealt a heavy blow to the export capacity of those countries in the region which were particularly dependent on foreign trade. Hungary furnishes a characteristic example: compared to prewar figures, it exported only 0.1 percent of wheat, 0.3 percent of flour, 2.1 percent of cattle, and 2.5 percent of meat. (By 1921, the figures were respectively 7.4, 33, 20, and 78.) Only the export of wine and feathers reached or exceeded the prewar volume. By 1920, the total export of agricultural produce reached 21 percent, and in the following year 41 percent of the prewar level. Given Hungary's economic structure, this enormous setback could not be compensated for by the export of manufactured goods; in any case, industrial exports had also declined. In 1920, they scarcely exceeded 40 percent, and in 1921 reached only 57 percent of the prewar totals. A vicious circle hindered the development of the export trade. For the economy to function and for industry to be put on its feet, foreign currency and raw materials were essential, but these could be secured only by the export of agricultural produce, which was then impossible; the place of these missing agricultural products could have been taken by competitively-priced manufactured goods, but to produce these was impossible without importing raw materials.[5]

In the nations of East Central Europe, the crippling of foreign trade created a catastrophic situation, for they had emerged from the breakup of the Monarchy with a so-called export-import sensitive economy. When Austria, Bohemia, and Hungary were parts of the old empire they did not have to cope with export problems, for a considerable proportion of Austrian and Czech industrial products – for instance, three-quarters of their textile manufactures – were marketed in the agricultural regions of the Monarchy, and the same in reverse applied to agricultural produce. For example, 80 percent of Hungarian agricultural exports (primarily grain and flour) had been marketed in the Austrian and Czech areas.

Thus, foreign trade – that is, exports to countries outside the Monarchy – had played a relatively subordinate role, given the variety of opportunity within the empire itself. In the new situation, the successor states disposed of one-sided, unbalanced productive capacities. Some of them had inherited relatively too much industry, others too little. But in both cases, within the new frontiers, only part of the commodities required to operate the national economy was present. Without these essential prerequisites, these economies could not function satisfactorily within the restricted national markets. For Czechoslovakia and Austria, this implied the export of manufactured goods and the import of agricultural products and many industrial raw materials; Hungary, on the other hand, had to export agricultural produce and import industrial raw materials and capital goods. Thus, for the successor states foreign trade became vitally important; all of them became to a large extent dependent on it.

The foreign trade problem in its turn posed in a new form the question of capital accumulation. The very importance of trade, the restricted outlets for exports, the unavoidable need for imports were in themselves enough to increase the need for capital to finance trade. But capital accumulation, which had always been small, sank even lower because of the decline in production and the rapid rate of currency depreciation. The fall in internal capital accumulation was particularly marked in the case of Austria, which had formerly been a relatively big exporter of capital and had played a leading role in supplying the capital needs of the more backward regions of the Monarchy. Inflation, always a corollary of economic exhaustion, had wiped out a large part of its monetary capital. In 1913, the deposits in the leading Vienese banks and in the savings banks of the capital and the countryside, came to 2.2 billion crowns. In 1923, this figure – converted to its gold value – had sunk to 8.7 million. The extraordinarily slow pace of recovery is demonstrated by the fact that even by the summer of 1925, average deposits stood at only 11 percent of prewar levels. All this was an inseparable part of the new problems of financing, and forced Austria as well as Hungary to seek large injections of capital from abroad. Their only means of recovery from the economic chaos of the postwar years was to tap foreign sources. Currency stabilization, based on credits from western countries and the loans which followed, became one of the most important factors in the consolidation of their economies. The situation in Yugoslavia, Romania, and Poland was very similar. Only Czechoslovakia, by its own unaided efforts, managed to extricate itself from the postwar confusion and to embark on a programme of independent development.[6]

However, the results of the breakup of the Austro-Hungarian Monarchy stretched much further than the short-term manifestations of economic chaos, or the troubles and convulsions caused by adjustment to new conditions. The confusion, which lasted for several years, was such as could lead both to great progress and to a state of permanent regression. When the Monarchy broke up, it was by no means clear which of these two possibilities would be realized, for conditions in the Monarchy had influenced the economic development of its constituent peoples in very diverse ways. Living together within a large area had brought both advantages and disadvantages. It had, for instance, been advantageous to Austrian and Czech industrialization, to the development of Hungary's agriculture and agricultural industries; it had been unfavourable to Austrian and Czech agriculture and to Hungary's consumer goods industry. In addition to these reciprocal advantages and disadvantages, the Monarchy had embodied a system based on the inequality of its constituent parts, as reflected in the division of labour. The economic unity of the empire had rested on the integration of backward agrarian regions with others which had attained a standard of industrial development comparable to that of Western Europe. Apart from the splitting up of an economic community which had endured for half a century, and of the capitalist development which had held it together, the end of the Monarchy denoted for the newly emerging states a release from both the favourable and the unfavourable aspects of the system through which this division of labour had been carried out. Thus, the longer-term developments in one or other of the successor states were not merely the result of the empire's disintegration, or of the economic potential which had been inherited, but were largely dependent on the path followed after the breakup and on the success of the economic strategy that was planned and pursued. Therefore, attention should be focused above all on the economic strategies of the various countries of the Danube Basin between the two World Wars.

In the economic chaos of the postwar period, the first efforts of the new states were directed towards making a clean break with their old economic ties and towards attaining, as far as possible, complete economic independence. They regarded it as their main task to eliminate the last traces of the division of labour prevailing in the former empire, and to make themselves independent of even those regions which had up till then been their natural market for some goods and their main source of supply for others. The value of the goods exported by Austria and Czechoslovakia to Hungary in 1924 – even taking postwar territorial changes into consideration – sank to 60 percent of the 1913 figure.

The newly independent states quickly walled themselves in with import prohibitions and high protective tariffs. For in the twenties, the European states – especially in Central and Eastern Europe – vied with each other in setting up the highest possible customs barriers. At the turn of the century, Hungary had already raised the cry for its own tariff system, and she could now turn this slogan into a practical economic policy. Although, by the conditions of the peace treaty, the customs duties of the erstwhile Austro-Hungarian Monarchy as set forth in Law no. 53 of 1907 were still obligatory for Hungary, Law no. 21 of 1920 gave the government the power to impose by decree new regulations for foreign trade. From July 1921 onwards, one decree after another was issued, placing ever larger numbers of commodities which had formerly been freely imported onto the list of prohibited goods. This applied above all to textile, iron, leather, and engineering products. Compared with the prewar 10-20 percent duty on consumer goods, the duty from 1925 onwards averaged 50 percent *ad valorem* and thus kept the principal imports of former days out of the Hungarian market.[7]

Of course, the Central and East European states intended these barriers around their national economies to act as a protection against all their trading partners equally. In practice, however, protection did not work in a uniform way; its impact was most marked on the neighbouring states. This was a natural outcome, for both in agriculture and industry these countries used less up-to-date techniques than did the more advanced nations; consequently, their goods were dearer and could not compete successfully on the world market. Thus, although at the Austrian and Czechoslovak frontiers the same duties were imposed on grain and flour irrespective of origin, these proved to be much more effective against Hungarian than against American produce, in spite of the higher transport costs of the latter. While the customs tariffs of the Balkan states imposed a heavy burden on imported machinery, they affected Austrian products much more than, for example, English and Belgian.

Thus, the barriers which had been erected to promote self-sufficiency unquestionably divided the Central and East European states more deeply from each other than from those of Western Europe. It is significant that between the wars, Yugoslavia's trade with its Balkan neighbours was quite small, exports and imports ranging between 5 and 9 percent of the total foreign trade turnover. Although immediately after the war Czechoslovakia, maintaning its old economic associations, still sold more than half of its exports to the Danubian states, by about the middle twenties the percentage had fallen to little more than a third. This process was reciprocal: parallel with this radical fall in exports to the Danubian states, Czechoslovakia, at the end of the decade (and partly for political reasons) was importing more than half its flour from overseas and not from its agrarian neighbours. The same situation developed in Austria, which was already buying a third of its wheat requirements in America, and during the same period was unable to sell the products of its engineering industry to its agrarian neighbours. Midway through the twenties, the Balkan states were buying French and English machine tools and equipment for their textile factories, at a time when Austria's engineering industry was producing hardly more than a third of its prewar output. In spite of geographical closeness, of historical tradition, and the existence of natural markets near at hand, trade between the eastern and southeastern European states shrank to a minimum: to about 10-15 percent of their total trade. An additional reason for this was that they all consistently and rigidly excluded the Soviet Union from their economic life. A large part of what was now Poland had formerly been part of the Russian Empire, and the greater part of its market lay, so to speak, on Russian soil; yet only 1.5 percent of Poland's export trade was carried on with the Soviet Union. Conditions were similar in Czechoslovakia; while in the other East European states, not even this figure was reached. Exports from East Central Europe were directed largely to Western Europe which, by the Second World War, took 75-80 percent of their export and supplied 70-80 percent of their imports.[8]

The economic policies pursued were naturally accompanied by the growth of autarkic tendencies. Austria and Czechoslovakia, for instance, made great efforts to increase their output of agricultural produce and livestock which they had formerly obtained from the agrarian districts of the Monarchy. In Austria, by 1934, the stock of pigs was almost double that of the postwar reconstruction period. About the middle of the twenties, home-grown wheat could hardly satisfy one-third of the domestic requirements, but ten years later, it was already covering more than half. In the middle of postwar decade, Czechoslovakia's production of wheat came to about 20 million hundredweight; ten years later, it had reached 34 million.

In a particularly favourable year, Czechoslovakia, ordinarily an importer of wheat, showed a surplus on its own harvest.

It is, therefore, not surprising that the markets which the Danubian countries could have offered each other shrank more and more as, following the 1929-33 overproduction crisis, still greater efforts were made to achieve self-sufficiency. After 1918, Hungary still sold a fifth or a sixth of its exports to Czechoslovakia; but by the middle thirties, this had fallen to 5 percent. On the other hand, it used as much of its available capital as possible to develop those consumer goods industries which it had formerly lacked.

In comparison with prewar levels, production in the Hungarian textile industry had doubled by 1925, trebled by 1929, and by the end of the thirties, had reached four times the prewar figure; textile imports, which in 1913 accounted for 70 percent of total home consumption, now covered only 2-3 percent. The most striking example of this severance of the associations based on the earlier division of labour can be found in the way Austria and Czechoslovakia developed their own industries. In the Monarchy, most of the spinning for the textile industry was done in Austria, while the weaving was concentrated in Bohemia. Each country wanted its textile industry to become independent of the other, so Austria began to enlarge its weaving industry, and by 1925 had already set up 5,000 looms, while Czechoslovakia, for its part, built spinning mills. Those Balkan states which had enjoyed independence before the war now also strove to consolidate their economic independence, but they were so backward industrially that international economic ties were not of paramount importance. Their efforts were in many ways successful, helping to correct the one-sidedness of their economies and to promote industrialization.[9]

Unfortunately, these methods of encouraging development were by no means the most efficacious. As the states – dazzled by national pride and driven by nationalist passion – began the all-round development of their economies, they paid no heed to the narrow and restricted basis of their economic potential as compared to that of the economic cooperation formerly practised with the neighbouring Danubian states. Thus, their ventures proved to be not only extremely costly, but also led to much overlapping of effort and superfluous parallel capacity. As a consequence, much of the economic capacity created earlier, both agricultural and industrial, was wasted. By the time Hungary's textile industry was built up, or Austria expanded its weaving, and Czechoslovakia its spinning mills, the old Austrian and Czech textile industries had lost a considerable part of their markets and had fallen into a critical condition. The same thing happened to Hungarian agriculture and flour milling which, deprived of a large part of their share of the Austrian and Czech markets, had also sunk into a state of chronic crisis. Austria tried to promote the cultivation of cereal crops and to develop its own milling industry. It introduced state subsidies, and in 1930 created a special fund by levying taxes on sugar, beer, and alcohol. Hungary's milling industry had supplied the total requirements of the Monarchy, but between the wars it could never, even in boom periods, produce more than three-quarters of its former output. The giant Hungarian mills, which had formerly worked for the export trade, closed down one after the other; their assets were disposed of, their empty premises were sold for conversion into textile factories, or were simply razed. Thus, apparently insurmountable difficulties in selling their products was one of the most obivous consequences of the developments in the agrarian countries of Central and Easter Europe after the First World War. The developed and even the less well developed countries soon discovered that part of their industrial capacity was superfluous.

This, together with the endeavour of each country to develop industries which already existed in neighbouring states at a level high enough to produce export surpluses hindered, indeed rendered impossible, the creation of national economies based on the newest technological achievements, or the development of modern industries capable of competing on the world market. In other words, the effort to achieve agricultural self-sufficiency in the more industrialized states and the industrial ambitions of the agrarian states had indeed contributed to their own economic development, but had, at the same time, aggravated the new contradictions in the economic development of the entire area.

True, the more backward countries, through state aid and protective tariffs, succeeded in reducing imports, and thus laid the foundations for the relatively rapid development of consumer goods industries. Throughout most of these East Central European states it was the textile and other light industries which showed the most substantial progress. In Hungary, as already mentioned, the textile industry was in a position to cover practically all domestic requirements, compared to the only one-third of former days. In Yugoslavia also, it was the textile industry which between the two World Wars showed the fastest development. In the first half of the twenties, textiles had accounted for almost a third of all imports; in the second half of the thirties, for no more than 10 percent. On the other hand, the import of machines and factory equipment doubled. In Romania, before the Second World War, textiles represented more than a fifth of the value of the total industrial output.[10]

This rapid advance in the production of textiles and other consumer goods undoubtedly gave a great impetus to the industrial development of Eastern Europe; but it served also to conceal the discrepancy between the obsolete manufacturing processes and the industrial needs of the age. For during the first half of the twentieth century, the textile industry, indeed, consumer goods industries as a whole, were, in the more developed countries of Western Europe, already entering a relative decline. For example, during the years immediately preceding the Second World War, the output of the textile industry in England sank from 19 percent to 11 percent of total industrial production; in continental Europe, from 18 to 11 percent. On the other hand, the share of the iron, steel, metal-working and chemical industries rose in England from 32 to 44 percent, and on the continent from 41 to 50 percent.[11]

After the First World War, industry underwent a radical transformation. Through the use of new techniques, it became possible to provide electricity much more cheaply; industry, therefore, used it on a steadily expanding scale, and electrical power entered on its triumphant course. The multi-purpose electric motor forged ahead in competition with the clumsier steam engine. At the same time, the second great factor in the transformation of industry was making itself felt: the internal combustion engine, the invention of which led to completely new methods of industrial mass production. The modern assembly line was used first of all in the automobile industry; it opened the path to modern factory organization and management techniques, and to new ways of increasing output. It is no coincidence that these new mass production methods quickly spread to other industries, first to the manufacture of machine tools, with a marked effect on costs of production. All these processes naturally caused changes in the whole structure of industry, and in the more advanced capitalist countries, heavy industry advanced by leaps and bounds. In Western Europe, its share of the total output rose from 25-30 to around 50 percent.

The majority of the Central and Eastern European states could not keep pace with this development; it was only the light industries which managed to increase production, while the potentially dynamic heavy industries, where the new technology could and should have been adopted, stagnated. In this part of Europe, there was practically no country which could adapt its engineering industries for modern mass production; with their small and restricted markets, they were unable to take advantage of the new developments in industrial technology. If we measure the advance of modern industry by the per capita consumption of steel, the increase in England and Sweden between 1913 and 1938 was between 50 and 100 percent; whereas even in Czechoslovakia and Poland, there was virtual stagnation.[12]

The exclusion of certain types of commodities and the effort of each country to produce goods which had formerly been imported meant that the advantages following from the intense efforts to increase production in certain branches of industry were counterbalanced by the recession in others for the lack of markets. The example of Hungary is typical and highly instructive: while textile production quadrupled, heavy industry made no progress, and the food processing industries showed a substantial decline; as a result, total industrial production rose very slowly indeed, by not quite 30 percent over a period of twenty years. Owing to the stagnation in agriculture, the annual rate of increase of the national income was only about 1.5 percent. In Austria, the rate of growth was similar, while Poland, which had regained its longed-for independence, was, between the two World Wars, quite unable to reach even that minimal economic growth. One important reason for Central and Eastern Europe's slow economic development was that these countries – though foreign sources of capital were less plentiful than before – still persisted in attempting to make themselves independent economically, and thus dissipated even the restricted opportunities of development open to them. Their exertions to promote economic development and industrialization were, therefore, bound to have only limited success.

In all the countries of the region, the problem of employment was the gravest. It was quite impossible to eliminate chronic unemployment; in Poland, Romania, Yugoslavia, and Bulgaria a fifth to a third of the rural population could find no work, and industry was in no position to absorb them.

Given the slow pace of economic development and the serious internal contradictions, there was, of course, no possibility of attaining the much desired economic independence, and in the end, little had been done to overcome the general backwardness. Before the outbreak of the Second World War, 75-80 percent of the population of Albania, Bulgaria, Yugoslavia, and Romania still earned their living on the land. Even in Poland, the rural population had only fallen from the 64 percent after the First World War to 61 percent. In Hungary, about half the country's population worked on the land.[13]

As a result of the policy of exclusion and autarky, of the consequent restriction of markets, and of the slow pace of industrial development and its consequences for capital accumulation, the economies of the Danubian countries remained extremely vulnerable and unstable. During the second half of the twenties, generous foreign credits and relatively favourable world market prices had enabled them to consolidate their economies; they even enjoyed a moderate prosperity. But when the temporary boom broke and the economic crisis of 1929-33 struck the world, all the economic problems flared up again more fiercely than ever before. Czechoslovakia, which had developed well during the twenties and appeared genuinely industrial; Austria, industrialized but stagnating after the First World War; Hungary, stuck in its old agrarian-industrial pattern; and the Balkan states, no longer facing competition from the Monarchy and longing for swifter industrialization – all fell into the most severe social and economic crisis, which, in its turn, brought to the fore the basic problem of their existence and progress. The dead-end reached in the thirties left only the choice between continuing as they were, or adapting themselves to be the *Lebensraum* of the new and frightening Germany of Hitler. The defencelessness of the Danube-Basin countries in the face of economic crisis did, indeed, prove fertile soil for the determined advance of the Germans. The rapid growth of German influence and her economic domination prepared the ground for the *Anschluss*, for the subjection of Czechoslovakia, and finally, for the Second World War. The incompetence and helplessness of the states of the Danube Basin on the eve of the war reflected the fiasco of the political pretensions, of the nationalist economic policies and of the plans for industrial development which they had clung to for twenty years. The economic problems created by the breakup of the Monarchy remained unsolved between the two World Wars.[14]

Notes

1. Alice Teichova, *An Economic Background to Munich International Business and Czechoslovakia 1918-1938* (Cambridge, 1978); R. Olsovsky, V. Prucha, *et al.*, *Prehled gospodursveho vyvoje Československa v letech 1918-1945* [Survey of the Economic Development of Czechoslovakia] (Prague. 1961).
2. Ivan Berend and György Ránki, *Magyarország gazdasága 1919-1929* [Hungary's Economy] (Budapest, 1965).

3. G. Gratz and R. Schuller, *Der Wirtschaftliche Zusammenbruch Oesterreich Ungarns* (Vienna, 1930); K. Rotschild, *Austria's Economic Development between the Two Wars* (London, 1946).
4. T. Faltus, *Povojnová hospodárska kriza v rokoch 1912-1923 v Československu* [Postwar Depression in Czechoslovakia] (Bratislava, 1966).
5. Iván Berend and György Ránki, *Hungary, Hundred Years of Economic Development* (London, 1974).
6. N. Layton and Ch. Rist, *The Economic Situation of Austria* (Geneva, 1923).
7. H. Liepmann, *Tariff Levels and the Economic Unity of Europe* (London, 1938).
8. A. Basch, *European Economic Nationalism* (Washington, 1943); L. Pasvolsky, *Economic Nationalism of the Danubian States* (New York, 1929).
9. W. Weber, *Oesterreichs Wirtschaftsstruktur gestern-heute-morgen* (Berlin, 1962); *Die Wirtschaft der Tschechoslowakei 1918-1928* (Prague, 1928).
10. V. Madgearu, *Evolutia economiei românesti dupa razboi mondial* [Evolution of the Romanian Economy after World War I] (Bucharest, 1940); M. Mirković, *Ekonomska Historija Yugoslavija* [The Economic History of Yugoslavia] (Belgrade, 1962).
11. A. Lewis, *Economic Survey 1919-1938* (London, 1932); A. Maisels, *Industrial Growth and World Trade* (Cambridge, 1974).
12. I. Svennilson, *Growth and Stagnation in the European Economy* (Geneva, 1954).
13. League of Nations, *Industrialisation and Foreign Trade* (Geneva, 1945).
14. Iván Berend and G. Ránki, *Economic Development of East Central Europe* (New York, 1974).

Peter Pastor

Hungarian Territorial Losses During the Liberal-Democratic Revolution of 1918–1919

Of the 13 clauses and 375 articles in the Treaty of Trianon, none has been considered more catastrophic by the war generation, and more unfair by the succeeding generations, than Clause II, articles 27-35. These defined the new frontiers of Hungary, reducing its imperium to one third of its prewar size. It doomed millions of Hungarians in the periphery to live under foreign sovereignty.

In 1921 these terms brought into question the viability of Hungary as a nation state. Hungarian public opinion embraced tenaciously the slogan "*nem, nem soha!*" [No, no, never!]; it became the rallying cry for territorial revisionism. This policy was eagerly adopted by the conservative Horthy regime, which recognized that revisionism helped to buttress an antiquated socio-economic system. As the slogan became synonymous with the Hungarian counter-revolution, few, if any, recalled that it was coined by government propagandists in Mihály Károlyi's revolutionary regime.

The revolution, with its liberal-democratic goals, broke out in the dying days of the Habsburg monarchy. From October 31 to March 20, 1919, the Revolutionary governments weighed options and searched for compromises as an alternative to territorial exactions which roughly overlapped with those that were stipulated in the Treaty of Trianon. The collapse of the Károlyi regime, and the rise of the communist regime of Béla Kun on March 21, 1919, was directly related to the refusal by Dénes Berinkey's liberal-democratic government to accept further territorial amputations spelled out in an Allied *démarche* known as the Vix Ultimatum.

It was the representatives of the counter-revolutionary Horthy regime who, however reluctantly, accepted and signed the punitive peace. This regime represented the interest of those circles which had been primarily responsible for Hungary's support of the war. Yet these groups showed their compatriots no remorse about being involved in a war that had led to Trianon. In a psychological climate receptive to scapegoat-seeking, official circles succeeded in accusing Mihály Károlyi and his supporters of being responsible for the territorial losses.[1]

Mihály Károlyi, then in foreign exile, was judged to be a traitor and his considerable wealth was confiscated. The historians of the era considered him and his government naive and held him responsible for the territorial losses, which was allegedly accepted as early as November 7, 1918.[2] This interpretation has been engraved in the Hungarian collective consciousness to such an extent that even today it finds broad acceptance among them.[3] Due to a similar evaluation found in Francis Deak's *Hungary at the Paris Peace Conference*,[4] this view has also influenced American scholars. Numerous publications of the last two decades, basing their findings on recently opened archival sources in Hungary, France and Britain, have challenged this view, and it is hoped that they will lay the old politically motivated charges to rest.[5]

The roots of the territorial clauses in the Treaty of Trianon could be found in the old adage on the consequence of war – "To the victors belong the spoils." World War I was no exception to this unwritten rule. The Entente powers offered large chunks of Austro-Hungarian territories to Italy (1915) and to Romania (1916) as a reward for joining the alliance in its struggle for victory. It is evident that the harshness of the territorial settlements made by the peace treaties of Brest-Litovsk (1918) and Bucharest (1918) would have been the same had the Central Powers won the war. The victors would have been different but spoils would have existed nevertheless.

Following the Bolshevik revolution of November 1917, Russia and the United States offered a challenge to traditional war aims. The Bolsheviks denounced the goals of the belligerents as being imperialistic. They called for the revolutionary overthrow of the warring regimes by the proletariat and the conclusion of a peace without indemnities or annexations.

President Woodrow Wilson introduced an equally radical program as the United States entered the war on the side of the Allies. He also called for peace without indemnities and annexations. Instead of proletarian revolutions, he called for the establishment of liberal-democratic regimes based on the American model. The right of self-determination for the peoples of the Austro-Hungarian monarchy was also part of this program. Wilson's call was based on a combination of idealism and diplomatic realism.[6] The collapse of the enemy governments, he believed, would force an end to the conflict.

On Wilson's urgings, the Entente abandoned traditional war aims. However, this did not assure the territorial status quo of the Austro-Hungarian empire.[7] Although the Wilsonian solution favored autonomous rights for the various nationalities within the Empire, spokesmen for the Czech and Slovak people, both in the west and in Russia, wanted more than that. They called for the creation of a Czechoslovak state; hence, the end of the Austro-Hungarian monarchy. Their views were influential because western governments relied on emigré specialists. What is more, the formation of volunteer Czechoslovak armies enabled the emigré leaders to make demands on the Allies; they could not be dismissed lightly.[8] The intervention of the Czechoslovak Legion on the side of the Anti-Bolshevik forces in Russia in June 1918 made the Czechoslovak cause even stronger.[9]

The Habsburg Emperor Karl, unable to achieve a separate peace, responded too late to the subversive, yet appealing, ideology originating from the West. Only in October 1918 – with his armies on the verge of collapse – did he call for the federalization of Austria. By then the Allies, including the United States, had abandoned their belief that Austria-Hungary's survival was desirable for the sake of international stability.[10]

To assure the decomposition of the realm through revolutions, the Allied leaders had even delayed the execution of a speedy armistice. Thus, when on November 3, 1918, the representatives of Austria-Hungary signed the armistice, the empire no longer existed. Since there was as yet no agreement on the geographical boundaries of the emerging successor states, the Armistice of Padua included purely military clauses, and it was not, therefore, a commitment for a specific type of peace agreement. This was to be worked out at the coming peace conference.[11]

In Hungary, a bloodless revolution brought to power a coalition on October 31 which represented the opposition in and outside of parliament. The head of the revolutionary government was Mihály Károlyi, the leader of the anti-war opposition Károlyi party since 1916. The most important member of the coalition was the Social Democratic party, with no parliamentary representation. The small Radical party rounded out the coalition. Its leader was the sociologist and specialist on the nationalities problems: Oszkár Jászi.

The revolutionary platform called for land and tax reforms and universal suffrage. In essence, it reflected positions held by the coalition members for some time. The platform also overlapped with the liberal-democratic program favored by President Wilson.[12]

For the nationalities of Hungary the government offered self-determination. It assumed that the Croats would secede, but that the others would support the plan of the Minister of Nationalities, Oszkár Jászi. It envisioned the reshaping of Hungary into a confederation, a kind of "Eastern Switzerland," which in turn would be part of a Danubian confederation of states.[13] This project clearly indicated that the leaders of the People's Republic of Hungary expected to preserve the frontiers of the former kingdom.

The ideology buttressing their efforts was Wilsonianism. The Hungarian policy, just as the American one in 1917, was based on idealism and diplomatic realism. The Hungarians were sincere partisans of the Wilsonian program, but they also knew that Hungary lay prostate before the victorious powers. It was incapable of resorting to arms in pursuit of its own interests. Therefore, it was believed that only a Wilsonian peace could extricate Hungary from its unenviable position.

The Hungarian ministers were not alone in their trust of Wilsonianism. A number of American and British officials also hoped that with the guns silent, a new Europe could be constructed,[14] and some type of confederation would replace the defunct Austro-Hungarian empire.[15] It was also believed, however, as Lewis Namier, a British specialist of the Foreign Office noted, that the Allies pledged themselves "to the entire independence of too many of Austria-Hungary's constituent elements to make it practicable."[16] This view reflected a degree of fatalism at a time when firmness by the leadership of the victorious great powers and a belief in confederation could have achieved better results.[17]

The great degree of disorganization among the peacemakers gathering in Paris also contributed to the lack of effectiveness of the Wilsonians.[18] Following the armistices, the threat of bolshevik-type revolutions hung over Europe, diverting the attention of the victorious Allies from the details of the peace terms.[19] Thus, peacemaking, just like warmaking during the previous four years, did not fulfill expectations and did not follow plans set earlier.

In East Central Europe, the intransigence of the Entente's small allies over territorial issues created further complications. Some of these touched Hungary directly. Romania, following the Armistice of Padua, broke the Peace Treaty of Bucharest and re-entered the war against Germany just three days before the armistice at Compiègne was signed. Romania's new declaration of war, however, was used not to further territorial demands against distant Germany, but against neighboring Hungary.

Romania's claims were based on the secret Treaty of Bucharest (1916) in which France and Russia promised Romania a large chunk of Hungary, including Transylvania. These exaggerated war-time promises which the Entente had no intention of fulfilling were also nullified. This was done because Romania had signed a separate peace with the Central Powers.[20]

Due to the anti-bolshevik stance of the Czechoslovak Legion in Russia, the Czechoslovak National Council in Paris was recognized as a government in exile.[21] The emigré government was promised and independent state within "historical boundaries." Although no Czechoslovak state had ever existed before 1918, establishing boundaries for such an entity meant territorial losses for Hungary.[22]

The Entente also had wartime commitments to Serbia on which she intended to cash in. On August 18, 1915, the Entente promised Serbia Fiume and the Banat of Southern Hungary. The same territories were also promised to Italy and Romania – Fiume, to the former, and Banat to the latter.

Under the circumstances, the Károlyi government had assumed a hopeless task when it insisted on the integrity of Hungary's frontiers. It was apparent that most nationality leaders in Hungary were hostile toward the idea of federalism and were enthusiastic about secession instead.[23] Therefore, whether the Allies acted along the principles of Wilsonian self-determination or according to traditional war-time practices, their major task was to redraw the boundaries at Hungary's expense.

Although the Hungarian government's position stated that the nationalities could be persuaded to stay within an integral democratic Hungary, its officials in the cabinet were quite realistic. They believed that territorial concessions were unavoidable. Thus, the avowed insistence on territorial integrity was a maximal position motivated by the desire to secure an advantageous compromise under adverse conditions.

The first occasion to deal with the boundary issue came up during the first week of November. Although the Austro-Hungarian representatives had signed the Armistice of Padua in the name of the Hungarians as well, the Commander-in-Chief of the Balkan front, General Louis Franchet d'Esperey, demanded a separate armistice from Budapest.[24] He was still on the offensive against the Germans and the 170,000 troops of General August von Mackensen were still in Transylvania.

An early meeting with Franchet d'Esperey was desirable for the Hungarians. Its purpose would be to secure a favorable demarcation line from this Allied arbiter before the Romanians had a chance to do the same. In conjunction with a mission to the Allied Commander, the government also wanted to send deputies to Romania. The pretext for the latter mission was based on a technicality. Since the Hungarian parliament had never ratified the Peace Treaty of Bucharest, a final settlement between Hungary and Romania was still needed. The Hungarians wanted to make a bilateral deal over territories before Romania's appetite was reawakened.[25] The fall of the Marghiloman cabinet in Jassy and Romania's reentry into the war, made the project superfluous.

The Hungarian cabinet faced the upcoming meeting with Franchet d'Esperey with reservation. Mihály Károlyi, the Prime Minister and Foreign Minister of Hungary, was advised by his colleagues not to take part in the negotiations. It was feared that if the Hungarians were given extremely unfavorable terms, Károlyi would be discredited and his government hopelessly weakened.

The deteriorating economic situation, however, forced the ministers to change their minds. It was concluded that Károlyi's presence was needed as he had a long-established pro-Entente reputation. Therefore, he was expected to prevail upon the Allied commander to lift the economic blockade of Hungary.[26] The considerable debate over the make-up of the mission indicates that neither Károlyi nor the other leaders had illusions about the bleak future facing Hungary.

The final decision to have Károlyi as the leader of the delegation turned out to be a good one. When the Hungarians met Franchet d'Esperey in Belgrade on November 7, it was only Károlyi who was treated with deference, while his entourage, including Jászi, was humiliated.[27] The French general noted in his report to Paris that he thought well of Károlyi, an aristocrat with pro-Entente sympathies, but that he considered his cabinet a bunch of second raters.[28].

Franchet d'Esperey considered the negotiations in line with the changed situation in East Central Europe. Since the Austro-Hungarian Empire had ceased to exist, he believed that the Padua Armistice, signed on the Italian front, needed updating. He considered the terms he was now giving to the Hungarians as an addendum to the armistice, a convention. The agreement was military in nature. It established a line of demarcation only in southern Hungary which put part of Transylvania under French occupation, with the Banat, and part of Baranya under French and Serb occupation.[29]

The Allied occupation of even this limited amount of Hungarian lands led to the insistence by Hungarian negotiators that the convention specify that the demarcation line could in no way be considered as a new political boundary. That was to be settled by the Peace Conference. This stipulation was swiftly accepted by Franchet d'Esperey with the blessing of his superiors in Paris.[30]

The Belgrade meeting indicated success for Károlyi. Franchet d'Esperey, following his government's instructions, did not recognize the Károlyi government *de jure*. Nevertheless, he was sufficiently impressed by it – so much so that he advised Paris that it was in the interest of the Allies to support Károlyi because the latter represented "the party of order."[31]

Fair treatment of the Hungarians was possible only at the cost of leaving some of Hungary's neighbors unsatisfied. Rewards, however, had to be given to the Czechoslovaks for their ongoing intervention in Russia. There was also the price to be paid to Romania if she were expected to do the same.

By the end of November, therefore, the French government, at the urgings of the Czechoslovak foreign minister, Eduard Beneš, broke the terms of the Belgrade Convention in the name of the Allies. It gave the Czechoslovaks a green light to occupy Slovakia without defining its borders. In order to camouflage this unilateral action, the French offered a false explanation. They indicated that Franchet d'Esperey had overstepped his duties at the Belgrade negotiations when he allowed the continuation of Hungarian administration over all territories formerly belonging to the old kingdom. There was also an effort mounted to discredit Károlyi as a "perfidious" leader of an anti-democratic Hungary bent on enslaving the non-Magyar nationalities.[32]

In fact, the Hungarians had attempted to come to an understanding with the nationalities through negotiations. When it was evident that the spokesmen for the Slovaks or the Romanians were unwilling to accept autonomy within Hungary, the cabinet searched for compromise solutions which would be based on the principle of self-determination.[33]

Negotations were undertaken with Milan Hodža, a representative of the Slovak National Council, and with Iuliu Maniu, a member of the Romanian National Council in Hungary. On December 6, Oszkár Jászi and Minister of War Albert Bartha came to an understanding with Hodža, who also represented the Czechoslovak government. A demarcation line was established in Slovakia which closely followed the ethnic boundaries. Yet Prague, aware that a more favorable line was being prepared in Paris, disavowed the Hodža-Bartha agreement.[34] On December 23, the Allied

Supreme Council, dominated by Marshal Ferdinand Foch, transmitted a new demarcation line. This line was similar to the frontier given to the Hungarians at Trianon.[35] It left close to a million Hungarians on the Slovak side.

The shaping of the demarcation line in northern Hungary reflected the apparent French decision favoring, in the words of Foreign Minister Stephen Pichon, a "purely Magyar" Hungary. He further announced that France had no intentions of supporting the principle of self-determination. Instead it favored strong East Central European states which could be the allies of France.[36] Since France was allowed to have primary responsibility for peacemaking in East Central Europe, the case of the Hungarian government became weaker than ever.

Negotiations with the Romanian National Council started on November 13 and 14. Jászi, the head of the Hungarian delegation, offered the abolition of the counties, the old administrative units of Hungary. In their stead, he proposed the creation of national areas which, like the Swiss cantons, would have cultural and administrative autonomy. These cantons were to send representatives to the central government in Budapest. As a temporary solution, he also suggested the transfer of administrative power to the Romanian council, where a Romanian majority existed.

The Romanian National Council, led by Iuliu Maniu, Alexandru Vaida Voevod, Vasile Goldis and Ioan Erdelyi, rejected the offer and demanded full sovereignty for the council. The Hungarian officials returned to Budapest empty-handed.[37] However, Maniu's visit to Budapest at the end of November and his conciliatory manner revived Hungarian hopes for a negotiated settlement.[38]

In response to Maniu's favorable stance, and expecting compromise, the Hungarian government agreed to provide transportation for the Romanians of Transylvania to attend a Popular Assembly sponsored by the Romanian National Council in Alba Iulia (Gyulafehérvár). On December 1, this meeting unilaterally decided to unite the twenty-six counties with the kingdom of Romania. Interwar Hungarian historiography branded the Hungarian government's willingness to provide trains to the Romanians as treachery.[39] It is evident, however, that the Hungarian officials acted in good faith and expected positive results.

Oszkár Jászi, as minister of nationalities, recognized that the government could do nothing if the nationalities decided to secede.[40] After the Alba Julia decision, he thought of other alternatives to confederation. He was prepared to consider that in the eventuality that Hungarian villages would come under Romanian control, the national rights of the Hungarian minority would be protected by the Hungarian government.[41] This indicated the consideration of overlapping sovereignty as another compromise solution to the territorial dispute. Put into practice, this concept could have reconciled the self-determination of the Romanians with the needs and expectations of the Hungarians.

Jászi's plan could be considered as the minimum program of the Hungarians. However, the maximum plan – a confederated Hungary – was not jettisoned. The government continued to press for the maximum, fully expecting this position to be challenged and chipped away at the Paris Peace Conference.[42] The weakness of this reasoning was the government's failure to realize that the victors, disregarding traditions, did not intend to invite the defeated to present their case and bargain over details.

The Hungarian government rejected the Alba Iulia decision. According to Jászi, the Romanian leaders could not speak in the name of the majority. The combined Hungarian and Saxon population represented a 57 percent majority in the contested area. Significantly, the Allies also questioned the legitimacy of the Romanian claim on the same basis.[43] The Royal Romanian government's response to the declaration of its co-nationals was guarded at first as it still intended to pursue territorial quests as outlined in the Bucharest Treaty of 1916.[44]

To counterweigh the Romanian National Council in Transylvania, the Hungarian government encouraged the Hungarian National Council in Transylvania to organize an assembly and to call for continued Hungarian sovereignty over the 26 counties. This tactic was to bring to the attention of the Allies the multi-ethnic character of the region. As another alternative, Budapest reluctantly supported the position of the Székely National Council. Spokesmen for this Hungarian-speaking group with their own distinct cultural traditions favored the formation of a Transylvanian Székely republic.[45]

In addition to these steps, preparations for military resistance were also undertaken. These were necessitated by the march of the Romanian army into Trasylvania. The first Romanian troops crossed the Carpathians on November 13. Marosvásárhely (Tîrgu Mureş) was occupied on December 2, Beszterce (Bistriţa) on December 4, and Brassó (Braşov) on December 7. By the middle of the month, the Romanians had reached the Transylvanian segment of the Belgrade demarcation line. By December 24 they surpassed it and occupied Kolozsvár (Cluj-Napoca).[46] In contradiction to the Belgrade Convention, the administration of the occupied areas was taken over by the Romanians.[47]

In northern Hungary, the French government approved the occupation of Slovakia in the name of the Allies. In Transylvania, on the other hand, the expansion of Romanian control was made without Allied sanction but with the support of General Henri Berthelot. Berthelot, as a commander of the Allied forces in Romania and in southern Russia, disregarded the orders of his commander-in-chief, Franchet d'Esperey, and gave unqualified support to Romanian expansionist designs.[48]

In response to the Romanian advances, the Hungarian Council of Ministers was forced to decide on appropriate measures. Consideration was given to the resignation of the government and a call was issued to the Entente to govern Hungary. As a result of the continued blockade and territorial losses, Hungary was on the brink of chaos. Passive or active resistance to the absorption of Hungarian lands by Romania was also discussed. Oszkár Jászi proposed that government ministers take personal leadership over a Hungary divided into ten regions. The socialist Minister of Welfare, Zsigmond Kunfi, proposed that, instead of decentralizing, the government should map out a new frontier along solidly ethnic lines. He concluded that this was the price Hungary would have to pay for the lost war.

The cabinet finally decided to issue instructions to the commissioner of the 26 counties, István Apáthy. He was advised to agree to the occupation of Transylvania by Romanian troops acting as Allied representatives. This occupation was already in effect. Apáthy was to insist on Romanian acquiescence to the retention of Hungarian police forces in the occupied areas. These were to be the symbolic representatives of the Hungarian authorities, as sanctioned in the Belgrade convention.[49]

Instead, on December 31, General Berthelot offered Apáthy a new demarcation line. Following negotiations in Kolozsvár, Apáthy accepted the terms on January 3, 1919. The new agreement allowed the Romanians to hold the Nagybánya (Baia Mare)-Kolozsvár-Dés (Dej) line. They were to be separated from the Hungarian troops by a 15-kilometer-wide neutral zone. Budapest, however, disavowed the agreement, claiming that Apáthy was not empowered to deal away the more favorable terms of the Belgrade Convention. The Romanians also disregarded the Apáthy-Berthelot agreement as it would have curtailed further expansion.[50]

General Franchet d'Esperey and even Prime Minister and Minister of War Georges Clemenceau were displeased with the unauthorized action of Berthelot. They did, however, accept the agreement *post facto*. Accordingly, Franchet d'Esperey expected that the new demarcation line would put an end to further Romanian expansion.[51]

On January 23, the government of Dénes Berinkey and Mihály Károlyi, who was now the President of the Republic, decided that it had no other choice but resort to armed resistance against Romanian expansion. To stop further Romanian advances, it was decided to dig in along the county lines of Bihar. An offensive was not planned – there were no reserves. The energy crisis caused by the blockade also precluded the transportation of supplies in large quantity.[52]

The Peace Conference, which opened in Paris in mid-January refused to accept the Entente commitments made to Romania in 1916. It also objected to the ongoing Romanian expansion. On January 25, the day after the Alba Iulia decision was enacted in the Romanian parliament, the peacemakers adopted President Wilson's resolution against the use of force for territorial acquisitions.[53] Special committees were set up to resolve the territorial questions. These committees were without either central direction or declared focus other than a resolution of border issues. They did not go about recommending general principles of settlement. They were restricted by the conflicting wishes of the great powers and the demands of the representatives of their small allies.[54] The committees were expected to write their reports in such a way that they could be incorporated directly into the treaty.[55] Since the reports of the committees were due by March 8, the territorial issues concerning Hungary, Czechoslovakia and Romania were decided during the tenure of the Károlyi regime.

Flouting Allied wishes to leave the territorial questions to the Peace Conference, Romanian troops continued to advance. By the end of January they held the Máramarossziget (Sighetul Marmaţiei), Zilah (Zalău), Csucsa (Ciucea), Zám (Zam) line. The Romanian occupation of most of Transylvania was complete. Military flare-ups between the Hungarians and the Romanians became frequent and further conflict was imminent.[56]

Franchet d'Esperey, therefore, requested that the peacemakers in Paris establish a neutral zone between the Romanians and the Hungarians. He expected that the Romanians would be told to withdraw to the Apáthy-Berthelot line. Instead, on February 26, the Commission to Study the Territorial Questions Relating to Romania accepted a demarcation line that allowed Romania to occupy a line north of the outlines of historic Transylvania. A neutral zone was established to separate the Hungarian and Romanian troops.

The demarcation lines were drawn upon the advice of the French General Staff. It put strategic railway lines under Romanian control. These additional gains, sanctioned by Paris, intended to assure the succes of Marshal Foch's projected grand alliance against Communist Russia. Romania, whose troops were already fighting the Bolsheviks, were natural allies. Hungarian territory was the price for continued Romanian intervention in Russia.[57] Although Foch's plan was soon rejected, the demarcation line assigned to the Romanians was not altered. Subsequently, the Hungarian-Romanian frontier of Trianon closely resembled the Romanian demarcation line as defined on February 26, 1919.

General Franchet d'Esperey was soon instructed to make military preparations for the execution of the decision. The Romanians were informed of the things to come, but the Hungarians were kept in the dark. The Hungarian government remained isolated. It was not recognized by the Allies who claimed that, without a territorial settlement, Budapest represented only a "local government."[58] Consequently, the government also lacked diplomatic accreditation abroad.

As a result of its isolation, which was compounded by a lack of information about the peacemaking spirit in Paris, the Hungarian government could not really formulate policies that would fit the new realities. By February 1919, it was evident that self-determination was "*demodé*," and that there was no aversion to assigning the Hungarian population in the periphery to the neighboring states.[59]

Charles Seymour, the chief of the Austro-Hungarian division of the American peace commission, recognized this problem. He saw the need to invite the Hungarians to Paris, if not for participation, then for consultation. He expected that in this fashion the Hungarian government could weather the shock which was awaiting it.[60]

The Hungarian government, however, was unable to learn the truth. To curtail further Romanian advances, it was preparing for military resistance. On March 2, Károlyi inspected the troops in Szatmárnémeti and in an address declared:

> If Wilson's principles do not materialize and, instead of a peace based on mutual agreement, a dictated peace demanding territorial dismemberment is offered, I promise you, soldiers, I will never sign such peace terms![61]

The Hungarians were not informed of the February 26 decision of the Peace Conference until the middle of March. Until then, there were only rumors about new demarcation lines.[62] It was during the visit of Halsey E. Yates, the American military attaché to Romania, that the truth was unofficially revealed.

Yates came to Budapest to learn about the position of the government on the border question and to demand 250 locomotives for the Romanians. It was claimed that these were needed for them to fight against the Bolsheviks. Yates, stationed in Bucharest, was influenced by the Romanian version of the conflict. He considered that some of the American peace commissioners who had visited Hungary and sent favorable report to Paris were biased in favor of the Hungarians. He intended to get an objective picture for his superiors in Paris and in Washington.[63]

On March 15, Yates met Károlyi. He learned that the Hungarians were reconciled to the loss of the Maros Valley, but intended to resist further Romanian demands by military force. Károlyi argued that additional territorial losses would ruin the country economically. This would cause trouble and discontent and would eventually throw Hungary into the arms of Germany.[64]

Yates told Károlyi that the Hungarians must accept the loss of Slovakia and Transylvania. With this he confirmed the rumors about the new demarcation lines. He warned that, even though the Allies did not have sufficient armies around Hungary to reply to Hungarian intransigence, there were other means at their disposal, such as food blockades and indemnities.[65]

Before leaving Budapest, Yates wired Paris that he "strongly recommended" that the existing lines not be changed until some 100 British and American officers supplied with automobiles could arrive. He also expressed the view that Hungarians could successfully resist the Romanians who could not be resupplied before May 15.[66]

Yates' proposal, however, was not considered. New developments in southern Russia pressed for the transmission of the terms for a neutral zone. By mid-March the French interventionist forces in the area of Odessa were facing the threat of defeat by the Bolsheviks. On March 13, Clemenceau ordered General Berthelot to use Romanian troops to defend the Tiraspol, Razdelnaya, Odessa railway line.[67]

The crisis in Russia gave the Romanians an opportunity to press for the execution of the February 26 decision. On March 14, the Romanian representative in Paris, Victor Antonescu, transmitted to Clemenceau his government's memorandum. In it the Romanians claimed that while Franchet d'Esperey was looking for a suitable French officer to carry out the terms of the Peace Confrence, the Hungarians were stripping Transylvania and spreading Bolshevik propaganda. Clemenceau's response came on the same day. Using almost the exact words of the Antonescu memorandum, Clemenceau referred to the alleged scorched-earth policy of the Hungarians. He ordered Franchet d'Esperey to avoid any further delay and carry out the decision of the Peace Conference.[68]

It is unlikely that Clemenceau bought Antonescu's argument about Bolshevism in Transylvania. However, he was cognizant of the fact that Romanian help in the new crisis in Russia was needed, and that the new demarcation line was the price for continued Romanian participation.

Colonel Yates, following his return to Bucharest on March 17, also saw the need to satisfy the Romanians in order to resolve the Russian problem. He wired to Paris:

> The Poles and Rumanians are willing to fight our battles for us but they must be given at once the necessary supplies; and the menaces on their other fronts must be removed by our establishing neutral zones.[69]

Franchet d'Esperey, who would have preferred to blame Romania's military involvement in Transylvania for the fiasco in Russia, had no choice but to order the transmission of the Peace Conference edict to the Hungarians at once. This was done in spite of Franchet d'Esperey's fears that the Hungarian-Romanian clashes above the neutral zone would continue. Furthermore, because of the crisis in Russia, no Allied troops were available to enforce the order in case of resistance.[70]

On March 20, Colonel Vix, in the presence of other Allied representatives, handed the Hungarians the order to withdraw to the new demarcation line. In his instructions, Vix was told to give the Hungarians 48 hours to reply. His directions further stated that in case the Hungarians turned down the ultimatum, no immediate war-like act would be instituted against them. Yet during his meeting with Károlyi and the other leaders, Vix threatened to pack his bags if the government did not acquiesce. This was tantamount to the threat of resumption of war.[71]

Following this meeting, the Council of Ministers and President Károlyi gathered to discuss the required response to the Vix Ultimatum. Károlyi informed the ministers that the *démarche* could not be accepted because it would make the Romanian demarcation line into a frontier, thus depriving Hungary of further territories. In the meantime, French troops in the neutral zone would prevent the Hungarians from using force against Romanian territorial expansion. Károlyi gathered that the territorial losses could not be reversed as the Entente intended to use the Serbs, Czechs and Romanians in a war against the Bolsheviks. Since the Peace Conference did not recognize the Wilsonian principles, Hungary needed new internal and external policies. He proposed the creation of a socialist government which could assure better productivity, hence increase the nation's economic strength. It could also gather the support of the international socialist movement. As the only mass party in Hungary, the Social Democratic Party could mobilize the workers and, subsequently, the middle classes to resistance. He also proposed that the socialists reach an understanding with the small Communist party, so that Hungary would not be attacked by the Russian Bolsheviks.[72]

The socialists, however, went further than was expected. They fused with the communists. On March 21, following the rejection of the Vix Ultimatum and the resignation of Károlyi and the cabinet, the socialists and the communists established a Soviet Republic. The new government was now dominated by the communist Béla Kun. In alliance with the Russian Bolsheviks, it aimed to undo the dictated frontiers in the north and the south by calling for a war against "Entente imperialism."[73]

The unsuccessful attempts of Károlyi's democratic regime to arrive at some understanding with its adversaries led to its demise. Neither its minimal nor maximal territorial solutions were found to be acceptable by its Czechoslovak and Romanian neighbors. The demarcation lines to which it objected and which it refused to accept became the frontiers that the Allies forced on a right-wing, authoritarian government. For a quarter of a century, the Horthy regime unjustifiably blamed the high price of defeat in war on a government which had actually refused to acquiesce to dictated territorial losses.

Notes

I wish to thank Montclair State College for granting release time for the work on this article.

1. Mária Ormos, "Még egyszer a Vix-jegyzékről" [Once More about the Vix Memorandum], *Századok*, vol. 113, no. 2 (1979), p. 314; Gyula Juhász, *Hungarian Foreign Policy 1919-1945* (Budapest, 1979), p. 39.

2. Zoltán Szende, "Count Michael Károlyi in Belgrade," *Hungarian Quarterly*, vol. 5, no. 3 (1939); Ferenc Nyékhegyi, *A Diaz-féle fegyverszüneti szerződés (a paduai fegyverszünet)* [The Diaz Armistice Treaty (The Armistice of Padua)] (Budapest, 1922); Jenő Horváth, *A trianoni békeszerződés megalkotása és a revízió útja* [The Creation of the Peace Treaty of Trianon and the Course of the Revision] (Budapest, 1939); Jenő László, *Erdély sorsa az Úniótól Trianonig* [The Fate of Transylvania from the Union to Trianon] (Budapest, 1940); a recent but similar view in Yves de Daruvar, *The Tragic Fate of Hungary* (Munich, 1974).
3. György Litván, *Magyar gondolat, szabad gondolat* [Hungarian Thought, Free Thought] (Budapest, 1978), pp. 144-145.
4. Francis Deak, *Hungary at the Paris Peace Conference* (New York, 1942, repr. 1972), p. 8; for recent and similar interpretations, see Bennett Kovrig, *Communism in Hungary* (Stanford, 1979), p. 37; Sándor Szilassy, *Revolutionary Hungary 1918-1921* (Astor Park, Fla., 1971), pp. 26-27.
5. Zsuzsa L. Nagy, *A párizsi békekonferencia és Magyarország 1918-1919* [The Peace Conference and Hungary 1918-1919] (Budapest, 1963); Tibor Hajdu, *Károlyi Mihály* (Budapest, 1978); Lajos Ardai, "Angol-Magyar viszony a polgári demokratikus forradalom idején az angol levéltári források tükrében (1918 október-1919 március)" [English-Hungarian Relations during the Bourgeois-Democratic Revolution in the Light of English Archival Sources] *Történelmi Szemle*, vol. 18, nos. 2-3 (1975); Peter Pastor, *Hungary between Wilson and Lenin: the Hungarian Revolution of 1918-1919 and the Big Three* (New York, 1976); Mária Ormos, " A belgrádi katonai konvencióról" [About the Belgrade Military Convention], *Történelmi Szemle*, vol. 22, no. 1 (1979).
6. Inga Floto, *Colonel House in Paris* (Copenhagen, 1973), p. 252; Arno Mayer, *Politics and Diplomacy of Peacemaking* (New York, 1965), p. 16.
7. Wilfried Fest, *Peace or Partition, The Habsburg Monarchy and British Policy 1914-1918* (New York, 1978), pp. 188-189.
8. Kenneth J. Calder, *Britain and the Origins of the New Europe, 1914-1918* (Cambridge, 1976), p. 218.
9. Josef Kalvoda, *Czechoslovakia's Role in Soviet Strategy* (Washington, 1978), p. 17; Fest, *Peace or Partition*, pp. 238-239.

10. Victor S. Mamatey, *The United States and East Central Europe, 1914-1918* (Princeton, 1957), pp. 333-334.
11. Fest, *Peace or Partition*, p. 253; M. L. Dockrill and Zara Steiner, "The Foreign Office at the Paris Peace Conference in 1919," *The International History Review*, vol. 2, no. 1, January (1980), p. 55.
12. Peter Pastor, "The Hungarian Revolution's Road from Wilsonianism to Leninism, 1918-1919," *East Central Europe*, vol. 3, no. 2, (1976), pp. 211-213.
13. Gabor Vermes, "The Agony of Federalism in Hungary under the Károlyi regime, 1918-1919," *East European Quarterly*, vol. 6, no. 4, (1972), p. 496; Béla K. Király, "The Danubian Problem in Oszkár Jászi's Political Thought," *The Hungarian Quarterly*, vol. 5, (1965), pp. 127-129.
14. Dockrill and Steiner, "The Foreign Office," p. 56; Zsuzsa L. Nagy, "Összeomlás és kiútkeresés 1918-1919-ben, Jászi Oszkár és a forradalmak" [Collapse and Search for Extrication in 1918-1919, Oszkár Jászi and the Revolutions], *Kritika*, no. 5, May (1978), 3; Charles L. Mee, Jr., *The End of Order: Versailles 1919* (New York, 1980), pp. 103-105.
15. Pastor, *Hungary between Wilson and Lenin*, p. 104.
16. As quoted in, Fest, *Peace or Partition*, p. 58.
17. Charles Seymour, *Letter from the Paris Peace Conference* (New Haven, 1965), p. XXX; Walter A. McDougall, "Political Economy versus National Sovereignty: French Structures for Economic Integration after Versailles," *Journal of Modern History*, vol. 51, no. 1 March, (1979), p. 11.
18. Dockrill and Steiner, *The Foreign Office*, pp. 67-68.
19. Mayer, *Politics and Diplomacy*, pp. 9-10.
20. Sherman D. Spector, *Rumania at the Paris Peace Conference: A Study of the Diplomacy of Ioan I. C. Brătianu* (New York, 1962), p. 37.
21. Josef Kalvoda, *Czechoslovakia's Role*, p. 15.
22. Zsuzsa L. Nagy, "Magyar határviták a párizsi békekonferencián" [Debates on the Hungarian Frontier Question at the Paris Peace Conference] *Történelmi Szemle*, vol. 21, no. 3-4 (1978), p. 443.
23. Béla Bellér, "A Magyar Népköztársaság és a Tanácsköztársaság nemzetiségi kultúrpolitikája" [The Cultural Politics of the Hungarian People's Republic and of the Soviet Republic toward the Nationalities] *Történelmi Szemle*, vol. 11, no. 1 (1968), p. 3.

24. Mária Ormos, "A belgrádi katonai konvencióról," p. 26.
25. Budapest, Országos Levéltár [National Archives], *Minisztertanácsi jegyzőkönyvek* [Minutes of the Council of Ministers] K 27 MT jkv. no. 40 (Nov. 4, 1918); no. 41 (Nov. 5, 1918).
26. Országos Levéltár, K 27 MT jkv. no. 41 (Nov. 5, 1918).
27. Michael Károlyi, *Memoirs of Michael Karolyi, Faith without Illusion* (London, 1957), pp. 130-137.
28. Jean Bernachot, ed., *Les armées alliées en Orient après l'armistice de 1918, comptes rendus mensuels adressés par le commandant en chef des armées alliées en Orient, à l'étàt major de l'armée à Paris, de décembre 1918 à octobre 1920* (Paris, 1972), p. 45.
29. Nagy, *A párizsi békekonferencia*, pp. 11-12.
30. Ormos, "A belgrádi katonai konvencióról," p. 29.
31. Bernachot, *Les armées alliées en Orient*, 45.
32. Ormos, "A belgrádi katonai konvencióról," p. 29; Peter Pastor, "The Diplomatic Fiasco of the Modern World's First Woman Ambassador, Róza Bédy-Schwimmer," *EEQ*, vol. 8, no. 3 (1974), 279.
33. Országos Levéltár, K 27 MT jkv. no. 59 (Nov. 29, 1918).
34. Ferenc Boros, *Magyar-csehszlovák kapcsolatok 1918-1921-ben* [Hungarian-Czechoslovak Relations in 1918-1921] (Budapest, 1970), pp. 46-47; Országos Levéltár, K 27 MT jkv. no. 58 (Nov. 28, 1918).
35. L. Nagy, "Magyar határviták," p. 444.
36. *Le Temps*, Dec. 31, 1918.
37. Pastor, *Hungary between Wilson and Lenin*, pp. 72-73.
38. Országos Levéltár, K 27 MT jkv. no. 58 (Nov. 28, 1918).
39. László, *Erdély sorsa*, p. 117.
40. Országos Levéltár, K 27 MT jkv. no. 59 (Nov. 29, 1918).
41. Budapest, Országos Levéltár [National Archives], *A Magyarországon élő nemzetek önrendelkezési joga előkészítésével megbízott miniszter* [The Minister in Charge of the Preparation of the Right of Self-determination of the Nations Living in Hungary], K 40, Erdődi Nemzeti Tanács to Jászi and reply (Dec. 3, 1918).
42. Országos Levéltár, K 27 MT jkv. no. 72 (Dec. 28, 1918); no. 58 (Nov. 28, 1918).
43. Spector, *Rumania*, p. 93.
44. Mária Ormos, "Az ukrajnai katonai intervencióról és hatásairól Közép-Európában, 1918 október-1919 április" [The Impact of the

French Intervention in the Ukraine and in Central Europe] *Történelmi Szemle*, vol. 20, nos. 3-4 (1977), p. 423, no. 56.
45. Országos Levéltár, K 40, Böhm to Jászi (Dec. 5, 1918); Minutes (Dec. 17, 1918).
46. György Ránki, ed., *Magyarország története, 1918-1919, 1919-1945*, vol. 8 [The History of Hungary, 1918-1919, 1919-1945] (Budapest, 1976), pp. 113-117.
47. Ránki, *Magyarország története*, p. 96.
48. Peter Pastor, "Franco-Rumanian Intervention in Russia and the *Vix Ultimatum*: Background to Hungary's Loss of Transylvania," *The Canadian-American Review of Hungarian Studies*, vol. 1, nos. 1-2 (1974), p. 14. This essay is based on unpublished archival sources from the French Military Archives and the Archives of the Ministry of Foreign Affairs, Paris.
49. Országos Levéltár, K 27 MT jkv. no. 69 (Dec. 18 and 19, 1918); Országos Széchényi Könyvtár kézirattára [Archives of the National Szechenyi Library], *Apáthy iratok* [Apathy Papers], Quart. Hung. 2455, "Erdély az összeomlás után" [Transylvania after the Collapse].
50. Országos Levéltár, K 27 MT jkv. no. 13 (Jan. 27, 1919); Ormos, "Még egyszer a Vix-jegyzékről," p. 327.
51. Bernachot, *Les armées alliées*, p. 164.
52. Országos Levéltár, K 27 MT jkv. no. 11 (Jan. 21, 1919).
53. Spector, *Rumania*, p. 80.
54. Dockrill and Steiner, "The Foreign Office," p. 66.
55. Dockrill and Steiner, "The Foreign Office," p. 69.
56. Ormos, "Az ukrajnai francia intervencióról," p. 427.
57. Pastor, "Franco-Rumanian Intervention," p. 20; Ormos, "Az ukrajnai katonai intervencióról," pp. 429-430.
58. Pastor, *Hungary between Wilson and Lenin*, p. 83.
59. Sir James Headlam-Morley, *A Memoir of the Paris Peace Conference 1919* (London, 1972), p. 27, 44.
60. Pastor, *Hungary between Wilson and Lenin*, p. 104.
61. Pastor, *Hungary between Wilson and Lenin*, p. 128.
62. Ormos, "Még egyszer a Vix-jegyzékről," p. 331.
63. Washington, National Archives, *War Department General Staff Military Intelligence Division 1917-1941*, MID 220 a 2266-V 174, Report of Yates (March 4, 1919).
64. National Archives, MID 239 2323-354, Yates to Brig. Gen. Churchill (March 15, 1919).

65. Paris, Archives historiques, *Ministère de la Guerre. Etat-Major de L'Armée, Campagne Contre Allemagne*, Carton 106, dossier 3, Vix to de Lobit (March 16, 1919).
66. National Archives, MID 239 2323-354, Yates to Brig. Gen. Churchill (March 15, 1919).
67. Pastor, "Franco-Rumanian Intervention," p. 20; Ormos, "Az ukrajnai francia intervencióról," pp. 435-436.
68. Pastor, "Franco-Rumanian Intervention," p. 21.
69. National Archives, MID 243 2069-98, Yates to Brig. Gen. Churchill (March 29, 1919).
70. Ormos, "Még egyszer a Vix-jegyzékről," p. 330.
71. Tibor Hajdu, *Március huszonegyedike* [The Twenty-First of March] (Budapest, 1979), pp. 54-57; for the French and Hungarian text of the Vix Ultimatum see György Litván, ed., *Károlyi Mihály levelezése I, 1905-1920* [The Correspondence of Mihály Károlyi I, 1905-1920] (Budapest, 1978), pp. 445-448; for the English version see Deak, *The Paris Peace Conference*, pp. 407-409.
72. Országos Levéltár, K 27 MT jkv. no. 29 (March 20, 1919); part of the minutes in Hajdu, *Március huszonegyedike*, pp. 59-73.
73. Tibor Hajdu, *The Hungarian Soviet Republic* (Budapest, 1979), pp. 28, 34-35.

Stephen Fischer-Galati

Trianon and Romania

The dismemberment of Hungary and corollary provisions of the Treaty of Trianon have rankled Hungarians for more than half a century.[1] Redressing the humiliation of Trianon was a cardinal aim of Hungarian political leaders of the interwar years. Crucial to Hungarian revisionism – the most extreme form of expression of Hungarian aspirations – has been the recovery of Transylvania from Romania. Even more moderate exponents of the need for rectification of the injustices inflicted upon historic Hungary at Trianon have, in their determination to keep the Transylvanian question in the forefront of international discussions, focused on actual or alleged abuses of the rights of the Hungarian minority in Transylvania by successive Romanian regimes. And there are good reasons for this preoccupation.

The singling out of Transylvania and of the Romanians as central to Hungarian aspirations is ultimately related to the historic contempt shown by Hungarian ruling classes, and even by many of the non-ruling ones, toward their Romanian counterparts. The Romanians, whether in Transylvania or in the Old Kingdom, have been traditionally viewed as uncivilized, unscrupulous, and inferior to the Hungarians. If Romanian leaders resented Tsar Nicholas's *bon mot* that being a Romanian is "a profession rather than a nationality", if they expressed outrage at the Germans' concept of the *"Unmensch"*, which embraced the Romanians with other peoples in Southeast Europe, it was the Hungarians' contempt for the Romanians that gave Romanian nationalism the greatest impetus since the late nineteenth century.[2] The "liberation" of Transylvania from Hungarian yoke was the primary goal of Romanian nationalists before Trianon, and conversely, the liberation of that province from the Romanian yoke became the primary goal of Hungarian nationalists after Trianon. Under these circumstances a review of the significance of Trianon for Romania is indeed desirable, particularly because of the continuing importance of the Transylvanian question in the 1980s to nationalists and communists alike.

In the last analysis, the decisions made by the Great Powers with respect of Hungary's dismemberment, and the determination of the Hungarians not to accept their validity, is the root cause of all problems related to Trianon. The Hungarian challenges to the legitimacy of Romanian rule in Transylvania invariably focused on violations by the Romanians of specific provisions of the Treaty of Trianon, particularly those related to the rights and treatment of national minorities.[3] Moreover, as these discriminatory, and thus illegal, practices provided the rationale for the Hungarians' seeking the physical reincorporation of at least those parts of Transylvania in which Hungarians constituted a majority of the population, all Romanian regimes of the interwar years – all committed to the maintenance of Greater Romania – defended their minority policies and rejected all accusations leveled against them as "external interference in domestic affairs." And in these respects, too, little has changed since World War II.

It would be erroneous to assume, however, that Romanian policies in Transylvania were primarily motivated by the need to safeguard the territorial integrity of the province against Hungarian irredentism. And it would also be incorrect to regard the anti-Hungarian policies in Transylvania as a prerequisite for maintaining the spirit of Romanian nationalism at a high pitch during the years when the euphoria of reunification of all Romanian territories into Greater Romania was blunted by the political and socioeconomic realities which faced all Romanians after World War I.[4] It is true that anti-Magyarism was an integral part of Romanian nationalism but it was not necessarily its principal component. It is also true that Hungarian revisionism was unwelcome to Romania's rulers but there was no apprehension over the territorial security of Transylvania. Other problems, some expressly related to Transylvania and others only peripherally so, were more relevant to an analysis of Romanian minority policies than have been suggested by individuals concerned with the Hungarian minority alone.

The primarily political issue in postwar Romania was that of consolidation of power by the "unifiers", identified with the political establishment of the Old Kingdom and particularly with Ioan I. C. Brătianu's "Liberals", who entertained the belief that Greater Romania was their own creation.[5] Brătianu's power base was, however, threatened by the proliferation of political organizations following the territorial expansion of the Old Kingdom and by the Great Powers' lack of confidence in his tactics and policies. His temporary absence from the premiership of Romania, between September 1919 and January 1922, following his resignation over a dispute with the Allies over peace settlements, allowed him to develop political positions designed to discredit his opponents and secure unrestricted power for himself and the Liberals. The main threat to the Liberals' interests was perceived to come from the National Party of Transylvania which, together with the Peasant Party of the Old Kingdom, sought to identify itself with the nationwide interests of the peasantry by advocating acceptance of the popular Transylvanian pattern of agrarian reform as the prototype for the whole Greater Romania.[6] Brătianu, fearful of a likely realignment of political forces, sought and secured the support of all conservative and nationalist forces of the Old Kingdom. In fact, it was the alteration by the Romanian parliament of the Transylvanian pattern of agrarian reform which paved the way for Brătianu's return to power as the protector of the traditional political interests of the creators of Greater Romania.

The anti-Transylvanian aspects of the political struggles of the immediate postwar years clearly transcended the Hungarian question in Transylvania. Whereas the reforms initiated by the Romanian National Party of Transylvania were indeed detrimental to the interests of the Hungarian latifundiaries, they were not adverse to the interests of the rank-and-file of the Hungarian peasantry. Moreover, the reforms were designed to be democratic and nondiscriminatory toward national minorities.[7] As such, they were unacceptable to Brătianu – the self-styled champion and protector of the Romanians' historic interests and guarantor of Romanian supremacy in the Greater Romanian state. Since Brătianu's political philosophy also entailed nonacceptance of "dictates" by the Great Powers in matters related to the rights of minorities and to any form of "external interference in Romania's internal affairs," the rights of the Hungarians in Transylvania became an *ipso facto* issue, but not the main issue, in post-Trianon Romanian politics.

Brătianu's policies toward Transylvania in general and toward national minorities in particular were also affected by external factors not directly related to Trianon. Brătianu was identified as the diagnostician and primary opponent of the "Judeo-Bolshevik conspiracy", both in Romania and abroad, largely because of his actions against Béla Kun's regime and his defiance of the Bolsheviks' demands for restitution of Bessarabia.[8] It was thus incumbent upon the Liberals to protect all Romanians – particularly those of Transylvania and Bessarabia – against Judeo-communists who, by definition, included most Hungarian Jews in Transylvania, most Russian Jews in Bessarabia, and most Jewish, pro-Jewish, or Jewlike intellectuals in all parts of Romania. Jews and communists thus provided a convenient link between internal politics and the primary and most persistent external problem of interwar Romania, that of Soviet revisionism in Bessarabia.

The Bolsheviks' insistence on the return of Bessarabia coupled with Romanian rejection of their demands boded ill for Soviet-Romanian relations.[9] It is not that in the early 1920s the Romanians feared seizure of Bessarabia by force of arms or even by externally-fomented revolutionary actions; yet, Brătianu as well as other Romanian political leaders realized that Soviet revisionism was not to be taken lightly. Whether Romania's rulers were fearful of an actual or potential link between Russian and Hungarian revisionism is uncertain. But they were aware of the Bolsheviks' anger over Romania's military intervention against Kun's forces which afforded the Russians with the opportunity of branding Romania as the enemy of the "democratic" Hungarian masses. They were also aware of the anti-Romanian sentiments of the Hungarian masses, whether "democratic" or not, and of the Hungarian bourgeoisie and aristocracy, who far from looking upon the Romanian armies as "liberators" from Bolshevism viewed the Romanians as rapists and plunderers of Hungarian property, not to mention of Hungarian territories secured by the Treaty of Trianon. Thus, revisionism – of the threatening Soviet variety as well as of the potentially-threatening Hungarian one – became the bugaboo of Romanian foreign policy in the twenties. And, in the process, the groups that could be labeled as supportive of external revisionist forces, specifically Hungarians and Jews, were singled out for discrimination by Brătianu and by other nationalist forces in Romania.

It is fair to say that the ensuing anti-Hungarian and anti-Jewish manifestations were largely based on guilt by association. It is true that there was little love lost between Hungarians and Romanians and between Romanians and Jews in Greater Romania. But it would be difficult to argue that the majority of the Hungarians were revisionists or that most of Romania's Jews were anti-Romanian or pro-Bolshevik. There can be little doubt, however, that most of the Hungarian bourgeoisie, functionaries, expropriated landlords, and intellectuals were anti-Romanian and that many of these educated Hungarians favored the reincorporation of Transylvania into Hungary. And it is also undeniable that most of Transylvania's Jews identified their interests with those of the Hungarians, as they considered themselves to be either Hungarian Jews or Jewish Hungarians.[10]

Whether reconciliation of disparate ethnic, socio-economic, and cultural differences could have been achieved within the Romanian body politic under more enlightened rule is a matter of conjecture. The fact is that since 1922, at least, Bucharest made no effort to secure the allegiance of the Hungarians and Jews of Transylvania and, if anything, made a conscious effort to Romanianize Transylvania in a manner detrimental to the interests of most of its inhabitants, regardless of their nationality or religion.

The ascendancy of Romanians over Hungarians in Transylvania would have occurred even if political power had been held by the Romanian National Party of Transylvania. The introduction of Romanian as official language, the replacement of Hungarian functionaries, the redistribution of wealth, and similarly radical alterations of previous relationships were prerequisites for the incorporation of Transylvania into the Greater Romanian body politic. It is possible, but not likely, that the resultant dislocations could have been made less painful had the process of Romanization been directed by Transylvanians for the benefit of the Romanians of Transylvania but in a spirit of reconciliation toward non-Romanians. But that was not to be since Brătianu and the Liberals were determined to integrate Transylvania into Greater Romania *à la roumanie*. In their dual opposition to both Hungarians and the National Party of Transylvania, the Liberals controlled the process of Romanianization from Bucharest by subordinating it to the central bureaucracy. Although Transylvanian Romanians participated in the transfer of political and economic power they did not direct it. Their displeasure with the arrogance and corruption identified with Brătianu's men became more pronounced as Bucharest continued to direct Transylvanian affairs even after the transfer was completed. As for the Hungarians, their bitterness toward Romanians was exacerbated by the need to deal with Bucharest-appointed functionaries and to cope with Bucharest methods of governance. Yet, from a Romanian political standpoint, the integration of Transylvania into Greater Romania and subordination of regional to central political interests was essential. Minority rights could be observed to the extent to which they would not affect the interests of the state. Or, in the view of Bucharest, the Hungarians were a potential Trojan Horse because of their presumed allegiance to Hungarian revisionism and, in any event, they and the Jew had to be humiliated because of their historic exploitation of the Romanian masses in Transylvania. Nevertheless, the rights of national minorities were formally respected by the Liberals and by their successors throughout most of the interwar period. Thus, the repeated complaints regarding actual or alleged violations of the provisions of the Treaty of Trianon addressed by the Hungarian government to the League of Nations or to Bucharest were readily refuted by the Romanian government.[11] In fact, such complaints tended to aid Bucharest as they gave credence to the official line that Hungarians, both outside and inside Romania, were revisionists and enemies of Greater Romania and of the Romanians. All the same, relations between the Hungarian minority and the Romanians in Transylvania were correct during the twenties and, if anything, even improved between 1928 and 1933 during the short-lived governance of the National Peasant Party.

Nevertheless, the prognosis for the solution of nationality and political problems in Transylvania was poor by the early 1930s for reasons not necessarily related to Transylvanian affairs. By then the problems of Greater Romania had become a function of major international crises related to the global economy and the corollary alteration of political structures.[12] The economic difficulties facing Romania in the twenties and early thirties were symptomatic of the general economic malaise which facilitated the rise of Mussolini and Hitler and which led to the Great Depression. The Romanian agrarian economy suffered less than the industrialized economies of other European countries in the interwar years, but the peasants' disillusionment with the agrarian reform, and the intellectuals' and students' with the inability of the Liberals and other political organizations to provide remedies for the economic stagnation and unemployment of university graduates and of the intellectual community in general, led to the formulation of Christian populist ideologies and the organization of extreme right-wing political groups whose proclaimed mission was to save Romania from Jews and communists. The virulently anti-Semitic and anti-communist ideology of the students and intellectuals, who supported Professor A. C. Cuza's League of National Christian Defense and Corneliu Zelea Codreanu's Legion of the Archangel Michael, was relatively ineffectual before the Depression but caused havoc in Romania by the mid-thirties.[13] Nevertheless, the established political parties, to counter the impact of Cuza's and Codreanu's appeal to the young, the unemployed, the intellectuals, and even the disgruntled peasants and industrial workers, became more and more committed to nationalist formulae in attempting to solve Romania's problems. And since the problems proved insoluble, the scapegoats were readily identified as non-Romanian and, presumably, anti-Romanian elements – the Jews and the Hungarians at home and the Russian communists and Hungarian revisionists abroad.

It is true that anti-Semitism and anti-Bolshevism ranked higher with Romanian nationalists than anti-Magyarism, but it is also true that the spreading of Codreanu's radical ideology into Transylvania led to a coupling of the anti-Jewish and anti-Hungarian attitudes of his supporters in that province. In Transylvania the Hungarians and the Jews, because of their preponderance in urban commercial and professional activities, were linked as common "exploiters of the Romanian masses". In Transylvania too the nationality problems were further aggravated by the presence of the Saxons and the political significance which that group assumed after the rise of Hitler in Germany.[14]

The Saxons had received preferential treatment from Romania's rulers even before the rise of Hitler because of their support of Bucharest and their sharing of a common antagonism toward Hungarians and Jews. With Hitler's advent and the corollary strengthening of the influence, if not yet the power, of the Romanian extreme right, the Saxons were regarded as a potential link, or at least contact, with Berlin for those political organizations that were in power, or seeking power, in Greater Romania. By 1936, as the first overt expressions of Hungarian revisionism were voiced by Budapest to its friends in Rome and Berlin, the importance of the Saxons as a possible counterweight to Hungarian revisionism in Transylvania and as supporters of Romanian positions in Berlin became more pronounced. Moreover, as the shift to the right in Romania in general gained momentum by 1937, the Saxons were used both by Nazi Germany and by pro-Nazi organizations such as Codreanu's Iron Guard as tools in their attempts to fulfil common political goals. It should be noted, however, that even during this period of sharpening of nationality conflicts in Transylvania, violations of the constitutional rights of Hungarians and of their alleged supporters, the Jews, were not legally evident. What was evident was the worsening of the psychological climate, the decline of the levels of toleration by Romanians of Hungarians and Jews. In fact, it was not until 1938 that overt legal violations of minority rights occurred in Greater Romania following the establishment of the first radical right-wing government – that of Goga-Cuza, following the national elections of December 1937.[15] But it should be noted that discriminatory measures against the Hungarians became evident only after the Munich and ensuing crises, which affected Romania's relations with Hungary, with the Soviet Union, with the Axis, and with her traditional allies.

Italian support of Hungarian revisionist claims and Russian reluctance to abandon its own revisionist claims to Bessarabia, so manifest in the 1930s, were taken in stride by Bucharest until German revisionism itself assumed significant proportions. Hitler's support of the Sudeten Germans' demands were perceived as ominous for Czechoslovakia, but the Czechoslovak contacts with Moscow and the Axis' with Budapest were deemed ominous for Romania. The First Vienna Award of 1938 which favored Hungary's claims to Czechoslovakia, caused panic in Bucharest and placed the question of maintenance of the territorial integrity of Greater Romania on the front burner of political activities and concerns. To most Romanian political leaders it was no longer a question of whether territorial revisions were to occur but of how to cut losses.[16]

Reconstruction of the political dynamics of Romania between the fall of 1938 and the fall of 1940, during which period the territorial integrity of the state was the paramount concern of all political forces, remains a difficult and controversial task.[17] It seems fair to say, however, that all political organizations – with the exception of the communists – were united in opposition to any territorial revisionism but aware of the likelihood of Hitler imposing a rectification of Romania's borders with Hungary in the foreseeable future. Few believed that France or England could effectively guarantee Romania's territorial integrity, but most were persuaded that Soviet revisionism could be contained because of Hitler's seemingly implacable hostility toward Stalin's Russia. In fact, the gradual abandonment of the French connection by King Carol II and other astute political leaders was largely based on the assumption that neither France nor Britain could safeguard Romania's integrity and that the French and the British, in their quest for an arrangement with Stalin, would be more likely to support Soviet revisionism against Romania than Hitler ever would.

In line with this general assessment of political realities, Bucharest entered into pourparlers with Budapest and with the Axis powers with a view to ascertaining the extent of likely losses of Transylvanian territory to Hungary. In this process the Romanians sought to exploit the often conflicting German and Italian interests in Eastern Europe in general and with respect to Hungary and Romania in particular. In this process too, Romanian political leaders found it necessary to proclaim their determination to maintain the territorial integrity of Romania and to rally the Romanian masses against revisionists and pro-revisionists, most notably against Jews and communists but also against Hungarians.

The juggling for the survival of Greater Romania and of its political leaders is well known except for one key aspect which affected the ultimate resolution of Hungary's territorial claims in Transylvania. It is clear that the destruction of Greater Romania which occured in 1940 was not due to Hungarian revisionism as such but to the fatal Hitler-Stalin pact of August 1939. As far as Romania was concerned this unimaginable agreement which rendered all game plans obsolete meant the inevitable loss of Bessarabia to the USSR.

It is uncertain just how many Romanian leaders were aware of the secret clauses of the agreement, but it is certain that many suspected the worst in August 1939. The Soviet occupation of Bessarabia and Northern Bukovina in June 1940 certainly came as no surprise to the communists who had been alerted to the Soviet move; it also failed to surprise political realists whose proverbial mistrust of Russia seemed vindicated by Stalin's action. What did surprise everyone, however, was the realization, soon after the occupation of the Romanian territories, of a connection between Soviet and Hungarian revisionism, which was to affect the ensuing negotiations between Hungary and her Axis partners and the Romanian government in Bucharest.

It has been ascertained by serious researchers of territorial revisionism in Eastern Europe that links between Hungarian and Soviet revisionism antedated June 1940; that, in fact, Moscow was supportive of Hungary's demands throughout the interwar years.[18] Such an interpretation of Russo-Hungarian relations is indeed plausible, given the antagonism shared by Moscow and Budapest toward Bucharest following the Romanian military intervention in Hungary before Trianon and the securing of territories deemed Hungarian, and respectively Russian, by Greater Romania after World War I. But pending publication of documented studies of these relations for the interwar years, it seems desirable to limit our observations to actual evidence related only to Russo-Hungarian relations in 1940. In this respect, the evidence is conclusive that Molotov encouraged the Hungarians to push their "legitimate" claims in Transylvania during the summer of 1940 in an obvious effort to lessen Hungary's dependence on the Axis and to so weaken a dismembered Romania as to preclude meaningful revanchist action by Bucharest. It is also clear that Budapest used Moscow's support as leverage in its own dealings with Berlin, Rome, and Bucharest and that the Moscow connection proved to be somewhat counterproductive.[19] Whether Hitler's blueprint for partition of Transylvania would have been more generous to Hungary had it not been for Russia's action in Romania and overtures to Budapest is uncertain, but it is evident that the Führer was anxious to prevent the total humiliation of Romania and to secure control over Romania's strategic resources, as well as to gain support for Germany's plans against the USSR and for Romania's participation therein by assuming the role of the "honest broker" in matters territorial. Thus, the Second Vienna Award of August 1940 whereby Northern Transylvania was returned to Hungary achieved Hitler's immediate goals but not the long-range ones of the principal parties involved, the Hungarians and the Romanians. The Treaty of Trianon may have been repudiated in 1940, but the fundamental problem of territorial allocations and rights of national minorities in Transylvania remained unsolved. It is thus not surprising that Trianon is still a household word in the vocabulary of international relations some sixty years after the dismemberment of the Austro-Hungarian conglomerate.

In truth, the Vienna Award was unsatisfactory to both Romania and Hungary.[20] The Romanians vowed to recoup the lost territories while the Hungarians thought that they were shortchanged by not receiving all of Transylvania. The treatment of Hungarians in Romanian Transylvania and of Romanians in Hungarian Transylvania was such as to raise animosities among nationalities and governments to historically-unsurpassed levels. Hungarian Jews or Jewish Hungarians suffered more in Hungarian Transylvania than in Romanian territories with the resultant virtual annihilation of that minority, ostensibly protected by the Treaty of Trianon and implementing accords. Only the Saxons benefitted from the repudiation of Trianon. As the protegés of Nazi Germany they enjoyed a privileged status unprecedented since medieval times. But all this was to change in 1945 when Stalin returned Northern Transylvania to Romania.

The repudiation of the Vienna Award was ostensibly based on the illegitimacy of Hitler's actions rather than on acceptance of the validity of Trianon.[21] In fact, Stalin's refusal to return Bessarabia and Northern Bukovina to Romania and Russia's seizure of territories in other parts of East Central Europe were conclusive proof of Stalin's continuing rejection of the legality of previous treaties affecting Eastern Europe. Reconciliation of political differences among nationalities and states concerned with Transylvania was assumed to be inevitable because of the commom rejection of fascism and acceptance of the comradely principles inherent to communist doctrine and practice. To demonstrate the validity of this dogma, the equality of rights among coinhabiting nationalities was repeated *ad nauseam* and, during the early years of communist rule, the

Romanian leaders extended unusual privileges to "democratic" Hungarians, to antifascist Jews, and even to repentant Saxons. Minority rights were given special attention in the Constitution of 1952 when the Hungarian Autonomous Region was established in the predominantly Hungarian-inhabited part of Transylvania.[22]

But reconciliation and harmony under communism proved to be even more ephemeral than under previous political systems. The harshness of communist rule was unacceptable to most inhabitants of Transylvania. Antagonisms were either papered over or temporarily suppressed but not forgotten. This is not to say that in the late forties and early fifties the Hungarians in Transylvania – or in Budapest for that matter – longed for reincorporation of Transylvania into the Hungarian body politic. It is to say, however, that dissatisfaction with communism in general was nearly all-pervasive among Transylvania's inhabitants and that any change within the extended Soviet empire in East Central Europe would have been welcomed by all nationalities. As it happened, following Stalin's death, limited options became available to the more mobile minorities – the Jews and the Saxons – and by 1956 they appeared to be available also to the Hungarians. And indeed, after the Hungarian Revolution of 1956, the Hungarian question in Transylvania was born again much in the mold of the interwar years, yet within the framework of new internal and external political orders.[23]

The Hungarian Revolution revealed the lack of acceptance of communist rule by Hungarians, whether in Hungary or in Transylvania. The Hungarians in Transylvania did not join the Hungarian revolutionaries but were clearly supportive of the aims of their conationals in Hungary. The anti-communist sentiments of the Hungarians in Transylvania were representative of that of other nationalities in that province but was singled out by the communist Romanian regime for political purposes essentially unrelated to nationality questions. Specifically, the Hungarian Revolution and its reverberations in Transylvania were exploited by Romania's leader Gheorghe Gheorghiu-Dej to secure his own power base which was threatened by Khrushchev's plans to replace the Stalinist Romanian leadership with one of his own choice. As self-styled protector and executor of Romanian national and communist interests, based on "objective Romanian conditions," the self-proclaimed architect of a Romanian road to socialism was able to justify the correctness of his own policies as opposed to the Hungarian ones which led to the threatening Hungarian Revolution. The Romanian road to socialism, after 1956, became increasingly more nationalist as its scope and validity were continually challenged by Khrushchev and his followers in the Kremlin. Thus, first Gheorghiu-Dej and later Nicolae Ceauşescu reverted more and more to traditional Romanian policies on matters related to the rights and privileges of national minorities. And, as pressures from Moscow mounted and a Romanian road to independence within the Soviet bloc emerged more clearly in the 1960s, the Romanian leadership adopted extreme nationalist positions commensurate with claims of execution of historic legacy rooted in the legitimacy of the entire Romanian historic experience since the days of the Dacian warrior Burebista.[24] In the process the Transylvania question, in all its historic aspects, became of paramount concern to Bucharest and, perhaps only to a slightly lesser one, also to Moscow and Budapest.

There are indeed very close similarities between contemporary Romanian positions and policies and those of the interwar years. The Romanianization of Transylvania and corresponding decline in rights and privileges enjoyed by coinhabiting nationalities – particularly the Hungarians – bears striking similarities to the policies of previous Romanian regimes. As in the past, the constitutional rights of the national minorities in Transylvania are being observed *de jure*, but the selective imposition of quotas based on nationality has reduced the one-time virtually unlimited opportunities for employment and political representation enjoyed by Hungarians, Saxons, and Jews. Romanianization has also affected educational and cultural opportunities for members of national minorities again not because of the elimination of schools, theaters, and publications in the languages of the minorities but because of the necessity of integration for possible advancement within the contemporary Romanian order.

The motivations for the adoption of restrictive minority policies, particularly against the Hungarians, are manifold. Apart from the need to pose as the defender of Romania's historic interests and traditions – which by definition entails acceptance of the nationalist historic tradition – Ceauşescu pursued a Romanian road to communism based on Romanian autarchic principles of long standing, as best expressed in the slogan of the 1920s: "By ourselves". As the implementing policies have been no more successful than those adopted by previous exponents of the same doctrine, Romanian economic conditions today are markedly worse than those of Hungary. Thus, the disaffection of Transylvania's Hungarians with Romanization is exacerbated by comparisons of their own living standards in Romania with those of their conationals in Hungary. Finally, Soviet exploitation of the disaffection of the Hungarian minority in Transylvania for the express purpose of checking Romanian deviations from policies devised by Moscow and accepted by faithful members of COMECON and the Warsaw Pact further aggravated the nationality problem in Transylvania.[25]

There was little talk of outright revisionism within the Soviet bloc, although fear of yet another repudiation of the Trianon treaty through a contemporary version of the Vienna Award was apparent in Romania. What tended to contribute to that fear were the activities of interested parties abroad which, in a manner reminiscent of similar attacks during the interwar years, steadily attacked Romania's policies toward national minorities on the grounds of their violating human rights. And, as in some instances, formulations of classical Hungarian revisionism with proper reinvocation of the "betrayal" of Trianon were becoming louder and clearer, the specter of actual revisionism reappeared on the East Central European political arena.

"*Plus ça change, plus c'est la même chose*" may not be an accurate historic slogan. It is, however, applicable to East Central Europe because the Soviet empire adopted the essential policies of the Tsarist, Habsburg, and Ottoman empires of yore for the attainment of its goals and because member nations – whether integral components or vassal states of that empire – have not forgotten the lessons of the past.

Notes

1. The text of the Treaty of Trianon will be found in *The Treaties of Peace 1919-1923* Vol. I compiled by Lt.-Col. Lawrence Martin (New York: Carnegie Endowment for International Peace, 1924), pp. 457-648.
2. A succinct study of these issues will be found in Stephen Fisher-Galati, "Romanian Nationalism," in Peter F. Sugar and Ivo J. Lederer, eds., *Nationalism in Eastern Europe* (Seattle: Univeristy of Washington Press, 1969), pp. 373-395.
3. R. W. Seton-Watson, *A History of the Roumanians* (Cambridge: Cambridge University Press, 1934), pp. 548-550.
4. The most complete and perceptive analysis of these problems will be found in Henry L. Roberts, *Rumania: Political Problems of an Agrarian State* (New Haven: Yale Univeristy Press, 1951), pp. 89 ff.

5. See especially the comprehensive study by Sherman D. Spector, *Rumania at the Paris Peace Conference: A Study of the Diplomacy of Ioan I. C. Brătianu* (New York: Bookman Associates, 1962), pp. 67 ff.
6. Roberts, *Rumania*, pp. 22 ff.
7. *Ibid.*, pp. 36-39.
8. Spector, *Rumania*, pp. 98 ff.
9. Important data will be found in Walter M. Bacon, Jr., *Behind Closed Doors: Secret Papers on the Failure of Romanian-Soviet Negotiations, 1931-1932* (Stanford: Hoover Institution Press, 1979), pp. 3 ff.
10. The most intelligent overview of these problems is by Eugen Weber, "Romania," in Hans Rogger and Eugen Weber, eds. *The European Right: A Historical Profile* (Berkeley: University of California Press, 1966), pp. 501-574.
11. See especially C. A. Macartney, *Hungary and Her Successors: The Treaty of Trianon and Its Consequences 1919-1937* (London: Oxford University Press, 1937), pp. 284 ff.
12. Stephen Fischer-Galati, *Twentieth Century Rumania* (New York: Columbia University Press, 1970), pp. 29 ff.
13. Weber, *Romania*, and the important study by Nicholas M. Nagy-Talavera, *The Green Shirts and the Others* (Stanford: Hoover Institution Press, 1970) are most informative on these topics.
14. See Macartney, *Hungary*, pp. 284 ff. and Hugh Seton-Watson, *Eastern Europe Between the Wars, 1918-1941* (Cambridge: Cambridge University Press, 1945), pp. 277 ff.
15. Roberts, *Rumania*, pp. 206 ff.
16. The essential study is by Béla Vágó, "Le Second Diktat de Vienne: Les Préliminaires," *East European Quarterly*, II:4, 1969, pp. 415-437. See also William O. Oldson, "Romania and the Munich Crisis: August-September 1938," *East European Quarterly*, XI:2, 1977, pp. 177-190.
17. Fischer-Galati, *Twentieth Century Rumania*, pp. 46 ff; Roberts, *Rumania*, pp. 206 ff. See also the interesting contemporary study by Al. Gh. Savu, *Dictatura regală, 1938-1940* (București: Editura Politică, 1970).
18. See Vágó, "*Le Second Diktat: Les Préliminaires*," pp. 415 ff. and especially his "Le Second Diktat de Vienne: Le partage de la Transylvanie," *East European Quarterly*, V:1, 1971, pp. 47-73.

19. *Ibid.* See also Savu, *Dictatura regală*, pp. 407 ff.
20. Seton-Watson, *Eastern Europe*, pp. 303 ff.
21. Ghita Ionescu, *Communism in Rumania 1944-1962* (London: Oxford University Press, 1964), pp. 107 ff.
22. *Ibid*, pp. 217 ff.
23. Stephen Fischer-Galati, "Rumania," in Béla K. Király and Paul Jónás, eds. *The Hungarian Revolution of 1956 in Retrospect* (Boulder, Colorado: East European Quarterly, 1977), pp. 95-101.
24. *Revista de Istorie*, 32:7, 1979, pp. 1215-1233 contains important data on this subject.
25. Robert F. King, *A History of the Romanian Communist Party* (Stanford: Hoover Institution Press, 1980), pp. 128-134.

Yeshayahu Jelinek

Trianon and Czechoslovakia: Reflections

The Treaty of Trianon was of major importance for the development of the Czechoslovak Republic.[1] It defined the Republic's borders with Hungary and fixed the fate of several nations and nationalities. This essay will place the problems of borders and nationalities in historical perspective; it will discuss their origin before the First World War, their formation during the years of 1918-1920, and their lasting impact.

The treaty merely rubberstamped a historical development. The new Czecho-Slovak state labored to establish facts long before the Hungarian delegation fixed its signature on the document.

According to Macartney, the Czechoslovak Foreign Minister Eduard Beneš, in a message to Karel Kramař, the Czechoslovak Premier, stated the need "...to occupy Slovakia *via facti* and create *faits accomplis;* we must command the situation..."[2] The Slovak leader Vavro Šrobár put it this way: "The one who first lays hands on Slovakia would have it for keeps..."[3] The new government strove from the outset to establish itself on Slovakia's territory; the southern border confronted it with a problem. Hence Hungarian-Czecho-Slovak military clashes started immediately with the formation of the state. The Czech and Slovak military strength was mostly inferior to the Hungarian, but it sufficed for the politicians to justify their territorial claims. In the last count, however, the decision of the Great Powers rather than the fragile *fait accomplis* brought about the final results. French adroitness and obstinacy was decisive, and therefore Paris was charged with the deliberate weakening of Hungary, with the purpose of curtailing its influence in East Central Europe.[4]

Whether the fate of Hungary is described as punishment, bad luck, the vindication of the victors, historical justice, or whatever, for Czecho-Slovakia the treaty meant the fulfillment of a dream. At an important consultation of Czecho-Slovak (but for all practical purposes, only Czech) political leaders on 2 January 1919, the attending parties learned that neither Germans nor Hungarians would be invited to participate in the treaty negotiations. "The conditions will be dictated to them, and it is only up to us to forward our demands."[5] Consequently, Prague coveted large chunks of their hapless neighbour. The contested area contained coal mines, industrial plants, railroad lines and strategic rail terminals, rich agricultural land and vineyards, as well as several hundreds of thousands Hungarians. The politicians attending the consultation were well aware that their demands contradicted the ethnic principle; they relied on the Entente's wish to weaken Hungary. President Thomas G. Masaryk already warned against the creation of a sizeable Hungarian minority within the Czecho-Slovak borders.[6] He would have preferred a border reflecting ethnic realities, one that would have left a smaller number of Hungarians on the Czechoslovak side. In spite of his conviction, however, he approved, when the time came, the incorporation of large Hungarian-populated areas into the new state.

Prague politicians cautioned the Slovaks to be realistic in their demands. One may doubt, however, whether the Slovak public figures possessed a clear enough picture, indeed any picture, of the future southern borders of their country. Enthusiastic but mostly inexperienced, naive and partly ignorant, the Slovaks relied on the judgement of their Czech brethren.

The Czecho-Slovak delegation in Paris included the talented young Slovak lawyer Štefan Osuský and several lesser Slovak consultants. Nonetheless the guiding directives came from Kramář and Beneš. The results of the skillfully managed campaign were quite impressive. To quote Macartney "...sympathy with the Magyars must blend with admiration for the skill of the Czech in negotiating successfully so many finesses and finally making a contract which their cards never seemed to justify."[7]

Because of the obstacle of the ethnic principle, the Czechs were forced to give in several times. While yielding on their most extremist demands, they were able to secure several purely Hungarian districts of economic and strategic importance. The Czech delegates reasoned that a large proportion of Hungarians were distributed over all of Slovakia, and that while they were taking on a large number of Hungarian people, numerous Slovaks would remain in Hungary. Also, the requested space consisted of a compact geographic unit. Some strategic considerations look ludicrous to us in view of contemporary military technology. In practical terms, the assigned regions granted Czechoslovakia a free and easy access to the Danube river, provided military advantages, enabled unhampered rail- and motor-transportation from the South West to the South East, and furnished mountainous Slovakia with a rich agricultural hinterland. The competent use of proper arguments advanced the Czecho-Slovak cause. The reasoning of historical justice proved to be somehow less convincing.[8]

The politicians alleged – and have done so with scholarly help up to the present – that a large proportion of the ethnic Slovak population to the south of the Slovak mountains underwent a process of Magyarization.[9] The previously solid Slovak regions lost their ancient homogenous character, and became Magyarized to varying degrees under the pressure of Hungarian national policies.[10]

Beneš was the architect of Czecho-Slovak victory. He enjoyed the full confidence and support of Prague. Yet the Czechs, much more then the Slovaks, understood the pernicious consequences of creating a huge bloc of a captive population, potentially hostile to the state. This internal opposition was different from the aggressive nationalism expressed in the slogan "*nem, nem, soha*" (no, no, never, i.e. never giving up the claim of a greater Hungary). Yet even urban, moderate, and sensible Hungarians whether living in Czechoslovakia or abroad, could not acquiesce to an arbitrary decision which created a large minority and forced it to live under alien rule. The Czechoslovak-Hungarian border constituted a permanent danger, an apple of discord. External enemies of both nations deployed this apple as a convenient tool for winning influence and facilitating intervention. The French were conscious of the advantage which the mutual hostility within the Danubian basin gave their policy-makers and their sympathizers in local capitals.

In a similar fashion the contested borders made Slovak dependence on Prague inevitable, and provided the Czechs with a stick for taming a rebellious Bratislava. Not by mere chance did President Beneš remind the Slovaks repeatedly during the last war of the fate of their southern territories, and of his activities to regain them. This, after the German-Italian "Arbitration of Vienna" of 2 November 1938, awarded to Hungary a larger part of the disputed Slovak regions,[11] with its predominantly Hungarian population.

Tensions in Slovakia's southern rim reoccurred periodically. (Let us recall only a few of the more significant dates: 1928, 1938, 1939-1945, 1946-1948, 1956, and 1980.) Those of the Czech politicians who understood the problem, and found the negative outweighting the positive, expressed a willingness to revise the borders.[12] The leading Czech Communist, Bohumir Šmeral, called for a revision of frontiers as early as 14 June 1921.[13] Naturally, it was easier for a Czech to agree to a revision of Slovak borders than to be challenged over the historic frontiers of his fatherland. It had to be rather entertaining to watch Slovaks, including rabid Czech-mongers and haters of Beneš and his memory, as they piously subscribed to the result of Czech diplomatic dexterity in Paris. In the eyes of many Slovaks, every inch of land obtained in Paris was sacrosanct, a part of the patrimony of the Slovak people, a gift of Providence – a ground drenched by the blood and sweat of Slovakia's children. Such was the attitude of Gustav Husák and his Communist friends in 1945.[14] While Hungarian nationalists lamented "the amputated, bleeding regions of the fatherland," Slovak patriots sang odes of joy. Orgies of chauvinism are alike. It is not without interest that a few Slovak nationalists, particularly during the existence of the Slovak state, saw Slovakia's allotment not extensive enough, and claimed Hungarian villages with an allegedly ethnic Slovak population as far south as the outskirts of Budapest. They resembled the Hungarian irredentists who aspired to regain the *Felvidék* (Upper Hungary, i.e. Slovakia).

Slovakia profited in many ways from the territorial expansion. The narrow mountain strip between Carpathians and Pannonia could hardly provide enough space for economic and social prosperity. The extensive agriculture of the southern lowlands supplied the country with food and with an outlet for redundant labor in the hills.

At Trianon the Great powers discriminated against Hungary in favor of Czecho-Slovakia. They awarded the Czechoslovak Republic with another prize at Hungary's expense: Transcarpathian Rus (Subcarpathian Ukraine). The St. Germain-en-Laye Peace Treaty with Austria of 10 September 1919 and its minority-rights paragraphs recorded this transfer reading. Leading Czecho-Slovak figures coveted this territory long before the end of the war. Masaryk started to negotiate with several Ruthene figures in the United States early in 1918, and others held similar talks with Ruthene dignitaries in the old country at a later date. Overriding opposition from various corners, Czechoslovaks succeeded in convincing their partners of the advantages of joining the new republic.[15]

The benefits of holding Transcarpathian Rus' were multiple and varied. The country served as a bridge between Czecho-Slovakia and Romania, two states hostile to Hungary. By holding on to it, Czecho-Slovakia prevented territorial contact between Hungary and Poland, something regarded as dangerous to the new state. The annexation of Transcarpathia to Czecho-Slovakia was preceded by thoughts of attaching it to Poland,[16] of making it independent under a United States governor,[17] and by other, even more colorful plans. Some Ruthenes appealed to Prague to cross the

Carpathian chain and absorb parts of Western Ukraine.[18] The solution eventually chosen worked well, however. Since there existed prospects, or dangers, of Russia becoming master of Eastern Galicia, the Great Powers saw in attaching the region to Czecho-Slovakia a way of preventing Bolshevik penetration of East Central Europe.[19]

Schools of Russian and of Ukrainian nationalism claimed alternatively the Ruthene population for themselves. Bolshevik troops could easily follow the precedent of the short-lived "West Ukrainian Republic" and try to conquer the strategic region. France in particular dreaded such a possibility, and supported Czechoslovak aspirations.

In addition to political-strategic considerations, the Czech politicians cherished the prospect of economic-commercial benefits. They habitually spoke about "expansion to the East," presumably through Slovakia and Transcarpathian Rus'. Direct connections with Romania promised uninterrupted railway transportation to the Black Sea ports and perhaps to the planned Transcaucasian line to the Middle and Far East. Czech business interests anticipated a significant increase in trade with Russia, and again the Transcarpathia was regarded to be the natural gate to East Slavonic markets.[20] For Hungary, loss of the territory meant a material disadvantage, for it left her bereft of the area of flood control of most of its rivers and deprived the mother country of further tens of thousands of her people.

The Treaty of Trianon solidified Czecho-Slovakia's territorial growth at the expense of Hungary. It had significant human-national ramifications, too.[21]

In some sense, Trianon could be regarded as a "nation building" instrument. This was true for Hungary, which for the first time in her history became a genuine nation-state, free of the ballast of subservient minority-nationalities. To a lesser degree (and perhaps as an irony of history) one cannot say the same about the other successor states. Neither Czechoslovakia nor Yugoslavia were ever genuine nation-states. Only Romania could assert that distinction, yet even her situation was checkered by the existence of considerable minorities and by the varied and contradictory traditions of the hodge-podge of regions composing that Balkan kingdom.

Slovaks could enjoy the full benefit of the new conditions. Hungarians and Germans living in Slovakia felt a considerable deterioration of status in comparison with the past. Ruthenes were still torn between the multitude schools of national identity. Although the state recognized Jews and Gypsies as independent nationalities, their particular social conditions do not allow us to judge them by general criteria.

Befor the war, the development of Slovak national consciousness was curtailed by Hungarian nationalism, and by the social environment in which Slovaks lived. These circumstances slowed down the process of self-determination and hampered the rise of indigenous nationalism. Certain regions of Western and Central Slovakia could boast a rather small, nationally awakened intelligentsia, ecclesiastic (Lutheran and Catholic) and secular; as well as moderate attention in the broad masses. Eastern Slovakia could not display even such modest achievements.[22] Impoverished and backward, speaking a dialect different from the rest of Slovakia, and worshiping in the Greek rite of Catholicism, the population stood apart from the majority of the Slovak people. Hungarians utilized the East Slovakian distinctions for further deepening the chasm within the Slovak people. A slight corrective was offered by expatriate emigrants (the region suffered from extensive emigration) who formed their national consciousness in America, and injected the newly gained convictions into the home population.[23] All in all, on the eve of the First World War Slovak nationalism was still underdeveloped and primitive.

During the process of the formation of the republic, the involved parties were aware of Slovakia's condition. Hence Hungarians insisted on a plebiscite to decide the country's future before signing the treaty,[24] while Czechs and Slovak activists resisted the proposal.[25] The deeply religious Slovak people were said to be unable to separate the political aspect of the cult of St. Stephen (the *Staatsidee* of the Hungarian state) from the spiritual one, and could be easily influenced in a pro-Hungarian direction, all the more so, if Hungarians were to be in charge of the plebiscite. Also, the vote of many Magyarized Slovaks augured ill for the national cause. Little wonder, then, that Czecho-Slovak authorities would have nothing to do with the plebiscite.[26] Aware of the realities,[27] and following the *fait accompli* strategy, they refused any sort of democratic decision-making. President Masaryk put it this way:[28]

> The Slovak nation was oppressed to such a degree that it never had an occasion for political thinking, and would not be able to decide its fate. Therefore it is only natural that the opinions of national leaders should be decisive.

The "national leaders" were of course self-appointed political figures without significant public influence and support. They gathered once only, on 30 October 1918 in the city of Turčiansky Sv. Martin in Central Slovakia, to vote on and to accept the "Declaration of the Slovak Nation".[29] That document defined Slovaks as a branch of the unified Czechoslovak nation, and for this nation it demanded the right of self-determination. Several members of the gathering, which came to be known as the Slovak National Council, represented political groups and clusters, while others were unaffiliated. The groups were inactive during the war, and represented largely Western and Central Slovakia. The Declaration reached the population in the form of leaflets. Local councils occasionally voiced their agreement with it; the populace expressed its approval, it was said, by manifestations of street violence,[30] hardly legal forms of self-determination.

Nevertheless, it would not be easy to argue against Slovakia's joining Bohemia and Moravia in a common state. In an age when self-determination and independence of nations was made into a sacred law, Slovakia's continued existence under Hungarian government made no sense. All the more so as the Hungarians had acquired the dubious fame of being inconsiderate and oppressive toward minorities. On the other hand, the Slovaks were not ready for any sort of independent life, and were by no means able to manage their country's existence by themselves. In fact, it was argued that those who were interested in returning Slovakia to Hungary's bosom were also the ones who invented and propagated the slogans of Slovakia's autonomy.[31]

The proposals coming from various corners to attach Slovakia to Poland remained barren. Poles had had only limited contacts with Slovaks in the past, partly because of the natural barrier which separated the two nations. Moreover, Poland on the eve of an independent life had no resources to spare and share with Slovakia. Evidently nobody but the Czechs could offer and advance Slovakia's separation from the Hungarians. But the country's entrance into the Republic did not come about because its national leaders desired it. It was a *via facti* strategy, as well as the Entente's fear of Hungarian Bolsheviks, that toppled the scales in the direction of Czecho-Slovakia. (At the same time, of course, we shouldn't underestimate the value of the wartime preparatory work carried out by Masaryk and his friends, or the importance of other diplomatic, military, and propagandistic activities abroad.)

Several local "republics" stood in the way of Slovakia's self-determination, and they were to be eliminated before further steps could be taken. The most dangerous was the Slovak Soviet Republic founded by Hungarian, Slovak, and Czech Communists in the city of Prešov in 1919; a motley group of Hungarian and pro-Hungarian patriots formed others. Martial law enforced by Czecho-Slovak occupation troops paved Slovakia's way into Czecho-Slovakia.

An accepted cliché had it that the Czechs and Czechoslovakia saved the Slovak people from national extinction. But this is a deterministic notion; it denies the existence of creative forces within a nation and predicts the future on the basis of narrowly subjective criteria. In an epoch of national awakening among small nations and stirring, even among very small ethnic groups (the Basques, Bretons, and Corsicans are cases in point), it would be presumptuous to presuppose the disappearance of an entire nation. The fable of "Slovak salvation" belongs to the realm of the propaganda whose aim was to justify the break-up of Austria-Hungary, the Peace of Trianon, and their outcome.

There is, however, little doubt that Slovak national survival was indeed in serious danger, and that the Hungarian denationalization drive could boast undeniable achievements. Czech public figures, more experienced in public relations and international politics, guided the Slovak attempt to overthrow Hungarian domination. The Czechs based their activity on the thesis of a single "Czechoslovak" nation with a Czech and a Slovak branch. In the coming years this thesis proved to be a serious blunder because of the threat it posed to Czech-Slovak coexistence. In addition, the Czechs' patronizing attitude toward the "poor tinkers" was not very helpful in developing a healthy relation between the two groups.

Slovak nationalists, especially the younger ones who had not experienced Hungarian supremacy, proved themselves to be ungrateful to the Czechs. The uninhibited behaviour of the followers of Hlinka's People Party and of the Communist Party, their blind hatred and hostility, called for resolute action. The essentially derogatory attitude and firm administrative methods of the departed Hungarian aristocratic rulers were apparently more efficient in dealing with some Slovak hot-heads than the conciliatory policies of the democratic Czech petit-bourgeois. Neither was the Czech expansion to the East as altruistic as occasionally presented. Prague reaped political, economic, territorial and psychological benefits from the annexation of Slovakia. Nonetheless, a denial of Czech compassion for their oppressed relatives would be an affront to historical truth. Slovakia needed Czech assistance and, in one way or the other, got it. Trianon contributed definitively to the nation-building of the Slovak people.

The Ruthenes were less close to Czech hearts than were the Slovaks. Abandoned and destitute, the Ruthenes suffered badly from Hungarian denationalization and dreaded continuous Hungarian domination.[32] (Described as *Natio Fidelissima*, the Ruthenes were entitled to a better treatment in Hungarian hands.) The un-Magyarized intelligentsia split over the question of ethnic-national allegiance. Divided into "Russian," "Ukrainian," and "Rusin" factions, the Ruthenes failed to offer a unified action of self defence. The Hungarians exploited the split thoroughly by a divide and rule strategy. Later the Czech masters borrowed a few pages from the Hungarian book of recipes.[33] The Ruthene assumption that all Slavonic Greek Catholics of the regions were co-nationals troubled their relations with the Slovaks. These relations suffered even more from the Ruthene claim on a considerable part of the territory that was thought to be Slovak. The others did not sit idle either, and portrayed Ruthenes as renegade Slovaks – at least the ones living in counties claimed by the Slovaks as well.[34] When drawing the borders between Slovakia and Ruthenia, the Czechs favored the Slovak side. Prague also did not honor the promises given to Ruthene dignitaries, and codified in the treaty of St. Germain and in the Czechoslovak constitution, to grant the people of Ruthenia autonomy and self-rule.[35] To summarize, the Ruthenes benefited less from the collapse of St. Stephan's kingdom. Part of the blame goes to the Czechs, the rest to the forever quarrelling Ruthenes. The *Tertium Gaudens* was Moscow, which annexed the country in 1945, and with that finally penetrated into East Central Europe. Quarrels among the Ruthenes, and with the Slovaks, go on happily among immigrants on the American continent.

Hungarians in Czechoslovakia were not beneficiaries of Trianon. On the contrary: as liberal as the Czech leadership might have been toward minorities, liberalism was not prized too highly by Slovak authorities. Hungarians in the country remained a visible symbol of Slovakia's past. They could easily become the whipping boy, the object of Slovak revenge, and the target of their suspicions. The Hungarian leadership too often sailed along winds blowing from Budapest, and these were not exactly friendly winds. Moreover, as the political conditions changed in East Central Europe, the minority moved toward radicalism.

The Hungarians were living in a democratic republic. They had political representation, and social and cultural institutions to satisfy their intellectual needs. The state's agencies respected their particularities, at least to a degree. Economically they were better off then many of their co-nationals in Hungary (although their living standards were somewhat below those of the Czech-Slovak population). Did the forced separation stimulate an independent ethnic development, a different ethos, a new consciousness? The interwar period was too short a time to observe such changes.

Some idiosyncracies did develop, however. At least a portion of the inhabitants was willing to assimilate, and some Magyarized Slovaks did revert to their native culture. A fraction of the minority acquiesced in the given realities, and the various minority rights helped to soothe the pains of others. Again it was the President Masaryk who from the outset labored for a better understanding. Yet, as István Borsody has observed, minority rights were never proved to be a satisfactory substitute for hoped for majority rights.[36]

The intensive propaganda warfare carried on over the heads of the minority by official agencies and private institutions in Hungary and Czechoslovakia, often had little to do with the actual frustration, worries, and joys of the people. Sometimes, though, the Czechoslovak Hungarians did produce ammunition for new battles, and other times intolerant Slovaks were the instigators. How convenient a tool was the ethnic minority itself in the hands of irredentist propaganda; Budapest and Prague spent enormous amounts of money to castigate the other side, in order of course to win sympathy abroad.

This duel kept the atmosphere tense, and decreased the likelihood of a rapprochement. It aided the anti-democratic elements in Hungary, as well as Slovak nationalists and Communists, in their attacks on liberals and in their defense of totalitarian values. The conflict offered the outside Fascist powers opportunities which they did not fail to grasp. Unfortunately, the liberals on both sides were unable to find a common language and to cooperate.

The authorities plainly regarded the Hungarian minority as hostage; their treatment of that minority depended on the well being of Slovaks in Hungary. The Slovak press started to discuss this unhuman principle as early as 1919.[37] Accordingly, minority rights could be granted or withdrawn on the basis of reciprocity. Hungary counted among her inhabitants Slovaks, who composed solid ethnic islands. However, the Slovaks in Hungary were a fraction of the mass of Hungarians who resided in Czechoslovakia. Their national life it is true, was not sheer pleasure, and complaints were frequent. A system of turning entire minorities into a football of high policies could not be easily appreciated. In the First Republic, the hostage principle was scarcely applied, if ever. But during the Second World War, when Slovakia turned into a *Schutzstaat* of Berlin, and when Hungarian revisionism reached the pinnacle of achievement and power, there was no limit to the barbarities on either side.

As stated above, Czechoslovak politicians and diplomats alleged in Paris that many of the Hungarian residents of southern Slovakia/northern Hungary were in reality Slovaks, who had become the victims of Budapest's Magyarization drive. Consequently, one may say, their incorporation into Slovakia would be an act of historical justice. Strangely enough, representatives of the Great Powers swallowed this bait, and its impact could occasionally be felt.[38]

Europe is still crowded with denationalized populations, and the process of denationalization is still going on. If each nation were to demand for itself its lost brothers, international life would turn into perpetual anarchy. In any case, Czechoslovakia promised to honor the rights of minorities, to abstain from challenging their nationality, and to give them schools in their own language.[39] What would not be done by the bourgeois governments of the First Republic, was accomplished by a Communist-led administration in Prague and Bratislava in 1947. The campaign of "Reslovakization" carried out under the premiership of the Communist Klement Gottwald was not any tamer than the work of the notorious HAKATA and other denationalization enterprises in modern Europe. The story of Hungarians in Czechoslovakia is a serialised one. New chapters appear at irregular intervals, though their appearance is more or less inevitable.

The Germans of Slovakia identified themselves with the Hungarian cause. By 1918 they were on the verge of losing their ethnic identity and becoming loyal Hungarians. The Germans regretted Trianon, supported Hungary as long as they could, and once they could not, they defended zealously their own minority rights.[40] In order to decrease the numerical strength of the Hungarians the Republic backed German efforts to preserve a separate German ethnic identity. In the long run the official policies backfired: being nationally conscious yet short of having a faithful and qualified intelligentsia, Germans of Slovakia imported teachers, administrators, and other professionals from Bohemia and Moravia. The newcomers brought along the political and social convictions prevalent in their milieu and imbued their co-nationals with these ideas. Thus, in the final analysis, the publicly encouraged and supported policies of de-Hungarization assisted in the Nazification of Slovak (and Transcarpathian) Germans, another unexpected and bizarre result of Trianon.

The Jews do not fit the regular definition of nationality in the terms discussed here (i.e. language, territorial concentration, and a mother country to look after them). They were, however, major beneficiaries of the change in the region after the First World War.

The Slovak population and its leaders accused Jews of prewar Hungary of a close cooperation with Budapest authorities in the denationalization process. František Votruba, a Czech author familiar with Slovak affairs, understood the Jewish dilemma well:[41] "All instincts of life preservation led the Slovak Jewry to secure the good will of those in power; above all it needed to liberate itself from conditions of illegality and dependence... There were few incentives to join the minute and powerless Slovak elite and the masses of ignorant population devoid of protection of law." What was comprehended by an objective Votruba could not be and would not be appreciated by the Slovak intelligentsia, and even less by the general population. The hatred of Jews, a heritage of centuries of religious and social indoctrination, frequently sought rational explanation and found it in all sorts of alleged sins. In Slovakia the Jews pursued their traditional professions, innkeeping probably being the bestknown among them. This trade, like the others forced on Jews during centuries of persecution was short on high ethic standards. Consequently the innate hatred of Jews received an objective boost. Also the acceptance of Hungarianhood by many Jews, as well as fanatical Magyarization activity by individuals, alienated the nationally conscious Slovak intelligentsia. Finally, Slovak spokesmen attacked Jews for allegedly serving as informers and stool pigeons to the wartime Hungarian authorities. This is another of the notorious defamations of Jews, used by all their adversaries (Slovaks *and* by Hungarians alike).

When in 1918 the whole of East Central Europe was hit by a wave of anti-Jewish riots, all regions of Czechoslovakia participated in the outrages. Often the wish to plunder Jewish – and non-Jewish – property sparked the riots, and even pre-programmed looting was recorded.[42] Czecho-Slovak officials and the press whitewashed the murder and the looting by describing it as a popular revenge for Jewish misconduct in the past and especially during the war. On the other hand, they omitted to mention the social and political unrest that gave impetus to the riots. Czechoslovak troops coming to secure Slovakia and Ruthenia for the new state made the Jews a special target of persecution, including summary executions on flimsy pretexts. Nevertheless, the authorities were reluctant to extend protection and help.[43] Vavro Šrobár, the Minister for Slovak Affairs in the government of Prague, justified violence and actually made the Jews responsible for it.[44] Even imprisoned Zionist leaders were found to be enemy agents.[45] Hungarian troops, occasionally commanded by Jewish officers and manned by Jewish soldiers, enforced law and order and assisted victims of the disturbances. During the Hungarian Bolshevik invasion Jews again drew the vindictiveness of Czecho-Slovak officials and troops. And agian they were between hammer of the Bolsheviks and anvil of their foes. All in all, the new Czechoslovak regime did not augur well for the Jews in Slovakia and Ruthenia. If Jews did nonetheless abandon their pro-Hungarian sentiments and eventually turned into constructive and faithful citizens of the Czechoslovak state it was to a great extent because of the good will shown by President Masaryk and his lieutenants.[46] Protests by Jewish and Zionist organizations from abroad, as well as local Jewish presentations, finally met with a favorable response.

The Republic introduced liberal policies toward the Jews, enabling them to assert their Jewish identity and choose their own representation. The recognition of Jewish nationality was designed also to reduce the number of citizens opting for German and Hungarian nationality. (Similarly, the Gypsies were given the choice of their own nationality.) In certain municipalities, Jews opting for their own nationality sharply reduced the number of Hungarians (and Germans) and hence put them all outside the bracket required for execution of the minority right as stipulated by the Republic's constitution.

The condition of Jews in the Republic worsened as one moved toward the East. Slovak nationalists in particular refused to recognize the benefits of cooperation with the Jewish population, and made them a convenient scape-goat for the country's ills. In Ruthenia the Czech authorities joined the local Jew-baiters. They tampered with legally granted rights and benefits, and through intimidation pressed the Jews to serve the needs of Czech political parties and of the central government.[47]

Jews of the eastern parts of Czechoslovakia however, reaped major rewards from Trianon. They grew nationally conscious, free of forced national identities. They learned to exercise the legal rights of independent citizens and ceased to be subservient petitioners. The liberal and humane policies accorded to the Jews by the central government made them into convinced believers in Czechoslovak democracy, although Jews were still subject to unfriendliness and discrimination by state agencies. Anti-Semitism did not disappear. In Slovakia Jewish interests paralleled those of the democratic pro-Czechoslovak elements, and Jews offered voluntarily to cooperate with governmental representatives and private institutions. The situation was less ideal in Transcarpathia, though nonetheless better than in the past. Many a Czechoslovak Jew did not regret the treaty of Trianon.

This essay reflected on the territorial and the national changes brought about in East Central Europe by the First World War and the Trianon Peace Treaty. The changes in the lives of millions of human beings who were the silent victims of developments beyond their comprehension, cannot be accurately recorded. It was they who nevertheless tried to make a new life for themselves in a radically altered political, social and psychological environment.

Notes

1. Originally, the name of the state was hyphenated (Czecho-Slovakia). The new constitution, accepted in Summer 1920, stipulated the unhyphenated name (Czechoslovakia).
2. C. A. Macartney, *Hungary and Her Successors* (London, Toronto, New York: Oxford University Press, 1937), p. 106.
3. Quoted by Dagmar Perman, *The Shaping of the Czechoslovak State* (Leiden: E. J. Brill, 1962), p. 78.
4. Stephen Borsody, "Czechoslovakia and Hungary", in Miloslav Rechcigl, Jr., ed., *Czechoslovakia Past and Present* vol. I (The Hague: Mouton, 1968), p. 666.
5. Prameny k ohlasu velké řijnové socialistické revoluce a vziku ČSR, *Boj o směr vývoje československého statu* vol. I (Prague: Nakladatelství Československé Akademie Vied, 1965), p. 38; document no. 26.
6. *Ibid*, p. 41; document no. 26.
7. Macartney, p. 103.
8. Slovensko, *L'ud* vol. I (Bratislava: Obzor, 1974), pp.440-51.
9. Prameny: p. 103.
10. Harold W. V. Temperley, ed., *A History of the Peace Conference of Paris* vol. IV (London: Henry Frowde and Hodder & Stoughton, 1921) p. 271; Joseph Chmelař, *National Minorities in Central Europe* (Prague: Orbis, 1937), p. 18.
11. Examples, see at the Balch Institute for Ethnic Studies, Philadelphia, PA, Hurban Papers, box 74-60, Extraordinary meeting of the government, President Beneš's report on his sojourn to the United States, London, June 17, 1943; President Beneš's address: Victory, Before the return home, London, March 28, 1945.
12. U.S. National Archives (Washington, D.C.) 860F.00/1-746, summary no. 377, December 19-25, 1946; 860F.00/9-564, airgram no.

A-1254, Jefferson Caffery to the Secretary of State, Paris, September 6, 1946.
13. *Rudé Právo* (Prague), June 14, 1921.
14. Marta Vartiková, "Československá pracovná konferencia KSS v Košiciach ako príos pri tvorbe vládneho programu prvéj vlády Národného Frontu Čechov a Slovákov," *Historický Časopis, XXIII*, 2 (1975), pp. 170-200.
15. Praměny, p. 43; document no. 28; *Národné Noviny* (Pittsburgh), January 23, March 13, and April 24, 1919.
16. *The New York Times*, January 2, 1920.
17. *The Times*, January 4, 1920.
18. Praměny, p. 79; document no. 54.
19. Praměny, p. 65; document no. 40; pp. 85-86; document no. 60.
20. Praměny, pp. 36-42; document no. 26.
21. In the 1821 census the following number of people reported their nationality as Slovak: 1,967,870; Magyar 744,621; Ruthene: 461,449; German: 139,880 (in Slovakia only); Jewish 70,522 (in Slovakia only). (Juraj Purgat, *Od Trianonu po Košice* (Bratislava: Epocha; 1970), p. 301.
22. Anton Štefánek et al., eds., *Milan Hodža* (Prague: Českomoravské podniky tiskarské, 1930), pp. 784-87; *NN*, February 20, 1919.
23. *NN*, January 2 and 25, 1919.
24. *Times*, April 14, 1920.
25. Czechoslovak statesmen traditionally disliked plebiscites, because of the inherent dangers in a territory that has national minorities.
26. According to Macartney (p. 103), Oszkár Jászi predicted the defeat of Hungarians in the proposed plebiscite. He also favored international supervision of the balloting.
27. Ferdiš Juriga, *Blahozvest' kriesenia Slovenského národa a Slovenskéj krajiny* (Trnava: Urbánek a spol., 1937), p. 194; *NN*, August 28, 1919.
28. *NN*, February 20, 1919.
29. Juriga, pp. 81, 82.
30. Štefánek, p. 236; Praměny, p. 21; document no. 11.
31. *NN*, April 3, and June 19, 1919.
32. Praměny, p. 136; document no. 120; *NN*, April 24, 1919.
33. Praměny, pp. 358, 359; document no. 28.
34. *NN*, July 17 and 27, 1919.

35. Prameny, p. 94; document no. 67; pp. 101, 102; document no. 75; pp. 364, 365.
36. Borsody, 670.
37. *NN*, March 27, 1919.
38. Temperley, p. 271; *NN*, April 17, 1919.
39. *NN*, August 28, and September 20, 1919.
40. *NN*, June 5, 1919.
41. Štefánek, p. 281.
42. *NN*, January 2, and 16, 1919. The parents of this writer often recalled the looting in their respective birthplaces, Žarnovica and Prievidza, and the preceding occurences.
43. The Slovak paper in Pittsburgh *Národné Noviny* (National Press), which regularly charged Jews with Magyarization and with exploitation of the Slovak people, did not hesitate to deny the occurrence of bloody pogroms in Poland and the Ukraine, and described them as Jewish falsehood and propaganda against the Slavonic people (June 5 and 12, 1919).
44. *The Jews of Czechoslovakia* vol. I (New York: Society for History of Czechoslovak Jews, 1968), pp. 225-27; Prameny, p. 192; document no. 167; *NN*, August 28, 1919.
45. *The Jews*, vol. I, pp. 223-25.
46. Jindřich Kohn, "Masaryk a slovenská otázka židovská," in Jozef Rudinský, ed., *Slovensko Masarykovi* (Prague: Nakladetel'stvo Vojtecha Tilkovského, 1930), pp. 213-18.
47. *NN* April 24, 1919; *Times,* March 7, 1920.

Thomas Karfunkel

The Impact of Trianon on the Jews of Hungary

The Jewish population of pre-Trianon Hungary enjoyed greater legal security, social acceptance and economic well-being than the Jewish communities of other East Central European states. However, anti-Semitism was present and affected, with varying degrees of intensity, all strata of society. It ranged from the cultural snobbery of the aristocracy to the crude popular stereotyping of the lower classes. During the last decades of the Dual Monarchy, to the more traditional, religion-based prejudice was added a politically motivated anti-Semitism that was the product of the reaction to the modernization that was slowly changing the character of society.

The century before World War I witnessed a rapid and fundamental improvement of the condition of the Jews of Hungary. The legislation promulgated, the economic opportunities created, the general absence of anti-Jewish agitation, the enlightened attitude of the ruling circles, all created a propitious atmosphere for growth for the Jewish community. This was noted in neighboring lands.[1] There was a massive migration of Jews into Hungary, primarily from Galicia. The estimated number of Jews in Hungary in 1787 was only 93,000. At the time of the Revolution of 1848, Jews numbered 336,000 by 1869, 542,000, and the census of 1910 showed the presence of 911,227 out of a total population of 18,265,493 in Hungary proper. This was a spectacular increase, an eloquent testimony of Hungary's appeal to the generally persecuted and shunned Jews of East Central Europe.

Numerical increase was accompanied by official acts leading toward legal equality. The Act of Emancipation was passed by the revolutionary government in 1849. In 1867 legal equality between Christian and Jews was promulgated, and in 1895 Judaism was granted the status of a "received religion," a designation that entitled it to government support and, ironically, a designation that was witheld from a number of Christian denominations.[2]

There were a number of factors that played a role in producing a favorable climate for Jews in Hungary. The Dual Monarchy was a multinational empire, a hopeless amalgamation of nationalities large and small, with conflicting aims and programs, and each with limited appreciation for the accomplishments and aspirations of neighboring groups. The national question, in the Age of Nationalism, was a simmering volcano ready to erupt and jeopardize not only the tranquility of the state, but the state itself. The two nationalities in power, when not preoccupied with their own conflict, were engaged in a perennial balancing act, with a constantly shifting program of concessions and threats vis à vis their minorities, to preserve the status quo. The Census of 1910, the last one held in Austria-Hungary, identified 54.5% of the population of Hungary as Hungarian. This majority status, extremely important for political as well as psychological reasons, was gained through the cooperation of Jews who were not classified as a separate national group and who overwhelmingly opted for Hungarian nationality. Jews constituted only 5% of the population, but it was the difference between a majority or a minority position for the Hungarians. A Hungarian-Jewish alliance was formed.

The Jewish self-identification as Hungarian was only partially motivated by the advantages such declaration produced. A large segment of the Jewish community enthusiastically and voluntarily submitted to the process of Magyarization. Jews in Hungary spoke the Hungarian language, championed the Hungarian culture, assimilated, intermarried and energetically supported the objectives of Hungarian nationalism.[3] This process of Jewish acculturation was encouraged and rewarded by the Hungarian establishment. In addition to offering badly needed numerical extension, it also confirmed the claim of Hungarian cultural superiority. It could, and did, serve as an example for the other minorities.

The Hungarian-Jewish alliance was a natural one, based on self-interest. The Hungarian squirearchy was primarily concerned about the perpetuation of its dominant political position, and it appreciated Jewish support. It was also very comfortable with this support, for the Jews could never mature into a threatening partner, with a political program calling for autonomy or separate existence. Simultaneously, the emergence of a Jewish capitalist class, and Jewish economic pursuits in general, received official encouragement. The Hungarian gentry was not overly attracted to these activities and Jewish penetration was preferred to that of any other ethnic group, including, or perhaps especially, that of the German minority.

The Hungarian-Jewish partnership was an effective combination for it blended political authority with economic power. The city of Budapest may be seen as the symbol of this viable and productive alliance. The city was the capital of a large, heterogeneous state ruled over by Hungarians, who controlled all the institutions and instruments of political power. Budapest was also the home of a large Jewish community, comprising almost a quarter of the population. The city and its environments were in the process of being developed into the industrial heartland of the state by a predominantly Jewish entrepreneurial class. Budapest was also the center of a secularized and Magyarized Jewish intelligentsia that played a very active role in the cultural life of the nation. It was a city where the social barriers separating Christian and Jew (especially in the upper segments of each group) were lowered, and many Jews completely abandoned their Jewish legacy and embraced a Hungarian identity.[4]

Anti-Semitism, and particularly its more violent and uncontrollable impulses, was frowned upon by the ruling establishment. The ruling circles perceived themselves as a part of the liberal tradition that endorsed the concept of toleration, and sensed that any attack on their junior partners was an attack on the system and on a Hungarian hegemony tenuously maintained. It may be suggested, even at this early point, that the chief component of the Hungarian policy toward Jews was not a very strong philosophical conviction, but rather a pragmatic understanding of national/class interest.

Before Trianon, Jews needed Hungarian assistance to gain legal and social acceptance and economic advancement, but the Hungarians also needed the Jews to maintain their monopoly on political power. C. A. Macartney concludes that

> The talent and industry of the Jewish industrial and financial bourgeoisie was indeed the most powerful prop to the ruling class, which could not otherwise have existed and developed as it did.[5]

Trianon was the watershed in the history of the Jews in Hungary. The pressure of domestic and international events that led to Trianon and its consequences destroyed the Hungarian-Jewish alliance and gradually wiped out all the benefits and advantages that it bestowed on Hungarian Jewry. Trianon-Hungary was a compact and homogenous state where the dominant nationality, the Hungarians, constituted approximately 90% of the population. The Jewish minority was not needed anymore to maintain a numerical superiority. In addition, Jews were now one of the two significant minorities in Hungary, the other being Germans.

Trianon-Hungary was the Hungary of Miklós Horthy. The Horthy regime was established by military force after the defeat of the Hungarian Soviet, primarily at the hands of a Romanian Interventionist Army. It was an authoritarian system of government, whose authoritarianism was unsuccessfully concealed by a facade of pseudo-parliamentarianism. It was not a totalitarian or fascist dictatorship; some opposition, in Parliament as well as in the Press, was tolerated. Horthy, as Regent, was the symbol and the final authority for a ruling group that was never monolithic in composition or with respect to its political orientation. It was a reactionary regime that moved ideologically further to the Right with the establishment of Nazi dictatorship and the growth of German influence in international relations.

Anti-Semitism was a basic doctrine of Horthy-Hungary. It appeared consistently, though in a variety of forms and with varying degrees of intensity during the life-span of the regime. Anti-Semitism is usually the product of a number of factors; political, socio-economic, religious or psychological, and the Hungarian version was no different. However, it is possible to isolate seven primary factors that produced the anti-Semitism of post-Trianon Hungary, and they were: the "Szeged idea"; domestic politicking; the identification of Jews with the dissemination of communist propaganda; the preponderance of Jewish capital in the economic life of the nation; the fear that the Jewish population was growing too rapidly and posed a threat to the character and identity of the nation; the belief that the Jews were an alien and unassimible minority and the conviction that anti-Jewish acts at home would earn diplomatic support for foreign policy objectives.

The "Szeged idea"

Szeged, a large city in Southern Hungary, was the headquarters of the Horthy-led counterrevolutionary forces. The "Szeged idea" was the philosophical underpinning of a movement that generally stressed action rather than thought. It was a program that envisioned specific and radical changes. It was the original program of the anti-democratic interests that sponsored and carried out the White Terror (Autumn 1919-Summer 1920), and established a dictatorship that ruled the state until the German military occupation in the final phase of World War II. The program, pre-dating the establishment of any fascist system of government, suggested a form of nascent fascism.[6]

Anti-Semitism was a central feature of the Szeged program. It expressed violent opposition to communism, and the Jews were identified as the prime supporters of that doctrine. The program promoted the idea of an exclusionary and racialist Hungarian state where Jews, by definition, could not fit in. It expressed hostility toward the feudal aristocracy that traditionally acted as both the ally and protector of the Jewish capitalist class. It promised jobs in the professions and commerce, where Jews predominated. It was a program appealing to Hungarians and directed against non-Hungarians, and in the long run against Magyarized non-Hungarians as well. There was a call for the radical transformation of Hungarian society, to a very great extent, at the expense of the Jewish community. It was essentially a class-oriented program with benefits offered to the middle classes, and it was also a classic right-radical manifesto, relying on revolutionary rhetoric – it promised fundamental changes, while at the same time making a commitment to preserve tradition. In practical terms little was offered to the urban and rural lower classes. The radical nature of the program was very much evident in the call for the solution of the Jewish problem. The idea was promptly translated into action by the Order Detachments that conducted a bloody pogrom against the Jews in the countryside while Horthy was still in the process of consolidating his power. The anti-Semitic credentials of the regime were solidly established.

The "Szeged idea" was promoted by a host of officially sanctioned overt and covert organizations. There were patriotic and secret societies, professional organizations, student federations, veterans' groups, irredentist and racist associations. The common feature of all of these formations was the ineligibility of Jews to become members. Some of the associations exercised considerable power. The most potent group was the Hungarian Association of National Defense (*Magyar Országos Véderő Egyesület* or MOVE), organized by officers but including civilians as well. It operated behind the scenes and served as both a pressure group and as a mutual help society. Its success was ensured by the high positions many of its leading members occupied in the regime. In January of 1919 Gyula Gömbös, the future Premier, was elected as the President. Militant anti-Semitism was a central feature of the movement. Gömbös issued anti-Semitic pamphlets with racialist overtones years before that kind of literature became politically fashionable. The civilian inner core of MOVE received the appropriate designation of the Hungarian Scientific Race-Protecting Society (*Magyar Tudományos Fajvédő Egyesület*).[7] The middle class ambitions of its supporters were expressed by attempts to squeeze the Jews out of the professions. In 1920 legislation was enacted, the notorious *numerus clausus,* that restricted the number of Jewish students in higher education to 5%, the approximate percentage of Jews in the total population.

The government did not always pursue policies that were consistent with the spirit of Szeged. The "idea" was often toned down and diluted by successive waves of officials who were forced to govern under the pressures of domestic and international considerations. The *numerus clausus* was not enforced. The degrees earned by Hungarian Jewish students at foreign universities were acknowledged without difficulty by the authorities. But the "Szeged idea" remained, sometimes only as an abstraction, the ideological foundation of the regime.

Domestic politicking

The Szeged movement, from its very beginning, was a coalition of forces. It was an umbrella designation, for under its banners there were different interest groups with different backgrounds and orientations. There was tension and constant jockeying for positions, power struggles between zealous and lukewarm supporters of the (Szeged) program. The latter would pay lip service to the ideals without any strong desire to implement many aspects of it. This, more moderate, wing was more concerned with the establishment of conservative orderliness, and regarded the radical pints of the program as sheer rhetoric. The militant wing, on the other hand, consisted of the true believers. There was also a class differentiation between the two groups. The lukewarm supporters of the program were led by representatives of the traditional upper classes, while the militants had a more bourgeois identification. The extreme Szeged orientation had great appeal to the embittered refugees from the successor states, who had comfortable pasts but dim prospects for the future, to the junior officers of the Army who had limited promotional opportunities, to the many jobless diploma-holders, to the struggling Christian commercial interests and to ambitious politicians on the fringes of the establishment. Anti-Semitism was the cutting edge, for it identified and it differentiated. Even so, the Bethlen era (1921-1931) was characterized by the ascendancy of the moderate wing. In the 1920's the Jewish question was downplayed, the Bethlen program was dedicated to consolidation and normalisation, and to the gaining of international support. Anti-Semitic acts did not fit into this scheme – the goals of the government would have been jeopardized by them. Militants, like Gömbös, felt betrayed. In 1923 the more resentful Szegedists temporarily seceeded from the Government Party and organized an opposition group: the Party of Racial Defence (*Fajvédő Párt*).

Tokenism on the Jewish question indicated indifference to the entire Szeged program. Attacks on the government on the Jewish question by supporters of the regime could mobilize support within the ruling establishment as well as attract popular support against policies and individual policy-makers. It is very much revealing of the ideological atmosphere prevailing in the Horthy establishment that even those individual officials who were not particularly anti-Semitic had to adopt an anti-Semitic posture to disarm potential critics. In the 1920's the government was controlled by "reasonable" anti-Semites. The Bethlenite definition of an anti-Semite as one who hates the Jews more than necessary exposed a mentality that tempered bias with doses of cynicism and pragmatism. The Jewish minority viewed the Bethlen period as an era of relief, a peaceful decade following the brutalities of the White Terror. In the 1930's the more militant Szegedists gained the upper hand and the consequences were inevitably harsh for the Jews.

The Jewish question, freely discussed in Parliament as in the Press, enabled opponents of the regime to agitate and to challenge the legitimacy of the system. Demands for anti-Semitic action served as a generally understood code-word for the dismantling of the existing system and substituting a radically reorganized Hungarian society. Supporters of the New Order indicted the anti-Semitic Horthy regime for not taking drastic action against the Jews. Radical anti-Semitism, therefore, was not only an attack on the Jews, but also on the regime itself. The government tried to outflank the opposition by becoming more militant on the Jewish question. The First Jewish Law passed in 1938 and the Second Jewish Law, enacted a year later, attempted to undercut the growing strength of the Radical-Right opposition. These anti-Jewish measures were denounced as inadequate by political leaders seeking power. Former Premier Béla Imrédy accused the government of not being genuinely anti-Semitic, at the very time anti-Jewish laws were promulgated by it. Ferenc Szálasi and the Arrow Cross movement spotlighted the cordial relationships that continued to exist between leading members of the regime, including the Regent, and Jewish capitalists.

The absence of a radical mass movement of the Left channeled the revolutionary impulses of the lower classes toward extremist right-wing parties, where the call for a radical overhaul of Hungarian society was expressed in politically and legally acceptable anti-Semitic terminology. The Arrow Cross, a violently anti-Semitic party, received massive support from the working classes. Its fanatical anti-Semitic slogans attracted the disenfranchised and the oppressed. In the 1939 election, despite an electoral system that was rigged against it, it gained 31 parliamentary seats. The Party did particularly well in industrial centers – in "red" Csepel for example. Indeed "The Arrow Cross performed a function that the socialists were unable to fulfil."[8]

The identification of Jews with the dissemination of communist propaganda

Anti-communism was an ideological mainstay of the Horthy period. Hatred and fear of communism was the catalyst that produced the counter-revolutionary Szeged movement. The anti-communism of the regime, unlike so many of the other postures periodically embraced, had a pure and pristine quality. The shortlived Soviet that pre-dated its coming to power, as well as the looming shadow of the Soviet Union, combined to produce a rigid brand of political intolerance. The Communist Party was driven underground, vigorously and successfully persecuted. Its leadership was either imprisoned or driven into exile. The Party was never able to establish a viable internal apparatus. Its membership in December of 1929 was down to 1,000.[9] The large majority of the population genuinely endorsed this crusading anti-Bolshevism.

The event which imprinted the idea that there was a connection between Jews and communists into the Hungarian mentality was the organization of the Hungarian Soviet in 1919. Jews played a very active role in the communist dictatorship.[10] As a group they made up a very small portion of the Jewish community, and they were all secularized, assimilated and Magyarized, but in the eyes of their opponents they were, first and foremost, Jews. The leader of the Soviet was Béla Kun, a Jew. The terror campaign against the opponents of the Revolution was conducted by Tibor Szamuely, a Jew. The Commissar of War and the organizer of the Red Army was Vilmos Böhm, a Jew. Most of the political commissars in the army and most of the judges and prosecutors of the revolutionary courts were Jewish. Leading roles were played by such future communist (and Jewish) luminaries as Mátyás Rákosi, the post World War II dictator, who served as Deputy Commissar of Commerce, György Lukács, Deputy Commissar of Public Education and József Révai, who was on the staff of the *Vörös Újság*, the communist newspaper.

The population at large was receptive to a campaign that condemned the entire Jewish community as sympathetic to communism. The spectre of Judeo-Bolshevism, a popular theme in many countries in the turbulent postwar years, was also raised in Hungary. The White Terror was directed against Jews in general, and most of the victims had nothing to do with the Soviet government. Organizations like the Awakening Magyars (*Ébredő Magyarok*) identified themselves as the champions of Hungarian nationalism in the face of Jewish promoted internationalist communism.

Horthy's anti-Semitism was also shaped by the Kun episode. In the safety of his asylum in authoritarian Portugal, he described his reaction to the communist interlude:

> The atrocities of the Bolsheviks filled the land with horror. The Jews who had long been settled among us were the first to condemn the crimes of their co-religionists, in whose hands the new regime almost exclusively rested.[11]

The Regent was less circumspect in a letter to Hitler written in July of 1940. He wrote "...when all decent men were on the front, the Jews engineered a revolution here and made Bolshevism."[12]

The preponderance of Jewish capital in the economic life of the nation

In the interwar period Hungary was still a predominantly agricultural society, and in the absence of any meaningful land reform the economy had a semi-feudal character with large landholdings controlled by a few noble families, while at the same time there were over one million landless peasants. Industry was developed and concentrated in a few areas, primarily in and around Budapest. The middle class was proportionately small and it included, in addition to the industrial bourgeoisie, the more traditional categories of merchants, professionals and civil servants.

Jews made up a large portion of the middle class. The Jewish community, for historic reasons, was more urbanized than the population at large.

In a country where 2/3 of the population was still rural, the majority of the Jews (56%) resided in Budapest and in the ten major cities.[13]

The Treaty of Trianon crippled the economic order. Hungarian manufacturing establishments were deprived of their markets. Hungarian refugees in large numbers fled the successor states. They were generally members of the former ruling circles, property owners, Imperial bureaucrats without an Empire to administer, army officers, teachers and politicians. They played a prominent role in the counterrevolution and were a major pillar of support of the Horthy regime. And now they demanded their rewards, seeking "respectable" and salaried positions in a shrunken, crisis-plagued economy oversaturated with practicing professionals, potential civil servants and people "with an education." The competition was brutal, there were simply not enough "*úri*" (gentlemanly) positions available to satisfy the expectations. The entrenched Jewish middle class stood in the way of the native bourgeoisie. Anti-Semitism was the outcome of this keen economic rivalry. The Christian Party, supported by the politically moderate Hungarian middle class, and quite powerful in Budapest, generally followed an anti-Semitic orientation that was akin to the anti-Semitism of more right-wing elements.

Hungarian-Jewish economic rivalry was made even more acute by the decision of large numbers of the "Swabians", Hungary's German minority, to Magyarize their names and emphasize the Christian nature of the struggle against the Jews. Public opinion was mobilized against the apparent Jewish domination of the economy.

The statistics of the period confirm the disproportionate role played by Jews in some sectors of the economy. At the same time, Jews were strongly underrepresented in a number of occupational categories where non-Jews were proportionately over-represented.[14] The statistical table reproduced below was slightly edited to eliminate some occupational categories and to include only three denominations. Roman Catholics, Evangelical Christians and Jews numbered 6,612,735 out of a total population of 8,688,319. The picture presented is not altered, however, by the abridgment.

OCCUPATIONAL CATEGORIES ACCORDING TO RELIGION IN 1930[15]

Category	Roman-Catholic	Evangelical	Israelite
Agriculture	2,895,199	299,999	12,976
Industry	1,304,474	107,076	143,687
Commerce & Credit	196,330	19,415	194,211
Military	50,054	4,087	236
Laborer	82,200	8,868	1,718
Domestics	136,890	11,821	2,012
Total Population	5,634,003	534,165	444,567

Roman Catholics formed the largest group in Hungary, approximately 2/3 of the entire population. Evangelical Christians (Lutherans) and Jews were roughly of the same number, and therefore an easy comparison is in order. (Calvinists, the second largest denomination, are not cited.) Note the slight presence of Jews in agriculture, the primary occupation in Hungary, and in the categories of laborers and domestics, the lowest rungs of the socio-economic order. Jews were (rigidly and arbitrarily) excluded by governmental fiats from military service. The number of Jews in commerce and credit, on the other hand, was spectacularly greater than their percentage in the total population would suggest. This fact enraged the Hungarian population, for it underscored the intolerable notion that Jews controlled the country.

Jewish industrialists played a dominant role in the developing industrial life of the nation. The statistical table below vividly illustrates this point. (Numerically small denominations, like the Greek Catholics, are not included in the chart, and therefore only 97% of the population is accounted for.

INDUSTRIAL CORPORATIONS IN 1935[16]

Position	Roman-Catholic (64.9%)		Reformed (20.9%)	
Owner or Renter	673	33.7%	150	7.6%
Director	789	36.6%	247	11.4%
Technical functionaries	2,517	54.5%	532	11.5%
Commercial functionaries	8,244	45.9%	1,497	8.4%

Position	Evangelical (6.1%)		Israelite (5.1%)	
Owner or Renter	146	7.4%	1,008	50.9%
Director	197	9.1%	900	41.6%
Technical functionaries	479	10.4%	1,021	22.1%
Commercial functionaries	1,115	6.2%	6,877	38.3%

The numbers in parentheses indicate the percentage of the total population. The low numbers certainly underline the weak development of Hungarian industry. In the most important category of Owner or Renter, Jews, but 5% of the population, were an absolute majority. It is important to bear in mind that these numbers speak of Jews from the religious point of view. It will be the contribution of the late 1930's in Hungary's history to introduce the Nazi concept of the racial Jew. A very significant portion of the non-Jewish capitalist class – and in the absence of specific statistics it is necessary to generalize – consisted of converted Jews. Extreme assimilation, including the abandonment of the Jewish faith, was most popular among the most successful and wealthiest segment of the community. Subsequently, to anti-Semites of the Nazi era the baptismal rite made no difference.

In Budapest 38.2% of the two-story buildings, 47.2% of the three-story and 57.5% of six or more story structures were owned by Jews.[17] Even in agriculture where Jews, as indicated above, were underrepresented, Jewish capital made significant inroads. 9.7% of all estates classified as "large" were controlled by Jews.[18] The great Jewish historian of the Holocaust, Jenő Lévai, speculated that about 20-25% of the total wealth of the country was controlled by Jews.[19] There was also great poverty in the Jewish community, a factor that did not lessen a hatred partially produced by the great wealth of some Jews.

The fear that the Jewish population was growing too rapidly and posed a threat to the character and identity of the nation

Anti-Semitism, indeed and all types of racial and ethnic intolerance pays special attention to the numbers game. There is always concern and anxiety, sometimes articulated and oftern simmering just beneath the surface, that the host population may be engulfed by a rapidly growing minority, and the character of the nation may be distorted, damaged, diluted or even destroyed. The feeling is often irrational – the root cause, perhaps, of its existence – because the evidence contradicts it. In Hungary, after World War I, the Jewish population was actually shrinking not only in terms of percentage but also in absolute numbers. The statistical table reproduced below clearly dispels the popular myth that Jewish growth threatened the Hungarian character of Hungary.

RELIGIONS IN HUNGARY[20]

Religion	1920		1930	
Roman-Catholic	5,105,375	(63.9%)	5,643,003	(64.9%)
Greek-Catholic	175,655	(2.2%)	201,093	(2.3%)
Reformed	1,671,052	(21.0%)	1,813,162	(20.9%)
Evangelical	497,126	(6.2%)	534,165	(6.1%)
Greek-Eastern	50,918	(0.6%)	39,839	(0.5%)
Israelite	473,355	(5.9%)	444,567	(5.1%)
Others	16,721	(0.2%)	21,490	(0.2%)

It is noteworthy that in a ten-year period, while every other group, with the exception of the small Greek-Eastern denomination, grew, the Jewish population decreased by about 30,000.

After 1938 Hungary, as an ally of Germany, territorially profited from both the Western policy appeasement and the subsequent establishment of German hegemony in East Central Europe. Some of the lost territories were regained. The dismemberment of Czechoslovakia returned the Hungarian inhabited portion of Slovakia, referrred to as Upper Hungary, and Ruthenia. Hungary also capitalized on the destruction of Yugoslavia and the Bácska region was reincorporated. Diplomatic support from Berlin compelled Romania to cede about half of Transylvania back to Hungary. These additions significantly enlarged the total as well as the Jewish population. In 1942 there were 725,007 Jews in Hungary, 4.9% of the population, a slight further proportional decrease.[21]

In the late 1930's and 40's anti-Semitic agitation was abetted by the "visibility" of the Jewish population. In Eastern Hungary and even more so in the "new territories," Jews tended to be more attached to Orthodox traditions. There were a great many Hasidic sects. The general appearance and lifestyle of these Jews; their Oriental caftans, beards and payes and Yiddish tongue, conspicuously set them apart from the rest of the population (including most of the Jews of Trianon Hungary). There was no fear of economic domination by these Jews, but, there seemed to be so many of them.[22] These Jews, with their large families, concentrated in Ruthenia and some parts of Transylvania, were seen as a direct and physical challenge to the Hungarian nation. In the counties of Bereg, Máramaros and Ugocsa they made up 17.8%, 18.4% and 13.3% of the population.

The "visibility" of Jews was further accentuated by their presence, in disproportionately large numbers, in the urban centers. This was a historic necessity reinforced by the logic of contemporary economics. It was a world-wide phenomenon, reflected in all the cities of Hungary. The Hungarian Nazi movements, including the Arrow Cross, by far the most popular, were primarily supported by the radicalized discontented lower classes of the big cities, where the large Jewish communities served as ready-made ammunition for the propaganda canons of anti-Semitic agitators.

JEWS IN LARGE CITIES[23]

City	Region	Jewish Population	% of Total Population
Budapest	Trianon-Hungary	184,453	15.8%
Miskolc	Trianon-Hungary	10,428	13.5%
Debrecen	Trianon-Hungary	9,142	7.3%
Kassa	Upper-Hungary	10,079	15.0%
Nagyvárad	Transylvania	21,333	22.9%
Szatmárnémeti	Transylvania	12,960	24.9%
Kolozsvár	Transylvania	16,763	15.1%
Ujvidék	Southern-Hungary	3,621	5.9%
Ungvár	Ruthenia	9,576	27.2%

Right-wing publicists inflated these figures. They attacked the reliability of the official statistics and proclaimed that there were far more Jews in Hungary than the actual number recorded by the census takers. It was also emphasized by them that there were many Jews who concealed their true identity and through intermarriage, conversion or the changing of family names, infiltrated into the Hungarian nation without surrendering the characteristics of their race, or that peculiar loyalty and mentality which sets Jews apart from their neighbors. It was declared that these crypto-Jews posed an even greater threat than their more readily identifiable brethren. A typical illustration of this mentality was a pamphlet published by the Arrow Cross Party that differentiated between the racial and the religious Jew, and thus was able to fortify the claim that the Jews were indeed a real and numerical menace to the nation. It is difficult to establish how the numbers were arrived at. However, it is illuminating to note that the allegations were made not only for Hungary, but for other European states as well.

JEWS IN EUROPE[24]

State	Racial Jews	Religious Jews
Hungary	1,300,000	500,000
Romania	3,200,000	1,000,000
Poland	6,100,000	3,500,000
England	1,200,000	300,000
France	2,900,000	725,000

Such allegations reflect the Hungarian racists' notion that anti-Semitism was a defensive measure whose aim was to preserve the Hungarian character of Hungary.

The belief that the Jews were an alien and unassimilable minority

Extreme nationalism was a basic component of the philosophy of the Horthy regime. Generations of schoolchildren were indoctrinated with the injustices of Trianon. Irredentism was the primary foreign policy objective of the government. In the charged emotional atmosphere of the era, all minorities would encounter difficulties. In addition, Hungarians were traditionally very conscious of the fact that they were a small nation, unique and unrelated to the neighboring ethnic groups. The doctrine of integral nationalism was translated into official policies that accentuated the Hungarian character of Hungary. Swabians, despite the presence of a powerful patron-state, were repeatedly victimized by a xenophobic regime.[25] The German minority had to wage an incessant struggle to protect its mother-tongue, school-system and cultural autonomy. Undoubtedly, Hungarian pride suffered in the interwar years as a result of the anti-Hungarian policies pursued by the dominant nationalities of the successor states, former victims of Hungarian intolerance themselves, against their large Hungarian minorities. However, Budapest could not retaliate. The Slovaks, Romanians, Croats and Serbians constituted only 2.4% of Hungary's population.

Hungarian nationalism was very much influenced by the racist theorizing, in vogue after World War I. It employed racist terminology and slogans. The Szeged movement was affiliated with race-protecting leagues. Racists occupied high positions in the government.

Jews were obvious targets and victims of this spirit and policy. It was possible for some of the minorities, like the Germans, to be accepted into the Hungarian nation if certain prerequisites, like family name, knowledge of the Hungarian language, were met.[26] However, Jews always remained Jews. They were perpetual outsiders, an alien minority; they could never become Hungarians. This sentiment was embraced not just by the apostles of marginal hate-groups, nor was it limited only to the leading spokesmen of the reactionary regime – it appealed to many liberal-thinking Hungarians as well. Jews were perceived as a separate nation within the body-politic of the Hungarian nation. They had a different mentality and different characteristics; they posed a permanent danger. In practical terms they were blamed for all the problems and ills of Hungary. On June 6, 1939, Zoltán Meskó, an Arrow Cross deputy, spoke on the floor of Parliament about a housing proposal. In his address he stated that "If we exterpate these [unmistaken reference to Jews] from the Hungarian society, then we will not have Social Democracy, or this party or that party; what we will have will be a nation of honest Christian Hungarians."[27]

People in responsible positions echoed, in a more cultured manner, this same sentiment. Premier Imrédy in a celebrated speech in the Upper House on May 20, 1938, spoke about the Jews.

> It is undeniable that among the Jews, this racial mentality presents itself rather sharply; therefore the assimilation of Jews is

> more difficult than that of other elements... The other side of the problem is the question of mentality... there slowly emerged and in Budapest especially took hold a mentality which in its perception of public, communal and moral problems does not always agree, indeed it frequently sharply differs from, with that Hungarian spirituality (mentality), which we inherited from our forbears and which we want to transmit to our descendants.[28]

It was particularly galling that this "different mentality" was so well entrenched in the cultural and intellectual life of the nation. Jews were very numerous among Hungary's intelligentsia. In 1930 49.2% of lawyers, 34.4% of doctors, 45.1% of private chemists, 31.7% of journalists, 28.9% of musicians, 24.7% of scholars and writers and 24.1% of all actors were Jewish.[29] These were the numbers after a decade of subtable and direct pressures by the regime on Jewish professionals. In 1930, while practically half of all jurists were Jews, those in governmental service, as judges, prosecutors, administrators, etc., were only 2% Jewish.[30] In the civil service Jewish bureaucrats constituted an insignificant 1.7% of the total number.[31] These "achievements" were not sufficient. Hungarian professionals continued to press for additional measures to ensure the further erosion of the Jewish role in these middle-class occupational categories.

Populist writers, generally of a leftist and reformist orientation, also picked up the theme of the endangerment of Hungarian culture by foreign influence. The Village Explorers (*Falukutatók*) not only revealed the shocking conditions of the Hungarian rural proletariat, the purest essence of the nation, but in their writings they mounted an offensive against the establishment that was responsible for the callous indifference exhibited toward Hungarians and Hungarian values. It was charged that the literary establishment was too attached to a non-Hungarian ethos. The dominant periodical and arbitrator of literary tastes was the *Nyugat* (West), a publication that transmitted Western ideals. The element of anti-Semitism was only implicit. By and large, these Hungarian narodniks were not specifically against Jews, but in their defense of Hungarian culture they identified the Jewish influence as another non-Hungarian factor that had to be eliminated. *Nyugat* for instance, was supported by Jewish financial interests and many of its contributors were Jewish writers.[32]

The conviction that anti-Jewish acts at home will earn diplomatic support for foreign policy objectives

The primary objective of Hungarian foreign policy, as stated above, was irredentism. To regain the lost territories, Hungary gradually drifted into the orbit of Nazi Germany, another revisionist Power. There were many sharp differences between the totalitarianism of the Third Reich and the authoritarianism of the Horthy regime. However, in order to enlist German support for Hungarian national objectives, the Hungarian government was prepared to ape the German system. There was an element of opportunism in this attitude. Berlin was always suspicious of the ideological purity of the Horthy clique. German-Hungarian relations were made even more complex by the presence, within and on the fringes of the Hungarian regime, of elements that were prepared to identify completely with the Nazi doctrine and objectives. (The Szeged militantas constituted one such group).

It was the expectation of Germany that Hungary, as a faithful ally, would adopt the anti-Semitism and specifically anti-Jewish measures of the Reich. At the same time, there was concern in Budapest that non-compliance would have negative consequences for Hungary's territorial ambitions. Romania, Slovakia and Croatia were implementing anti-Jewish measures on the Nazi model; Hungary could not afford to do otherwise. The decision to enact the First Jewish Law was made to assure German support in the negotiations over the partition of Czechoslovakia.[33] The Third Jewish Law, passed on August 8, 1941, when Hungary, as an ally of Germany had already declared war on the Soviet Union, was a race-protecting measure that received its inspiration from the Nuremberg Laws. With the cooperation of native Nazis, overwhelming pressure was applied by Germany on the Hungarian government to pursue a more and more radical anti-Jewish policy. The anti-Semitism of the Horthy regime was not the anti-Semitism of Adolf Hitler. In the beginning Hungary was prepared to sacrifice the rights and well-being of her Jews to accomplish foreign policy objectives, but as the war progressed and the benefits of being a German ally diminished, her attitude changed. The Horthy regime, especially during the tenure of Premier Miklós Kállay (March, 1942-March, 1944), effectively resisted participation in the Final solution.[34] The Jews of Budapest escaped deportation to the death camps because of the personal protection extended by the Regent. The mass murder of Hungarian Jewry would take place only after German military occupation of the country.

The anti-Semitism of Horthy-Hungary was a consistent policy. It was an integral part of the ideology of the regime. There were acts of great brutality (The White Terror, the Kamenec-Podolsk massacre of July, 1941), as well as periods of relaxation (1920s), and periods of tension (1930s), but there was always a preoccupation with the "Jewish question." Trianon Hungary was not always a bad place for the Jews, and Jews survived there longer than in Poland, Slovakia or even the Netherlands. The mass destruction of the Jews of Hungary was promoted, supervised and executed by officials of Nazi Germany, but Hungarian anti-Semitism shares in the moral responsibility for the Holocaust.

Notes

1. See Hugh Seton-Watson, *Eastern Europe Between the Wars 1918-1941* (New York, 1967), p. 291.
2. Denominations received official classification. The highest level was that of a "received religion," a less favorable one was that of a "recognized religion," with the right to exercise a degree of self-government, and the lowest level was that of a "non-recognized confession," denominations under police supervision.
3. A unique phenomenon among the Jews of Eastern Europe was the inability of most Magyar Jews, including the religiously observant, to speak Yiddish. See Ivan Sanders, "Tétova vonzalmak" [Tentative Affinities] in *Új Látóhatár* (5 Munich, 1975), p. 441.
4. For an illuminating dicourse on the subject, see George Barany, "Magyar Jew or Jewish Magyar? Reflections on the Question of Assimilation" in Béla Vágó and George L. Mosse, eds., *Jews and Non-Jews in Eastern Europe 1918-1945* (New York, 1974).
5. C. A. Macartney, *October Fifteenth* (Edinburgh, 1956), p. 20.
6. For such an interpretation see Nicholas M. Nagy-Talavera, *The Green Shirts and the Others* (Stanford, 1970).
7. For a Marxist treatment of the organization see Rudolfné Dosa, *A Move. Egy jellegzetes magyar fasiszta szervezet 1918-1944* [The MOVE. A Characteristic Magyar Fascist Organization 1918-1944] (Budapest, 1972).

8. István Deák, "Hungary" in H. Rogger and E. Weber eds, *The European Right* (Berkely, 1965) p. 397.
9. Benett Kovrig, *Communism in Hungary. From Kun to Kádár* appendix 2 (Stanford, 1979).
10. Rudolf L. Tőkés, *Béla Kun and the Hungarian Soviet Republic* (Stanford, 1967), p. 193.
11. Nicholas Horthy, *Memoirs* (New York, 1957), p. 98.
12. Nicholas Horthy, *The Confidential Papers of Admiral Horthy* ed. M. Szinai and L. Szűcs (Budapest, 1965), p. 131.
13. Iván T. Berend and György Ránki, "A magyar társadalom a két világháború között" [Magyar Society Between the Two World Wars], *Új Irás* 10 (1973), p. 100.
14. There is a striking similarity between the roles played by Jews in Hungary and the contemporary roles of Chinese in many Far Eastern countries.
15. *Hungarian Statistical Yearbook* (1935), p. 18.
16. *Ibid.*, p. 136.
17. Alajos Kovács, *A Csonkamagyarországi zsidóság a statisztika tükrében* [The Jews of Dismembered Hungary in a Statistical Mirror] (Budapest, 1938), p. 48.
18. *Ibid.*, pp. 13-L1.
19. Eugene Lévai, *Black Book on the Martyrdom of Hungarian Jewry.* Edited by Lawrence P. Davis (Zurich, 1948), p. 37.
20. *Hungarian Statistical Yearbook* (1939), p. 18.
21. *Hungarian Statistical Yearbook* (1942), pp. 14-17.
22. A very skeptical Mark Twain reacted to the official census figures in the United States by writing the following disclaimer in the September 1899 issue of *Harper's Magazine* under the title "Concerning th Jews"; "Look at the city of New York; and look at Boston, and Philadelphia ... how your race swarms in those places!" p. 533.
23. *Hungarian Statistical Yearbook* (1942), pp. 16-17.
24. Mátyás Matolcsi (comp.), *A Zsidók útja* [The Way of the Jews] (Budapest, 1943), p. 11.
25. For a detailed treatment of the subject see Thomas Spira, *German-Hungarian Relations and the Swabian Problem from Károlyi to Gömbös 1919-1936* (New York, 1977).
26. Gömbös was of German background and Szálasi's non-Magyar ancestry included Armenians. However, when it was revealed, by po-

litical opponents, that Imrédy had some Jewish ancestry, he was forced out of office.
27. Hungary. Parliament, Proceedings, I., p. 195.
28. Béla Imrédy, *Múlt és Jövő határán* [On the Boundary Between Past and Future] (Budapest, 1938), p. 36.
29. Kovács, *op.cit.*, pp. 18-19.
30. Berend and Ránki, *op.cit.*, p. 100.
31. *Ibid.*
32. I am indebted to my good friend Ivan Sanders for his helpful comments on the village explorers.
33. C. A. Macartney "Hungarian Foreign Policy During the Interwar Period, With Special Reference to the Jewish Question" in *Jews and Non-Jews in Eastern Europe 1918-1945* (New York, 1974), p. 134.
34. There is extensive primary and secondary literature on this sensitive subject. Helpful sources would include the captured documents of the German Foreign Office, Randolph L. Braham (comp.), *The Destruction of Hungarian Jewry. A Documentary Account,* Jenő Lévai, ed., *Eichman in Hungary. Documents,* the private papers and memoirs, generally self-serving but always revealing of the decision-makers, like Nicholas Kállay, Hungarian Premier.

István I. Mócsy

Partition of Hungary and the Origins of the Refugee Problem

The refugee problem is more than a historical accident, more than a humanitarian issue. In fact, if Heinrich Böll, the German Nobel laureate is correct, the refugee phenomenon is symptomatic of our age. He has written: "When the time comes to seek a name for our century, it will probably be called the Century of Expellees and Prisoners. When people begin trying to add up the worldwide total of these unfortunate people, they will arrive at a number of displaced human beings big enough to populate entire continents."[1] As all such characterizations of an epoch, this is an overstatement. Nevertheless, it does focus attention on a new phenomenon: the systematic dislocation and persecution of civilians in modern states. Not that displacement of civilians is in itself new - in the past peasants, for example, regularly fled from the path of approaching armies; religious persecutions often forced the flight of sizable groups of religous dissenters. But the disturbing regularity of population displacement, the sheer magnitude of the refugee problem, suggests that massive uprooting of civilians is no longer only the occasional and accidental by-product of military or political struggles, but an integral part of the modern system of conflict-resolution. The problem seems to arise either from the contradictory principles upon which modern nation-states are established, or form irreconcilable ideological divisions which often accompany social change. In the first case, the principle of national self-determination may contradict the rights of national minorities, while in the second, the right of the sovereign state to demand ideological conformity from its citizens comes into conflict with the basic rights of individuals.

The subjects of this essay is one such group: the Hungarian refugees who, after 1918, fled or were expelled to Hungary from areas awarded in the Treaty of Trianon to the successor states of Czechoslovakia, Romania and Yugoslavia. These refugees fell victim to the national as well as ideological intolerance of the new regimes. As victims of persecutions, the refugees in Hungary became symbols of the injustices of the Treaty of Trianon; and as a group radicalized by their own misfortunes, they left their mark on Hungary's history as supporters, and often leaders, of the new Radical Right.

The disintegration of the Austro-Hungarian Empire was completed by a two-pronged revolution – a social revolution in Hungary, which in the minority areas was quickly transformed into a national revolution. In the October 1918 revolution the moderate left came to power, the genuine liberals: the Bourgeois Radicals and the Social Democrats. During the previous decades the leaders of these groups had been consistent opponents of Hungarian supremacy, and offered a solution to the minority question based on principles of complete equality and democracy; they hoped to achieve their goals through fundamental economic and social reforms. A few years earlier even a more modest program of reform would have satisfied the national minorities, but conservative Hungarian leaders of the time, defending the political and social predominance of the nobility within the Hungarian nation-state, ruled out democratic reforms. The main reason for conservative opposition was a fear that granting political equality to the minorities would unleash a social and economic revolution which would abolish both the Hungarian character of the state and the dominant role of the traditional ruling classes.[2]

In November 1918, however, a policy of reconciliation of all the nationalities of Hungary through prudent political and economic reforms was no longer viable. The same forces which radicalized the Hungarian population, brought to power the moderate left and made meaningful reforms possible, also radicalized the minorities and created for them a more appealing alternative.

The First World War brought deprivations and massive suffering to both the military and civilians, regardless of nationality.[3] This, combined with repressive measures directed against some of the minorities,[4] completed the alienation of a large segment of the non-Hungarian population and accelerated the growth of national consciousness and resistance. The time favored virulent nationalism and national confrontation, and the fate of the country ceased to depend upon the policies of the Hungarian government. The initiative passed to the victorious Western Powers and to their East Central European allies and, to a lesser degree, to some of the well-placed representatives of the national minorities. During the war the Allies committed themselves to certain territorial changes and to a set of general principles that was to be followed during a post-war reorganization of East Central Europe, though this is not to assert that the Great Powers possessed a coherent plan for the region. Short range objectives, the pressures of immediate events, as well as concessions forced by the successor states were just as influential in shaping the final settlement as the designs of the Great Powers. On one principle the Allies and the successor states were in agreement: as the end of the war approached, both became determined to satisfy the national ambitions of the former minorities of the Austro-Hungarian Empire, not through mere reform, but through a recognition of the right of minorities to form independent nation-states.[5] The failure to realize the non-viability of the idea of nation-states in a multi-national region led to a reversal of the previous situation. In the territories detached from Hungary, Hungarian supremacy was replaced by Serbian, Czechoslovak or Romanian supremacy, and the formerly dominant Hungarians became an oppressed national minority, whose right to national self-determination was denied. Just as in 1867-68, the minority issue was to be resolved by means of limited legal guarantees, but once again such attempts were doomed to failure. Not surprisingly, reconciliation between the new majorities and minorities became even less likely than during the Dualist Era.[6]

In 1918-1919 the successor states were little concerned with the establishment of a system that would assure long range cooperation between the small states of the region. They realized that the Western Allies were not in a position to fill the power vacuum left by the defeat of the Central Powers, and seized upon this unique opportunity to guarantee their security through territorial expansion. The goals of the successor states were simple: they wished to bring under their control the territories sought immediately and to secure maximum economic and military advantage for themselves, even if in the process a substantial number of presumably hostile minorities had to be incorporated in their states. Without awaiting the final decision of the Paris Peace Conference the successor states, supported partially by the Great Powers, moved to occupy the demanded territories. Between November 1918 and March 1919 most of these areas were indeed brought under their jurisdiction. At first, Hungarian resistance was only sporadic. But after the establishment of the Hungarian Soviet Republic in March 1919, and until its defeat in August of that year, further encroachment on Hungarian territories was forcefully opposed.[7]

The flight of the Hungarian population from the minority areas paralleled the changing fortunes of their respective regions. Some fled even before the arrival of the occupation forces, while others decided to leave only after repressive measures directed against the Hungarian minority and economic and administrative changes introduced by the new governments directly affected their lives, and made their continued existence in the successor states precarious or impossible. In all, an estimated 426,000 individuals left the lost territories between 1918 and 1924. Of these, the National Refugee Office (*Országos Menekültügyi Hivatal* or *OMH*) registered about 350,000 individuals. Their distribution according to the country of origin was as follows:

TABLE I

Number of Refugees
From Territories Ceded to *OMH* Figures Estimated Actual Numbers

Czechoslovakia	106,841	147,000
Romania	197,035	222,000
Yugoslavia	44,903	55,000
Austria	1,221	2,000
Total	350,000	426,000

As a result of the flight of the refugees, the population of Trianon Hungary increased by about 5.3 percent, while the size of the Hungarian population in the successor states was reduced: by 13.7 percent in Czechoslovakia, by 13.4 percent in Romania, and by 9.5 percent in Yugoslavia.[9] According to the *OMH*, the flow of refugees was the heaviest in the last two months of 1918, when about 58,000 arrived in Hungary, and continued at a high rate during the early months of 1919. After a temporary slowdown in refugee arrivals during the four-month existence of the Soviet Republic, the tempo once again picked up and began to decline only during 1921. (Table II.)

TABLE II

Year	Number of Refugees	Year	Number of Refugees
1918	58,784	1922	21,242
1919	110,573	1923	9,041
1920	121,930	1924	2,307
1921	26,123		

In general, the refugees represented the former social and political elite of the lost territories, the past beneficiaries of Hungarian hegemony in the old minority areas of the country. Their livelihood was tied to the continued existence of the Hungarian nation-state, and with its break-up they lost both their political power and economic footing. The largest single group among the refugees were the former state and county officials: judges, prosecutors, court clerks, village notaries, police officers and gendarmes, state pensioners, teachers and professors, officials and workers of the state railroad and other state enterprises. The second largest group consisted of the employees of privately owned Hungarian banks, commercial or industrial enterprises and small business owners or craftsmen. A sizable group of gentry and aristocratic landowners also left the successor states. Though numerically inferior to the previous groups, this third group was the politically most active and powerful. While the ranks of the Hungarian upper and middle classes were seriously depleted in the lost territories, relatively few peasants chose to leave their homelands. Those who did left mainly for practical economic reasons, in most cases when they found that the new frontiers separated them from their holdings.

Out of the 350,000 registered refugees, 160,271 were housewives and other dependents; 86,375 were pupils or university students. The occupation of the remaining 103,254 refugees fit in the following categories:[11]

TABLE III

Occupational Group	Number in Group	Percentage of Total
Public Employees	44,253	42.9%
Commerce and Industry	35,553	34.4%
Landowners	10,376	10.0%
Gentlemen	8,323	8.1%
Professionals	621	0.6%
Other	4,128	4.0%
Total:	103,254	100.0%

To give up ancestral estates, to leave homelands rich in cultural and historical traditions and memories is always painful. The decision to depart was made by many Hungarians only after all hopes for a reversal of Hungarian fortunes dimmed, or if economic necessity made it unavoidable. We can identify four causes which at various times influenced individuals of families to leave the old minority areas. First, the fear of physical violence by the occupation armies, or of retribution by the local population for past grievances, real or imagined; second, an ardent Hungarian nationalism which led many people to reject a life under foreign domination; third, loss of economic security; and finally, the inability of many to accept a loss of social status.

For some of the Hungarian officials the terror began with the collapse of the Austro-Hungarian Empire. The disintegration of the armies at the front paralleled the lost of control of population within Hungary. By September 1918 an estimated 400,000 men deserted from the Army[12] and during the last month of the war the pace of desertions accelerated. From the approximately 2.1 million Austro-Hungarian soldiers taken prisoner of war in Russia by the fall of 1918, about 725,000 soldiers were allowed to return. Of these about 152,000 were Hungarian, 94,000 Romanian, 80,000 Croatian, 44,000 Slovakian and 4,000 Serbian.[13] From the fronts soldiers streamed home in great disarray, often in rags and without food supplies. By the end of November 1918 about 700,000 soldiers from Hungary were demobilized and by the end of December their number grew to 1,200,000.[14] Upon hearing the news of the end of the war, the "Green Companies", made up of thousands of army deserters, emerged from their mountain hiding places and joined hands with the returning soldiers, unemployed former prisoners of war and rebellious peasants, and plundered the countryside. Count Tivadar Batthyány, the Hungarian Minister of Interior wrote: "A veritable flood of complaints poured in from every direction that armed groups, small and large, as well as bands of returning soldiers were causing havoc, seizing property, robbing, using force, and even committing murders."[15] In Transylvania returning soldiers, peasants and the hastily formed Romanian National Guards seized entire districts. In every region of the country peasants, both Hungarian and non-Hungarian, attacked, looted and in some cases, burnt down the châteaux and manor houses of the nobility, in the process killing or severely beating some of the overseers who tried in vain to protect their masters' properties. Occasionally landless peasants, fired by the news of an impending land reform, began to divide the nobles' estates among themselves.[16] Great estates were assaulted in northern Hungary, Croatia, Transylvania, Transdanubia and on the Hungarian Plain. For example, some of the Transylvanian estates of the Teleki, Haller, Zichy, Kemény, Hirsch and Bethlen families were attacked and ransacked.[17] The same fate befell the Andrássy château at Tiszadob.[18] Not even Mihály Károlyi's estate at

Parádfürdő escaped the rage of the peasants.[19] Though peasant attacks were random and disorganized, their pattern was fairly uniform. Disturbances were begun mostly by radicalized and armed peasant soldiers who won over the support of the local population for attacks on the estates.[20] Many of the peasant soldiers arrived in their native villages ready to settle old scores, or to take revenge upon local officials for abusing their families during their absence. Also, because the landlords were absent or were the first to flee, the hatred of the peasants, especially in the minority areas, was vented upon the remaining lesser officials: village notaries, teachers, gendarmes, and even priests, men, that is, who symbolized to them the authority of the old Hungarian state. Since in the minority areas most of the landlords and officials were Hungarian, the social revolution of the peasants in those regions acquired a national character. The notaries and gendarmes were especially harshly treated. According to Oszkár Jászi, during the first few days of the revolution alone, one third of the notaries were forced to flee.[21] According to another estimate, about one third of notaries fled from Hungarian villages – one half from Slovak-populated areas and about nine-tenths from Romanian regions.[22] In many villages the notaries were beaten to death or shot; in one instance the deceased notary's body was disinterned and dumped into a ditch.[23] In vain did the notaries protest at their December 5th congress that they were "robbed of their property, vilified," and had become the "persecuted martyrs" of the revolution.[24] A main goal of the government was restoration of order, though it was powerless to protect its isolated officials in the villages. Most of the rural gendarmerie stations had to be abandoned and the personnel concentrated in larger towns. On a number of occasions regular military units were called out to restore order. At time aristocrats organized independent armed detachments to recapture their estates and to take bloody revenge on the offending peasants.[25] But repressive measures could not permanently reinstate local officials.

Peasant attacks on estates and officials, as well as reactions to them, were part of a social revolution. This is born out by the fact that Romanian and Serbian national guard units were also active in repressing rebellious peasants. What turned the social revolution into a national one, and at the same time sealed the fate of the Hungarian officials and that of the Hungarian middle classes, was the invasion of the country by the Serbian, Czech and Romanian armies. Following the arrival of occupying forces, arrests, murders, and taking of hostages were frequent. News of these incidents spread rapidly and became amplified as they were passed on.

Rumors of planned bloody revenges that were to follow the arrival of the Serbian, Romanian or Czech armies were often sufficient to cause many officials, landowners, estate managers, and police officials to seek safety in central Hungary. Some of the desperate officials tried to organize the local population into a military force to resist the invaders, but all such attempts in northern Hungary and most in Transylvania ended in failure. The Hungarian peasantry looked upon these efforts with suspicion and remained passive, while in the urban areas, workers and some of the intellectuals were openly hostile to the noble officer recruiters, suspecting, not without justification, that such a force would quickly become a conterrevolutionary army. Moreover, the Hungarian government of Mihály Károlyi, more clearly appreciating the hopeless military position of the country and still clinging to a hope of peaceful, negotiated settlement, discouraged active resistance by the population.[26]

The upper classes and the most exposed champions of Hungarian nationalism mostly left during the chaotic first few months after the armistice. With the establishment of military control by the successor states, overt acts of violence against the Hungarian population subsided, though they by no means ceased completely. Pressure on the remaining Hungarian minority changed in character; persecution and discrimination became more subtle, systematic and selective, and more a consequence of government policies than of popular hatred. The governments of the successor states welcomed, actively encouraged, and at times forced the departure of Hungarian families or individuals, partly to reduce the overall size of the Hungarian minority and thereby to strengthen their claims to the territories seized, and, more importantly, to bring about a change in the social composition of the population in the newly acquired territories. Most of the cities in these areas had Hungarian and German majorities, with the Hungarian element dominating. To fully control the new provinces, the political influence and economic role of the Hungarian middle classes had to be broken and if possible, Hungarians had to be replaced with newly transplanted, loyal Serbians, Romanians, or Czechs. In each of the successor states the prime target of continued persecutions was the gentry-dominated middle class, which was the backbone of authority in the old Hungarian state. It was the politically most conscious, best organized, and therefore most dangerous group, from whose ranks the potential leaders of a national resistance movement could emerge. This class, however, was particularly vulnerable to attacks because of the excessive dependence of its members upon the old Hungarian state.[27] A continued domination of the administrative hierarchy was inconceivable to the leaders of the new states. Technically, according to the terms of the Belgrade Armistice Agreement of 13 November 1918, the contested areas were to remain an integral part of the Hungarian state until the signing of a peace treaty, even though these areas were under military occupation. Accordingly, at first, Hungary was ordered to evacuate only its military forces beyond the line of demarcation, but "Civil Administration" was to "remain in the hands of the [Hungarian] Government." Naturally, the laws of Hungary were to continue to be in force. Similarly, "being indispensable to the maintenance of order ..." the Hungarian police and gendarmerie were to be "retained in the evacuated zone."[28]

The successor states ignored these provisions and severed the occupied regions' ties with Budapest. Elimination of the Hungarian administrative structure and reform of the educational system was completed even before the signing of the Treaty of Trianon. Serbia acted with the greatest efficiency. The first task of most military commanders was to oust the old Hungarian administration. Often this was not necessary, because many of the old officials fled or were already replaced by the spontaneously formed South Slav Councils even before the arrival of the Serbian Army.[29] The purges conducted in Slovakia and Transylvania were less thorough and more drawn out. In Slovakia, a desperate shortage of qualified replacements slowed down the transition. Then too, the greater concentration of Hungarian population, especially in Transylvania where entire counties were solidly Hungarian, made a complete de-Magyarization of the administration impractical. Thus, while the higher posts were taken away from Hungarians, some lower officials were retained. But during various screening procedures many were weeded out as security risks. Others were dismissed on the pretext of reorganization of the administrative structure, or as a result of alleged failure to meet some new standard required of all officials.[30] Such was the language requirement, which made it mandatory for all state officials to learn within a year the new, official Czech/Slovak, Serbian, or Romanian language.[31] Another device was to demand a loyalty oath from all officials, which confronted every Hungarian employee with a difficult choice of conscience as well as with a practical problem.[32] As Hungarian partriots they could not renounce their loyalty to Hungary and as employees of the old Hungarian state many feared the loss of their pensions if such oath was taken. The Károlyi government, recognizing the dilemma of the Hungarian officials, gave its permission to those in the zone of occupation to take, under compulsion, such oaths, and extended a guarantee of a continued payment of salaries to those who refused.[33] This guarantee tended to encourage the flight of the state employees.

One of the most bitter blows to the Hungarian minorities was the de-Magyarization of the educational system in the lost areas. On the other hand, few institutions of old Hungary were as much in need of reform as its school system. To the old subject nationalities of Hungary, the most visible sign of their second class status and of their oppression was the disparity between the numbers and quality of the Hungarian and non-Hungarian schools.[34] The reform of the educational system, therefore, was high on the agenda of every one of the successor states. In practice, however, the Hungarian population's loss of schools did not always represent a gain for the old minorities. In Yugoslavia, the Hungarian educational system was abolished during 1919, and over two-thirds of the more than 1,800 Hungarian teachers were dismissed; the Hungarian schools were reduced to one-sixth of their former capacity.[35] In Czechoslovakia the number of Hungarian schools was reduced from nearly 4,000 to less than 700, and nearly three-fourths of the Hungarian teachers lost their jobs.[36] Out of about 1,600 state-operated schools of Transylvania, only 562 were allowed to retain Hungarian as language of instruction.[37] One result of this de-Magyarization of the educational institutions in the successor states was that over two-thirds of the dismissed teachers, some 8,870, left or were expelled from their homelands by 1920.[38] Deprived of educational opportunities for their children, many Hungarian families, especially those of middle class origins, fled or at least sent their children to Hungary to be educated.

Thus, even before the decision of the Western Powers sealed the fate of Hungary and of the Hungarian population of the occupied areas, the successor states, through forced de-Magyarization of the administrative and educational institutions, through seizures of Hungarian, mostly noble, estates, as well as through outright expulsions, achieved a dramatic reduction in the size of the remaining Hungarian minorities. Moreover, the political and economic power of the Hungarian minorities was broken and their social and cultural leadership destroyed. The Hungarian minorities became a socially more homogeneous, overwhelmingly agricultural group, which could be more easily controlled and managed.

The last illusory hope of the Hungarians was a reprieve from the Great Powers during the long delayed peace negotiations. But the ratification of the Treaty of Trianon in June 1920 merely sanctioned the dismemberment of Hungary and the discriminatory and repressive policies of the successor states. At the Peace Conference the Western Powers rejected every request of the Hungarian delegation for substantive change in the draft treaty.[39] Hungary had to accept the position that in her case, because she was a defeated state, historical rights, economic needs, or ethnic principles did not apply. The collective right to national self-determination of the Hungarian majorities in some of the disputed areas, the right to determine the fate of their region, was denied. The only concession to the transferred Hungarian population was extended to them as individuals, and this concession involved the right to depart. Article 63 of the Treaty of Trianon, the so-called optant clause, stated: "Persons ... losing their Hungarian nationality ... shall be entitled within a period of one year from the coming into force of the present Treaty to opt for the nationality of the State in which they possessed rights of citizenship before acquring such rights in the territory transferred ..."[40] This clause triggered the last major wave of refugees. Those who up to this point still clung to illusions about the future of their homelands, were forced to face reality. Over 100,000 individuals chose to exercise their right to depart.

From the very beginning, the reception of the refugees in Hungary was mixed. As suffering human beings and as the visible symbols of the nation's tragedy, many of the refugees became beneficiaries of the personal generosity of the more affluent classes. At the same time, the country was in the midst of a social revolution, and refugees as a group were often viewed with suspicion and hostility as representatives of the old ruling and official classes, and as champions of bankrupt conservative politics. The massive influx of refugees also created an intolerable economic burden for Hungary and intensified internal social tensions. With its economy at a stand-still, beset by widespread unemployment and shortages of every kind, including food, fuel, and clothing, and without hope of relief from the West due to a continuation of the Allied economic blockade, the government was incapable of satisfying even the minimum needs of the refugees. Moreover, for the Left aid to the refugees was an ideological issue. They could not justify the squandering of the meagre resources of the state on their former class enemies when their own long deprived supporters, the workers and the lower classes, were equally destitute. The same view was taken when the few vacated bureaucratic posts were to be filled or when the even rarer apartments were to be assigned.[42] As a result, refugees had to struggle for even a single room apartment, and thousands were forced to live, often for years, in the same railroad cattle cars (now shunted to the side tracks of the main railroad stations) in which they arrived.[43] The misery of the population was greatest in Budapest. Yet, the demobilized refugee soldiers and officers, the refugee students and officials, naturally flocked to the capital, either to continue their education there or to press the ministries, usually without success, with their demands for aid or jobs.

The refugees left a deep imprint on the postwar history of Hungary; they were heavily involved in the counterrevolution, helped to consolidate the Horthy regime, participated in the establishment of the first fascist groups, and markedly influenced the formulation of the ideology of Hungarian fascism. The reasons for their deep political involvement is not hard to see. The experiences of the refugees – their desperate economic situation and their destroyed political and social roles – primed them for radical action. In an increasingly polarized society the refugees were the most traumatized group who eagerly joined, and often led, the many newly-formed Right wing organizations. Even more than the defeated aristocracy and gentry of inner Hungary, they were prepared to counter the nation's social revolution, and the national revolutions of the former minorities, with a revolution of the Right.

Notes

1. Heinrich Böll, "Hymn to a New Homeland," *Saturday Review* (May 3, 1975).
2. Even the eleventh-hour attempt to grant political equality to all citizens of Hungary was rejected by the conservative leaders. During the February 1918 parliamentary debates on voting rights Count István Tisza declared: "From 1848 until recent times everyone agreed that radical electoral right is the doom of the Hungarian nation, the Hungarian nation-state.... It is the enemies of the nation-state who want, desire, demand universal franchise.... " *Budapesti Hírlap,* 26 February 1918. On the same subject the leader of the Transylvanian Hungarians Count István Bethlen said: "In Transylvania ... electoral right is not a question of democracy, nor of conservatism; it is not even a question of class, but a question of survival." *Ibid.,* 2 March 1918.
3. The massive disruption of civilian lives can be illustrated by the size of the military mobilization. Of the 7,264,861 men who were made available for military service in the Monarchy by July 31, 1917, 3,243,323 came from Hungary, representing 72.88 percent of the 18

to 50-year-old male population of the country registered in the 1910 census. Antal Józsa, *Háború, hadifogság, forradalom. Magyar Internacionalista hadifoglyok az 1917-es oroszországi forradalmakban* [War, Captivity, Revolution. Hungarian Internationalist Prisoners of War in Russian Revolutions of 1917] (Budapest, 1970), p. 36. Proportionately, the contribution of the Hungarians was the highest. The Romanians and Germans were also declared fit for military service at a rate higher (and the Slavs at a rate lower) than their proportion out of the total population. Wilhelm Winkler, *Der Anteil der nichtdeutschen Volksstämme an der öst.-ung. Wehrmacht* (Vienna, 1919), pp. 1-2; cited in *ibid.*, p. 34.
4. The policy of the Hungarian government towards the national minorities during the war needs clarification. The selective harsh treatment of the minorities was not racially motivated, but grew out of the security requirements of the state, and out of attempts to arrest separatist tendencies among some of the nationalities. Accordingly, repressive measures were not uniformly applied, and paralleled the military fortunes of the country. At the outset of the war the policy towards the Slovaks and Croatians, who were considered to be trustworthy, changed but little. However, in areas which came under the military jurisdiction as zones of operations, military authorities, at times independently of the government, resorted to bloody repression. Such was the case particularly along the Serbian frontier, in Serbia itself, as well as in the Ukrainian-populated regions at the time of the Russian invasion of Hungary. Treatment of Romanians changed only after the 1916 Romanian invasion of Transylvania. Though the Romanian population remained generally passive, many Romanians, especially members of the intelligentsia, compromised themselves with the result that tens of thousands fled with the retreating Romanian Army. Thousands of those who remained were subsequently interned and hundreds were charged with treason. For a detailed account of Hungarian policy towards the minorities during the war see József Galántai, *Magyarország az Első Világháborúban, 1914-1918* (Budapest, 1974), [in English Hungary in World War I, Budapest, 1989], especially pp. 175-182, 190-195, 224-225, and 351-352. See also, Zoltán Szász, "Az erdélyi román polgárság szerepéről 1918 őszén," [On the Role of the Romanian Bourgeoisie of Transylvania in the Fall of 1918] *Századok* no. 2 (1972), pp. 309-310; Miron Constantinescu, *et. al.*, *Unification of the Romanian*

National State: The Union of Transylvania with Old Romania (Bucharest, 1971), pp. 100-101.
5. Not until 1918 did the Allies abandon their plans for reorganizing the Austro-Hungarian Empire, allowing "the freest opportunity for autonomous development" among the minorities, in favor of the complete dismemberment of the Empire. But the dissolution of the Empire was already implied in the earlier secret agreements with Serbia and Romania. Alfred D. Low, *The Soviet Hungarian Republic and the Paris Peace Conference* (Philadelphia, 1963), pp. 8-9. For the changing attitudes of the Western Powers towards the future of Austria-Hungary, see Wilfred Fest, *Peace or Partition: The Habsburg Monarchy and British Policy, 1914-1918* (New York, 1978). See also, Kenneth J. Calder, *Britain and the Origins of the New Europe. 1914-1918* (Cambridge, 1976); W. H. Rothwell, *British War Aims and Peace Diplomacy. 1914-1918* (Oxford, 1971).
6. For the text of minority treaties, see H.W.V. Temperley, ed., *A History of the Peace Conference of Paris* vol. 5: *Economic Reconstruction and Protection of Minorities* (London, 1924), pp. 446-470.
7. See the essay by Pastor.
8. Baron Emil Petrichevich-Horváth, ed., *Jelentés az Országos Menekültügyi Hivatal négy évi működéséről* [Four Year Activity Report of the National Refugee Office] (Budapest, 1924), p. 37. Hereinafter cited as *OMH Report*. In estimating the number of refugees, the various postwar censuses and the 1910 Hungarian census were used.
9. As compared to the 1910 census figures.
10. *OMH Report*, p. 37. It seems that most of the estimated 76,000 individuals who escaped registration by the OMH reached inner Hungary during the last months of 1918 or during early 1919. Many of these individuals were already in central Hungary at the time of the occupation of their homelands and simply chose to remain. Others were soldiers and officers returning from the front or released or escaping prisoners of war.
11. *Ibid.*
12. Galántai, *Magyarország az Első Világháborúban*, p. 397.
13. Antal Józsa, *Háború, hadifogság, forradalom: Magyar Internacionalista hadifoglyok az 1917-es oroszországi forradalmakban* (Budapest, 1970), pp. 101-103.
14. József Breit, *A Magyarországi 1918/19 évi forradalmi mozgalom és a vörös háború története* [History of the Revolutionary Movement

of 1918-1919 and of the Red War in Hungary] vol. I (Budapest, 1929), p. 37. See also Ervin Liptai, *Vöröskatonák Előre! A magyar Vörös Hadsereg harcai, 1919.* [Soldiers of the Red Army Ahead! Wars of the Hungarian Red Army] (Budapest, 1969), p. 12.
15. Tivadar Batthyány, *Beszámolóm* [My Account] vol. I (Budapest, n.d.), p. 294.
16. Zoltán Szász, "Az erdélyi román polgárság," p. 317.
17. *Ibid.*, p. 316.
18. *Vörös Ujság,* February 15, 1919. Article reproduced in László Remete, "Rengj csak, Föld!" [Let the Earth Quake] (Budapest, 1968), pp. 272-275.
19. Tibor Hajdu, *Károlyi Mihály* [Mihály Károlyi] (Budapest, 1978), p. 285.
20. Szász, "Az erdély román polgárság," p. 317.
21. Oscar Jászi, *Revolution and Counter-Revolution in Hungary* (New York, 1969), p. 61. (Originally published in 1924.)
22. Tibor Hajdu, *Az 1918-as magyarországi polgári demokratikus forradalom* [The Hungarian Bourgeois Democratic Revolution of 1918] (Budapest, 1968), p. 98.
23. Miklós Kozma, *Az összeomlás: 1918-19* [The Collapse: 1918-1919] (Budapest, 1934[?]), Journal entries for December 2 and 5, 1918, pp. 51 and 63. See also, Liptai, *Vöröskatonák,* p. 13.
24. János Kende, *Forradalomról forradalomra* [Revolution by Revolution] (Budapest, 1979), p. 88. See also, Batthyány, *Beszámolóm* vol. I., pp. 294, 303. Indeed no other class was treated as harshly during the revolution as notaries. Though some abused their greatly increased powers during the war, most simply carried out state policies. Handling military draft exemptions, forced food requisitions and similar measures inevitably made them many enemies.
25. Szász, "Az erdélyi román polgárság," p. 319. See also Constantinescu et. al., *Unification of the Romanian National State,* p. 248. *Vörös Ujság,* February 15, 1919. György Ránki *et al., Magyarország története vol. 8: 1919-1945* (Budapest, 1976), p. 81. Also, László Kővágó, *A magyarországi délszlávok 1918-1919-ben* [South Slavs in Hungary in 1918-1919] (Budapest, 1964), p. 103. Kende, *Forradalomról forradalomra,* p. 63.
26. Only the formation of the Székely Division received official sanction. Its function was to guard the official line of demarcation between the Romanian occupied territories and Hungary, though it also con-

ducted unofficial raids and rescue missions across that line. After the dissolution of the Division in April 1919, a large number of its soldiers became refugees and joined the counterrevolutionary army of Admiral Horthy.
27. The reason for that dependence lies in the decline of the gentry. After 1867 the smaller, less efficient noble estates lost their economic viability and the bankrupt owners joined the ranks of the already sizable class of landless nobles. The state compensated them for their losses by offering them posts defitting their station in a greatly expanded bureaucracy.
28. For the text of the Agreement see Temperley, *History of the Peace Conference of Paris* vol. 4, pp. 509-511.
29. Kővágó, *A magyarországi délszlávok*, pp. 95-96. See also, C. A. Macartney, *Hungary and Her Successors; The Treaty of Trianon and Its Consequences, 1919-1937* (Oxford, 1937), p. 409.
30. In Slovakia, for example, three conditions were set for continued employment of Hungarian officials: first, the taking of a loyalty oath to the new Czechoslovak constitution; second, passing of Czech/Slovak language examinations within one year; and, finally, meeting unstated qualifications for holding a specific office. R. W. Seton-Watson, *Slovakia, Then and Now* (London, 1931), pp. 217, 221.
31. Zsombor Szász, *Erdély Romániában. Népkisebbségi Tanulmány* [Transylvania in Romania. A Nationality Paper] (Budapest, 1927), pp. 83-84.
32. In vain did the Hungarian government protest to the Western Powers that "the Czecho-Slovak and the Romanian Governments compel the Hungarian officials, professors and teachers – under charge of instant dismissal and expulsion – to take the oath of allegiance to the Czecho-Slovak and Roumanian State[s]" and that this was "a manifest infraction of Article 45 of the Hague Convention." Peace Conference Delegation, *Atrocities Committed by Roumanians and Czechs. Memorandum to the mandatories of the Associated Powers at Budapest regarding the abuses perpetrated by the Powers of occupation in the territories subjected to Czecho-Slovak and Roumanian administration* (n.p., n.d. [1920?]), p. 1. See also, Macartney, *Hungary and Her Successors*, p. 413 and Szász, *Erdély Romániában*, p. 55.

33. According to Batthyány, Károlyi's Minister of Interior, around 8-10 November 1918 he personally issued an order to all state officials authorizing them to take the loyalty oath, but only as a last resort and under duress. Batthány, *Beszámolóm* vol. I, pp. 298-299. See also, Tibor Hajdu, *Az 1918-as magyarországi polgári demokratikus forradalom*, p. 163. Subsequently, the counterrevolutionary government of Szeged gave similar assurances, though, at the same time, urged the officials to take the oath and remain at their posts. Béla Kelemen, ed., *Adatok a szegedi ellenforradalom és a szegedi kormány történetéhez. 1919. (Naplójegyzetek és okiratok)* [Data on the History of the Counterrevolution in Szeged and the Szeged Government, 1919. Diary Notes and Documents] (Szeged, 1923), pp. 243,269.
34. As a negative result of the educational reform of 1907, the number of schools where instruction was offered in the languages of the minorities declined from about 6,000 in 1899 to a little over 3,300 by 1914, representing about 20 percent of the approximately 16,600 schools of the country. These schools offered education in their native tongues to about 35 percent of the minority students. Péter Hanák, ed., *Magyarország története, 1890-1918* vol. 7/2 (Budapest, 1978), p. 641. Differences in literacy rates between the different ethnic groups are another indication of the inequities of the educational opportunities. In 1910, while 79 percent of the Hungarian and 82 percent of the German population of Hungary were literate, only 65 percent of the Slovaks, 48.5 percent of the Serbs and 36 percent of the Romanians could read and write. It should be noted that national discrimination was far from being the only cause of the higher rate of illiteracy among the minorities. Also, low as the literacy rate was for the Romanian population, it was still higher than in the Kingdom of Romania.
35. *A jugoszláviai magyarság helyzete* (Budapest, 1941), p. 14.
36. Jozeph Mikus, *Slovakia: A Political History, 1918-1950* (Milwaukee, 1963), p. 29. Also R. W. Seton-Watson, ed., *Slovakia: Then and Now; A Political Survey* (London, 1931), p. 125.
37. Szász, *Erdély Romániában*, pp. 232-233.
38. László Buday, *Megcsonkított Magyarország* [Hungary Dismembered] (Budapest, 1921), p. 260.
39. The unbending attitudes of the Western Powers may be understandable in the case of the original Hungarian proposal for a com-

plete restoration of Hungary's former territories. Less justifiable was the refusal of the Great Powers to consider any modifications in the proposed borders whose aim was to achieve a greater correspondence between the prevailing ethnic and the new political boundaires.

40. Fred L. Israel, ed., *Major Peace Treaties of Modern History, 1648-1967* vol. III (New York, 1967), p. 1888. The optant clause already appeared in the minority treaties signed by all three of the successor states in 1919.
41. Article 63 of the Treaty of Trianon also guaranteed a right to the optant "to retain their immovable property in the territory of the other State where they had their place of residence before exercising their right to opt." *Ibid.*, p. 1889. This clause became the subject of a major international controversy after the successor states, and specifically Romania, expropriated Hungarian refugee estates for the purpose of land reform. Hungary sued and won her case, but without a satisfactory compensation for the refugees.
42. Not surprisingly, when the Hungarian Soviet Republic, in a fit of egalitarianism, declared the palaces and townhouses of the aristocracy as well as the spacious apartments of the upper and middle classes underutilized, it was not the refugees but the lower classes of the slums who were allowed to move in.
43. *OMH Report*, p. 38.

Lóránd Dombrády

Trianon and Hungarian National Defense

The military clauses of the peace treaty signed in Trianon on 4 June 1920 were aimed at securing the total military superiority of the victorious Allies over Hungary and the absolute protection of the territories ceded to them. For this reason it only allowed Hungary to maintain an army which – due to its size, composition, command and equipment – could not go on the offensive nor even provide minimal protection for a country which, without natural borders, was endangered from three sides.

Part V of the treaty included the military, naval and air clauses.[1] It abolished universal compulsory military service and declared that in the future the Hungarian army could only be constituted and recruited on a voluntary basis. It would only be used for internal peace keeping and for frontier control. It would not be allowed more than 35,000 men, of which only 1,750 could be officers. Each division could be established freely within the set limits of numbers and armament available. It was forbidden to establish or to maintain any organizations (headquarters) for preparing or conducting a war. All preliminary mobilization measures and preparations, and the establishment of a reserve body of officers and other ranks were prohibited. The peace treaty fixed the time of service in the ranks at 12 years and that of the officers at 20 years.

According to the peace treaty, the army was able to have 15 machine guns, 4 trench mortars and 3 artillery pieces per 1000 soldiers and in total 40,250 rifles, 525 machine guns, 140 trench mortars and 105 light cannons (10.5 centimeters maximum). The storable quantity of the ammunition for each type of weapon was fixed precisely. Weapons and ammunition were only to be manufactured by the state and then only to replace munitions which had been used. Exporting and importing weapons and ammunition was banned.

Within three months of the date when the treaty had come into force weapons, ammunition and equipment over the permitted amount had to be handed over to the Inter-Allied Control Commission and all factories capable of producing, maintaining and storing these had to be closed or rebuilt for commercial purposes.

An especially rigorous condition of the treaty, which had a paralyzing effect on the army, banned the keeping, manufacturing and importing of armored vehicles, and of all other forms of transport capable of military uses, such as airplanes and airships. The Hungarian army was not to have a military or naval air service. As part of the Austrian-Hungarian Navy, the Danube Flotilla had to be handed over. From the Danube Flotilla, only three patrol boats could be kept.

The implementation of the military regulations of the peace treaty was supervised by the Inter-Allied Control Commission assigned to Hungary for this purpose.

Although the Hungarian delegation at the Peace Conference tried to mitigate serious conditions, such as the military restrictions of the treaty, their propositions were refused. Among their proposals, that for permission to have a conscripted peace-time army of 85,000 minimum was not even given a hearing. The delegation clearly pointed out that a smaller army was not sufficient for internal order and for fighting effectively against Bolshevism. This, however, was disregarded. The argument that the country would be left without an army, since it could not keep up a professional army, much more expensive than a conscript army, and that it also was not able to recruit a sufficient number of reliable people, since the army had been discredited by the war and the revolution, was not accepted either.

As far as they were able to, the Hungarian government and military leadership tried to delay the execution of the requirements of the peace treaty. Act no.1921:XXXIII., on the peace treaty, accepted by Parliament after its third reading on 15th November 1920, enacted on 26th July 1921 and published on 31st July 1921 was followed in November 1921 by Act no.1921:XLIX. on the Hungarian Army; this made arrangements for the Royal Hungarian Honvéd Army to succeed the National Army from 4th January 1922, in accordance with the regulations of the peace treaty.[2]

During negotiations with the Control Commission, the military leadership, working on the implementation of the military clauses of the treaty – it could not be postponed any further – still tried to achieve smaller, and for the army beneficial, changes in the text of the treaty. They also tried to counteract the efforts of the Control Commission and gain time in order to hide as much as possible of the small amount of weapons to be handed over. With an eye to the opportunities developments in foreign affairs offered, they did not give up the idea that by getting round the regulations and controls, they could establish the foundations of a future army based on two years of military service and conscription. Steps were taken for certain military institutions to be disbanded. Others such as medical institutions, food stores, cartographic institutes, etc., were placed under the authority of other ministries, while at the same time they secretly remained under the authority of the Ministry of Defense.

Act no.1922:III. issued on 22 February 1922, modified some of the regulations of Act no.1921:XLIX. Thus, the numbers of effectives were: 1,750 officers, 2,334 non-commissioned officers and 30,916 men. Students of the Ludovika Academy were counted among the men.[3]

This was followed by Act no.1922:X. which made provisions for the training of officers, limiting it to the Ludovika Academy.[4] The training of general staff officers and thus the maintenance of general staff academy for this purpose was banned. For this reason during this surreptitious period, the institute was called for training in military regulations.

Act no.1922:XI., for the execution of some prohibitions and restrictions of the peace treaty, was issued on 25th February. This laid down the final amount of ammunition the army was allowed to store: 57,776 rifles, 28,822 pistols, 560 machine guns, 600 submachine guns, 70 trench mortars, 129 guns. It also confirmed that weapons and ammunition could only be manufactured in the military factory run by the state. The amount permitted per month was as follows: 300 pcs of small arms, 80 pistols, 5 machine guns, 5 submachine guns. Only two artillery pieces and trench mortars were allowed to be manufactured yearly. The act also made provisions for setting up a state military ammunition factory.[5]

Finally in April 1922, nothing further prevented the Ministry's national defence regulation coming into force in May. The Hungarian army was to be newly structured according to the provisions of the peace treaty and could not be changed in the forseeable future.[6] The elimination of the remaining troops and organisations over the permitted limit could not be postponed any longer. It was typical of the delays and arguments about the structuring of the new military formation that in spite of the careful "assistance" of the Commission, modification was already needed in June. The most important modification was the abolition of military districts; these were later described by the control Commission as organizations which were the equivalent of the army corps.

The structure of the Hungarian Army consisted of 7 mixed brigades, 4 cavalry regiments under the supreme command, 4 independent batteries and 3 sapper battalions. These consisted of 1,750 officers – 23 generals, 119 colonels and lieutenant colonels, 192 majors and 1,416 subalterns – 2,334 non-commissioned officers, 30,916 men. Part of the force consisted of civilians, to a total of 1,300 members.

Separate provisions applied to different military institutions, such as the military office of the Regent, the Ludovika Academy, the ranges, health institutions, etc.

The mixed brigades consisted of 2 infantry regiments – each of 3 battalions – 1 bicycle battalion, 1 cavalry squadron, 1 trench mortar company, 1 artillery battalion (3 batteries with 6 guns in total) 1 signal company, 1 train detachment and 1 car detachment. Each mixed brigade had 30,053 rifles, 42 machine guns, 12 artillery pieces and 10 trench mortars. (The artillery was only permitted to have guns of 7.5-10.5 cm in calibre).

Armored, motorized and air formations were, of course, not included in the military structure.

Since the army, according to the peace treaty, was not permitted to have a general staff, this could only exist secretly, as Section number VI of the Ministry of Defense. This included all the general staff subdivisions essential for commanding the army.

The Hungarian Army could only have professional soldiers. Although the departmental order, which demanded 12 years of service, had been issued in December 1921, interest was smaller than expected. By 15th January 1922 not even half of the required number had joined up. The government asked to be allowed to change over gradually to a conscription system over 12 years. Seeing the situation, the Control Commission was inclined to allow the changes during a period of 6 years, but the Council of Ambassadors was very much against all kinds of concessions and obliged the Hungarian government to observe the peace treaty in its entirety.[7]

There was no other option but to get round these restrictions and complete the numbers by giving quotas to the local authorities of the counties for compulsory conscription ("C"). The men conscripted this way were born mainly in 1901 and had to serve 2 years. Because of the restrictions, even this method was not successful at the beginning. Even in 1925 the effective force was only 22,000 strong, i.e. 60% of establishment. On the basis of the report of the Control Commission, that between 1924 and 1926, 9,500 men had gone into the army in a way not permitted, the Council of Ambassadors suspended conscription and required an explanation from the Hungarian government in 1926. In 1927, after long negotiations, when the Military Control Commission had left Hungary and there was no direct control, the government was allowed to go on with conscription.[8]

Even while the Military Control Commission was operating, the police and other armed organisations of the state made it possible to disguise the size of the army. In January 1921 the Council of Ministers made provisions for the structure and size of the gendarmerie, the police and border guards. The army sent 70 officers and 600 men to the police as police reserves. The gendarmerie also hid 38 officers and 301 soldiers under a similar title. A total of 878 officers of the Hungarian Army came under the command of the customs guards, who were under the supervision of the Finance Ministry; this was several times more than the permitted number. The Air Department was regarded as a civil institution and the 548 members of its "air gendarmerie" were the training cadre of the future Hungarian Air Force. The river forces were also partly a cover organization; its 1,947 members hid members of sapper units.[9] Because of the restrictions, these possibilities could only be used effectively after 1927.

The paralysis of the army was eased by the decision of the Council of Ministers which brought an end to the operation of the Military Control Commission from 31st March 1927. Through this, permanent local controls were stopped, and a system of occassional checks was introduced. As a result of political and economic consolidation, the country was able to free itself from total isolation in foreign affairs and to express its political interest in restoring its former powers and territory. In the autumn of 1926, Prime Minister István Bethlen pointed out that the next step in establishing stability was to stop military control as soon as possible and to build up armaments whenever the chance arose. The need to take a direction in foreign affairs which would maintain an equilibrium with the Little Entente, and win Italy as a suitable partner for this, was discussed.

The Little Entente reacted to these efforts of Hungary's. Pacts between them were renewed and in 1929 they confirmed and harmonized their military cooperation. They also made plans for a mutual military measures against Hungary.

The direct military steps of the Allies were mainly caused by the secretive decisions and arrangements of the Hungarian government to lay the foundations for an army which could be used in peace and war. If the military restrictions of the peace treaty became less rigid or ceased to exist as a result of favorable changes in foreign relations, this would be the basis for quickly developing a new, efficient army which would be able to support the restoration of Hungarian power and territory. On 23 December 1927, the Crown Council made a decision about army development to be completed between 1928 and 1930. They also decided to stop hireing and to use the "C" recruitment *i.e.*, conscription. In spite of the restricted number laid down by the treaty, the Crown Council fixed the size of the army at 62,500, to be reached by 1930. A large part of this force was hidden in the organization of the police, the gendarmerie and the frontier guards. The neccessary budgets were hidden within different ministries.[10]

Decisions were made to establish experimentally the foundations for the new branches of the service, for armored troops and for the air force.

As a result of the difficult economic situation and of the difficulty in hiding the numbers involved, the military leadership could neither recruit the required number of people nor obtain the amount of equipment needed, consequent by the effectives in 1930 ammounted to 57,648, which was less than planned. Careful steps were taken to train the age groups so far unconscripted, in a very short period of time, generally within a few weeks.

All these steps were reacted to by the Little Entente, who increased their armed forces. By the beginning of the 1930s, they were 20 times stronger than Hungary, which made it possible for them to launch an immediate attack and to occupy the country unhindered, if Hungarian policy or the Hungarian army decided to make a threatening move towards them. The secretive militarization, if it exceeded the limit acceptable to them, was regarded as one such move. The Hungarian leadership was aware of this. At the meeting of the Supreme Council of Defense in April 1929, in his speech on military preparations, General Vilmos Rőder, deputy chief of general staff (i.e. deputy chief of Section VI) pointed out that the condition of preparedness was the relaxation of the provisions of the peace treaty and the prevention of any negative consequences in case these provisions were violated. If these could not be granted, then aims should be limited or changed completely. The political and military leadership had to work in close collaboration: "The most important point of our military policy situation is in the field of foreign affairs: without favourable preliminary conditions in foreign relations, we cannot think of an offensive war, cannot use the advantages of a given situation and cannot even make military preparations needed for it."[11]

Although the prohibitions did not change, and the Allies reacted threateningly to all the vibrations of Hungarian politics, the Supreme Council of Defense accepted a plan for the future development of the Hungarian Army. Because of the difficult circumstances, the pace of this development could only be very slow. Only favourable effect of the political and economic circumstances could speed up this development. So, only 7 of the planned 21 infantry divisions were to be set up within an unspecified time. Besides these, the first air force units and a tank unit of the mobile units needed to be established according to the development plan.[12]

In 1932 in spite of the prohibitions, compulsory military service was introduced in connection with the development of the military structure. The regulation issued in July 1932 defined the order of recruitment. Earlier "C" recruits had been drafted several times a year. From now on, they had to join up on 1 October each year. Those who did not respond were arrested by the police. The duration of service was 19 months but after 12 months the soldiers could opt out. This method was intended to ensure that, within the limitations on numbers, a big proportion of all age groups were conscripted and trained.

Until 1938 the circumstances did not make it possible to conscript and check all the people liable for military service. From 1932 to 1935 the number of men in the army rose from 66,500 to 67,900. It was only between 1936 and 1938 that changes in foreign affairs and economic circumstances resulted in a rise from 72,300 to 85,200 per year. By then, it was possible to manufacture reasonable amounts of ammunition in the country and to import it from Italy and Germany.

After the changes in the system, the original volunteers were released from service.

In the first part of the 1930s, the Allies followed Hungary's military moves with close attention, ready to react immediately. They tried to use a scandal over a consignment of weapons from Italy to Hungary, detected by the Austrian Social Democrats in Hirtenberg in 1933, to prove the existence of Hungarian military preparations, which were an obstacle to their own disarmament. In February the members of the Little Entente concluded a pact, which replaced several bilateral treaties with a multilateral alliance.[13]

Partial or full cancellation of the military restrictions of the peace treaty might have led to the revisions of the territorial decisions of the treaty. Consequently, in spite of the efforts of the Hungarian Committee, the Disarmament Conference at Geneva which had been in existence since

1933 excluded the possibility of any development favorable to Hungary. The Allies were only ready to approve equal rights for Hungarian armament, if Hungary signed a mutual non-aggression agreement with them. But since by doing this Hungary would have given up its demand for a revision of the treaty, any such agreement was rejected.

The Little Entente's policy convinced the Hungarian government that the only possible solution was to retain old allies and seek new ones; political and military cooperation with a new ally would prevent the danger of any pre-emptive action against the secretive or arbitrary armament of Hungary and would apply pressure for its acceptance. After winning the right to re-arm, the new ally would have to support Hungary in its revisional steps. It seemed to the Hungarian goverment that the Nazi take-over in Germany would give them this opportunity. Besides Italy, Germany, who wanted to dismantle the peace system and to rearrange the Central-East-European region, seemed to be the main supporter of Hungarian rearmament and demands for territorial revision.

In 1934 the situation report of the General Staff stated that Hungary's policy of territorial revision against a unified and strong Little Entente was not in accord with Hungary's military strength nor with the support of its allies – at this time; meaning Italy alone. Although the possibility of war for Hungary still existed, it was "not in a position to be able to make war", because "geographical and military potentials"[14] made it impossible. The most important political aim was to create the chance to make war, to establish an army, with the help of a reliable ally. Existing relations with Italy, which involved the Germans, needed to be made into an alliance. All efforts had to be made to destroy the unity of the Allies, so that it would only be necessary to fight one of them.

The rapid rearmament encouraged by Germany, a quick political and economic development of the region, and through the failure of the Eastern security policy, the growth of German hostility against Czechoslovakia, along with the signs of disintegration among the Allies, all made it clear to the Hungarian military leadership and to the government headed by Gyula Gömbös that "sooner or later Germany would decide the pending questions by force. The quick recognition and evaluation of Germany's efforts and aims would be decisive for Hungary's future."[15] From 1935 General Jenő Rátz, Commander of the General Staff thought that the aim to strive for was a flexible Hungarian-German military cooperation built on the old brotherhood in arms against Czechoslovakia and Bolshevism. If Hungarian policy towards Germany became clear, Germany would give quick and effective support to establishing the army. These steps needed to be taken even if it meant making concessions to Germany. General Rátz tried to make an alliance with Germany the leading idea in Hungarian military policy: "Now it is clear that we have to be on the German side, because it is the only side from which we can benefit. Just imagine if Germany was our enemy."[16] The developments in foreign affairs urged Rátz and the General Staff to start rearming, making up for lost years and to have the army ready to fight as soon as possible. Delay would make it impossible to take advantage of the situation. Rátz came to the conclusion that war would break out around 1940, that Hungary needed to fight on the German side, because only the Germans would support Hungarian political aims. The government needed to take steps to establish the political and economic potential to start immediate armament.

From 1936 the military leadership was of the opinion that even the weakening of Allied unity provided them with the opportunity to rearm. In spite of the conflicts amongst themselves, the Allies were united against Hungarian demands, but aggressive action against Hungary's re-arment was not likely.

The prospects and the possible effects of Hungary's realization of her right to rearm were outlined in a study by the General Staff, made at the request of the Defense Minister in spring 1937.[17] The study stated that

> although between 1934 and 1936 the Allies would have started a military action, had Hungary openly proclaimed her program of armament, in 1937 in a different political situation caused by the consolidation and union of Germany and Italy, they would only take diplomatic and economic steps and might turn to the League of Nations. They would not apply any military restrictions, and would not order military action, until they had found out how Germany and Italy would react to that. The reason why the Allies did not want to start negotiations on Hungary's right to rearm was the improvement in Hungarian foreign relations caused by her growing relationship with the fascist powers and this determined the future direction of Hungarian foreign affairs.

According to Rátz, the League of Nations was also to be avoided when trying to acquire the right to rearm, because it would lead to long negotiations without any result and "because of the policy of Germany and Italy, against the League of Nations." Although the Western powers preferred to settle things with the help of the League of Nations, any other solution would also encounter difficulties, bringing up the danger of war or making the economic situation worse. According to the Chief of General Staff, the proclamation of the right to rearm would only be needed, if "the lack of this right held up the quick development of the army." Since armament was already in progress with the tacit knowledge of the Allies, it was unnecessary to proclaim it and provoke action on the part of the Allies. In any case, large concessions, such as a non-aggression pact could not be the price of the right to rearm.

With an eye on the above points and on the basis of the 1932 concepts, the General Staff made their new plan for reorganizing the military. This consisted of 21 infantry divisions, 4 cavalry brigades, 1 air force division, and the necessary arms. The sum of 1.7 million was considered necessary to put this into practice. Rátz asked General Vilmos Rőder to submit the plan to the Council of Ministers urgently.

Though the government led by Darányi, which succeeded the Gömbös government, thought that the approach to Germany was of importance, yet it proceeded with more caution not to jeopardize the relations with other European powers. The government tried to find out British and French views on Hungary's aspirations towards the right to rearm and towards the revision of the treaty. The Hungarian government also wanted to know how tolerant the British and French were of the political ambitions of Germany, how far Hungary was able to go in cooperation with Germany without becoming involved in a military conflict, and what level of consensus existed between the weakened Allies. At the beginning of 1937, to show its goodwill, the government started to negotiate with the Little Entente on Hungarian rights to rearm. The negotiations were not successful. As the result of the general pressure of foreign affairs, the Little Entente was likely to give concessions, but insisted on a mutual non-aggression pact. The Hungarian government wanted to revise the treaty, even by force; since Germany disapproved of Hungarian negotiations with the Little Entente, Hungary refused the non-aggression pact. Negotiations stopped. This led to the growth of German political influence over Hungary. Germany, counting on Hungarian support, prepared to move against Czechoslovakia.

In the winter of 1937, on a visit to Berlin, Prime Minister Darányi was informed by Hitler that Germany would soon take action against Czechoslovakia and that Hungarian military support would not be refused. At the same time Hitler called Darányi's attention to the importance of Hungarian – Yugoslav rapprochement and to the necessity of positive development of Hungarian – Romanian relations. This made it clear that Hungarian military preparations could be continued without proclaiming the right to rearm and without the danger of any repercussions, and that according to Germany, rearmament was necessary.

After this, on 5 May 1938, a new rearmament program costing billions, urged by the military leadership, was introduced. The carrying out of this program, *i.e.*, the open flouting of the military clauses of the peace treaty – as was expected – was not followed by any action from the Little Entente or the Great Powers. They acknowledged it.

However, quickly worsening German – Czechoslovak relations disturbed the Hungarian government. Although Hitler told Horthy that Germany would approve of Hungary initiating military action to seize of the Eastern areas of Czechoslovakia, because it would give Germany a good opportunity to intervene, the government and the military leadership did not want to take risks with an underdeveloped army. The possibility that the Western powers would intervene on the side of Czechoslovakia also made the government uncertain. An intervention could lead to war, and this Hungary wanted to avoid.

In this uncertain situation the Hungarian government thought that it was neccesary to renew negotiations with the Entente. The aim was to acquire *de jure* recognition of Hungary's right to rearm. As a gesture of reconciliation, Czechoslovakia, which was in a difficult situation, had the Little Entente sign the agreement in Bled on 22 August 1938. In the agreement, the Allies recognized Hungary's right to rearm and showed willingness to grant further concessions to Hungarian minorities. Hungary formally renounced the use of force.

The agreement immediately gave rise to German dissatisfaction, which was firmly made known to Horthy and Prime Minister Béla Imrédy, who were in Berlin at this time. Germany considered this step, which had made Czechoslovakia happy, a very unfriendly and unreasonable betrayal of the revision of the treaty. This made an already difficult situation, caused by Hungarian unwillingness to take military action against Czechoslovakia, even worse.

The Bled Agreement recognised Hungary's previously proclaimed right to rearm, which the Little Entente opposed previously so much but was not able to prevent. The agreement between Hungary and Czechoslovakia, which was constantly under the threat of war, and between Yugoslavia and Romania, drawn away from her Western allies by Germany's influence, did not relax the tension between them, but made the differences even worse.

Notes

1. *Hungarian Legislative Records*, Act no.1921:XXXIII.
2. *Ibid.*, Act no.1921:XLIX.
3. *Ibid.*, Act no.1922:III.
4. *Ibid.*, Act no.1922:III.
5. *Ibid.*, Act no.1922:XI.
6. War History Archives (WHA), Ministry of Defence(MD), Presidential Documents (PD) no.1500/1922 and no.12000/1922
7. WHA, MD,PD no.VI-1. 1999/1929 Defence Regulations (DR)
8. *Ibid.*
9. *Ibid.*
10. WHA, MD,PD no.VI-1. 1999/I/1929 DR
11. WHA Collection of Studies, no. 2015
12. WHA, MD,PD no.VI-1. 9135/1932 DR
13. WHA, MD,PD no.VI-2. 119421/1933
14. WHA, MD,PD no.VI-1. 4010/1935 DR
15. WHA, MD,PD no.VI-1. 9205/1935 DR
16. *Ibid.*
17. WHA, MD,PD no.VI-1. 2237/1937

CONCLUSIONS

Béla K. Király

Total War and Peacemaking

War, if reason prevails, is waged to obtain a better peace than that which existed prior to the hostilities. During the 19th and early 20th century – an era of balance of power and limited wars – the victor usually attained his goals or at least part of them, through peace negotiations, which often contained compromises. During the last cycle of wars which preceeded World War I, this was still the case. In the Crimean War Russia lost; consequently she had to give up the southern part of Bessarabia and demilitarize her Black Sea shores. In 1859, France and its Sardinian ally won. As a result, Austria had to give up Lombardy, satisfying part of the victor's goal. In 1866 Prussia won; consequently Austria was expelled from Germany and the German Confederation was dissolved. In 1870 the Germans won, and France had to give up Alsace and Lorraine and reconcile itself to the unification of Germany. In 1905 Russia lost, resulting in Japan's expansion of its possessions in the Pacific area at the expense of Russia. In the two Balkan wars, the Balkan states won. The consequence was the virtual elimination of the Ottoman Empire from the Balkans.

In all these wars the belligerents entered the war with a design for the post-war peace and attained all or part of what they intended to gain. Thus the resulting peace was, without exception, better for the victors than what they had enjoyed prior to the wars.

This was not, however, the case in World War I. None of the great powers started hostilities in 1914 with a definitive design for the post-war peace.[1] In fact, not one of the belligerents, victors, or vanquished envisaged in 1914 anything resembling the consequences of World War I. Except for a small band who followed Pitsudski into Russia even before the official declaration of war in 1914, no one went to war to restitute Poland nor to create a Yugoslavia. Even the small group of political and military leaders in Belgrade, who wanted the war more than anyone else, envisaged in a possible victory only the enlargement of Serbia. Nor did anyone enter the war to create Czechoslovakia. Even Masaryk went into exile in the fall of 1914 to propagate the transformation of the Habsburg monarchy from its dualistic into a trialistic form, to achieve for the Czechs rights identical to those that the Hungarians had achieved in 1867. No one went to war to destroy the German, Russian, Ottoman or Habsburg Empires, and most certainly, no one sought to create the first socialistic state – the USSR. Not even Lenin had dreamed of its rise in the near future. Yet these were the wholly unexpected results of World War I.

After the war, considerable scholarship was devoted to substantiating the supposition that the dissolution of the four empires and the inevitable creation or enlargement of various East Central European states were the result of organic historical processes.[2] Inevitability is a questionable assumption in history. While economic, social and other forces certainly dominate historical developments, they do not predetermine them. Among other considerations, the effect of the individual on historical evolution is enormous. Simply consider the course of the French Revolution without Robespierre or Napoleon; 1917 without Lenin; the USSR without Stalin; or, for that matter, German National Socialism without Hitler.

The thesis that the reorganization of East Central Europe after World War I was an inevitable culmination of organic developments, determined by forces accumulated through generations, is questionable. These forces had only a moderate effect on developments, and came to play a role only when the character of war changed to totality. This, in turn, defeated any effort to conclude a rational peace.

Until 1916, excepting a few peace feelers, no meaningful peace proposal was made by belligerent governments. In late 1916 a series of peace proposals were suddenly put forward, all of them without exception advocating compromises. They contained no demands for unconditional surrender or a dictated peace.

On November 14, 1916, Lord Landsdowne,[3] a minister without portfolio in the Asquith cabinet, put forward a memorandum on the need for peace negotiations. The Landsdowne memorandum recommended a serious investigation of the possibility of a peace and advocated that a statement be made by the British goverment indicating that the destruction of the German Empire was not her goal. He favored a peace on the basis of *status quo ante bellum*. The fall of the Asquith government and the installation of the Lloyd George cabinet on December 16 put an end to Landsdowne's activities,[4] at least temporarily. However, the affair did not die without vitriolic attacks being later made on Landsdowne.[5]

Shortly after the Landsdowne memorandum was drafted, Francis Joseph I died. The date was November 21, 1916. Upon ascending the throne, the new Emperor and King, Karl, declared in a manifesto[6] his desire to do everything in his power to end as soon as possible the horrors and sacrifices of the war. Germany, embarrassed by the statement, felt obliged to issue a memorandum. It proposed that the belligerents bring forward recommendations for a post-World War peace. The Reichstag passed a peace resolution on July 1917.[7]

Shortly after the German announcement, President Wilson proposed[8] that as an essential prerequisite to peace negotiations, the belligerents state their war aims. Several other propositions followed, including a papal Encyclical,[9] whose aim was to promote the cause of peace. None of these propositions negated with greater force all the heretofore universally accepted theses – among them the idea of the inevitability of a factual peace arrangement for East Central Europe and the thesis of the inevitability of the dissolution of empires – than did the Sixtus affair.[10] Emperor and King Karl asked his brother-in-law, Prince Sixtus of Bourbon, an officer in the Belgian army, to forward his peace proposals to the British and French governments. The Prince accepted the mission and made several trips to Vienna, Paris and London. As the particulars of the affair are well known, a detailed exposition is unnecessary; only a few points need be emphasized. Above all, the Habsburg Emperor and King was the first among all the belligerent heads of state who offered to give up territories under his own sovereignty for the sake of peace. He proposed the establishment of a South Slavic monarchy that would include Serbia, Montenegro, Albania and the two Austro-Hungarian provinces of Bosnia and Herzegovina. After long and arduous negotiations, in early August 1917, the Entente powers' reply was positive. It contained nothing about unconditional surrender or the dissolution of the Habsburg Empire, and recommended that only Trentino should be ceded to Italy. Even Trieste was to remain a free port. Instead of the dissolution of the Austro-Hungarian monarchy, the Entente powers proposed the enlargement of the dual state by the addition of Silesia and Bavaria. Even resurrected Poland was to become, within her 1772 borders, a monarchy under a Habsburg king.

During the Sixtus negotiations, a number of new, concrete peace proposals emerged. Prior to the Brest-Litovsk Treaty on February 9, 1918, none of them was other than a compromise peace proposal. For example, Prime Minister Lloyd George declared in January 1918 that the breakup of Austria-Hungary was not Britain's aim. Even according to President Wilson's fourteen points, promulgated on January 18, 1918, the place of Austria-Hungary was to be safeguarded among the nations.[11]

Two facts are demonstrated here. First, that the Eentente intention was to negotiate a peace with possible compromises. Second, and more important, the dissolution of Austria-Hungary was not contemplated by the Western powers until early 1918. The question arises: why did a multitude of peace proposals begin to emerge in late 1916, whereas none had been put forward before. One can also question why the original spirit of compromise changed in 1917 to a determination to fight to the bitter end, and to impose a treaty on the vanquished rather than to negotiate with them.

With no intent at oversimplification, it should be emphasized that one of the major causes of this change of attitudes and purposes was the change in the nature of warfare in 1916 and 1917 – a period when World War I changed into a total war.

Total war is an armed combat waged with all national resources: human, as well as material. In total war, big batallions are neither more nor less important than energy and financial resources such as farms, factories, mines, transportation systems, research establishments. All these become elements in waging the war and, subsequently, legitimate targets of hostile action. The unrestricted British blockade of the Central Powers and the German reply – unrestricted submarine warfare – are cases in point. Since all citizen soldiers and civilians participate in the war effort in total war, the maintenance of morale, the efforts to increase the population's will to fight and destroy the enemy, became pivotal. Thus, psychological warfare is a basic ingredient of the war effort, and it is not any less important than armed combat and economic warfare.[12]

Whether World War I was a total war is a question that can be resolved by analyzing the events of 1916 and early 1917. Between February 1916 and mid-May of 1917, three battles changed the face of World War I. In the battle of Verdun 522,000 Frenchmen and 434,000 Germans died. In the battle of Somme 615,000 allied soldiers (420,000 British and 195,000 French) and 650,000 Germans died. The Nivelle offensive, which lasted from April 29 to May 20, 1917, and was supposed to break through the German position, resulted in the death of 120,000 Frenchmen in five days. It did not result in any mentionable advance on the front.[13] This outcome precipitated widespread mutiny in the French Army.[14] Only the extraordinary discipline of the Entente media and the deficiency of the German intelligence service prevented the German High Command from learning that the French sectors of the western front were virtually denuded. These battles, with their unprecedented waste of human lives and material, and their remarkable lack of success, revealed that the war was hopelessly stalemated. Rapid industrial development and technological advances prior to and during the war created formidable fire power. They did not at the same time produce equivalent means of mobility. (This happened only later, in the interwar decades.) The result was a deadlock in the trenches. Statesmen saw but two alternatives: either to start peace negotiations and accept compromises, or to push the war effort to its extreme limits, and dictate peace to the vanquished. This explains the multitude of peace proposals, most of which date from late 1916.

Since all the compromise efforts failed for one reason or another, only the second alternative appeared to remain open. Subsequently, the world was dragged into the continuation of the first total war in modern times. As it was already indicated, a basic ingredient of total war is psychological warfare. Propaganda is a major weapon in this warfare, thus it is not surprising that the role of propaganda grew by leaps and bounds, to the point of madness. In a life and death struggle, propaganda served no other purpose but to strengthen the morale of its own and undermine the enemy's will to fight. In such efforts truth plays no role.[15] War propaganda on both sides fostered the belief that one's own side was without flaw while the enemy was the embodiment of evil. It created a state of mind which tolerated no compromise and which was slow in yielding its distortions. This war propaganda poisoned European minds and created a cancer more harmful and more lasting than the physical losses caused by the war. The failure of compromises led to the intensification of combat in a total war. And total war shaped total victory, and led to a reflex action: dictated peace, a peace that saw no victors. Even though the victorious leaders foresaw that a dictated peace would be the harbinger of future wars, they seemed to be unwilling or incapable of overcoming its momentum. The statesmen of the victors could have shaped history in harmony with their beliefs. They rather declined that august role. World War I, therefore, became what Raymond Aron has called a "hyperbolic war,"[16] one that created more problems than it resolved. Among the problems created was Trianon.

Notes

1. Kenneth J. Calder, *Britain and the Origins of New Europe, 1914-1918* (London, 1976), p. 8.

2. Wilfried Fest, *Peace or Partition* (New York, 1978), pp. 7-9. For a brief but excellent summary of the war aims see Gerhard Schulz, *Revolutions and the Peace Treaties*. This book also identifies peace feelers in 1915; first swallows that did not herald the arrival of the spring of peace. On war aims see A.J.P. Taylor, eds., *Essays presented to Sir Lewis Namier*. (London, 1956). For Hungary's position see Norman Stone "Hungary and the Crisis of July, 1914" in Walter Laquer and George L. Mosse, eds., *1914 The Coming of the First World War* (New York, 1966), pp. 147-64.
3. Sir Charles Petrie, *Diplomatic History, 1713-1933* (London, 1944), pp. 316, 317, 322. For the increasing interest in peace in 1916, see also Z.A.B. Zeman, *The Gentlemen Negotiators: A Diplomatic History of the First World War* (New York, 1971).
4. Lloyd George, *War Memoirs* (London, 1933-36). W.S. Churchill, *The World Crisis* (London, 1923-31). A.J.P. Taylor, *English History, 1914-45* (New York, 1965), p. 65.
5. Gordon A. Craig, "The Revolution in War and Diplomacy" in Jack J. Roth, ed., *World War I: A Turning Point in Modern History* (New York, 1967), p. 16.
6. Petrie, *Diplomatic History*, p. 317.
7. *Verhandlungen des Deutschen Reichstages* (1917), July 19, 1917. See also Zeman, *The Gentlemen Negotiators*, p. 116.
8. R. S. Baker, *Woodrow Wilson: Life and Letters* (New York, 1927-39).
9. Pope Benedict XV's Peace Proposal, August 1, 1917. Sidney Z. Ehler and John B. Morall, *Church and State Through the Centuries* (Westminster, Maryland, 1954), pp. 374-377.
10. Robert A. Kann, *Die Sixtus Affäre und die geheimen Friedensverhandlungen Österreich-Ungarns im ersten Weltkrieg* (Wien, 1966); Fest, pp. 64-76.
11. *Congressional Record*, vol LVI (1918), part I., pp. 680-81. Richard B. Morris, ed., *Basic Documents in American History* (New York, 1956), pp. 153-57.
12. Charles Roetter, *The Art of Psychological Warfare, 1914-1945* (New York, 1974), pp. 27-94.
13. For the place of World War I in the framework of wars since the defeat of Napoleon see J. David Singer and Melvin Small, *The Wages of War 1816-1965; A Statistical Handbook*.
14. Richard M. Watt, *Dare Call It Treason* (New York, 1963).

15. Arthur Ponsonby, M.P., *Falsehood in War Time. Containing an Assortment of Lies Circulated Throughout the Nations during the Great War* (Torrance, Cal., 1980). First published in Britain in 1928.
16. Raymond Aron, *The Century of Total War* (Boston, 1955), pp. 24-31.

Maps

1. Ethnic Hungarian Population of the Kingdom of Hungary in 1910 and of Partitioned Hungary After 1920
2. American Boundary Recommendations and the Trianon Borders of Hungary
3. Transylvania and Southeastern Europe
4. The Vix and Other Demarcation Lines

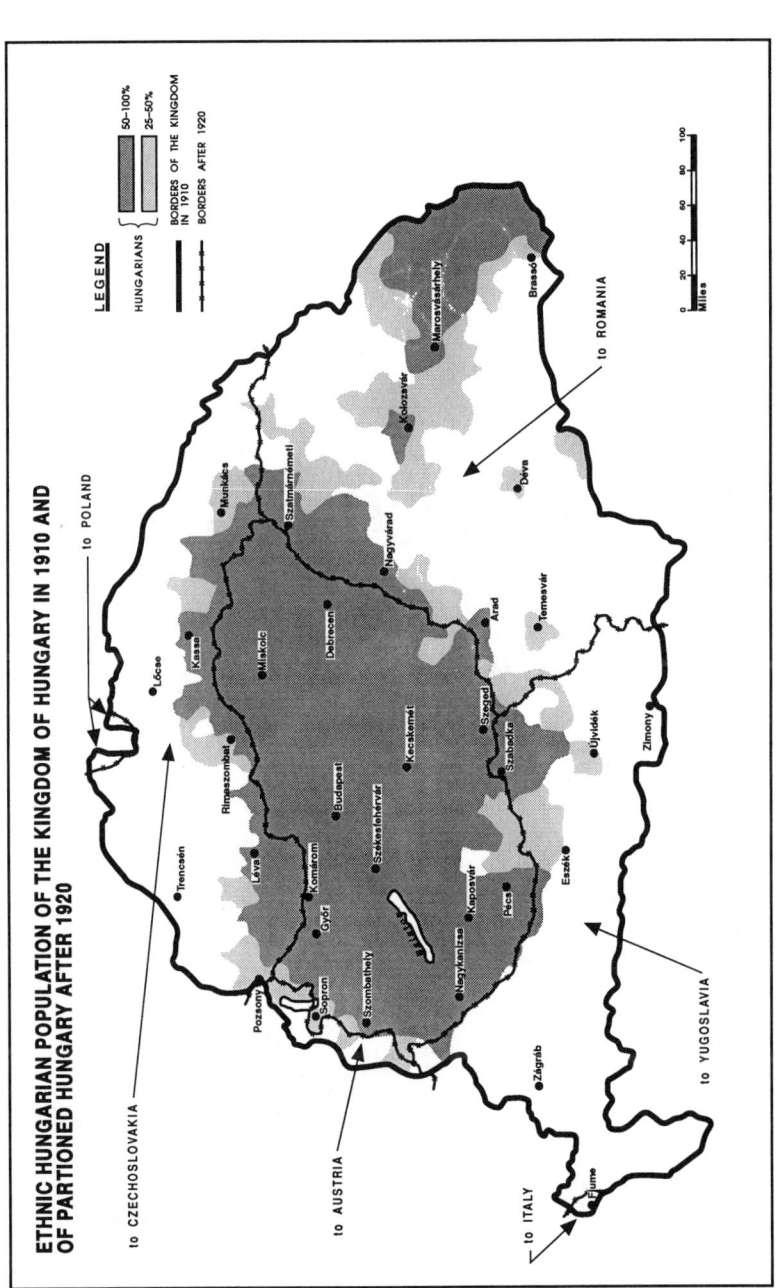

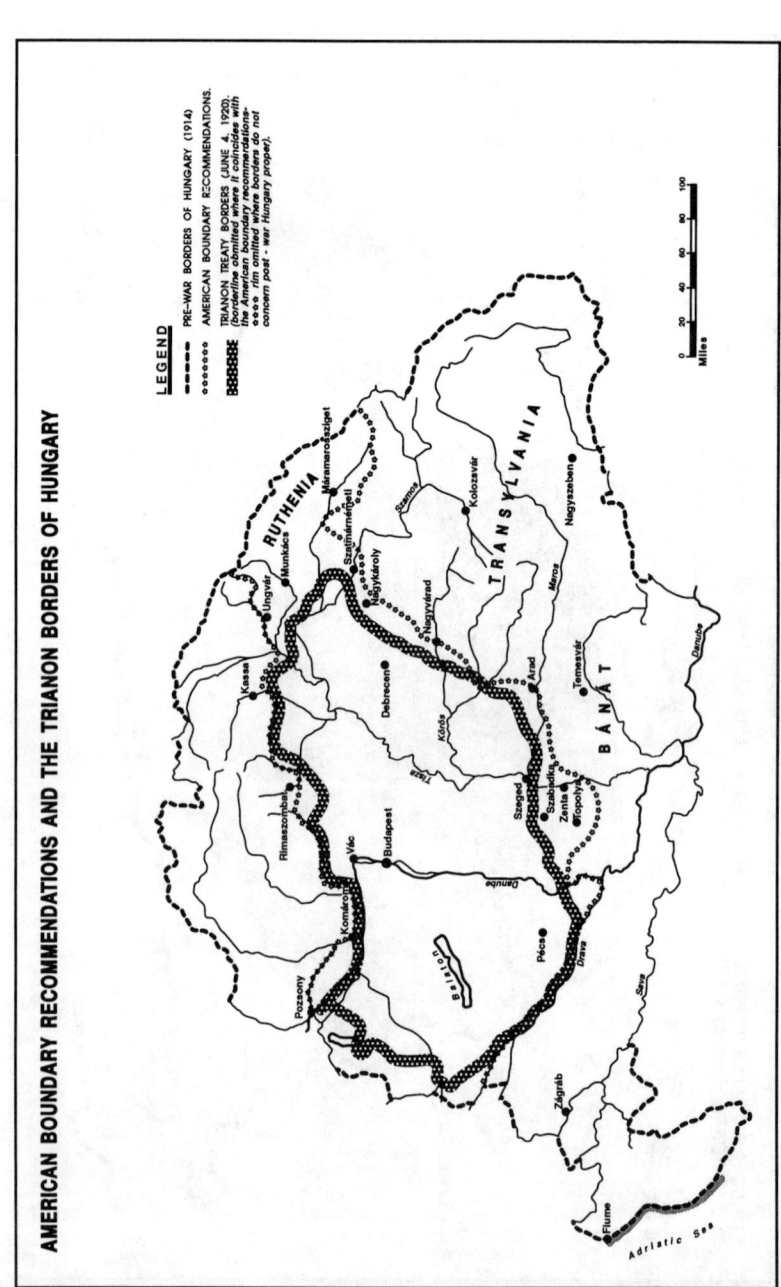

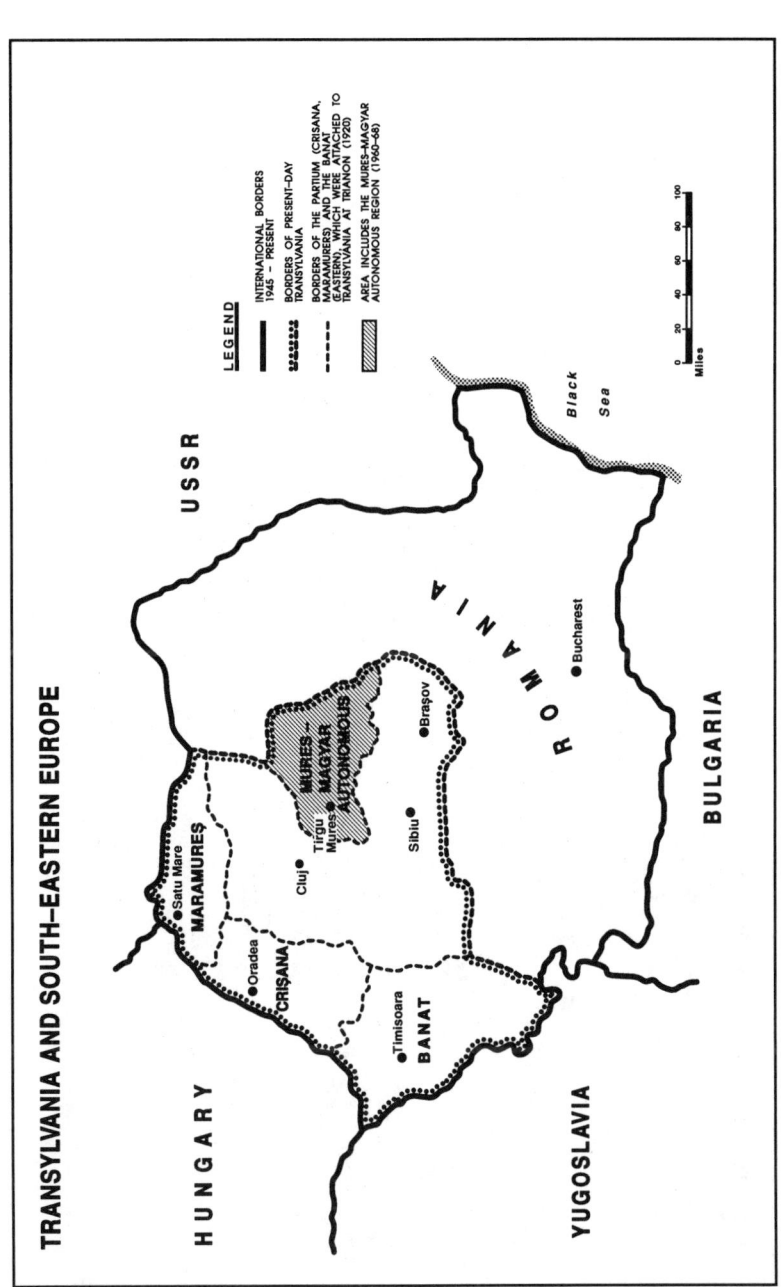

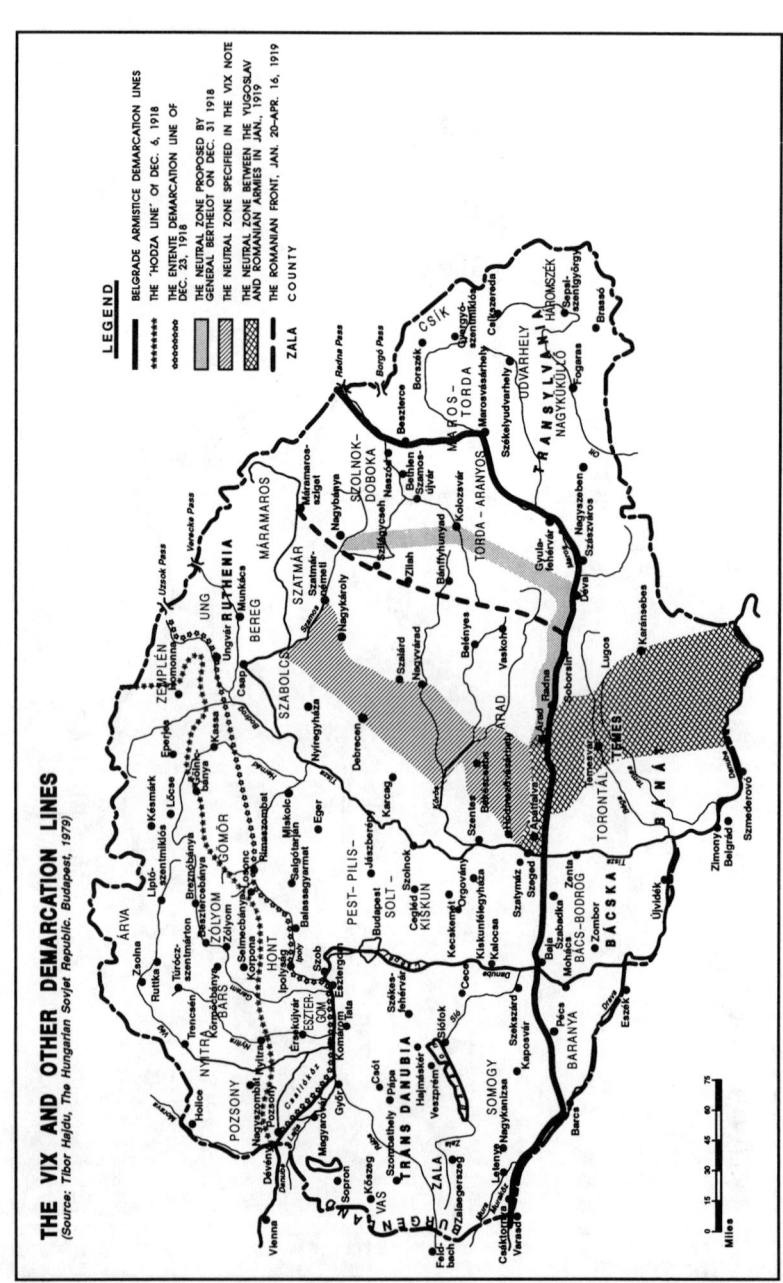

Biographical Index

Alexander I (1884-1934)
Regent, 1918-1921, then King of the Serbs, Croats, Slovenes 1921-1929. King of Yugoslavia, 1929-1934.

Allizé, Henry (1860-1930)
Head of the French military mission in Vienna, 1918-1919.

Amendola, Giovanni (1886-1926)
Italian publicist and politician. Cabinet Minister in the Nitti, Bonomi and Facta governments, 1919-1921.

Andrássy, Count Gyula (1860-1929)
Minister of Foreign Affairs of the Austro-Hungarian Monarchy, 1918, Minister of the Royal Household, 1894-95, Minister of Interior 1906-1910. After 1918 a monarchist politician in Hungary.

Antonescu, Ion (1882-1946)
Romanian Colonel, general staff operations officer, 1917-1920. Later Chief of the General Staff, 1933 and Marshal. Head of State, 1940-1944.

Antonescu, Victor
Romanian envoy to France, 1919.

Apáthy, István (1863-1922)
Biologist, political leader of the Hungarians in Transylvania, December, 1918.

Apponyi, Count Albert (1846-1933)
Hungarian politician and statesman. Minister of Education, 1906-1910, 1917-1918. Chairman of the Hungarian peace delegation, 1919-1920. Head of Hungarian delegation to the League of Nations, 1925-1933.

Ardeleanu (Erdélyi), Ioan
Leader of the Romanians in pre-war Hungary, Member of the Romanian National Committee.

Asquith, Herbert Henry (1852-1928)
Prime Minister of Great Britain, 1908-1916.

Balfour, Arthur J. (1848-1930)
British Secretary of State for Foreign Affairs, 1916-1919.

Bánffy, Count Miklós (1873-1950)
Minister of Foreign Affairs in Hungary ,1921-1922, Minister of Nationalities, 1921-1922.

Bartha, Albert (1877-1960)
Minister of War in Hungary, 1918, Minister of Defence, 1946-1947.

Battyány, Count Tivadar (1859-1931)
Hungarian politician, Minister of the Royal Household, 1917-1918, Minister of Interior of the Károlyi government, 1918.

Beneš, Eduard (1884-1948)
Minister of Foreign Affairs, later President of Czechoslovakia, 1935-1938.

Berinkey, Dénes (1871-1944)
Minister of Justice of the Károlyi government, 1918-1919, Prime Minister of Hungary, 1919, Minister of Foreign Affairs, 1919.

Berthelot, Henri-Mathias (1861-1931)
French general, reorganized the Romanian Army, 1917, commander of the Allied forces in Romania and Southern Russia, 1918-1919.

Berthelot, Philippe (1866-1934)
Secretary-General, Ministry of Foreign Affairs in France, 1920-1921, 1925-1932.

Bethlen, Count István (1874-1946)
Member of the Hungarian Peace delegation, 1920, Prime Minister of Hungary, 1921-1931., Minister of Finance, 1921, Minister of Justice 1924, 1929, Minister of Foreign Affairs, 1924, Minister of Agriculture 1924.

Böhm, Vilmos (1880-1948)
Hungarian socialist politician. Secretary of War, 1918-1919, Minister of War of the Berinkey governemnt, 1919, Commissar of War, Commissar of Collectivizing of the Hungarian Soviet Republic, 1919, Ambassador to Vienna, 1919, Ambassador, 1946-1948.

Borghese, Prince Livio
Italian diplomat and representative in Budapest, 1919

Biographical Index

Brătianu, Ioan I. C. (1864-1927)
Romanian political leader, Prime Minister of Romania 1908-1910, 1914-1919, 1922-1926, 1927., Minister of Foreign Affairs, 1918-19, 1927.

Cambon, Paul (1843-1924)
French diplomat, ambassador to London, 1898-1920.

Carol II (1893-1953)
King of Romania, 1930-1940.

Ceauşescu, Nicolae (1918-1989)
Leader of the Communist Party in Romania, 1965-1989.

Charmant, Oszkár (1860-1925)
Attorney to the Károlyi familiy. Representative of the Károlyi government in Vienna, 1918-1919.

Clemanceau, Georges (1841-1929)
French politician and statesman. Prime Minister,1906-1909, 1917-1920, Minister of War, 1917-1920, Chairman of the Paris Peace Conference,1919.

Clément-Simon, Gustave (1833-1937)
French diplomat. Minister plenipotentiary in Prague, 1918 and in Belgrade, 1921.

Clerk, George R. (1874-1951)
Head of Allied Mission in Hungary, 1919.

Coandă, Constantin General
Prime Minister of Romania, 1918, Minister of Foreign Affairs, 1918.

Codreanu, Corneliu Zelea (1899-1933)
Political leader of the Romanian Iron Guard.

Csáky, Count Imre (1882-1961)
Austro-Hungarian Diplomat, Head of the Political Department of Károlyi's Ministry of Foreign Affairs, 1918-1919, Minister of Foreign Affairs, 1920.

Cuza, A. C. (1857-1940)
Romanian politician, Head of the League of National Christian Defense.

D'Annunzio, Gabriele (1864-1938)
Italian novelist, poet, profascist politician. Occupied Fiume, 1919.

Darányi, Kálmán (1886-1939)
Prime Minister of Hungary, 1936-1938, Minister of Agriculture, 1935-38, Minister of Interior, 1937.

Deák, Francis (1899-)
International law specialist, who held various academic posts in the USA

Denikin, Anton Ivanovich (1872-1947)
Lt. general, military commander against communist revolution in Russia, 1918-1919, Head of anti-Bolshevist governments, 1919.

Derby, Earl of (1865-1948)
British ambassador to France, 1918-1920.

Ferdinand (Hohenzollern) (1865-1927)
King of Romania, 1914-1927.

Foch, Ferdinand (1851-1929)
French marshal, chief of the French General Staff, Commander-in-Chief of the Allied forces, 1918

Franchet d'Esperey, Louis Felix (1856-1942)
General, later Marshal of France, Commander-in-Chief of the Allied forces in the Balkans, 1917-1919.

Franz Ferdinand, Archduke (1863-1914)
Heir to the Austro-Hungarian Monarchy, assassinated in Sarajevo, Bosnia, 1914.

Friedrich, István (1883-1951)
Prime Minister of Hungary, 1919, Secretary of the Ministry of War, 1918-1919, Minister of War, 1919-1920, Minister of Commerce, 1919, Minister of Interior, 1919.

Fülep, Lajos (1885-1970)
Hungarian philosopher, art historian, sent to diplomatic missions to Fiume because of his Italian contacts, 1918-1919.

Gheorghiu-Dej, Gheorghe (1908-1965)
First Secretary of the Romanian Communist Party, 1944-1965, Prime Minister, 1954-1955, Head of State, 1961-1965.

Goga, Octavian (1881-1938)
Romanian poet, politician. Prime Minister, 1938, Minister of Education, 1920, Minister of Interior, 1926-1927, founder of National Agrarian Party.

Goldis, Vasile (1861-1934)
    Romanian political leader from Arad.
Gömbös, Gyula (1886-1936)
    Hungarian politician of extreme-right. Secretary of the Ministry of War of governments in Szeged, Prime Minister, 1932-1936, Minister of Defence, 1929-1936,
Gottwald, Klement (1896-1953)
    Leader of the Communist Party of Czechoslovakia, 1919-1923, third President of Czechoslovakia, 1948-1953.
Grey, Sir Edward (1862-1933)
    British statesman, Foreign Secretary, 1905-1916.
Gyárfás, Elemér (1884-1945)
    Lord Lieutenant of Kis-Küküllő county in Transylvania, after 1918 Hungarian politician living in Transylvania.
Heinrich, Ferenc (1866-1925)
    Hungarian politician, designated Prime Minister, 1919, Minister of Commerce 1919. 1919-1920.
Hitler, Adolf (1889-1945)
    German Chancellor, 1933, Führer of the Third Reich, 1934-1945.
Hlinka, Andrej (1864-1938)
    Slovak Roman Catholic priest and nationalities leader.
Hodža, Milan (1878-1944)
    Slovak politician in prewar Hungary, Czecho-Slovak representative in Hungary, December 1918, Prime Minister of Czechoslovakia, 1936-1938.
Horthy, Miklós Nagybányai (1868-1957)
    Regent of Hungary, 1920-1944.
House, Colonel Edward Mandell (1853-1938)
    Leader of the Inquiry, a close advisor to President Wilson.
Husák, Gustav (1913-1991)
    Czechoslovak and Slovak politician, First Secretary of the Communist Party, the 7th president of Czechoslovakia, 1975-
Ionescu, Dumitriu Take (1858-1922)
    Prime Minister of Romania, 1921-22, Minister of Foreign Affairs, 1920-1921, Minister of Education,1899-1900, Minister of Finance, 1900, 1904-1907, Minister of Interior, 1912.

Jászi, Oszkár (1875-1957)
Sociologist, political writer, Minister of Nationalities in the Károlyi government, Head of the Council of Foreign Affairs, 1919

Joseph August, Archduke (1872-1962)
Homo regius of King Karl (q.v.) in Hungary, October, 1918, reclaimed this title in August 1919 and appointed the Friedrich government. Resigned from his position on August 25, 1919.

Kánya, Kálmán (1869-1945)
Hungarian politician and diplomat. Ambassador to Mexico, 1913-1918, Ambassador to Berlin, 1925-1933, Secretary of Foreign Affairs, 1920-1925, Minister of Foreign Affairs, 1933-1938.

Karl (1887-1922)
Austrian Emperor as Karl I, Hungarian King as Karl IV., 1916-1918.

Károlyi, Count Mihály (1875-1955)
Hungarian politician and statesman, leader of the October revolutiuon in Hungary, Prime Minister, 1918-1919, Minister of Finance, 1918, Minister of War, 1918, provisory President of the Republic, 1919, Ambassador to Paris, 1947-1949.

Keynes, John Maynard (1883-1955)
Economist and economic philosopher, principal representative of the Treasury on the British Delegation at Paris, Member of the Supreme Economic Council.

Kramař, Karel (1860-1937)
First Prime Minister of Czechoslovakia, 1918-1920.

Kun, Béla (1886-1939)
Leader of the Hungarian Soviet Republic, 1919, Commissar of Foreign Affairs, Commissar of War, 1919.

Kunfi, Zsigmond (1879-1929)
Hungarian Social Democrat politician, Minister of Public Welfare, 1918-1919, Minister of Education, Commissar of Education, 1919.

Lansdowne, Henry Petty-Fitzmaurice, Marquess (1845-1927)
British statesman, Minister without portfolio in the Asquith government, 1915-1916.

Lansing, Robert L. (1868-1928)
American politician, Secretary of State under President Wilson, 1915-1920.

Lenin, Vladimir Ilyich (1870-1924)
Russian communist revolutionary, Leader of the Communist Party, 1917-1924.

Linder, Béla (1876-1962)
Staff officer of the Austro-Hungarian Army, Minister of War of the Károlyi government and Minister in charge of the conclusion of peace, 1918.

Lloyd George, David (1863-1945)
British Prime Minister, 1916-1922.

Mackensen, August von (1849-1945)
German general, Commander of German forces in occupied Romania, 1916-1918.

Macartney, Carlile Aylmer (1895-1978)
British historian of the Danube region, an Eastern Europe expert of the Foreign Office during World War II.

Maniu, Iuliu (1873-1953)
Member of prewar Hungarian Parliament, Leader of the Romanian National Peasant Party, Prime Minister of Romania, 1928-1930, 1932-33, 1944.

Masaryk, Tomáš Garrigue (1850-1937)
Founder and first President of Czechoslovakia, 1918-1935.

Meskó, Zoltán (1883-1959)
Hungarian politician of extreme right, participant of the Arrow Cross movement, founder of the Hungarian National Socialist Party in 1933.

Millerand, Alexandre (1859-1943)
French Prime Minister, 1920, President of France, 1920-1924, President of the Council of Ambassadors of the Peace Conference.

Mišić, Živojin (1855-1921)
Serbian voivode, military commander during the Balkan Wars, Commander of the First Army, 1914, Chief-of-staff on the Salonika front, 1918.

Mussolini, Benito (1883-1945)
Italian fascist dictator, Prime Minister, 1922-1943.

Nagyatádi Szabó, István (1863-1924)
Hungarian agrarian politician, Minister of Agriculture, 1919-1924 (several times)

Namier, Lewis B. (1888-1960)
Temporary Clerk in the Foreign Office, 1918-1920, Member of the Intelligence Bureau and the P.I.D.

Napoleon, Bonaparte (1769-1821)
French Emperor, 1804-1814,1815.

Nicholas, II (1868-1918)
Russian Tsar, 1894-1917, executed.

Nitti, Francesco Saverio (1868-1953)
Italian liberal politician, Prime Minister, 1919-1920.

Northcliffe, Viscount Alfred Charles W. Harmsworth (1865-1922)
British newspaper publisher, Director of the Department of Enemy Propaganda during World War I.

Orlando, Vittorio Emanuele (1860-1952)
Italian Prime Minister, 1917-1919.

Osuský, Štefan (1889-1973)
Slovak supporter of Masaryk during World War I., Secretary general of the Czecho-Slovak delegation at the Paris Peace Conference, later Ambassador to France.

Paléologue, Maurice (1859-1944)
Secretary-General, French Ministry of Foreign Affairs, 1920.

Pallavicini, Marquis György (1881-1946)
Hungarian Secretary of State, 1917-1918, monarchist politician of the postwar period.

Pellé, Maurice (1863-1924)
French general, Commander of the French military mission in Czechoslovakia, 1919-1920.

Pichon, Stephen (1857-1933)
French politician, Minister of Foreign Affairs, 1906-1911, 1913, 1917-1920.

Piłsudski, Józef (1867-1935)
Polish statesman, leader of Polish Socialist Party, during the First World War leader of the Polish Legion, Head of state, 1918-1922, Commander-in-Chief in war with Russia, virtual dictator after coup of 1926.

Prešan, Constantin General
Commander-in-Chief of the Romanian army in Hungary,1919.

Rákosi, Mátyás (1892-1971)
Commissar of social production of the Kun regime, 1919, Prime Minister of Hungary, 1952-1953, General secretary of the Hungarian Communist Party, 1945-1956.

Rátz, Jenő (1882-1952)
Leading military posts after 1923, Minister of Defense, 1936-1938, Minister without Portfolio, 1944, in 1945 condemned as a war criminal.

Révai, József (1898-1959)
Hungarian writer, communist party theoretician, Minister of Education, 1949-1953.

Ribbentrop, Joachim von (1893-1945)
Minister of Foreign Affairs under the Nazi regime

Rőder, Vilmos (1881-1969)
Chief of Staff, 1930-1935, Minister of Defense, 1936-1938.

Romanelli, Guido (1876-)
Italian general, leader of the Italian military mission to Hungary, 1919.

Rothermere, Harold Sidney Harmsworth, Viscount (1868-1940)
Conservative British politician and publisher.

Rugonfalvi Kiss, István (1881-1957)
President of the Székely National Committee in 1918, later a traditionalist historian of the National Romantic School at the University of Debrecen.

Schnetzer, Ferenc (1867-1944)
Minister of War in Hungary, 1919.

Schuschnigg, Kurt von (1897-1972)
Chancellor of Austria, 1934-1938.

Scialoja, Vittorio (1856-1933)
Italian senator and Minister of Foreign Affairs of the Nitti government, 1919-1920, Delegate to the Peace Conference, Representative to the League of Nations, 1921-1932.

Setan-Watson, Robert W. (1879-1951)
British scholar, founder and editor of *The New Europe*.

Seymour, Charles (1885-1963)
Scholar, American member of the Territorial Commission for Romania.

Sixtus, Robert Bourbon, Count of Parma (1886-1934)
Brother-in-law of Emperor Karl, go-between during the secret peace feelers between Austria-Hungary and France.

Šmeral, Bohumir (1880-1941)
Left-wing socialist, founder of the Czechoslovak Communist Party.

Smuts, Jan Christian (1870-1950)
South African politician and general, Minister in the Lloyd George cabinet, sent to Hungary by the Peace Conference, April 1919.

Somssich, Count József (1864-1941)
Hungarian Diplomat, Minister of Foreign Affairs, 1919-1920, Ambassador to the Vatican, 1920-1924.

Sonnino, Baron Giorgio Sidney (1847-1922)
Minister of Finance, 1893-1894, 1894-1896, Minister of Foreign Affairs of the Orlando government, 1914-1919.

Soós, Károly (1869-1953)
Minister of Defence in Hungary, 1920, Military commander in South Hungary, 1921-1922.

Šrobar, Vavro (1876-1950)
Slovak politician, Minister plenipotentiary for Slovak affairs, 1918-1920.

Stalin, Iosif Visarionovich (1879-1953)
Soviet dictator, 1922-1953.

Steed, Henry Wickham (1871-1956)
British publicist and Times journalist, notorious for anti-Austro-Hungarian sentiments.

Szamuely, Tibor (1890-1919)
Deputy Commissar of War, Commissar of Education in the Hungarian Sovie Republik. 1919.

Tardieu, André (1876-1945)
President of the Territorial Commission for Romania of the Paris Peace Conference, French Prime Minister, 1929-1930,1932.

Teleki, Count Pál (1879-1941)
Noted geographer, conservative Hungarian politician, Minister of Foreign Affairs, 1920-1921, 1941, Minister of the Hungarian Nationalities, 1920-1921, Minister of Education, 1938-39, Prime Minister, 1920-1921, 1939-1941, committed suicide.

Tiso, Msgr. Jozef (1887-1947)
Slovak clergyman and populist leader, President of the Slovak State, executed in 1947.

Tisza, Count István(1861-1918)
Leading Hungarian politician and statesman, Prime Minister, 1903-1905, 1913-1917, Minister of Interior, 1903-1905, Minister of the Royal Household, 1903-1904, 1915.

Titulescu, Nicolae (1882-1941)
Minister of Finance in Romania, 1917-1918, 1920-1922., Delegate to the Peace Conference, one of the signers of the Treaty, Minister of Foreign Affairs, 1927-1928, 1932-1936.

Troubridge, Sir Ernest (1862-1926)
British admiral, officer commanding on the Danube, 1919.

Vaida-Voievod, Alexandru (1872-1950)
Member of the prewar Hungarian Parliament, Member of the Romanian National Committee, Prime Minister of Romania, 1919, 1932-33, Minister of Foreign Affairs, 1919-1920, 1932.

Vesnić, Milenko (1862-1921)
Yugoslav statesman, Representative of Yugoslavia to the Peace Conference, 1919-1920.

Vix, Fernand (1872-)
Lieutenant-Colonel, Head of the Allied Military Mission in Hungary, 1918-1919.

Wilson, Woodrow (1856-1924)
President of the United States, 1913-1921.

Wrangel, Baron Pietr (1878-1928)
Commander of Russian White armies, 1920.

Yates, Halsey E.
American military attaché to Bucharest, 1919.

László Veszprémy

Selected Reading List on Trianon

Ádám, Magda, et al., eds., *Documents diplomatiques français sur l'histoire du Basin des Carpates 1918-1932*, vol.1 (October 1918 – August 1919) (Budapest, 1993).

Ádám, Magda, "New Sources on Trianon," *The New Hungarian Quaterly* 32 (1991): pp. 91-97.

Ádám, Magda, *The Little Entente and Europe 1920–1929* (Budapest, 1993).

Arday, Lajos, *Map After a Battle. Hungary in British Foreign Policy 1918-1919* [in Hungarian] (Budapest, 1990).

Barczy, Zoltán, "The Development and Concealment of Hungarian Antiaircraft Artillery, 1922–1938," [in Hungarian] *Hadtörténelmi Közlemények* 32 (1985): pp. 877–891.

Berend T., Iván, and Ránki, György, *The Hungarian Economy in the Twentieth Century* (New York, 1983).

Bíró, Sándor, *The Nationalities Problem in Transylvania 1867–1940* (New York, 1992).

Blanke, Richard, *Orphans of Versailles: The Germans in Western Poland 1918–1939* (Lexington, 1993).

Bödy, Paul, ed., *Hungarian Statesmen of Destiny: 1860–1960* (New York, 1989).

Borsányi, György, *The Life of a Communist Revolutionary, Béla Kun* (New York, 1993).

Borsody, Stephen, ed., *The Hungarians: A Divided Nation* (New Haven, 1988).

Braham, R. L., *The Politics of Genocide: The Holocaust in Hungary*, 2 vols. (New York, 1981).

Ciobanu, N. and Botoran, C., "The 1918 Decisions for Union at Chişianu, Cernăuţi and Alba Iulia," *Revue International d'Histoire Militaire*, no.77 (1992): pp. 95-108.

Crampton, R. J., *Eastern Europe in the Twentieth Century* (New York, 1994).

Dagan, Avigdor, ed., *The Jews of Czechoslovakia: Historical Studies and Surveys* (Philadelphia, 1984).

Deák, István, "Historical Foundations: The Development of Hungary from 1918 until 1945," in Klaus-Detlev Grothusen ed., *Südosteuropa Handbuch* vol. 5 (Göttingen,1987), pp. 36-66.

Di Biagio, Anna, "I bolscevichi e il sistema de Versailles 1919-1923," *Studi Storici* 27 (1986): pp. 453-502.

Dobrinescu, Valeriu, "Romania's Diplomacy and the Great Union of 1918," *Transylvanian Review* 2 (1993): pp.55-62.

Dockerill, Michael and Goold, J. Douglas, eds., *Peace without Promise: Britain and the Peace Conferences 1919-1923* (London, 1981).

Dogan, Mattei, "Romania 1919-1938," in Myron Weiner and Ergun Ozbuden, eds., *Competitive Elections in Developing Countries* (Durham, 1987), pp. 369-389.

Dombrády, Lóránd and Tóth, Sándor, *The Hungarian Honvéd Army 1919-1945* [in Hungarian] (Budapest, 1987).

Egerton, G. W., *Great Britain and the Creation of the League of Nations: Strategy, Politics and International Organization 1914-1919* (Chapel Hill, 1981).

Galántai, József, *Hungary in World War I* (Budapest, 1989).

Galántai, József, *Trianon and the Protection of Minorities* (New York, 1991).

Guida, Francesco, "Ungheria e Italia dalla fine del primo conflitto mondiale al Trattato del Trianon," *Storia Contemporanea* 19 (1988): pp. 381-418.

Hidas, Péter I., ed., *Minorities and the Law* (Toronto, 1986).

Iancu, Gheorghe and Mîndruţ, Stalian, "Genesis and Circulation of a Book: R. W. Seton-Watson, Corruption and Reform in Hungary," *Transylvanian Review* 2 (1993): pp. 84-90.

Jelinek, Yeshayahu, "Thomas G. Masaryk and the British Foreign Office," in Eva Schmidt-Hartmann and Stanley B. Winters, eds., *Great Britain, the United States and the Bohemian Lands 1848-1938* (München, 1991), pp. 277-284.

Kalvoda, J., *The Genesis of Czechoslovakia* (Boulder, 1986).

Karski, Jan, *The Great Powers and Poland 1919-1945* (Lanham, 1985).

Kaser, M. C., ed., *The Economic History of Eastern Europe: 1919-1975*, 5 vols. (Oxford, 1985-).

Katzburg, N., *Hungary and the Jews: Policy and Legislation 1920-1943* (Ramat-Gan, 1981).

Király, Béla K. and Dreisziger, N.F., eds., *East Central European Society in World War I* (New York, 1985).

Király, Béla K. and Nofi, Walter, eds., *East Central European War Leaders* (New York, 1988).

Király, Béla K. and Fischer-Galati, Stephen, eds., *Essays on East Central European Society and War 1740-1920* (New York, 1988)

Király, B., Pastor, P., and Sanders, I., eds., *Essays on World War I: Total War and Peacemaking, A Case Study on Trianon* (New York, 1982).

Latawski, Paul, "Lewis Namier and the Criteria of State Building: The Construction of Czechoslovakia and Poland 1915-1920" in Eva Schmidt-Hartmann and Stanley B. Winters, eds., *Great Britain, the United States and the Bohemian Lands 1848-1938* (München, 1991), pp. 143-152.

Liptai, Ervin, ed., *Military History of Hungary*, vol 2 [in Hungarian] (Budapest, 1985).

Litván, György, "Oscar Jászi, 1875-1957," *The New Hungarian Quaterly* 32 (1991): pp. 16-29.

Mendelsohn, Ezra, *The Jews of East Central Europe between the Wars* (Bloomington, 1983).

Mócsy, István, *The Effects of World War I. The Uprooted: Hungarian Refugees and Their Impact on Hungary's Domestic Politics* (New York, 1983).

Nagy, Zsuzsa L, "Peacemaking after Word War I: The Western Democracies and the Hungarian Question," in Borsody, Stephen, ed., *The Hungarians: A Divided Nation* (New Haven, 1988), pp. 32-52.

Ormos, Mária, *From Padova to the Trianon 1918–1920* (New York, 1990).
Pastor, Peter, ed., *Revolutions and Interventions in Hungary and Its Neighbor States* (New York, 1988).
Rothschild, Joseph, *Return to Diversity: A Political History of East Central Europe since World War II* (New York, 1990).
Sharp, Alan, *The Versailles Settlement: Peacemaking in Paris, 1919.* (New York, 1991).
Siklós, András, *Revolution in Hungary and the Dissolution of the Multinational State 1918* (Budapest, 1988).
Silverman, D.P., *Reconstructing Europe after the Great War* (Harvard University Press, 1982).
Spira, Thomas, "The Reaction of Hungary's German Minorities to Oscar Jaszi's Plan for an 'Eastern Switzerland'," *Hungarian Studies Review* 18, nos. 1–2 (1991): pp. 27–42. [Special Issue: *Oscar Jaszi: Visionary, Reformer, and Political Activist*].
Stevenson, David, "Reading History. The Treaty of Versailles," *History Today* 36 (Oct. 1986): pp.50–52.
Sukiennnicki, Wiktor, *East Central Europe during World War I*, 2 vols. (Boulder, 1986).
Teichová, Alice, *The Czechoslovak Economy 1918–1980* (New York, 1988).
Tomaszewski, Jerzy, *The Polish Economy in the 20th Century* (London, 1985).
Tomaszewski, Jerzy, "Some Methodological Problems of the Study of Jewish History in Poland between the Two World Wars," *Polin: A Journal of Polish-Jewish Studies* 1 (1986): pp. 163–175.
Trachtenberg, M., *Reparation in World Politics: France and European Economic Diplomacy 1916–1923* (New York, 1980).
Vermes, Gábor, *István Tisza. The Liberal Vision and Conservative Statecraft of a Magyar Nationalist* (New York, 1985).
Wandycz, Piotr, *France and Her Eastern Alliances 1926–1936* (Princeton, 1988).
Wandycz, Piotr, *The Price of Freedom. A History of East Central Europe From the Middle Ages to the Present* (New York, 1992).

Winters, S., Pysant, R. B. and Hanak, H., eds., *T.G. Masaryk 1850–1937*, 3 vols. (New York, 1989).

Zarnowski, J., ed., *Dictatorship in East Central Europe 1918–1939* (Wrocław, 1983).

Name Index

Alby, General Henri Edouard, 97, 105
Alexander, Serbian King, 46, 50, 96
Allizé, Henri, 116
Ameil, Captain, 73
Andrássy, Count Gyula, 116, 124, 142, 244
Antonescu, Ion, 7, 139, 178
Antonescu, Victor, 84, 177
Apáthy, István, 174, 183
Apponyi, Count Albert, 23, 49
Ardeleanu, Ioan, 38, 116, 172
Aron, Raymond, 275, 277
Asquith, Herbert Henry, 272
Balfour, Arthur, 70, 103
Bánffy, Count Miklós, 126, 143
Bartha, Albert, 171
Batthyány, Count Tivadar, 244, 253, 255
Békési, András, 109, 141
Belin, General, 99, 105
Beneš, Eduard, 18, 21, 26, 46, 50, 91, 102, 171, 201, 202, 203, 204, 214
Berinkey, Dénes, 165, 175
Berthelot, 19, 26, 63, 81, 82, 84, 89, 91, 174, 175, 177

Bethlen, Count István, 50, 52, 116, 120, 124, 128, 134, 135, 136, 138, 144, 222, 223, 244, 250, 261
Böhm, Vilmos, 78, 104, 183, 224
Böll, Heinrich, 239, 250
Borghese, Prince Livio, 111, 117
Borsody, István, 13, 38, 210, 214, 216
Brătianu, Ioan I.C., 14, 17, 50, 63, 83, 115, 119, 123, 125, 129, 131, 139, 181, 186, 187, 188, 189, 198
Burebista, 196
Cambon, Paul, 80
Cambon, Jules-Martin, 19, 102
Carol II., Romanian king, 50, 138, 192
Ceauşescu, Nicolae, 196
Charmant, Oszkár, 110, 111, 112, 113, 115, 128, 141
Clemenceau, Georges, 17, 18, 19, 23, 24, 25, 58, 60, 67, 70, 71, 74, 75, 76, 81, 83, 84, 85, 87, 88, 89, 90, 91, 96, 97, 99, 100, 101, 103, 104, 105, 174, 177, 178

Clément-Simon, Gustave, 99, 105
Clerk, Sir George, 125, 142
Cnobloch, Hans, 124
Coandă, General Constantin, 97
Codreanu, Corneliu Zelea, 190, 191
Contarini, 134
Csáky, Count Imre, 116, 129
Cuza, A.C., 190
D'Annunzio, Gabriele, 118
Darányi, Kálmán, 266
Davis, John William, 27
de Caix, 69, 82, 83, 88
Deák, Ferenc, 141, 143
Deák, István, 236
Denikin, General Anton Ivanovich, 95
Diamandi, Constantin, 117, 120, 124
Diaz, General Armando Vittorio, 56, 64, 67, 78, 87, 88, 180
Dormándy, Lieutenant Colonel Géza, 87
Erdelyi, Ioan, see Ardeleanu
Ferdinand, Romanian king, 118, 127, 130, 132
Foch, Marshal Ferdinand, 58, 60, 76, 79, 80, 89, 91, 96, 102, 172, 176
Franchet d'Esperey, General Louis, 18, 19, 57, 64, 66, 67, 68, 69, 71, 73, 74, 75, 76, 79, 84, 87, 88, 89, 90, 91, 96, 97, 99, 101, 105, 169, 170, 171, 174, 175, 176, 178
Francis Ferdinand, Archduke, 44, 53
Francis Joseph I, Austrian emperor, 272
Friedrich, István, 23, 117, 118, 120
Fülep, Lajos, 108
Fürstenberg, Prince Egon von, 130, 136, 143
Georges, General Joseph, 73
Gheorghiu-Dej, Gheorghe, 195, 196
Goga, Octavian, 191
Goldis, Vasile, 172
Gömbös, Gyula, 50, 144, 221, 223, 236, 264, 266
Gottwald, Klement, 211
Grandi, Dino, 136
Guillaumat, General Marie-Louis, 64, 72, 86
Gyárfás, Elemér, 110
Hajdu, Tibor, 180, 184, 253, 255
Heinrich, Ferenc, 119, 120, 126
Henrys, General Paul-Prosper, 19, 55, 68, 73, 74, 90
Hirsch, (family), 244
Hitler, Adolf, 7, 10, 13, 14, 35, 50, 51, 162, 190, 191, 192, 193, 194, 225, 234, 266, 267, 272
Hlinka, Andrej, 208

Name Index

Hodža, Milan, 44, 45, 171, 215
Holbán, General, 120
Horthy, Miklós, 7, 27, 31, 48, 49, 55, 104, 126, 130, 132, 133, 140, 165, 179, 220, 221, 223, 224, 225, 226, 231, 234, 235, 236, 250, 254, 267
Hóry, András, 132, 144
House, Colonel Edward M., 57, 59, 80, 81, 180
Husák, Gustav, 204
Imrédy, Béla, 223, 232, 237, 267
Ionescu, Take, 53, 63, 115, 129, 130, 131, 132, 139, 143
Isopescul-Grecul, Constantin, 116, 128
Jászi, Oszkár (Oscar), 5, 12, 13, 39, 45, 48, 51, 52, 53, 78, 109, 110, 114, 167, 168, 170, 171, 172, 173, 174, 181, 182, 183, 215, 245, 253
Joseph, Archduke, 23, 26
Kalergi, Count Coudenhove, 12
Kánya, Kálmán, 139
Karl, Austrian emperor, Hungarian king, 58, 167, 273
Károlyi, Count Mihály, 18, 22, 23, 25, 39, 48, 51, 55, 56, 66, 67, 68, 69, 73, 74, 75, 76, 77, 78, 79, 88, 90, 91, 104, 108, 110, 111, 112, 114, 118, 140, 165, 166, 167, 169, 170, 171, 175, 176, 177, 178, 179, 180, 181, 182, 184, 236, 244, 246, 247, 253, 255
Kemény, Gábor, 37
Kemény (family), 244
Keynes, John Maynard, 48
Khrushchev, Nikita S., 195, 196
Kovács, Alajos, 236, 237
Kozmovszky, Lieutenant Colonel József, 87
Kun, Béla, 22, 23, 48, 52, 79, 96, 99, 127, 165, 179, 187, 188, 224, 225, 236
Kunfi, Zsigmond, 174
Landsdowne, Henry Petty-Fitzmaurice, Lord, 272
Lansing, Robert L., 75, 80, 91
Lehár, Antal, 133, 144
Lenin, Vladimir I., 60, 78, 180, 181, 182, 183, 272
Lévai, Jenő (Eugene), 228, 236, 237
Linder, Béla, 55, 73, 90
Livio, Borghese Prince, see Borghese
Lloyd George, David, 9, 21, 23, 24, 27, 71, 81, 86, 128, 272, 273, 276
Lobit, Paul de, General, 19, 184
Lovászy, Márton, 118, 123
Lukács, György, 225
Macartney, C.A., 51, 140, 198, 201, 202, 214, 215, 219, 235, 237, 254

Machioro, 114
Mackensen, General August von, 66, 67, 71, 74, 169
Maniu, Iuliu, 50, 115, 116, 124, 131, 132, 136, 171, 172
Marghiloman, Alexandru, 170
Masaryk, Tomáš G., 26, 35, 39, 45, 46, 50, 102, 202, 204, 206, 207, 210, 213, 216, 271
Meskó, Zoltán, 232
Mihali, Teodor (Tivadar), 115, 124
Millerand, Alexandre, 18, 24, 25, 27, 29, 32, 37, 38, 128
Mironescu, Georghe, 137, 139
Mišić, Živojin, 55
Molotov, Viacheslav M., 10, 14, 193
Mombelli, General Ernesto, 124
Monzie, Anatole de, 133
Mussolini, Benito, 14, 50, 134, 135, 136, 138, 140, 190
Nagyatádi Szabó, István, 118
Namier, Lewis B., 168, 276
Napoleon, Bonaparte 272, 276
Nicholas, Tsar, 185
Nitti, Francesco, 23, 24, 128, 143
Northcliffe, Lord Alfred Charles, 46
Orlando, Vittorio Emanuele, 108
Osusky, Štefan, 202
Paléologue, Maurice, 18, 24, 27, 129

Pallavicini, Marquis György, 116
Pellé, General Maurice, 19, 99, 101, 105
Pichon, Stephen, 58, 61, 81, 82, 83, 84, 86, 91, 99, 105, 172
Prešan, General Constantin, 98
Raffay, Ernő, 25, 39, 141
Rákosi, Mátyás, 52, 225
Rattigan, William, 119
Rátz, Jenő, 264, 265, 266
Révai, József, 225
Ribbentrop, Joachim von, 10, 14
Robespierre, Maximilien, 272
Romanelli, Lieutenant Colonel Guido, 124, 126
Rossi, General, 111
Rothermere, Lord Harold Sidney, 50
Rubinek, Gyula, 126
Rugonfalvy Kiss, István, 115, 141
Schnetzer, Ferenc, 118
Schuschnigg, Kurt von, 151
Scialoja, Vittorio, 24, 128
Seton-Watson, Robert W., 43, 44, 45, 46, 47, 48, 49, 50, 51, 52, 53, 197, 199, 254, 255
Seton-Watson, Hugh, 13, 43, 198, 235
Seymour, Charles, 16, 81, 89, 113, 141, 176, 181
Sixtus, Prince Robert, of Bourbon, 273, 276

Šmeral, Bohumir, 203
Smuts, General Jan Christian, 96
Somssich, Count József, 123, 124, 126, 128
Sonnino, Baron Giorgio Sidney, 108, 113, 114
Soós, Károly, 128
Šrobár, Vavro, 38, 201, 212
Stalin, Iosif V., 14, 192, 193, 194, 195, 272
Steed, Henry Wickham, 47
Szabó, István, see Nagyatádi Szabó
Szamuely, Tibor, 224
Tacoli, Marquis de, 111, 112, 113
Tardieu, André, 19, 89
Teleki, Pál, 23, 40, 120, 124, 128
Teleki (family), 244
Tiso, Jozsef, Msgr., 7
Tisza, István, 5, 13, 31, 52, 108, 140, 250
Titulescu, Nicolae, 136, 139

Troubridge, Admiral Sir Ernest, 119, 124, 126, 142
Vaida-Voevod, Alexandru, 44, 125, 172
Vajda, Sándor, see Vaida-Voevod
Vesnić, Milenko, 70
Vix, Lieutenant Colonel Fernand, 19, 25, 74, 79, 90, 91, 97, 117, 165, 178, 179, 183, 184
Votruba, Prantišek, 212
Weber, General Victor, 65, 66, 87, 163, 198, 236
Wilson, Woodrow, 10, 16, 25, 57, 58, 59, 61, 78, 80, 166, 167, 175, 176, 180, 181, 182, 183, 273, 276
Wrangel, Pietr, 127
Yates, Halsey E., 177, 178, 183, 184
Zaleski, August, 137
Zichy (family), 244

Place Index

Alba Iulia, see Gyulafehérvár
Arad (Rom.: Arad), 109, 114, 120
Baia Mare, see Nagybánya
Baja, 108
Báziás (Rom.: Bazias), 64
Békéscsaba, 117, 120, 124
Belgrade, 17, 18, 55, 56, 57, 59, 61, 63, 65, 66, 67, 68, 69, 70, 71, 73, 74, 75, 77, 87, 88, 89, 96, 97, 100, 107, 108, 117, 118, 163, 170, 171, 173, 174, 180, 247, 271
Berchtesgaden, 138
Berlin, 43, 163, 191, 193, 210, 229, 234, 266, 267
Beszterce (Rom.: Bistriţa, Germ.: Bistritz), 173
Bled, 267
Braşov, see Brassó
Brassó (Rom.: Braşov, Ger.: Kronstadt), 173
Bratislava, see Pozsony
Brest-Litovsk, 16, 166, 273
Bucharest, 9, 17, 20, 46, 62, 64, 95, 102, 109, 111, 113, 115, 116, 117, 118, 119, 122, 123, 124, 125, 126, 127, 128, 130, 131, 132, 135, 136, 137, 139, 144, 166, 168, 169, 170, 173, 177, 178, 189, 190, 191, 192, 193, 196
Budapest, 14, 21, 22, 27, 31, 34, 35, 43, 44, 45, 53, 66, 72, 73, 74, 75, 76, 77, 87, 88, 89, 90, 91, 94, 96, 98, 99, 107, 108, 109, 111, 112, 113, 115, 117, 118, 119, 120, 124, 125, 127, 130, 133, 145, 169, 172, 173, 174, 176, 177, 191, 192, 193, 194, 195, 196, 204, 209, 210, 211, 212, 219, 225, 226, 228, 230, 232, 233, 234, 250, 254
Cluj-Napoca, see Kolozsvár
Csallóköz (Slov.: Žitný ostrov, Germ.: Grosse Schüttinsel), 31, 32, 38
Csepel, 224
Csucsa (Rom.: Ciucea), 114, 175
Debrecen, 95, 115, 116, 141, 230
Dej, see Dés
Dés (Rom.: Dej, Germ.: Desch), 174

Fiume, 74, 90, 107, 108, 112, 113, 118, 122, 133, 134, 169
Fünfkirchen, see Pécs
Geneva, 35, 263
Gödöllő, 129
Graz, 128
Grosse Schütt, see Csallóköz
Gyulafehérvár (Rom.: Alba Iulia, Germ.: Karlsburg, Weissenburg), 109, 172
Hajmáskér, 128
Hirtenberg, 263
Jassy, 84, 170
Kassa (Slov.: Košice, Germ.: Kaschau), 13, 230
Kolozsvár (Rom.: Cluj-Napoca, Germ.: Klausenburg), 33, 173, 174, 230
Košice, see Kassa
Kovin, see Kubin
Kragujevac, 46
Kubin (Serb.: Kovin), 64
London, 23, 24, 26, 27, 45, 50, 52, 62, 107, 273
Makó, 117, 120
Máramarossziget (Rom.: Sighetul Marmaţiei), 175
Marosújvár (Rom.: Ocna Mureş, Germ.: Maroschujvar), 130
Marosvásárhely (Rom.: Tîrgu Mureş, Germ.: Neumarkt am Muresch), 173

Milan, 135
Minsk, 127
Miskolc (also Miskolcz), 32, 49, 102, 230
Moscow, 4, 11, 52, 127, 192, 193, 196, 197, 209
Munich, 10, 11, 14, 51, 52, 79, 83, 162, 191, 198
Nagybánya (Rom.: Baia Mare, Germ.: Frauenbach, Neustadt), 63, 73, 77, 174
Nagykanizsa, 46
Nagyszeben (Rom.: Sibiu, Germ.: Hermannstadt), 73, 115
Nagyvárad (Rom.: Oradea, Germ.: Grosswardein), 63, 64, 73, 77, 113, 120, 230
Nanterre, 15
Novi Sad, see Újvidék
Odessa, 94, 95, 96, 97, 177
Oradea, see Nagyvárad
Oxford, 43, 52
Padua, 38, 55, 56, 65, 66, 67, 68, 69, 70, 77, 78, 82, 87, 141, 167, 168, 169, 170, 180
Palánka (Serb.: Banatska Palanka), 64
Pancsova (Serb.: Pančevo), 64
Parád, 130
Parádfürdő, 245
Paris, 4, 12, 13, 14, 21, 22, 23, 24, 27, 33, 39, 43, 47, 48, 58, 60, 61, 63, 67, 68, 69, 76,

77, 83, 84, 86, 97, 98, 101, 103, 104, 111, 115, 118, 123, 124, 131, 133, 140, 141, 142, 166, 168, 169, 170, 171, 173, 175, 176, 177, 178, 180, 181, 182, 183, 184, 198, 201, 202, 204, 211, 214, 215, 241, 252, 254, 273
Pécs, 46, 49, 108
Petrozsény (Rom.: Petroşani, Germ.: Petroscheni), 130
Pittsburgh, 7, 8, 215, 216
Pozsony (Slov.: Bratislava, Germ.: Pressburg), 33, 39
Prague, 35, 48, 71, 99, 102, 129, 171, 202, 203, 204, 208, 209, 210, 211, 212
Pressburg, see Pozsony
Rapallo, 133, 135
Razdelnaya, 177
Rome, 24, 84, 107, 108, 109, 111, 112, 127, 133, 134, 135, 191, 193
Salgótarján, 32, 49, 102
Sátoraljaújhely, 102
Satu Mare, see Szatmárnémeti
Semmering, 128
Sibiu, see Nagyszeben
Sighetul Marmaţiei, see Máramarossziget
Skalica, see Szakolca
Sopron, 33, 134
St. Germain-en-Laye, 204

Subotica, see Szabadka
Syrmia (Srem), 62
Szabadka (Serb.: Subotica), 49, 73, 90
Szakolca (Slov.: Skalica), 44
Szatmárnémeti (Rom.: Satu Mare, Germ.: Sathmar), 77, 113, 120, 176, 230
Szeged, 95, 98, 108, 116, 124, 141, 142, 220, 221, 222, 223, 224, 232, 234, 255
Temesvár (Rom.: Timişoara, Germ.: Temeschwar), 63, 64, 73
Theiss, see Tisza (river)
Timişoara, see Temesvár
Tirana, 133
Tiraspol, 177
Tisza (also Theiss river), 17, 19, 95, 97, 98, 115, 117, 122, 125, 128
Tiszadob, 244
Tîrgu Mureş, see Marosvásárhely
Tokaj, 102
Trieste (Hung.: Trieszt), 107, 113, 273
Újvidék (Serb.: Novi Sad), 64, 73
Ungvár (Ukr.: Uzhgorod), 230
Uzhgorod, see Ungvár
Vác, 102
Valona, 107, 133
Vásárosnamény, 95
Venice, 134
Verdun, 274

Vienna, 43, 44, 47, 61, 65, 72, 74,
    78, 89, 104, 110, 112, 114,
    116, 117, 128, 129, 143,
    151, 192, 194, 197, 203,
    273
Warsaw, 130, 131, 144, 197
Washington, 4, 58, 84, 177, 183

Zadar, 133
Zám (Rom.: Zam, Germ.: Sameschdorf), 175
Zilah (Rom.: Zalău, Germ.: Waltenberg, Zillenmarkt), 175
Žitný ostrov, see Csallóköz

List of Contributors

Ádám Magda – Professor of History, Eötvös Loránd Tudományegyetem, Budapest, Senior Research Fellow, Hungarian Academy of Sciences, Institute of History, Budapest

Iván T. Berend – Professor of History, University of California, Berkeley, Member of the Hungarian Academy of Sciences

Lóránd Dombrády – former Director of the Institute of War History, Budapest

Stephen Fischer-Galati – Professor Emeritus of History, University of Colorado

Yeshayahu Jelinek – Senior Lecturer, Ben Gurion Research Institute, Sdeh Boker, Israel

Thomas Karfunkel – Professor of History, New York City Technical College of CUNY

Béla K. Király – Professor Emeritus of History, Brooklyn College and the Graduate School and University Center, CUNY

István I. Mócsy – Professor of History, The University of Santa Clara, California

Zsuzsa L. Nagy – Professor of History, Head of the Department of Modern Hungarian History, Kossuth Lajos University, Debrecen

Mária Ormos – Professor of History, Janus Pannonius University, Pécs, Member of the Hungarian Academy of Sciences

György Ránki – former Deputy Director, Hungarian Academy of Sciences, Institue of History, former Director, Hungarian Chair, University of Indiana, deceased.

Ignác Romsics – Professor of History, Eötvös Loránd University, Budapest, Hungarian Chair Professor at Indiana University, Bloomington, USA

Peter Pastor – Professor of History, Montclair State University, New Jersey

Hugh Seton-Watson – former Professor of Russian History, School of Slavonic and East European Studies, University of London, deceased.

László Szarka – Research Fellow, Hungarian Academy of Sciences, Institute of History, Budapest

László Veszprémy – Director, Library of Military Sciences, Budapest

Volumes Published in "Atlantic Studies on Society in Change"

A Series distributed by Columbia University Press

No. 1	*Tolerance and Movements of Religious Dissent in Eastern Europe.* Edited by Béla K. Király. 1977.
No. 2	*The Habsburg Empire in World War I.* Edited by R. A. Kann. 1978
No. 3	*The Mutual Effects of the Islamic and Judeo-Christian Worlds: The East European Pattern.* Edited by A. Ascher, T. Halasi-Kun, B. K. Király. 1979.
No. 4	*Before Watergate: Problems of Corruption in American Society.* Edited by A. S. Eisenstadt, A. Hoogenboom, H. L. Trefousse. 1979.
No. 5	*East Central European Perceptions of Early America.* Edited by B. K. Király and G. Barány. 1977.
No. 6	*The Hungarian Revolution of 1956 in Retrospect.* Edited by B. K. Király and Paul Jónás. 1978.
No. 7	*Brooklyn U.S.A.: Fourth Largest City in America.* Edited by Rita S. Miller. 1979.
No. 8	*Prime Minister Gyula Andrássy's Influence on Habsburg Foreign Policy.* János Decsy. 1979.
No. 9	*The Great Impeacher: A Political Biography of James M. Ashley.* Robert F. Horowitz. 1979.
No. 10 Vol. I*	*Special Topics and Generalizations on the Eighteenth and Nineteenth Century.* Edited by Béla K. Király and Gunther E. Rothenberg. 1979.

---

* Volumes Nos. I through XXXIII refer to the series *War and Society in East Central Europe.*

No. 11 Vol. II	*East Central European Society and War in the Pre-Revolutionary 18th-Century.* Edited by Gunther E. Rothenberg, Béla K. Király, and Peter F. Sugar. 1982.
No. 12 Vol. III	*From Hunyadi to Rákóczi: War and Society in Late Medieval and Early Modern Hungary.* Edited by János M. Bak and Béla K. Király. 1982.
No. 13 Vol. IV	*East Central European Society and War in the Era of Revolutions: 1775-1856.* Edited by B. K. Király. 1984.
No. 14 Vol. V	*Essays on World War I: Origins and Prisoners of War.* Edited by Samuel R. Williamson, Jr. and Peter Pastor. 1983.
No. 15 Vol. VI	*Essays on World War I: Total War and Peacemaking, A Case Study on Trianon.* Edited by B. K. Király, Peter Pastor, and Ivan Sanders. 1982.
No. 16 Vol. VII	*Army, Aristocracy, Monarchy: War, Society and Government in Austria, 1618-1780.* Edited by Thomas M. Barker. 1982.
No. 17 Vol. VIII	*The First Serbian Uprising 1804-1813.* Edited by Wayne S. Vucinich. 1982.
No. 18 Vol. IX	*Czechoslovak Policy and the Hungarian Minority 1945-1948.* Kálmán Janics. Edited by Stephen Borsody. 1982.
No. 19 Vol. X	*At the Brink of War and Peace: The Tito-Stalin Split in a Historic Perspective.* Edited by Wayne S. Vucinich. 1982.
No. 20	*Inflation Through the Ages: Economic, Social, Psychological and Historical Aspects.* Edited by Edward Marcus and Nathan Schmuckler. 1981.
No. 21	*Germany and America: Essays on Problems of International Relations and Immigration.* Edited by Hans L. Trefousse. 1980.
No. 22	*Brooklyn College: The First Half Century.* Murray M. Horowitz. 1981.
No. 23	*A New Deal for the World: Eleanor Roosevelt and American Foreign Policy.* Jason Berger. 1981.

No. 24	*The Legacy of Jewish Migration: 1881 and Its Impact.* Edited by David Berger. 1982.
No. 25	*The Road to Bellapais: Cypriot Exodus to Northern Cyprus.* Pierre Oberling. 1982.
No. 26	*New Hungarian Peasants: An East Central European Experience with Collectivization.* Edited by Marida Hollos and Béla C. Maday. 1983.
No. 27	*Germans in America: Aspects of German-American Relations in the Nineteenth Century.* Edited by Allen McCormick. 1983.
No. 28	*A Question of Empire: Leopold I and the War of Spanish Succession, 1701-1705.* Linda and Marsha Frey. 1983.
No. 29	*The Beginning of Cyrillic Printing — Cracow, 1491. From the Orthodox Past in Poland.* Szczepan K. Zimmer. Edited by Ludwik Krzyzanowski and Irene Nagurski. 1983.
No. 29a	*A Grand Ecole for the Grand Corps: The Recruitment and Training of the French Administration.* Thomas R. Osborne. 1983.
No. 30 Vol. XI	*The First War between Socialist States: The Hungarian Revolution of 1956 and Its Impact.* Edited by Béla K. Király, Barbara Lotze, Nandor Dreisziger. 1984.
No. 31 Vol. XII	*The Effects of World War I, The Uprooted: Hungarian Refugees and Their Impact on Hungary's Domestic Politics.* István Mócsy. 1983.
No. 32 Vol. XIII	*The Effects of World War I: The Class War after the Great War: The Rise Of Communist Parties in East Central Europe, 1918-1921.* Edited by Ivo Banac. 1983.
No. 33 Vol. XIV	*The Crucial Decade: East Central European Society and National Defense, 1859-1870.* Edited by Béla K. Király. 1984.
No. 35 Vol. XVI	*Effects of World War I: War Communism in Hungary, 1919.* György Péteri. 1984.
No. 36 Vol. XVII	*Insurrections, Wars, and the Eastern Crisis in the 1870s.* Edited by B. K. Király and Gale Stokes. 1985.

No. 37 Vol. XVIII	*East Central European Society and the Balkan Wars, 1912-1913.* Edited by B. K. Király and Dimitrije Djordjevic. 1986.
No. 38 Vol. XIX	*East Central European Society in World War I.* Edited by B. K. Király and N. F. Dreisziger, Assistant Editor Albert A. Nofi. 1985.
No. 39 Vol. XX	*Revolutions and Interventions in Hungary and Its Neighbor States, 1918-1919.* Edited by Peter Pastor. 1988.
No. 40 Vol. XXI	*East Central European Society and War, 1750-1920. Bibliography and Historiography.* Complied and edited by László Alföldi. Pending.
No. 41 Vol. XXII	*Essays on East Central European Society and War, 1740-1920.* Edited by Stephen Fischer-Galati and Béla K. Király. 1988.
No. 42 Vol. XXIII	*East Central European Maritime Commerce and Naval Policies, 1789-1913.* Edited by Apostolos E. Vacalopoulos, Constantinos D. Svolopoulos, and Béla K. Király. 1988.
No. 43 Vol. XXIV	*Selections, Social Origins, Education and Training of East Central European Officers Corps.* Edited by Béla K. Király and Walter Scott Dillard. 1988.
No. 44 Vol. XXV	*East Central European War Leaders: Civilian and Military.* Edited by Béla K. Király and Albert Nofi. 1988.
No. 46	*Germany's International Monetary Policy and the European Monetary System.* Hugo Kaufmann. 1985.
No. 47	*Iran Since the Revolution — Internal Dynamics, Regional Conflicts and the Superpowers.* Edited by Barry M. Rosen. 1985.
No. 48 Vol. XXVII	*The Press During the Hungarian Revolution of 1848-1849.* Domokos Kosáry. 1986.
No. 49	*The Spanish Inquisition and the Inquisitional Mind.* Edited by Angel Alcala. 1987.
No. 50	*Catholics, the State and the European Radical Right, 1919-1945.* Edited by Richard Wolff and Jorg K. Hoensch. 1987.

No. 51 Vol. XXVIII	*The Boer War and Military Reforms.* Jay Stone and Erwin A. Schmidl. 1987.
No. 52	*Baron Joseph Eötvös, A Literary Biography.* Steven B. Várdy. 1987.
No. 53	*Towards the Renaissance of Puerto Rican Studies: Ethnic and Area Studies in University Education.* Maria Sanchez and Antonio M. Stevens. 1987.
No. 54	*The Brazilian Diamonds in Contracts, Contraband and Capital.* Harry Bernstein. 1987.
No. 55	*Christians, Jews and Other Worlds: Patterns of Conflict and Accommodation.* Edited by Phillip F. Gallagher. 1988.
No. 56 Vol. XXVI	*The Fall of the Medieval Kingdom of Hungary: Mohács, 1526, Buda, 1541.* Géza Perjés. 1989.
No. 57	*The Lord Mayor of Lisbon: The Portuguese Tribune of the People and His 24 Guilds.* Harry Bernstein. 1989.
No. 58	*Hungarian Statesmen of Destiny: 1860-1960.* Edited by Paul Bödy. 1989.
No. 59	*For China: The Memoirs of T. G. Li, former Major General in the Chinese Nationist Army.* T. G. Li. Written in collaboration with Roman Rome. 1989.
No. 60	*Politics in Hungary: For A Democratic Alternative.* János Kis, with an Introduction by Timothy Garton Ash. 1989.
No. 61	*Hungarian Worker's Councils in 1956.* Edited by Bill Lomax. 1990.
No. 62	*Essays on the Structure and Reform of Centrally Planned Economic Systems.* Paul Jonas. A joint publication with Corvina Kiadó, Budapest. 1990.
No. 63	*Kossuth as a Journalist in England.* Éva H. Haraszti. A joint publication with Akadémiai Kiadó, Budapest. 1990.
No. 64	*From Padua to the Trianon, 1918-1920.* Mária Ormos. A joint publication with Akadémiai Kiadó, Budapest. 1990.
No. 65	*Towns in Medieval Hungary.* Edited by László Gerevich. A joint publication with Akadémiai Kiadó, Budapest. 1990.

No. 66	*The Nationalities Problem in Transylvania, 1867-1940.* Sándor Bíró. 1992.
No. 67	*Hungarian Exiles and the Romanian National Movement, 1849-1867.* Béla Borsi-Kálmán. 1991.
No. 68	*The Hungarian Minority's Situation in Ceausescu's Romania.* Edited by Rudolf Joó and Andrew Ludanyi. 1994.
No. 69	*Democracy, Revolution, Self-Determination. Selected Writings.* István Bibó. Edited by Károly Nagy. 1991.
No. 70	*Trianon and the Protection of Minorities.* József Galántai. A joint publication with Corvina Kiadó, Budapest. 1991.
No. 71	*King Saint Stephen of Hungary.* György Györffy. 1994.
No. 72	*Dynasty, Politics and Culture. Selected Essays.* Robert A. Kann. Edited by Stanley B. Winters. 1991.
No. 73	*Jadwiga of Anjou and the Rise of East Central Europe.* Oscar Halecki. Edited by Thaddeus V. Gromada. A joint publication with the Polish Institute of Arts and Sciences of America, New York. 1991.
No. 74 Vol. XXIX	*Hungarian Economy and Society During World War Two.* Edited by György Lengyel. 1993.
No. 75	*The Life of a Communist Revolutionary, Béla Kun.* György Borsányi. 1993.
No. 76	*Yugoslavia: The Process of Disintegration.* Laslo Sekelj. 1993.
No. 77 Vol. XXX	*Wartime American Plans for a New Hungary. Documents from the U.S. Department of State, 1942-1944.* Edited by Ignác Romsics. 1992.
No.78 Vol. XXXI	*Planning for War against Russia and Serbia. Austro-Hungarian and German Military Strategies, 1871-1914.* Graydon A. Tunstall, Jr. 1993.
No. 79	*American Effects on Hungarian Imagination and Political Thought, 1559-1848.* Géza Závodszky. 1995.
No. 80 Vol. XXXII	*Trianon and East Central Europe: Antecedents and Repercussions.* Edited by Béla K. Király and László Veszprémy. 1995.

No. 81	*Hungarians and Their Neighbors in Modern Times, 1867-1950.* Edited by Ferenc Glatz. 1995.
No. 82	*István Bethlen: A Great Conservative Statesman of Hungary, 1874-1946.* Ignác Romsics. 1995.
No. 83 Vol. XXXIII	*20th Century Hungary and the Great Powers.* Edited by Ignác Romsics. 1995.
No. 84	*Lawful Revolution in Hungary, 1989-1994.* Edited by Béla K. Király. András Bozóki Assistant Editor. 1995.